NINETY-SIXTH ANNUAL REPORT

OF THE

Comptroller of the Currency

1958

WASHINGTON : 1959

Treasury Department

Document No. 3212

Comptroller of the Currency

LETTER OF TRANSMITTAL

TREASURY DEPARTMENT,
OFFICE OF THE COMPTROLLER OF THE CURRENCY,
Washington, D.C., June 15, 1959.

SIRS: In accordance with the provisions of section 333 of the United States Revised Statutes, I have the honor to submit the following report covering the activities of the Bureau of the Comptroller of the Currency for the year 1958.

Respectfully,

RAY M. GIDNEY,
Comptroller of the Currency.

THE PRESIDENT OF THE SENATE.
THE SPEAKER OF THE HOUSE OF REPRESENTATIVES.

III

ANNUAL REPORT

OF THE

COMPTROLLER OF THE CURRENCY

STATUS OF NATIONAL BANKING SYSTEM

On December 31, 1958, total assets of the 4,593 banks supervised by the Comptroller of the Currency were $129.5 billion. The national banking system maintained its relative position with 46.6 percent of the banking assets in the commercial and savings banks of the Nation, and 53.9 percent of the commercial banking assets. Commercial banks numbering 8,921 which are supervised by the respective 48 State banking authorities held assets of $110.6 billion, and 520 State-chartered and supervised mutual savings banks had assets of $37.8 billion. For all banks, assets were $277.9 billion, an increase of $18.7 billion for the year, which were held in the following types and categories of banks.

All operating banks—Continental United States and other areas

[Figures in millions of dollars]

Type of bank	Members of both the Federal Reserve System and Federal Deposit Insurance Corporation		Members of Federal Deposit Insurance Corporation only		Not members of Federal Reserve or Federal Deposit Insurance Corporation	
	Number	Total assets	Number	Total assets	Number	Total assets
National banks	4,582	[1] 128,881	[2] 10	[1] 364	[2] 1	[1] 259
State commercial banks	1,727	[3] 73,107	6,806	[4] 35,122	388	[5] 2,368
Mutual savings banks	3	[3] 29	238	[4] 30,160	279	[5] 7,590
Total	6,312	202,017	7,054	65,646	668	10,217

Recapitulation

	Number	Branches	Total assets	Increase for 1958
National banks	[1] 4,593	4,401	129,504	8,404
State commercial banks	8,921	4,388	110,597	7,677
Mutual savings banks	520	425	37,779	2,611
Head offices	14,034	9,214	277,880	18,692
Branches	9,214			
Total banking offices	23,248			

[1] Supervised by Comptroller of the Currency. (Includes 8 nonnational banks in the District of Columbia, 4 member and 4 nonmember insured banks with 27 branches.)
[2] Includes 7 national banks outside continental United States.
[3] Supervised by State banking departments and the Federal Reserve System. (Includes 1 member nondeposit trust company.)
[4] Supervised by State banking departments and Federal Deposit Insurance Corporation.
[5] Supervised by State banking departments only.

Growth of Financial Institutions

Commercial bank assets increased $16.1 billion during 1958 as compared to $5.4 billion in 1957 and $6.8 billion in 1956. The increase of 7.2 percent in 1958 was the largest increase for any year during the past decade which had an average annual growth of commercial bank assets of 5.4 percent per year. The growth of financial institutions during the past 10-year period was at a rapid rate, with the most rapid growth occurring in savings and loan associations and mutual savings banks which have been in a position to offer more attractive savings interest rates because of their favorable tax status and lower liquidity requirements. Relative growth by classes during the past 10-year period is presented in the following table.

Financial institutions

[Total assets]

	Dec. 31, 1948	Dec. 31, 1958	Percentage of increase
	(In billions of dollars)		
Commercial banks	155, 602	240, 101	54. 3
Mutual savings banks	20, 474	37, 779	84. 5
Savings and loan associations	13, 028	55, 114	323. 0

Status of National Banks

The number of operating national banks was reduced during 1958 from 4,627 at the close of 1957 to 4,585, a net change of 42. This compares with reductions of 32 in 1957, 41 in 1956, 96 in 1955, 68 in 1954, and 52 in 1953. The total assets of the national banking system continued upward in 1958 to $128.8 billion compared with $120.5 billion at the close of 1957, a gain of $8.3 billion or 6.9 percent. The system absorbed 45 state banks in 1958 which had total assets of $1.1 billion, through consolidations, mergers, purchases, and conversions; State systems absorbed by the same routes 25 national banks with resources of $484 million. A net gain of $609 million in assets accrued from these sources for the national banking system. Thus, the substantial gain in total assets for the system in 1958 occurred almost wholly through normal deposit growth.

Based upon managerial competence, asset soundness, adequacy of capital funds and reserves, and earning capacity as the fundamental considerations, the national banking system continues in excellent condition, the only exceptions being a few small banks which require and are receiving close and effective supervisory attention.

Deposits

During the year 1958 the national banking system showed the most significant gain in deposits for many years reaching a new high of $117 billion, an increase of $7.6 billion or 7 percent over the prior year end

The gain in time deposits of $4.2 billion in the same period accounted for a little more than 55 percent of the total upswing.

The total deposits of national banks and the average effective interest rate paid on time and savings deposits are set forth below for the years 1955 through 1958.

[In millions of dollars]

Total deposits	Dec. 31, 1955	Dec. 31, 1956	Dec. 31, 1957	Dec. 31, 1958
Demand_____	$76,894.6	$79,027.5	$77,881.0	$81,351.8
Time and savings#	27,323.4	28,467.3	31,555.3	35,734.3
Total___	104,218.0	107,494.8	109,436.3	117,086.1
#Interest paid___	374.0	437.0	636.0	762.3
Average rate (percent)___	1.37	1.54	2.02	2.13

Loans

The national banking system, at the end of 1958, held net loans of $52.8 billion after deducting reserves for bad debts and valuation reserves of $1.1 billion. The increase in net loans during 1958 amounted to $2.3 billion or 4.54 percent. As in the past, loans to commercial and industrial type borrowers continue to make up the major segment of the composite portfolio and constitute $22.4 billion or nearly 42 percent of $53.9 billion gross loans held by national banks. The increase in such loans during the year was relatively slight at $194 million or 0.88 percent.

New construction activity continued to rise though less spectacularly in 1958 and the aggregate of all types was valued at $49 billion, a gain of $865 million. Private activity of this kind was valued at $33.9 billion, practically unchanged from 1957. Permanent nonfarm dwelling units started during 1958 totalled 1,209 thousand in number, an increase of 167 thousand compared to a 76 thousand decrease in 1957.

The Nation's mortgage debt on nonfarm one to four-family properties continued to rise. A total of $118 billion was reached by the close of 1958, a gain of $10.4 billion over $107.6 billion reported in 1957. Conventional loans still make up the largest portion at 57 percent and aggregate $67.8 billion. Farm mortgage debt in the nation stood at $11.2 billion at the year end, up $700 million over 1957 or an increase of 6.7 percent.

By law, each national bank must restrict its aggregate investment in real estate mortgage loans, with the exception of those which are insured or guaranteed to the extent of not less than 20 percent by the Veterans' Administration, to an amount not in excess of 60 percent of its time and savings deposits or 100 percent of its capital and surplus, whichever is the greater. The $11.7 billion of real estate mortgage loans which are subject to this limitation equal 32.8 percent of the $35.7 billion of time and savings deposits held by the national banking system.

National banks held loans secured by real estate at the end of the years 1957 and 1958 as follows:

[Figures in millions of dollars]

Type	Dec. 31, 1957	Dec. 31, 1958	Dollar increase, decrease —
Conventional—residence	4,212	4,790	578
Conventional—other properties	2,521	2,904	383
Conventional—farm	523	562	39
Insured—Federal Housing Administration	3,068	3,470	402
Insured or guaranteed—Veterans' Administration	2,156	1,988	−168
Total	12,480	13,714	1,234

At the close of 1958 commercial bank mortgage loan holdings aggregated $25.5 billion; up $2.2 billion from the $23.3 billion at the 1957 year end. In relation to all commercial banks, national banks held nearly 54 percent of such loans with their total of $13.7 billion, a gain of 10 percent or $1.2 billion over the $12.5 billion held at the end of 1957. Such loans held by all national banks constituted 25.4 percent of their gross loans. Of the Nation's $171.2 billion total mortgage debt, national banks held 8 percent and they accounted for close to 8.2 percent of the national increase in such debt in 1958.

In late November 1958, the Comptroller of the Currency was informed that the Federal Housing Administration was approaching its statutory limitation on insurance in force and outstanding commitments and had adopted a new procedure which contemplates that firm commitments will continue to be issued in cases where there is a buyer at hand, but that with respect to commitments in the name of mortgagors who are not home buyers the Administration would henceforth issue an agreement to insure instead of a firm commitment. The agreement to insure obligates the Administration to issue its usual commitment, but it will be conditioned upon the availability of authorization at the time a lender holding the agreement requests its conversion to a commitment. The Commissioner informed the Comptroller of his belief that in all respects agreements to insure are valid and binding obligations upon the Administration and it is legally obligated to honor the agreements. The new procedure was conceived as a workable plan to meet temporary problems which the Federal Housing Administration anticipated would be promptly cured by Congress and the Commissioner asked the Comptroller to rule that agreements to insure should be treated by national bank examiners as the equivalent of an FHA firm commitment. It has been the position of the Comptroller of the Currency that when FHA has issued its firm commitment to insure, the loan covered thereby is exempt from the maturity and percentage limitations of the first paragraph of Section 24 of the Federal Reserve Act.

After careful consideration of the factors involved, on November 4, 1958, the Comptroller of the Currency issued instructions to national bank examiners to treat FHA Agreements to Insure already made and to be made during the next 120 days as the equivalent of firm commitments to insure for the purposes of Section 24 of the Federal Reserve Act.   On March 9, 1959, and in response to a further request from the Commissioner, these instructions were extended for an additional 90 days.

The first reduction in instalment debt since 1943 permitted the year 1958 to close with a total less than that of the prior year.   The modest reduction of $230 million from the 1957 total of $34.1 billion ended 1958 with the aggregate standing at $33.9 billion.   However, the Nation's consumer debt (instalment debt plus noninstalment debt in the form of single payment loans for the purchase of consumer goods, charge accounts, and debt incurred for the payment of services rendered) continued to rise to a new high of $45.1 billion at the year end, a gain of $291 million over the $44.8 billion at the close of 1957.   Instalment loans to finance the purchase of automobiles continue as the largest segment of instalment credit.   Such loans decreased by $1,278 million from $15.4 billion in 1957 to $14.1 billion at the close of 1958.   All other types of instalment credit increased slightly over 1957 levels.

Instalment type personal and consumer loans held by the national banking system aggregated $8.1 billion at the close of 1958, practically the same amount held at the 1957 year end.   This level of instalment loans constitutes 28 percent of the $28.9 billion of such loans held by financial institutions and 63.8 percent of the $12.7 billion of such loans held by commercial banks at the end of 1958.   Included in the instalment loan holdings of national banks at the year end was $3.8 billion of automobile loans, decreased $99 million from the previous year's close.   Of the total instalment type personal and consumer loans held by national banks, automobile paper constitutes 47 percent as compared to 48.1 percent in 1957.

Loan delinquencies of 90 or more days duration shown in reports of examination made in 1958 increased slightly.   This observation is based upon data accumulated as of the respective dates of examination.   In the following table the total unpaid balances of such delinquent loans is expressed as a percentage of the total outstandings of the group of national banks which segregate instalment loans in loan portfolios or hold such paper in an aggregate amount equal to or exceeding 10 percent of their loan accounts.

Instalment loan delinquencies

Year	Number of banks	Total instalment loans (A)	Auto-mobile loans	Floor plan Loans (B)	Loans collateraled by instal-ment obliga-tions (C)	Total (A) (B) (C)
		Percent	*Percent*	*Percent*	*Percent*	*Percent*
1956	4,073	0.56	0.33	0.19	0.12	0.50
1957	4,032	.36	.20	.13	.16	.34
1958	4,113	.45	.28	.17	.16	.43

Because of the rapid expansion in instalment credit which reached significant proportions in the early fifties, the increasing number of national banks engaged in this type of lending, and the need for better information as to lending practices and experience, a special section dealing with instalment credit was added to the report of examination in August 1955. For several years detailed schedules have been incorporated in annual reports showing the policies and range of terms followed by national banks in making and servicing instalment loans. It appears clear on the basis of the studies previously made that, generally, national banks are following sound policies in making and servicing these loans. The study made in 1958 supports the same conclusion although there has been a slight increase in the number of banks that now lend on 36 months' maturity on new- and late-model used automobiles. In 1957, 18 percent of all national banks in the study made such loans up to 36 months; in 1958 the number was up to 23 percent. Other terms remain fairly constant.

The following schedule divided into three size groups was prepared on the basis of the most recent report of examination in 1958 and shows the details of the down payment and maturity policies of the 4,113 national banks examined which segregate instalment paper in their loan portfolios or hold such paper in an aggregate amount equal to 10 percent or more of their loan accounts.

GROUP I BANKS

(Resources under $10MM)

NEW AUTOS

Term (number of months)	Percent of down payment					Total number of banks
	20	25	30	33⅓	Over	
18 and under	0	8	3	192	10	213
24	2	34	8	1,263	20	1,327
30	0	39	15	689	2	745
36	2	26	8	467	7	510
Total	4	107	34	2,611	39	2,795

USED AUTOS—LESS THAN 1 YEAR OLD

18 and under	0	1	1	145	28	175
24	0	9	7	409	10	435
30	0	16	0	126	0	142
36	0	2	1	66	1	70
Total	0	28	9	746	39	822

USED AUTOS—1 TO 2 YEARS OLD

18 and under	1	13	11	992	192	1,209
24	0	22	9	1,189	66	1,286
30	1	6	3	113	1	124
36	1	1	1	23	0	26
Total	3	42	24	2,317	259	2,645

USED AUTOS—2 TO 3 YEARS OLD

18 and under	2	18	16	1,527	380	1,943
24	0	14	3	558	35	610
30	0	1	0	21	0	22
36	1	1	0	6	0	8
Total	3	34	19	2,112	415	2,583

USED AUTOS—3 TO 4 YEARS OLD

18 and under	1	23	15	1,617	483	2,139
24	0	5	1	217	20	243
30	0	1	0	9	0	10
36	1	0	0	2	0	3
Total	2	29	16	1,845	503	2,395

USED AUTOS—OVER 4 YEARS OLD

18 and under	1	20	11	1,212	448	1,692
24	0	2	0	84	9	95
30	0	0	0	3	0	3
36	1	0	0	0	0	1
Total	2	22	11	1,299	457	1,791

GROUP II BANKS

(Resources between $10MM and $50MM)

NEW AUTOS

Term (number of months)	Percent of down payment					Total number of banks
	20	25	30	33⅓	Over	
18 and under	0	0	0	16	2	18
24	1	12	5	317	3	338
30	1	16	11	314	6	348
36	4	23	13	276	9	325
Total	6	51	29	923	20	1,029

USED AUTOS—LESS THAN 1 YEAR OLD

	20	25	30	33⅓	Over	
18 and under	0	0	0	22	4	26
24	2	2	1	107	5	117
30	0	1	3	80	0	84
36	1	4	4	39	2	50
Total	3	7	8	248	11	277

USED AUTOS—1 TO 2 YEARS OLD

	20	25	30	33⅓	Over	
18 and under	1	4	2	227	40	274
24	0	6	6	554	35	601
30	0	2	2	103	1	108
36	1	0	0	8	0	9
Total	2	12	10	892	76	992

USED AUTOS—2 TO 3 YEARS OLD

	20	25	30	33⅓	Over	
18 and under	1	6	6	467	99	579
24	0	3	3	364	20	390
30	0	0	1	12	0	13
36	0	0	0	1	0	1
Total	1	9	10	844	119	983

USED AUTOS—3 TO 4 YEARS OLD

	20	25	30	33⅓	Over	
18 and under	0	7	5	626	158	796
24	0	2	4	105	7	118
30	0	0	0	3	0	3
36	0	0	0	1	0	1
Total	0	9	9	735	165	918

USED AUTOS—OVER 4 YEARS OLD

	20	25	30	33⅓	Over	
18 and under	0	7	4	525	163	699
24	0	1	1	29	2	33
30	0	0	0	1	0	1
36	0	0	0	1	0	1
Total	0	8	5	556	165	734

GROUP III BANKS

(Resources $50MM and over)

NEW AUTOS

Term (number of months)	Percent of down payment					Total number of banks
	20	25	30	33⅓	Over	
18 and under	0	0	0	2	0	2
24	0	3	0	40	1	44
30	0	7	13	78	2	100
36	2	21	11	86	8	128
Total	2	31	24	206	11	274

USED AUTOS—LESS THAN 1 YEAR OLD

	20	25	30	33⅓	Over	
18 and under	0	0	0	1	1	2
24	0	1	1	23	1	26
30	0	3	4	18	1	26
36	1	2	2	16	0	21
Total	1	6	7	58	3	75

USED AUTOS—1 TO 2 YEARS OLD

	20	25	30	33⅓	Over	
18 and under	0	0	0	37	8	45
24	0	7	4	153	14	178
30	0	4	4	32	1	41
36	0	0	0	4	0	4
Total	0	11	8	226	23	268

USED AUTOS—2 TO 3 YEARS OLD

	20	25	30	33⅓	Over	
18 and under	0	3	2	99	21	125
24	0	7	2	119	9	137
30	0	0	0	2	0	2
36	0	0	0	1	0	1
Total	0	10	4	221	30	265

USED AUTOS—3 TO 4 YEARS OLD

	20	25	30	33⅓	Over	
18 and under	0	5	3	180	32	220
24	0	3	1	33	2	39
30	0	0	0	0	0	0
36	0	0	0	0	0	0
Total	0	8	4	213	34	259

USED AUTOS—OVER 4 YEARS OLD

	20	25	30	33⅓	Over	
18 and under	1	5	1	138	49	194
24	0	1	0	4	0	5
30	0	0	0	0	0	0
36	0	0	0	0	0	0
Total	1	6	1	142	49	199

Liquidity

Cash, balances with other banks, including reserve balances and cash items in process of collection, and obligations of the United States held by national banks at the close of 1958 totalled $62.7 billion, an increase of $4.5 billion over the 1957 year end total. Such assets are equal to 77 percent of demand deposits and 53.5 percent of total deposits at the close of 1958 compared to 74.7 percent and 53.2 percent, respectively, at the end of 1957, 74 percent and 54.7 percent in 1956, and 77 percent and 57 percent in 1955.

The full reserve requirements of national banks and State bank members of the Federal Reserve System must be maintained on deposit at the Federal Reserve Bank of the district in which such a bank is located and no allowance is made for holdings of vault cash. The Comptroller has favored enactment of a proposal under consideration in the Congress to amend Section 19 of the Federal Reserve Act so as to permit vault cash to be considered a part of the legal reserve.

Investment Accounts

The year 1958 saw a continuous and steady increase in the investment accounts of national banks with their security holdings at the end of the year totaling $46.5 billion, up $5.8 billion for the period. Of this increase United States Treasury obligations accounted for $4.5 billion.

Additions to the investment account were made possible by a deposit increase of $7.6 billion which also provided funds for the major portion of the increase in loans of $2.4 billion.

For the third successive year additions to United States Treasury investments have been in the shorter maturities although the year also produced an increase in the medium term holdings as reflected by the schedule below.

The foregoing changes were accompanied by profit taking of $298.1 million which was after net losses of $55.0 million. Due to income tax considerations, a practice has developed in many banks of taking bond profits in one year and losses in another according to market trends and opportunities. As indicated, 1958 was a profit year while in 1957 national banks took a net loss of $114.3 million in securities transactions. The latter figure is net after profits of $31.1 million.

The high investment quality in national bank portfolios, noted in previous years, continued through 1958.

[In millions of dollars]

	United States bonds			
	Dec. 31, 1955	Dec. 31, 1956	Dec. 31, 1957	Dec. 31, 1958
Short term	18, 982	22, 363	23, 924	26, 667
Medium term	11, 951	6, 321	4, 710	6, 632
Long term	2, 754	2, 992	2, 702	2, 522
Total	33, 687	31, 676	31, 336	35, 821

Recapitulation by maturities

(United States Bonds as of Dec. 31, 1958; municipal and other bonds as of most recent examination reports—adjusted)

[In millions of dollars]

	United States bonds	General obligation municipal bonds	Special revenue municipal authority and corporate bonds	Total
Short term (maturing up to 5 years)	[1] 26, 667	3, 942	2, 087	32, 696
Medium term (maturing between 5 and 10 years)	6, 632	2, 341	498	9, 471
Long term (maturing after 10 years)	2, 522	1, 351	464	4, 337
Total	35, 821	[2] 7, 634	[3] 3, 049	46, 504

[1] Includes $609 million of nonmarketable United States bonds.
[2] Includes $1,442 million of general obligations of States and $694 million of housing authority obligations.
[3] Includes $1,111 million of special revenue municipal authority obligations and $1,341 million of Federal Corporation (not guaranteed) bonds.

Capital Structure

Continued progress was made during 1958 by national banks in building stronger capital structures. Capital adequacy has always been considered to be of major importance, both by the Comptroller's office and bankers generally, and this common interest has made for strength and stability in the national banking system.

During 1958 the capital structures, including reserves for bad debts, of national banks increased $667 million. Of this increase $101 million resulted from capital revision programs undertaken by shareholders of 172 national banks who supplied additional proprietary funds through subscription to new stock. During the 10-year period from 1949 to 1958, 1,753 national banks fortified their capital structures $1,351 million through the sale of additional common stock.

With the sanction of the Comptroller, shareholders of 393 national banks approved dividends payable in common stock having a total par value of $108 million.

The 4,585 national banks had capital, surplus, undivided profits and reserves of $9,669 million as of December 31, 1958 and their reserves for bad debts and other valuation reserves on loans amounted to $1,056 million, making an aggregate total of capital funds and reserves of $10.7 billion. This represents 9.1 percent of deposit liabilities and 8.2 percent of total resources. Gross assets at the year end (reserves for bad debts and valuation reserves not deducted) were $129.9 billion. After deducting $68.1 billion, representing cash or its equivalent, United States Government obligations, and loans or portions of loans guaranteed or insured by Federal Government agencies, there remains $61.8 billion of the national banking system's funds placed in loans, municipal and corporate bonds, and other assets. Against each $5.78 invested in these types of assets there is held $1 of capital funds and reserves ($5.80 at the close of 1957, $5.88 at the close of 1956, and $5.80 at the close of 1955).

National bank examiners' reports of examination reveal that the volume of assets containing substantial or unwarranted degree of risk remain negligible in relation to the protection offered by the proprietary funds of national banks.

Earnings and net Additions to Reserves

The 4,585 national banks paid a total of $2,842 million in salaries and wages, taxes, and interest on deposits in 1958. Salaries and wages amounted to $1,264 million, of which $829 million went to 242,312 employees, $413 million was paid to 45,254 officers, and fees to directors accounted for $22 million. National banks paid $658 million in Federal income taxes, $32 million in State income taxes, and $126 million in various local taxes on property, etc., for a total tax payment of $816 million. Interest on savings and other time deposits of $762 million approximated 2.13% on total time deposits of $35.7 billion outstanding at the year end, compared to $636 million interest paid in 1957 on year-end time money of $31.5 billion, which approximated 2.02%.

The sources and disposition of the income dollar of all national banks in 1958 is shown by the following illustration:

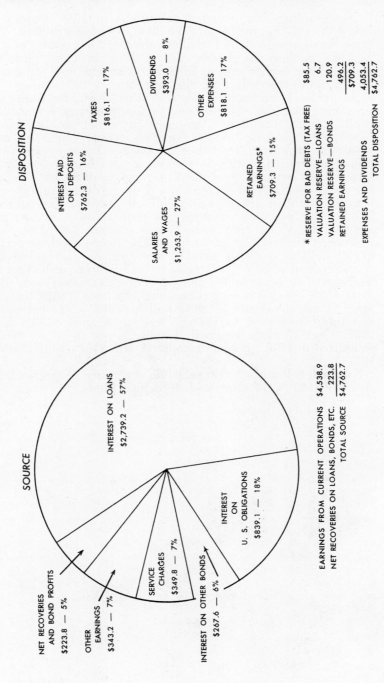

NATIONAL BANKS—1958

SOURCE AND DISPOSITION OF THE INCOME DOLLAR
(in millions of dollars and percent of one dollar)

DISPOSITION

DIVIDENDS $393.0 — 8%

TAXES $816.1 — 17%

OTHER EXPENSES $818.1 — 17%

INTEREST PAID ON DEPOSITS $762.3 — 16%

RETAINED EARNINGS* $709.3 — 15%

SALARIES AND WAGES $1,253.9 — 27%

*RESERVE FOR BAD DEBTS (TAX FREE) $85.5
VALUATION RESERVE—LOANS   6.7
VALUATION RESERVE—BONDS   120.9
RETAINED EARNINGS   496.2
                                        $709.3

EXPENSES AND DIVIDENDS   4,053.4
TOTAL DISPOSITION $4,762.7

SOURCE

INTEREST ON LOANS $2,739.2 — 57%

INTEREST ON U. S. OBLIGATIONS $839.1 — 18%

SERVICE CHARGES $349.8 — 7%

INTEREST ON OTHER BONDS $267.6 — 6%

OTHER EARNINGS $343.2 — 7%

NET RECOVERIES AND BOND PROFITS $223.8 — 5%

EARNINGS FROM CURRENT OPERATIONS $4,538.9
NET RECOVERIES ON LOANS, BONDS, ETC.   223.8
TOTAL SOURCE $4,762.7

Net earnings from current operations in 1958 dropped slightly below the 1957 figure of $1,576.6 million to $1,568.7 million. Although gross income rose $255.1 million above 1957 results, and reached $4,538.9 million, the greater cost of doing business, particularly in wages and a higher rate of interest on an enlarged volume of time money, more than offset the rise in income.

Actual losses on loans, bonds and other assets, recoveries on assets previously charged off, and bond profits, produced a net addition to profits of $223.8 million. This grew out of net profits on the sale of securities amounting to $298.1 million, reduced by $74.3 million of losses on various other types of assets. Income taxes of $690.3 million amounted to 40% on taxable income of $1,707 million. The latter figure consists of net operating income of $1,568.7 million, plus the above-mentioned $223.8 million of net recoveries and bond profits, less $85.5 million net increase in initially tax-free bad debt reserves.

After the payment of taxes net profits before dividends for all national banks in 1958 were $889.1 million, compared to $729.9 million in 1957, a rise of 21.8%. The figure given is exclusive of $213.1 million of both taxable and initially nontaxable earnings transferred to effect a net increase in bad debt and valuation reserves. The sum of such net profits and net additions to reserves is equivalent to 11.4% of year-end capital accounts, up from 9.36% the preceding year. Cash dividends of $393 million (4.06% of year-end capital accounts) were paid to shareholders, as against $363.8 million in 1957. Net earnings retained, including net additions to reserves, amounted to $709.3 million, compared with $487.6 million retained in 1957.

Set forth below is a 5-year schedule of earnings, expenses, dividends, etc., per $100 (1) of assets and (2) capital funds,

Earnings, expenses, etc., of national banks for the years ended Dec. 31, 1954, 1955, 1956, 1957, and 1958

[*Indicates amounts in millions of dollars]

	1954	1955	1956	1957	1958
*Total assets at close of year	116,151	113,750	117,702	120,523	128,797
*Total capital accounts at close of year	8,104	7,936	8,472	9,093	9,669
*Gross earnings	3,226	3,437	3,833	4,284	4,539
Per $100 of assets	$2.78	$3.02	$3.26	$3.55	$3.52
Per $100 of capital funds	$39.81	$43.31	$45.24	$47.11	$46.94
*Gross expenses	1,996	2,105	2,336	2,707	2,970
Per $100 of assets	$1.72	$1.85	$1.99	$2.25	$2.30
Per $100 of capital funds	$24.63	$26.53	$27.57	$29.77	$30.71
*Net earnings from operations	1,230	1,332	1,497	1,577	1,569
Per $100 of assets	$1.06	$1.17	$1.27	$1.31	$1.22
Per $100 of capital funds	$15.18	$16.78	$17.67	$17.34	$16.23
*Net asset losses or recoveries (including bond profits, etc.) [1]	+149	−154	−275	−180	+224
Per $100 of assets	+$0.13	−$0.14	−$0.23	−$0.15	+$0.17
Per $100 of capital funds	+$1.84	−$1.94	−$3.25	−$1.98	+$2.31
*Taxes (income)	532	446	432	545	690
Per $100 of assets	$0.46	$0.39	$0.37	$0.45	$0.54
Per $100 of capital funds	$6.56	$5.62	$5.10	$5.99	$7.14
*Net profits before dividends	847	732	790	852	1,103
Per $100 of assets	$0.73	$0.64	$0.67	$0.71	$0.85
Per $100 of capital funds	$10.46	$9.22	$9.32	$9.37	$11.40
*Cash dividends	300	310	330	364	393
Per $100 of assets	$0.26	$0.27	$0.28	$0.30	$0.30
Per $100 of capital funds	$3.70	$3.90	$3.89	$4.00	$4.06
*Retained earnings	[2] 547	[2] 422	[2] 460	[2] 488	[2] 710
Per $100 of assets	$0.47	$0.37	$0.39	$0.40	$0.55
Per $100 of capital funds	$6.76	$5.32	$5.43	$5.37	$7.34

[1] Exclusive of transfers to and from reserve for bad debts and other valuation reserves on loans and securities but including net losses charged to these reserves.

[2] Includes funds transferred to reserve for bad debts and valuation reserves less the amount of assets charged off against such reserve accounts. Includes $106 million in 1954, $89 million in 1955, $143 million in 1956, $121 million in 1957, and $213 million in 1958 transferred to effect a net increase in reserves for bad debts and valuation reserves. (Taxes would have absorbed a portion of these amounts had the transfers not been made.)

Reserve For Bad Debts

At the end of 1958, 2,843 national banks with gross loans of $50.5 billion or approximately 94% of the loans of the 4,585 national banks in the system, were maintaining reserves for bad debt losses on loans aggregating $1,005.0 million or 1.99% of the loans held by them.

There was a net increase of $85.5 million during the year in amount of the reserves for bad debt losses on loans maintained by the national banks. This increase resulted from banks leaving and entering the system, additional banks, adopting the reserve method of accounting for bad debt losses on loans and transactions within the accounts. Losses charged to the reserve account totaled $75.9 million and recoveries aggregating $37.9 million were credited. Net transfers to the reserve from undivided profits aggregated $123.5 million.

Branch Banking

There were 499 de novo branch applications received during 1958, as compared to 487 received during 1957, 524 during 1956, 532 during 1955 and 382 during 1954.

The following represents the disposition made of the 499 de novo branch applications received during 1958:

	Number	Percentage
Approved (primary approvals of applications for permission to establish branches)_	317	64
Rejected_____	99	20
Withdrawn_____	37	7
In process of investigation and study_____	46	9
	499	100

In 1958, certificates of authorization for the establishment and operation of 413 branches were issued, including 7 which had not yet opened for business on Dec. 31, 1958. Eleven branches which were authorized in 1957 did not open for business until 1958. This resulted in 417 branches opening for business during 1958. During this same period of time changes took place in existing branches, and at year end there were 4,401 branches, including 4 seasonal agencies, being operated by 743 of the total 4,585 active national banks, and 7 nonnational banks in the District of Columbia, reconciled as follows:

State	Branches in operation Dec. 31, 1957	Branches opened for business during 1958	Existing branches discontinued or consolidated during 1958	Branches in operation Dec. 31, 1958
Alabama_____	47	3		50
Arizona_____	92	12		104
Arkansas_____	4	4		8
California_____	1,017	64	4	1,077
Connecticut_____	60	18	2	76
Delaware_____		1		1
District of Columbia_____	52	6	3	1 55
Georgia_____	37	3		40
Idaho_____	65	1		66
Indiana_____	109	15		124
Kansas_____	2	5		7
Kentucky_____	49	4		53
Louisiana_____	74	9		83
Maine_____	31	4		35
Maryland_____	53	9	5	57
Massachusetts_____	158	16	7	167
Michigan_____	164	16	6	174
Minnesota_____	2 6			6
Mississippi_____	15	2		17
Nebraska_____	2 1			1
Nevada_____	19			19
New Hampshire_____	2 1			1
New Jersey_____	186	28	6	208
New Mexico_____	18	1		19
New York_____	361	30	6	385
North Carolina_____	78	12	4	86
North Dakota_____		2	1	1
Ohio_____	234	31	1	264
Oklahoma_____		8		8
Oregon_____	138	4		142
Pennsylvania_____	341	50	16	375
Rhode Island_____	43	4		47
South Carolina_____	76	11		87
South Dakota_____	23			23
Tennessee_____	92	11	1	102
Utah_____	37			37
Vermont_____	6	10		16
Virginia_____	96	10		106
Washington_____	214	8		222
Wisconsin_____	16			16
Alaska_____	8	3		11
Hawaii_____	22	2		24
Virgin Islands_____	1			1
Total_____	4,046	417	−62	4,401

1 Includes 27 branches in operation by 7 nonnational banks in the District of Columbia under the supervision of the Comptroller of the Currency.
2 Established prior to enactment of McFadden Act, Feb. 25, 1927.

The continuing large number of branch offices established during 1958 is largely attributable to the shift of population to suburban areas, requiring new or additional banking services, and the growing volume of business conducted by many banks which could not be adequately accommodated in existing quarters. Competition between banks has also prompted a large number of applications. Traffic congestion and parking problems in urban business sections continued to promote the need for drive-in banking service, and 127 of the 417 branches opened for business during 1958 provided for this type of service. Seventy-seven communities without previous banking service were provided with branch offices.

Branches opened for business during 1958 were distributed among areas with various population density, and established by banks of various sizes, as follows:

In suburban areas of large cities_____ 27
In cities with population less than 5,000_____ 105
In cities with population from 5,000 to 25,000_____ 119
In cities with population from 25,000 to 50,000_____ 54
In cities with population over 50,000_____ 112

    Total_____ 417

By banks with less than $10MM total resources_____ 57
By banks with total resources of $10MM to $25MM_____ 83
By banks with total resources over $25MM_____ 277

    Total_____ 417

During the current year new legislation was enacted by several States permitting the establishment of limited facilities beyond the confines of the bank's place of business. The following tabulation briefly summarizes the current status of branch banking statutes of States and Territories including those changes.

State	Number of all banks	Number of all branches	Total banking units as of Dec. 31, 1958	Number of all banking units in relation to population	Total banking resources (in millions of dollars)
States permitting statewide branch banking:					
Arizona_____	8	137	145	1 per 8,100	1,137
California_____	124	1,427	1,551	1 per 9,400	24,864
Connecticut_____	80	159	239	1 per 9,800	2,550
Delaware_____	27	43	70	1 per 6,900	726
District of Columbia_____	13	55	68	1 per 11,900	1,630
Idaho_____	28	80	108	1 per 6,200	686
Louisiana_____	186	152	338	1 per 9,300	3,050
Maine_____	55	116	171	1 per 5,600	699
Maryland_____	142	194	336	1 per 8,900	2,522
Nevada_____	6	31	37	1 per 7,300	402
North Carolina_____	203	407	610	1 per 7,600	3,021
Oregon_____	55	165	220	1 per 8,200	2,151
Rhode Island_____	9	84	93	1 per 9,500	947
South Carolina_____	144	122	266	1 per 9,200	1,043
Utah_____	49	63	112	1 per 7,900	994
Vermont_____	58	29	87	1 per 4,300	421
Washington_____	89	247	336	1 per 8,300	2,895
Total_____	1,276	3,511	4,787	1 per 8,600	49,738

State	Number of all banks	Number of all branches	Total banking units as of Dec. 31, 1958	Number of all banking units in relation to population	Total banking resources (in millions of dollars)
States permitting branch banking within limited areas:					
Alabama	239	56	295	1 per 11,000	2,137
Arkansas	237	34	271	1 per 6,500	1,273
Georgia	394	68	462	1 per 8,400	3,004
Indiana	459	244	703	1 per 6,600	4,906
Iowa	669	163	832	1 per 3,400	3,434
Kansas	593	11	604	1 per 3,500	2,468
Kentucky	360	113	473	1 per 6,600	2,463
Massachusetts	170	320	490	1 per 10,000	5,913
Michigan	393	491	884	1 per 9,000	8,963
Mississippi	194	121	315	1 per 7,000	1,336
New Jersey	262	360	622	1 per 9,400	7,238
New Mexico	53	38	91	1 per 9,500	714
New York	433	1,222	1,655	1 per 9,900	48,361
North Dakota	155	27	182	1 per 3,600	832
Ohio	606	548	1,154	1 per 8,200	11,584
Oklahoma	387	10	397	1 per 5,800	2,799
Pennsylvania	743	663	1,406	1 per 8,000	15,318
South Dakota	172	53	225	1 per 3,100	788
Tennessee	298	177	475	1 per 7,400	3,340
Virginia	312	217	529	1 per 7,600	3,420
Wisconsin	552	152	704	1 per 5,700	4,713
Total	7,681	5,088	12,769	1 per 7,500	135,004
States prohibiting branch banking, or with no laws regarding branch banking:					
Colorado	175		175	1 per 10,000	2,045
Florida	280		280	1 per 16,400	4,888
Illinois	946		946	1 per 10,600	18,435
Minnesota	686	6	692	1 per 4,900	4,447
Missouri	613	2	615	1 per 7,000	6,518
Montana	115		115	1 per 6,100	874
Nebraska	423	1	424	1 per 3,500	1,827
New Hampshire [1]	75	2	77	1 per 7,700	430
Texas	968	3	971	1 per 9,800	12,621
West Virginia	183		183	1 per 10,800	1,368
Wyoming [1]	52		52	1 per 6,200	433
Total	4,516	14	4,530	1 per 8,500	53,886
Total—United States	13,473	8,613	22,086	1 per 7,950	238,628
Possessions:					
Alaska	18	13	31	1 per 5,500	192
Canal Zone [2]					20
Guam [2]					22
Hawaii	10	64	74	1 per 8,000	628
Puerto Rico [3]	10	95	105	1 per 22,100	585
American Samoa	1		1	1 per 21,000	2
Virgin Islands	2	4	6	1 per 4,000	24
Total possessions	41	176	217	1 per 14,800	1,473
Total—United States and possessions	13,514	8,789	22,303	1 per 8,000	240,101

[1] State laws silent regarding branch banking.
[2] Figures represent branches of domestic banks.
[3] Figures include branches of domestic banks.

NOTE: Above data do not include 520 mutual savings banks operating 425 branches with total resources of $37,779 million.

Applications to Organize National Banks

Forty-eight applications to organize national banks were received during 1958. Primary approval was granted to 18 applications, 11 were disapproved, 7 were withdrawn or abandoned, and 12 continue under investigation and study. The 18 approved cases have resulted in, or are expected to result in, the organization of new national banks in the following 10 States.

State	Number of approvals	Number of banks opened	Approvals total capital structure	Banks opened total capital structure
			Thousands	*Thousands*
Colorado	1	2	400	550
Florida	4	3	2,500	2,600
Idaho	1		400	
Iowa		1		275
Maryland	2	1	1,750	750
Massachusetts		1		450
Michigan	1	1	350	350
Minnesota		1		200
Missouri	3		1,300	
New Hampshire		1		130
New Mexico		1		500
Oregon	1		500	
Tennessee		1		300
Texas	3	4	1,125	1,500
Virginia		1		900
Washington	1		750	
Wisconsin	1	1	350	400
Total	[1] 18	[2] 19	9,425	8,905

[1] Approvals include six which actually opened for business during 1958. The remaining 12 had not completed organization.

[2] Includes 13 that were originally approved in 1956 or 1957, but did not open for business until 1958.

Bank Consolidations, Mergers and Sales

During 1958 the Comptroller approved 83 consolidations, mergers or cash absorptions. An identical number was approved during the previous year. In 1958, 80 national banks absorbed 42 national and 39 State banks. In addition, one District of Columbia national bank and one District of Columbia nonnational bank were purchased by two District of Columbia nonnational banks. Twenty-two national banks and 46 State banks were absorbed by other State banks as compared to 82 such absorptions the previous year. The following schedule contains details of the absorptions which occurred during 1958:

Consolidations, mergers, purchases—1958

Number of banks	Type	Total resources (in millions of dollars)
29	National banks consolidated or merged with and into 29 national banks	513
24	State banks consolidated or merged with and into 23 national banks	568
13	National banks purchased by 13 national banks	88
15	State banks purchased by 15 national banks	422
1	District of Columbia national bank purchased by District of Columbia nonnational bank	75
1	District of Columbia nonnational bank purchased by District of Columbia nonnational bank	39
83	Approved by Comptroller of Currency	1,705
17	National banks consolidated or merged with and into 16 State banks	453
5	National banks purchased by 5 State banks	18
46	State banks consolidated, merged, or purchased with or about the same number of State banks	383
68	Approved by State banking departments	854
151	Grand total	2,559

Conversions

	Number	Resources (in millions of dollars)	Capital structure (in millions of dollars)
State banks converted into national banks.	6	102. 5	9.4—converted into 6 national banks.
National banks converted into State banks.	3	12. 5	.8—converted into 3 State banks.
	9	115. 0	10.2*

*Reserves included in capital structure.

The shareholders of 53 national and State banks consolidated with 52 national banks received cash and book value stock from the 52 continuing banks aggregating $103,514,550 or $12,453,218 in excess of the aggregate book value of assets which those banks contributed to the consolidations. The excess amounted, on the average, to 1.26 percent of the aggregate deposits acquired by the continuing banks. On an estimated fair valuation basis, the shareholders of the 53 absorbed banks contributed assets having an estimated fair value, in excess of liability to creditors, of $101,990,336 and received cash and fair value stock of the continuing banks aggregating $109,507,522 or $7,517,186 in excess of the aggregate fair value of assets which those banks contributed to the mergers or consolidations. The difference is accounted for through an estimated or fair appraisal value of fixed assets (bank premises, furniture and fixtures), bond appreciation or depreciation, allowances for pension fund adjustments, excess reserves for taxes, etc., and amounted on the average to approximately .76 percent of the aggregate deposits acquired by the continuing banks.

The shareholders of 13 national banks and 15 State banks which were purchased by 28 national banks, and the shareholders of one District of Columbia national bank and one District of Columbia nonnational bank, which were purchased by two District of Columbia nonnational banks, received $58,636,258 in cash, or $4,815,407 in excess of the selling banks' aggregate capital structures. This amounted, on the average, to .854 percent of the selling banks' deposits.

In the 9-year period from January 1, 1950 to December 31, 1958, the Comptroller's office approved the acquisition by national banks of 351 national banks and 377 State-chartered banks through consolidation, merger, or sale. After approval by their respective State banking departments, State-chartered banks absorbed 227 national banks. In addition 374 State-chartered banks consolidated or merged with or were purchased by other State-chartered institutions. The following table shows the number of banks which have been absorbed since 1950 and their total resources:

Data on consolidations, mergers, purchases and sales, and conversions—1950 to Dec. 31, 1958

Number of banks	Type	Total resources (in millions of dollars)
144	National banks consolidated with and into other national banks	3,615
62	National banks merged with other national banks	1,641
145	National banks purchased by other national banks	1,400
351	Total	6,656
124	State-chartered banks consolidated with and into national banks	2,363
60	State-chartered banks merged with national banks	796
193	State-chartered banks purchased by national banks	1,322
377	Total	4,481
1	District of Columbia non-national bank consolidated with and into District of Columbia national bank	55
1	District of Columbia national bank purchased by District of Columbia non-national bank	75
1	District of Columbia non-national bank purchased by District of Columbia non-national bank	39
3	Total	169
731	Approved by Comptroller of the Currency	11,306
133	National banks consolidated or merged with State-chartered banks	9,003
94	National banks purchased by State-chartered banks	909
374	State banks merged, consolidated, or purchased with or by other State-chartered banks	5,214
601	Approved by State banking departments	15,126
1,332	Total for absorbed banks	26,432

CONVERSIONS—1950 TO DEC. 31, 1958

23	National banks converted into State-chartered banks	179
49	State-chartered banks converted into national banks	549

Fiduciary Activities of National Banks

As of December 31, 1958, there were 1,724 national banks which had been authorized by the Board of Governors of the Federal Reserve System to exercise trust powers either full, limited or specific and one national bank was authorized under title 12, U.S.C., section 342, to continue administration of the trust account acquired from a State bank by consolidation. Trust departments were being operated in 109 branches. 248 national banks or 14.38 percent were not exercising any of the trust powers granted.

During the year 1958 the Board of Governors granted 37 original and 5 supplemental permits to national banks and the trust powers of 27 national banks were absorbed by consolidation or merger.

There is no uniform system for carrying values of trust department assets among corporate fiduciaries. Essentially there are two systems employed which are the cost or appraised value of the asset and unit value. The cost or appraised value system needs no explanation. Unit value systems carry bonds at $1 per $1,000 and stock at $1 per share or sometimes par value is used. A combination of both systems is usually found in any trust department and figures taken from trust ledgers have little meaning in relation to the actual value of the property held. The unit value system has the advantage of permitting assets to be set up immediately at a permanent carrying figure but usually requires the keeping of another set of books for tax purposes.

The trust figures as to dollar value which appear in this report and its appendix, except for figures on employee welfare and pension benefit plans, are valuable primarily for comparative purposes from year to year. We feel that to require national banks to furnish market values as of any given date would place a substantial and unjustified burden upon the banks.

Of the total liabilities for accounts held by trust departments of national banks as of December 31, 1958, 25.10 percent was in living trusts, 13.24 percent in court accounts, 53.40 percent in agency, escrow, custodianship type accounts, and 8.26 percent in all other liabilities. Figures compiled from trust departments with total assets of $75 million and over show that 83.68 percent of the total assets is held by 6.80 percent of the number of active trust departments. Gross earnings for 1958 were $141,473,000 which is an increase of $12,040,000 over the previous year and an all-time high.

Common trust funds numbering 165 were operated under section 17(c) of Regulation F in 132 national banks. They showed total ledger values for all assets of $517,345,980. Three nonnational banks in the District of Columbia operated 3 such funds with assets of $15,781,303 at the end of 1958.

Following a change in the report of trust examinations in the second half of 1957, we now have available market values during 1958 for employee benefit and pension plans of which national banks are the trustee. These figures appear in tables 22 and 23 of the appendix.

Emergency Preparedness

In 1956, under an order issued by the Director of the Office of Defense Mobilization (now Office of Civil and Defense Mobilization), the Treasury Department, the Comptroller of the Currency, the Board of Governors of the Federal Reserve System, and the Federal Deposit Insurance Corporation are responsible for the development of plans to encourage preparedness measures by commercial banks, designed to insure continuity of the operations of the Nation's banking system in the event of enemy attack. In carrying out this responsibility an Advisory Committee on Commercial Bank Preparedness was appointed. In turn, that committee established a subcommittee, Banking Committee on Emergency Operations, to develop a program to guide and assist banks in planning and taking defense preparedness measures suited to their individual requirements and intended to enable them to continue or resume their operations in event of damage or destruction resulting from attack on the United States.

The committees, composed of leading bankers and representatives of the American Bankers Association, prepared and published five booklets dealing with the subjects, Organization and Administration of the Program in Your Bank, Personnel Protection, Continuity of Management and Alternate Headquarters, Physical Properties, and Duplicate or Alternate Records, and early in 1958 copies of these booklets were distributed free of charge to every bank in the Nation.

Since 1956, national bank examiners have been inquiring informally of national banks located in cities where there is at least one bank, national or state, with deposits aggregating $50 million or more, as to their plans in the event of an emergency. Beginning at the end of March 1958 these inquires were formalized by including a separate page "Emergency Preparedness Measures" in reports of examination so as to record with respect to each national bank the answer to a primary question as to whether an emergency preparedness program has been formulated and, if so, the answers on a "Yes" and "No" basis to 25 questions based upon recommendations contained in the five booklets.

As in the case of the informal inquiries, all of the Federal bank supervisory agencies cooperated in this effort in the examination of banks under their respective supervision. Since this is a voluntary program to be fitted to the needs of the individual banks, examiners have thus far refrained from being critical of failure of any bank to initiate action.

As of the end of 1958, the constructive results of the program are less than might be desired. From May 1, 1958, through April 10, 1959, reports of examination of 9,000 insured commercial banks show that only 129 of 13,124 such banks, less than 1 percent, have record protection programs in full operation.

National Banks Acting As Travel Agents

For some time the Comptroller of the Currency has had under review the question of whether national banks may act as travel agents and whether they may participate in the carriers' conference system which establishes uniform rates of compensation, and uniform obligations to perform, on all participating travel agents.

After careful study it was concluded that national banks may, as an incidental power, provide travel services for their customers, as they have been doing for many years, and that they may have the reasonable rights and benefits that flow therefrom. It was further concluded that whether national banks may participate in the carriers' conference system and whether they can or should enter into agreements in this connection should properly be determined by the banks concerned and their representative counsel, based upon the facts and circumstances of each particular case.

Advisory Boards

A survey was made to determine the extent that advisory boards have been appointed by national banks. Only 98 national banks, in 28 States and the District of Columbia, have appointed such boards, other than in instances connected with branch banking activities. The largest number in one State is Texas, with 17 advisory boards, followed by Alabama, Massachusetts, New York, Pennsylvania, and Tennessee with five each. Twenty-two other States and the District of Columbia have four or less. The largest membership on an advisory board was 25 in 1 instance, followed by 2 at 24, and 1 at 20. Ten had memberships between 10 and 19, and the remainder ranged between 1 and 9.

Litigation

In February 1958 the Milwaukee Western Bank of Milwaukee, Wisconsin brought suit in the United States District Court for the District of Columbia challenging the legality of the Comptroller's approval of a change of location of a branch of the First Wisconsin National Bank of Milwaukee, Wisconsin. The Comptroller, acting under the authority contained in subsection (f) of R.S. 5155, as amended (12 U.S.C. 36(f)), had approved the removal of a branch of the First Wisconsin National Bank from one location within the City of Milwaukee to another location within the same city. Plaintiff's motions for a temporary restraining order, and for a preliminary injunction were denied by the court. Subsequently plaintiff moved for an order for voluntary dismissal and in November 1958 an order was entered dismissing the complaint.

In June 1958, Miss Claudia Walker, a former employee of the Bank of America National Trust and Savings Association, San Francisco, Calif., filed in the United States District Court for the District of Columbia, a mandamus action against the Comptroller of the Currency to compel him to bring an action for the liquidation of the Bank of America National Trust & Savings Association for alleged violations of banking statutes. A motion to dismiss filed on behalf of the Comptroller was granted in November 1958.

Legislation

During the year 1958 the Banking and Currency Committee of the House of Representatives continued its consideration of the proposed Financial Institutions Act, S. 1451 and H.R. 7026. However, this bill was not reported out of committee and was not enacted.

Legislation Enacted

Public Law 85–508, approved July 7, 1958, provided for the admission of the State of Alaska into the Union. This act contained an amendment to the Federal Reserve Act to provide that every national bank in any State should, within 90 days after admission into the Union of the State in which it was located, become a member bank of the Federal Reserve System. As a result of this legislation the nonmember national banks located in Alaska all became member banks of the Federal Reserve System.

Public Law 85–536, approved July 18, 1958, amended Section 24 of the Federal Reserve Act by providing that loans in which the Small Business Administration cooperates through agreements to participate on an immediate or deferred basis under the Small Business Act shall not be subject to the restrictions or limitations imposed upon loans secured by real estate. The effect of this amendment was to eliminate the requirement that in order to qualify for exemption from section 24 loans made by national banks with the cooperation or participation of the Small Business Administration must be made to established industrial or commercial businesses.

Public Law 85–699, approved August 21, 1958, the Small Business Investment Act of 1958, provided for the establishment of small business investment companies, the primary function of which shall be to provide a source of needed equity capital for small business concerns in the manner and subject to the conditions prescribed in the Act. This Act provides that shares of stock in small business investment companies shall be eligible for purchase by national banks, except that no national bank may hold shares in small business investment companies in an amount aggregating more than 1% of its capital and surplus.

Public Law 85–748, approved August 25, 1958, amended R.S. 5200, as amended (12 U.S.C. 84), limiting loans by national banks to any one borrower to 10% of capital and surplus, by adding a new exception as follows:

"Obligations insured by the Secretary of Agriculture pursuant to the Bankhead–Jones Farm Tenant Act, as amended, or the Act of August 28, 1937, as amended (relating to the conservation of water resources), shall be subject under this section to a limitation of 15 per centum of such capital and surplus in addition to such 10 per centum of such capital and surplus."

Public Law 85–836, approved August 28, 1958, the Welfare and Pension Plans Disclosure Act, provided that each administrator of an employee welfare benefit plan or an employee pension benefit plan as defined in the act shall publish in accordance with the terms of the act to each participant or beneficiary covered thereunder (1) a description of the plan and (2) an annual financial report, containing information prescribed in the act. Each such administrator is also required to file with the Secretary of Labor two copies of the description of the plan and each annual report thereon.

The act provides that it shall not apply to an employee welfare or pension benefit plan if such plan is administered by an instrumentality of the Federal Government. Since national banks have been held to be instrumentalities of the United States the extent to which this act applies to plans administered by national banks is unclear.

National Banks Placed in Receivership

There was only one national bank placed in receivership during the current year. On March 17, 1958 the Comptroller of the Currency appointed the Federal Deposit Insurance Corporation as receiver of the insolvent First National Bank of Halfway, Halfway, Oreg. By December 1, 1958 all creditors' proven claims had been paid in full with accrued interest from liquidation of the bank's assets, collections from a defaulting officer, and the surety on his bond. The Comptroller of the Currency on that date called a meeting of shareholders for January 9, 1959, as required under the provisions of 12 U.S.C., section 197, in order that they might vote either to have the receivership continued for their benefit, or to elect an agent who would assume the final liquidation responsibilities.

Examinations Conducted

The National Bank Act requires that each national bank be examined at least twice each year in order that the Comptroller may be kept currently informed of its condition and require such corrections as are deemed necessary with a view to maintaining each bank in sound condition. However, the Comptroller is authorized to waive an examination with respect to any particular bank not more frequently than once in any 2-year period. In addition to the regular examinations, special examinations are conducted of banks the condition of which is regarded as unsatisfactory. Also, the District Code authorizes the Comptroller to examine each nonnational bank and trust company in the District of Columbia.

During the year ended December 31, 1958, 7,142 examinations of banks, 6,104 examinations of branches, 1,566 examinations of trust departments, and 62 examinations of affiliates were conducted. Four State banks were examined in connection with consolidations and mergers with, or purchase by, national banks, and 11 State banks were examined in connection with conversions to national banks. Investigations were conducted in connection with applications for 32 new charters and 467 new branches.

Organization and Staff

On December 31, 1958, the total personnel of the Office of the Comptroller of the Currency consisted of 1,144 persons, 195 of whom were employed in the Washington office, including 32 in the Federal Reserve Issue and Redemption Division, the operating expense of which is borne by the Federal Reserve Banks. The total number employed in the Washington office increased by one during the year. The total number in the field increased by 37 during the year 1958.

The major segment of the field personnel consists of the national bank examining staff and, during the year, 18 national bank examiners left the service by resignation, retirement, and due to deaths, and 1 was promoted to Assistant Chief National Bank Examiner in the Washington office. Also during the year, 28 assistant examiners were promoted to examiner status, resulting in a net increase of 9 examiners. As to the staff of assistant examiners, 69 left the service during the year by resignation, retirement, promotion to examiner, etc., and 97 new assistant examiners were added to the staff, a net increase of 28. There were 12 District Chief National Bank examiners, 250 National Bank examiners, and 574 assistant National Bank examiners in the field service at the end of the year.

District Chief National Bank Examiner William B. Baker, who was in charge of the Philadelphia office, retired on September 30, 1958, and was succeeded by Marshall Abrahamson, who had been serving as an Assistant Chief National Bank Examiner in the Washington office. William A. Robson, a national bank examiner from the Kansas City district, succeeded Mr. Abrahamson as Assistant Chief National Bank Examiner.

The employee training programs for examiners and assistants, mentioned in previous reports, were continued during the year, and at the year end 288 examiners and assistants had completed the courses given in the interagency school established jointly in 1952 by the Comptroller of the Currency, the Board of Governors of the Federal Reserve System, and the Federal Deposit Insurance Corporation. Courses at the Graduate Schools of Banking, given at Rutgers University, the University of Wisconsin, the University of Washington, the University of Louisiana, and Southern Methodist University, had been completed by 68 examining staff members at the year end and 18 were still enrolled in courses at these schools. Extension courses given by the American Institute of Banking had been completed by 302 members of the examining staff at the year end and 246 were still enrolled in these courses.

In conformity with a Federal Government-wide program to reduce to writing promotion procedures so that all employees might be familiar with promotion requirements and the standards applied in making promotions, such plans were formulated and circulated to all employees during the year for their review and comment following which the plans were adopted, effective January 1, 1959.

The following table which has appeared in previous reports is again included to demonstrate how the work of the 1,144 employees is organized and their services utilized:

Division	Executive or supervisory	Assistant examiners, assistant counsel, administrative assistants, auditors, secretaries, typists, clerks	Total
I. EXECUTIVE ORGANIZATION			
(Policy and general supervision, all located in Washington, D.C.)			
Comptroller of the Currency	1	[1] 2	3
Deputy Comptrollers	3	[1] 3	6
Chief National Bank Examiner	1	[1] 1	2
	5	6	11
II. FIELD ORGANIZATION			
(Located in 12 Federal Reserve districts)			
District Chief National Bank Examiners	12	[1][2][3] 113	125
Policy and supervision, subject to executive staff in group I, above, of all field activities.			
National Bank Examiners	250		250
Perform examinations of 4,593 banks, 4,401 branch offices, and make investigations of new branch and charter applications, etc.			
Assistant National Bank Examiners		574	574
Assist National Bank Examiners.			
	262	687	949
III. WASHINGTON STAFF ORGANIZATION			
(a) Examining Division	8	[1][2][3][4] 26	34
Assistant Chief National Bank Examiners. Receive and analyze all reports of examination of national and District banks, and investigation reports on new branches and charters. Make recommendations to executive staff in group I, above, as to dispositions of cases, and prepare letters to banks, District Chiefs, and others. Confer with bankers, executive and staff representatives of the Federal Reserve System and the Federal Deposit Insurance Corporation, and District Chief National Bank Examiners, regarding banking and supervisory matters. One Assistant Chief also serves as head of the Personnel and Administrative Division, and one also serves as head of the field organization educational programs.			

See footnotes at end of table.

Division	Executive or supervisory	Assistant examiners, assistant counsel, administrative assistants, auditors, secretaries, typists, clerks	Total
III. WASHINGTON STAFF ORGANIZATION—continued			
(b) Organization Division Supervises activities of all national and District banks as to corporate and organization matters; i.e., new charters, branches, consolidations, mergers, purchase and assumption cases, sale of new capital stock, stock dividends, articles of association, etc. Final decisions made by executive staff in group I, above, after review with recommendations by Assistant Chief National Bank Examiners, and usually with the benefit of facts and recommendations furnished by District Chief National Bank Examiners and National Bank Examiners.	4	[1][2][3][4] 18	22
(c) Legal Division Serves as counsel for the Comptroller of the Currency. Considers all legal matters arising in the organization, operation, merging, and discontinuance of national and District banks. Prepares opinions, rulings, and correspondence on legal questions. Assists on all legislative matters. Exercises general supervision over conduct of litigation.	1	[1] 4 [5] 3	8
(d) Personnel and Administrative Division Performs functions relating to recruitment, transfer, promotion, separation, retirement, time and leave. Supervises and includes personnel in mail and files section, supply and duplicating section, stenographic pool, and messenger pool.	1	[1][2][3][4][6] 24	25
(e) Reports and Precedents Division Maintains all legal and policy precedents; receives reports of examination of all national and District banks from District Chief National Bank Examiners for binding, recording, and distribution. Supervises and places orders for printing work that pertains to examining division and the field organization.	1	[1][2][3] 3	4
(f) Statistical Division Compiles data indicative of banking trends for the information of the Comptroller and his staff, Congress, other banking agencies, bankers, economists, and others through examination and tabulation of data incorporated in call reports of condition and reports of earnings and dividends of national and District banks.	2	[1][2][3] 21	23
(g) Auditor for the Comptroller Accountable to the Comptroller of the Currency only. Maintains audits for the Comptroller of all accounts covering funds under control of the Disbursing Office including detailed audits of all collections and disbursements of funds; prepares and submits periodic audit reports to Comptroller; tabulates information and statistics on special subjects.	2	[1][2][3][7] 9	11
(h) Disbursing Division Receives all checks in payment of fees for examinations and makes deposits to the Comptroller's Treasury account. Maintains accounts covering funds of Examining Division and of Federal Reserve Issue and Redemption Division and makes all disbursements from these accounts covering payrolls, travel vouchers, and miscellaneous expenses. Makes all purchases of equipment and supplies from Examining Division funds.	2	[1][2][3][6] 23	25
(i) Federal Reserve Issue and Redemption Division All expenses of this division paid by Federal Reserve banks. Handles the issuance and redemption of Federal Reserve currency as provided under the Federal Reserve Act. Maintains detailed records of all shipments of original currency issues and of unfit currency notes destroyed.	2	[1][2][3][8] 30	32
	23	161	184
Grand total	290	854	1,144

[1] Secretarial.   [3] Clerical.   [5] Attorney.   [7] Accountants.
[2] Typists.   [4] Administrative.   [6] Messengers.   [8] Money counters.

Expenses of the Bureau

The total cost of bank supervision for the current year was $1,340,838.42 more than the total cost for the year 1957, although certain expense items showed decreases for the year 1958.   Increases in salaries of $925,478.46 for the year 1958, are very largely the result of the Federal Employees Salary Increase Act of 1958, approved June 20, 1958, increasing salaries of Federal employees retroactively to January 12, 1958.   Increases in Employer's Civil Service Retirement contributions of $286,842.84 for the year 1958, resulted from provisions of an amendment to the Civil Service Retirement Act, effective July 14, 1957, requiring such contributions of funds.   An increase of $138,090.02 in per diem costs for the year 1958, is largely attributable to a statutory increase in per diem allowances from $10 to $12, which was made effective in the Comptroller's office on May 1, 1957. Increases in additional expense categories aggregated $24,346.55. The decreases in other cost items amounted to $33,919.45.

Funds used in payment of the bank supervision costs are derived from assessments against the banks supervised.   All costs of operating the division which handles the currency issue and redemption functions are paid by the Federal Reserve banks.

Summary statement of the operating expenses of the Bureau for the year ended Dec. 31, 1958

	Bank supervision	Currency issue and redemption	Total
Salaries	$7,459,908.86	$152,265.93	$7,612,174.79
Per diem	1,544,780.75	0	1,544,780.75
Transportation	549,037.44	0	549,037.44
Supplies	22,235.64	434.72	22,670.36
Printing, books, and periodicals	65,368.25	0	65,368.25
Rent	146,756.61	0	146,756.61
Furniture and fixtures	29,241.32	0	29,241.32
Communications	51,998.54	475.01	52,473.55
Fixed charges	0	14,761.08	14,761.08
Maintenance	0	4,981.05	4,981.05
Treasurer's Federal Reserve note vault expense	0	11,628.00	11,628.00
Employer's F.I.C.A. and insurance fund contributions	23,741.15	464.61	24,205.76
Employer's civil service retirement contributions	479,418.95	9,851.11	489,270.06
Miscellaneous	28,367.85	5,590.26	33,958.11
Total	10,400,855.36	200,451.77	10,601,307.13

A comparison of the assets and liabilities of the banks in the national banking system as of December 31, 1957, March 4, June 23, September 24, and December 31, 1958, reported pursuant to calls for condition statements by the Comptroller of the Currency, is shown in the following table.

Assets and liabilities of national banks on dates indicated

[In thousands of dollars]

	Dec. 31, 1957 (4,627 banks)	Mar. 4, 1958 (4,622 banks)	June 23, 1958 (4,606 banks)	Sept. 24, 1958 (4,590 banks)	Dec. 31, 1958 (4,585 banks)
ASSETS					
Loans and discounts, including overdrafts	50,502,277	49,688,857	50,902,433	50,664,772	52,796,224
U.S. Government securities, direct obligations	31,335,767	31,795,874	34,599,192	35,281,644	35,821,327
Obligations guaranteed by U.S. Government	2,309	2,393	2,813	3,430	3,433
Obligations of States and political subdivisions	7,495,878	7,626,441	8,364,896	8,688,802	8,845,522
Other bonds, notes, and debentures	1,880,706	1,927,818	2,045,247	1,948,482	1,836,523
Corporate stocks, including stocks of Federal Reserve banks	267,049	271,708	274,438	277,829	281,419
Total loans and securities	*91,483,986*	*91,313,091*	*96,189,019*	*96,864,959*	*99,584,448*
Cash, balances with other banks, including reserve balances, and cash items in process of collection	26,865,134	23,633,476	24,032,436	23,361,568	26,864,820
Bank premises owned, furniture and fixtures	1,187,155	1,212,207	1,252,651	1,292,535	1,326,352
Real estate owned other than bank premises	36,487	35,386	40,958	38,664	33,575
Investments and other assets indirectly representing bank premises or other real estate	116,139	118,621	121,766	126,150	127,075
Customers' liability on acceptances	374,518	437,646	334,949	288,394	321,852
Income accrued but not yet collected	272,846	276,359	263,311	272,093	} 538,844
Other assets	186,375	212,350	233,825	210,456	
Total assets	120,522,640	117,242,136	122,468,815	122,454,819	128,796,966
LIABILITIES					
Demand deposits of individuals, partnerships, and corporations	58,715,522	55,043,742	55,115,495	56,580,477	61,785,222
Time deposits of individuals, partnerships, and corporations	29,138,727	29,882,234	31,329,692	32,215,034	32,614,707
Deposits of U.S. Government and postal savings	2,424,137	2,174,693	4,994,800	2,569,006	2,574,937
Deposits of States and political subdivisions	7,878,315	8,018,405	8,611,982	8,042,579	8,426,763
Deposits of banks	9,483,436	8,688,328	8,685,161	8,959,581	9,809,186
Other deposits (certified and cashiers' checks, etc.)	1,796,174	1,418,851	1,669,619	1,430,623	1,875,313
Total deposits	109,436,311	105,226,253	110,406,749	109,797,300	117,086,128
Demand deposits	*77,880,965*	*72,437,659*	*75,681,195*	*74,335,501*	*81,351,799*
Time deposits	*31,555,346*	*32,788,594*	*34,725,554*	*35,463,799*	*35,734,329*
Bills payable, rediscounts, and other liabilities for borrowed money	38,324	610,019	491,502	998,291	43,035
Mortgages or other liens on bank premises and other real estate	1,522	1,034	1,062	1,475	1,626
Acceptances outstanding	388,516	449,038	345,382	299,253	330,616
Income collected but not yet earned	576,713	566,634	593,004	620,649	} 1,666,760
Expenses accrued and unpaid	557,082	722,667	621,317	682,941	
Other liabilities	430,955	423,669	534,145	434,126	
Total liabilities	111,429,423	107,999,314	112,993,161	112,834,035	119,128,165

CAPITAL ACCOUNTS					
Capital stock (see memoranda below)	2,806,213	2,842,903	2,867,859	2,930,459	2,951,279
Surplus	4,416,426	4,448,129	4,514,485	4,558,635	4,718,459
Undivided profits	1,618,887	1,694,533	1,839,600	1,862,819	1,711,435
Reserves and retirement account for preferred stock	251,721	257,257	253,710	268,871	287,628
Total capital accounts	9,093,217	9,242,822	9,475,654	9,620,784	9,668,801
Total liabilities and capital accounts	120,522,640	117,242,136	122,468,815	122,454,819	128,796,966

MEMORANDA

Par value of capital stock:					
Class A preferred stock	3,585	2,568	2,743	3,492	3,492
Class B preferred stock	175	175			
Common stock	2,802,453	2,840,160	2,855,116	2,926,967	2,947,787
Total	2,806,213	2,842,903	2,867,859	2,930,459	2,951,279
Retirable value of preferred capital stock:					
Class A preferred stock	3,760	2,743	2,943	3,692	3,692
Class B preferred stock	200	200			
Total	3,960	2,943	2,943	3,692	3,692
Assets pledged or assigned to secure liabilities and for other purposes (including notes and bills rediscounted and securities sold with agreement to repurchase)	14,507,686	14,749,503	17,339,672	16,444,619	15,977,013

TRENDS IN BANKING

The following table shows the changes that have occurred in recent years in the relationships of the major asset and liability accounts of national banks to the aggregate of assets and liabilities.

Distribution of assets and liabilities of national banks, Dec. 31, 1955–58

	1955	1956	1957	1958
ASSETS				
Securities:	*Percent*	*Percent*	*Percent*	*Percent*
U.S. Government, direct and guaranteed	29.62	26.91	26.00	27.81
Obligations of States and political subdivisions	6.15	5.97	6.22	6.87
Stock of Federal Reserve banks	.17	.17	.18	.18
Other bonds and securities	1.74	1.36	1.60	1.47
Total securities	37.68	34.41	34.00	36.33
Loans and discounts	38.29	40.99	41.90	40.99
Cash and balances with other banks, excluding reserves	12.68	13.27	12.77	12.21
Reserve with Reserve banks	9.97	9.74	9.53	8.65
Bank premises, furniture and fixtures	.85	.93	.98	1.03
Other real estate owned	.02	.03	.03	.03
All other assets	.51	.63	.79	.76
Total assets	100.00	100.00	100.00	100.00
LIABILITIES				
Deposits:				
Demand of individuals, partnerships, and corporations	51.16	50.62	48.72	47.97
Time of individuals, partnerships, and corporations	22.11	22.32	24.18	25.32
U.S. Government	2.07	2.00	2.00	1.99
States and political subdivisions	6.45	6.34	6.53	6.54
Banks	8.19	8.37	7.87	7.62
Other deposits (including postal savings)	1.64	1.68	1.50	1.46
Total deposits	91.62	91.33	90.80	90.90
Demand deposits	*67.60*	*67.14*	*64.62*	*63.16*
Time deposits	*24.02*	*24.19*	*26.18*	*27.74*
Other liabilities	1.40	1.47	1.65	1.59
Capital funds:				
Capital stock	2.17	2.24	2.33	2.29
Surplus	3.37	3.52	3.67	3.67
Undivided profits and reserves	1.44	1.44	1.55	1.55
Total capital funds	6.98	7.20	7.55	7.51
Total liabilities and capital funds	100.00	100.00	100.00	100.00

EARNINGS, EXPENSES, AND DIVIDENDS OF NATIONAL BANKS FOR YEAR ENDED DECEMBER 31, 1958

Summaries of the earnings, expenses, and dividends of national banks for the years ended December 31, 1957 and 1958, are shown in the following table.

Earnings, expenses, and dividends of national banks for years ended Dec. 31, 1957 and 1958

[In millions of dollars]

	1958	1957	Change since 1957
Number of banks [1]	4, 585	4, 627	−42
Capital stock (par value)[2]	2, 875. 1	2, 716. 9	+158. 2
Capital accounts [2]	9, 412. 6	8, 769. 8	+642. 8
Earnings from current operations:			
Interest and dividends on—			
U.S. Government obligations	839. 1	782. 1	+57. 0
Other securities	267. 6	225. 4	+42. 2
Interest and discount on loans	2, 739. 2	2, 631. 1	+108. 1
Service charges on deposit accounts	269. 6	244. 1	+25. 5
Other current earnings	423. 4	401. 1	+22. 3
Total	4, 538. 9	4, 283. 8	+255. 1
Current operating expenses:			
Salaries, wages, and fees	1, 263. 9	1, 189. 4	+74. 5
Interest on time deposits (including savings deposits)	762. 3	635. 8	+126. 5
Taxes other than on net income	125. 9	116. 3	+9. 6
Recurring depreciation on banking house, furniture, and fixtures	91. 2	79. 5	+11. 7
Other current operating expenses	726. 9	686. 2	+40. 7
Total	2, 970. 2	2, 707. 2	+263. 0
Net earnings from current operations	1, 568. 7	1, 576. 6	−7. 9
Recoveries, transfers from valuation reserves, and profits:			
On securities:			
Recoveries	5. 5	4. 2	+1. 3
Transfers from valuation reserves	33. 1	14. 3	+18. 8
Profits on securities sold or redeemed	353. 1	31. 1	+322. 0
On loans:			
Recoveries	11. 3	9. 5	+1. 8
Transfers from valuation reserves	27. 6	15. 1	+12. 5
All other	30. 6	17. 4	+13. 2
Total	461. 1	91. 6	+369. 5
Losses, charge-offs, and transfers to valuation reserves:			
On securities:			
Losses and charge-offs	54. 8	119. 0	−64. 2
Transfers to valuation reserves	159. 7	37. 9	+121. 8
On loans:			
Losses and charge-offs	11. 6	11. 7	−. 1
Transfers to valuation reserves	157. 7	177. 2	−19. 5
All other	66. 6	47. 2	+19. 4
Total	450. 4	393. 1	+57. 3
Profits before income taxes	1, 579. 4	1, 275. 1	+304. 3
Taxes on net income:			
Federal	658. 6	522. 7	+135. 9
State	31. 7	22. 5	+9. 2
Total	690. 3	545. 2	+145. 1

See footnotes at end of table.

Earnings, expenses, and dividends of national banks for years ended Dec. 31, 1957 and 1958—Continued

[In millions of dollars]

	1958	1957	Change since 1957
Net profits before dividends_____	889. 1	729. 9	+159. 2
Cash dividends declared:			
On preferred stock_____	. 2	³. 2	. 0
On common stock_____	392. 8	363. 7	+29. 1
Total_____	393. 0	363. 9	+29. 1
Memoranda items:			
Recoveries credited to valuation reserves (not included in recoveries above):			
On securities_____	6. 9	1. 6	+5. 3
On loans_____	38. 9	29. 5	+9. 4
Losses charged to valuation reserves (not included in losses above):			
On securities_____	12. 6	32. 1	−19. 5
On loans_____	76. 8	62. 7	+14. 1
Stock dividends (increases in capital stock)_____	108. 5	64. 7	+43. 8
Ratios:	*Percent*	*Percent*	*Percent*
Expenses to gross earnings_____	65. 44	63. 20	+2. 24
Net profits before dividends to capital accounts_____	9. 45	8. 32	+1. 13
Cash dividends to capital stock_____	13. 67⅜	13. 39	+. 28
Cash dividends to capital accounts_____	4. 18	4. 15	+. 03

¹ Number at end of period. Remaining figures include earnings, expenses, etc., of those banks which were in operation a part of the year but were inactive at the close of the year.

² Figures are averages of amounts reported for the June and December call dates in the current year and the December call date in the previous year.

³ Revised.

NOTE.—Figures are rounded to the nearest tenth of a million and may not equal totals.

STRUCTURAL CHANGES IN THE NATIONAL BANKING SYSTEM

The authorized capital stock of the 4,581 national banks in existence on December 31, 1958, consisted of common capital stock aggregating $2,958,859,229, a net increase during the year of $156,408,877, and preferred capital stock of $3,491,670, a net decrease during the year of $268,000. These figures exclude four banks which furnished reports of condition in response to the call, although two of them had converted into State banks, one had consolidated with another national bank, and one had gone into voluntary liquidation and was succeeded by another national bank, all effective as of the close of business on December 31.

In addition to the 43 applications with proposed common capital stock of $9,450,000 carried over from the previous year, 60 applications were received to organize national banks and to convert State banks into national banking associations with proposed capital stock of $28,578,000. Of these applications, 26 with proposed common capital stock of $21,565,000 were approved; 13 with proposed common capital stock of $3,325,000 were rejected; and the remainder had been abandoned or were still pending on December 31. From the applications carried over from the previous year and those approved during 1958, 24 national banking associations with common capital stock of $7,650,000 were authorized to commence business. Of the charters issued, six with common capital stock of $3,200,000 resulted from the conversions of State banks.

Changes in the number and capital stock of national banks during the year ended December 31, 1958, are shown in the following summary.

Organization, capital stock changes, and national banks closed as reported during the year ended Dec. 31, 1958

	Number of banks	Capital stock	
		Common	Preferred
Increases:			
Banks newly chartered:			
Primary organizations	18	$4,450,000	
Reorganizations			
Conversions of State banks	6	3,200,000	
Capital stock:			
Preferred: 1 case by new issue			$800,000
Common:			
172 cases by statutory sale		38,913,756	
393 cases by statutory stock dividend		108,471,131	
1 case by stock dividend under articles of association		35,000	
22 cases by statutory consolidation		13,520,000	
18 cases by statutory merger		4,531,500	
Total increases	24	173,121,387	800,000
Decreases:			
Banks ceasing operations:			
Voluntary liquidations:			
Succeeded by national banks	13	2,850,000	
Succeeded by State banks	6	2,245,000	
Statutory consolidations	15		
Statutory mergers	14		
Conversions into State banks	3	275,000	
Merged or consolidated with State banks (Public Law 706)	17	10,875,000	
Receivership	1	25,000	
Capital stock:			
Preferred: 4 cases by retirement			1,068,000
Common:			
3 cases by statutory reduction		89,010	
3 cases by statutory consolidation		257,500	
2 cases by statutory merger		96,000	
Total decreases	69	16,712,510	1,068,000
Net change	−45	156,408,877	−268,000
Charters in force Dec. 31, 1957, and authorized capital stock	4,626	2,802,450,352	3,759,670
Charters in force Dec. 31, 1958, and authorized capital stock	4,581	2,958,859,229	3,491,670

NATIONAL BANK NOTES OUTSTANDING

There were, as of December 31, 1958, $58,709,057 of national bank notes outstanding.

ASSETS AND LIABILITIES OF ALL BANKS IN THE UNITED STATES AND POSSESSIONS

The total assets of all classes of active banks in the United States and possessions on December 31, 1958, amounted to $277,880 million, an increase of $18,692 million since December 31, 1957.

The total deposits at the end of 1958 amounted to $251,332 million, an increase of $17,154 million over 1957. Included in the latter aggregate are deposits of individuals, partnerships, and corporations of $209,676 million, an increase of $14,134 million in the year. Deposits of the U.S. Government, including postal savings deposits, were $4,666 million, an increase of $373 million; deposits of States and political subdivisions amounting to $14,722 million showed an increase of $1,067 million, and deposits of banks of $18,204 million were $1,157 million more than in 1957.

Loans and discounts amounted to $122,287 million in December 1958 after deducting reserves of $2,188 million for possible future losses. The net loans were $6,527 million over the amount reported as of the end of 1957. Commercial and industrial loans of $40,771 million were $54 million less than the 1957 figure; real estate loans of $48,786 million were up $4,280 million, and all other loans of $34,918 million increased $2,489 million.

The banks held obligations of the U.S. Government, direct and guaranteed, of $73,935 million in December 1958, an increase of $7,869 million in the year. Obligations of States and political subdivisions held amounted to $17,311 million, an increase of $2,641 million, and other securities held amounted to $9,079 million, an increase of $697 million. The total of all securities held at the end of 1958 was $100,325 million, and represented 36 percent of the banks' total assets. At the end of the previous year the ratio was 34 percent.

Cash and balances with other banks, including reserve balances, in 1958 were $50,147 million, an increase of $608 million since the previous year end.

Total capital accounts were $21,822 million, compared to $20,537 million at the end of 1957, an increase of 6 percent.

A statement of the assets and liabilities of all classes of active banks at the end of December 1957 and 1958 follows.

Assets and liabilities of all banks in the United States and possessions, 1957 and 1958

[In millions of dollars

	Dec. 31, 1958	Dec. 31, 1957	Change since 1957
Number of banks	14,034	14,103	−69
ASSETS			
Real estate loans	48,786	44,506	+4,280
Loans to banks	723	731	−8
Loans to brokers and dealers in securities and other loans for the purpose of purchasing or carrying securities	4,698	4,250	+448
Loans to farmers directly guaranteed by the Commodity Credit Corporation	814	462	+352
Other loans to farmers	4,179	3,624	+555
Commercial and industrial loans (including open-market paper)	40,771	40,825	−54
Other loans to individuals	21,034	20,512	+522
All other loans (including overdrafts)	3,470	2,850	+620
Total gross loans	124,475	117,760	+6,715
Less valuation reserves	2,188	2,000	+188
Net loans	122,287	115,760	+6,527
U.S. Government obligations, direct and guaranteed	73,935	66,066	+7,869
Obligations of States and political subdivisions	17,311	14,670	+2,641
Other bonds, notes, and debentures	7,661	7,092	+569
Corporate stocks, including stocks of Federal Reserve banks	1,418	1,290	+128
Total securities	100,325	89,118	+11,207
Currency and coin	3,452	3,533	−81
Balances with other banks, including reserve balances, and cash items in process of collection	46,695	46,006	+689
Bank premises owned, furniture and fixtures	2,578	2,330	+248
Real estate owned other than bank premises	66	63	+3
Investments and other assets indirectly representing bank premises or other real estate	204	175	+29
Customers' liability on acceptances outstanding	868	1,004	−136
Other assets	1,405	1,199	+206
Total assets	277,880	259,188	+18,692
LIABILITIES			
Demand deposits of individuals, partnerships, and corporations	115,664	110,139	+5,525
Time deposits of individuals, partnerships, and corporations	94,012	85,403	+8,609
U.S. Government and postal savings deposits	4,666	4,293	+373
Deposits of States and political subdivisions	14,722	13,655	+1,067
Deposits of banks	18,204	17,047	+1,157
Other deposits (certified and cashiers' checks, etc.)	4,064	3,641	+423
Total deposits	251,332	234,178	+17,154
Demand deposits	150,902	144,210	+6,692
Time deposits	100,430	89,968	+10,462
Bills payable, rediscounts, and other liabilities for borrowed money	96	98	−2
Acceptances executed by or for account of reporting banks and outstanding	907	1,048	−141
Other liabilities	3,723	3,327	+396
Total liabilities	256,058	238,651	+17,407
CAPITAL ACCOUNTS			
Capital notes and debentures	58	49	+9
Preferred stock	19	18	+1
Common stock	5,491	5,241	+250
Surplus	11,207	10,547	+660
Undivided profits	4,258	4,010	+248
Reserves and retirement account for preferred stock and capital notes and debentures	789	672	+117
Total capital accounts	21,822	20,537	+1,285
Total liabilities and capital accounts	277,880	259,188	+18,692

NOTE.—Figures for nonnational banks obtained from the Federal Deposit Insurance Corporation.

REPORTS FROM BANKS

National banks in the continental United States, Alaska, the Territory of Hawaii, and the Virgin Islands of the United States were, in accordance with the provisions of Section 5211 of the Revised Statutes, called upon to submit four reports of condition during the year ended December 31, 1958. Reports were required as of March 4, June 23, September 24, and December 31. Summaries from all condition reports, by States, are published in pamphlet form. National banks were also required by statute to obtain reports, unless waived by the Comptroller, of their affiliates and holding company affiliates other than member banks as of the four dates for which condition reports of the banks were obtained and to submit such reports to the Comptroller.

Under the general powers conferred upon him by law, the Comptroller obtained from each national bank during the period indicated semiannual reports of earnings, expenses, and dividends; also reports of condition of foreign branches as of December 31, 1958.

National banking associations authorized to act in a fiduciary capacity were called upon to submit reports of their trust departments as of the close of business on December 31, 1958.

In accordance with the code of law for the District of Columbia, banks other than national in the District were required to make to the Comptroller condition reports and reports of earnings, expenses, and dividends identical with those obtained from national banks during the year.

Detailed figures from reports of condition and earnings and dividends will be found in the appendix of this report.

AFFILIATES AND HOLDING COMPANY AFFILIATES OF NATIONAL BANKS

The Federal statute requires each national bank to obtain and submit to the Comptroller periodically reports of its affiliates, as defined in sections 2 (b) and (c) of the Banking Act of 1933, as amended. However section 21 of the Federal Reserve Act, as amended, provides in part that the Comptroller may waive the requirement for the submission of the report of an affiliate if in his judgment such a report is not necessary to disclose fully the relations between an affiliate and a bank and the effect thereof upon the affairs of the bank. Pursuant to this latter section the Comptroller's waiver of requirement for reports of affiliates provides principally that reports of affiliates (other than holding company affiliates) need not be submitted and published in a newspaper unless the affiliate is indebted to the national bank or the bank owns obligations of the affiliate and the aggregate of such indebtedness and/or investment is carried as an asset on the bank's books at a value in excess of $5,000, or 1 percent of the bank's capital and surplus, whichever is the greater.

At the end of December 1958, 365 member national banks in the United States submitted 412 reports of affiliates. Included in these figures are 205 banks in 28 States which are members of 29 holding company groups. The number of banks in each holding company group varied from 1 to 58. The actual number of reporting affiliates and holding company affiliates was 242.

In addition there was one nonnational bank in the District of Columbia which is a member of the Federal Reserve System that reported one affiliate to the Comptroller pursuant to the provisions of the code of law for the District of Columbia.

ISSUE AND REDEMPTION OF NOTES

There were 668 shipments of new Federal Reserve notes (458,567,000 notes—aggregate value $5,585,420,000) made to Federal Reserve agents and Federal Reserve branch banks. In addition, there were 29 deliveries of such notes (10,722,000 notes—aggregate value $189,-100,000) made to the Treasurer of the United States.

There was a total of 5,212 lots of unfit Federal Reserve notes and Federal Reserve bank notes (490,342,204 notes—aggregate value $5,914,582,789) received for verification and certification for destruction.

There were 30 lots of national bank notes (124,979 notes— aggregate value $2,141,890) received for verification and certification for destruction.

There was a total of 231,968 badly damaged Federal Reserve notes, Federal Reserve bank notes and national bank notes (aggregate value $4,075,401) presented, by the Treasurer of the United States, for identification approval.

APPENDIX

APPENDIX

CONTENTS

TABLES

43

TABLE No. 1.—*Comptrollers and Deputy Comptrollers of the Currency, dates of appointment and resignation, and States whence appointed*

No.	Name	Date of appointment	Date of resignation	State
	COMPTROLLERS OF THE CURRENCY			
1	McCulloch, Hugh	May 9, 1863	Mar. 8, 1865	Indiana.
2	Clarke, Freeman	Mar. 21, 1865	July 24, 1866	New York.
3	Hulburd, Hiland R	Feb. 1, 1867	Apr. 3, 1872	Ohio.
4	Knox, John Jay	Apr. 25, 1872	Apr. 30, 1884	Minnesota.
5	Cannon, Henry W	May 12, 1884	Mar. 1, 1886	Do.
6	Trenholm, William L	Apr. 20, 1886	Apr. 30, 1889	South Carolina.
7	Lacey, Edward S	May 1, 1889	June 30, 1892	Michigan.
8	Hepburn, A. Barton	Aug. 2, 1892	Apr. 25, 1893	New York.
9	Eckels, James H	Apr. 26, 1893	Dec. 31, 1897	Illinois.
10	Dawes, Charles G	Jan. 1, 1898	Sept. 30, 1901	Do.
11	Ridgely, William Barret	Oct. 1, 1901	Mar. 28, 1908	Do.
12	Murray, Lawrence O	Apr. 27, 1908	[1] Apr. 27, 1913	New York.
13	Williams, John Skelton	Feb. 2, 1914	Mar. 2, 1921	Virginia.
14	Crissinger, D. R	Mar. 17, 1921	Apr. 30, 1923	Ohio.
15	Dawes, Henry M	May 1, 1923	Dec. 17, 1924	Illinois.
16	McIntosh, Joseph W	Dec. 20, 1924	Nov. 20, 1928	Do.
17	Pole, John W	Nov. 21. 1928	Sept. 20, 1932	Ohio.
18	O'Connor, J. F. T	May 11, 1933	Apr. 16, 1938	California.
19	Delano, Preston	Oct. 24, 1938	Feb. 15, 1953	Massachusetts.
20	Gidney, Ray M	Apr. 16, 1953	_____	Ohio.
	DEPUTY COMPTROLLERS OF THE CURRENCY			
1	Howard, Samuel T	May 9, 1863	Aug. 1, 1865	New York.
2	Hulburd, Hiland R	Aug. 1, 1865	Jan. 31, 1867	Ohio.
3	Knox, John Jay	Mar. 12, 1867	Apr. 24, 1872	Minnesota.
4	Langworthy, John S	Aug. 8, 1872	Jan. 3, 1886	New York.
5	Snyder, V. P	Jan. 5, 1886	Jan. 3, 1887	Do.
6	Abrahams, J. D	Jan. 27, 1887	May 25, 1890	Virginia.
7	Nixon, R. M	Aug. 11, 1890	Mar. 16, 1893	Indiana.
8	Tucker, Oliver P	Apr. 7, 1893	Mar. 11, 1896	Kentucky.
9	Coffin, George M	Mar. 12, 1896	Aug. 31, 1898	South Carolina.
10	Murray, Lawrence O	Sept. 1, 1898	June 27, 1899	New York.
11	Kane, Thomas P	June 29, 1899	[2] Mar. 2, 1923	District of Columbia.
12	Fowler, Willis J	July 1, 1908	Feb. 14, 1927	Indiana.
13	McIntosh, Joseph W	May 21, 1923	Dec. 19, 1924	Illinois.
14	Collins, Charles W	July 1, 1923	June 30, 1927	Do.
15	Stearns, E. W	Jan. 6, 1925	Nov. 30, 1928	Virginia.
16	Awalt, F. G	July 1, 1927	Feb. 15, 1936	Maryland.
17	Gough, E. H	July 6, 1927	Oct. 16, 1941	Indiana.
18	Proctor, John L	Dec. 1, 1928	Jan. 23, 1933	Washington.
19	Lyons, Gibbs	Jan. 24, 1933	Jan. 15, 1938	Georgia.
20	Prentiss, William Jr	Feb. 24, 1936	____do____	California.
21	Diggs, Marshall R	Jan. 16, 1938	Sept. 30, 1938	Texas.
22	Oppegard, G. J	____do____	____do____	California.
23	Upham, C. B	Oct. 1, 1938	Dec. 31, 1948	Iowa.
24	Mulroney, A. J	May 1, 1939	Aug. 31, 1941	Do.
25	McCandless, R. B	July 7, 1941	Mar. 1, 1951	Do.
26	Sedlacek, L. H	Sept. 1, 1941	Sept. 30, 1944	Nebraska.
27	Robertson, J. L	Oct. 1, 1944	Feb. 17, 1952	Do.
28	Hudspeth, J. W	Jan. 1, 1949	Aug. 31, 1950	Texas.
29	Jennings, L. A	Sept. 1, 1950	_____	New York.
30	Taylor, W. M	Mar. 1, 1951	_____	Virginia.
31	Garwood, G. W	Feb. 18, 1952	_____	Colorado.

[1] Term expired.
[2] Died Mar. 2, 1923.

TABLE No. 2.—*Total number of national banks organized, consolidated and merged under Act Nov. 7, 1918, as amended, insolvent, in voluntary liquidation, converted into and merged or consolidated with State banks under Public Law 706 (12 U.S.C. 214), and in existence Dec. 31, 1958*

Location	Organized	Consolidated and merged under Act Nov. 7, 1918, as amended		Insolvent	In liquidation	Public Law 706 (12 U.S.C. 214)		In existence
		Consolidations under secs. 1, 2, and 3	Mergers under secs. 4 and 5			Converted to State banks	Merged or consolidated with State banks	
Maine	127	5	1	13	79			29
New Hampshire	81	3		5	22			51
Vermont	85	3		17	29		4	32
Massachusetts	375	30	1	28	207		2	107
Rhode Island	67	3		2	58			4
Connecticut	125	9	4	7	67		8	30
Total New England States	860	53	6	72	462		14	253
New York	998	101	22	130	437	4	46	258
New Jersey	419	33	3	59	149		8	167
Pennsylvania	1,283	79	11	211	465		32	485
Delaware	30			1	18		4	7
Maryland	142	2	1	17	66		3	53
District of Columbia	32	7		7	13			5
Total Eastern States	2,904	222	37	425	1,148	4	93	975
Virginia	253	19	1	28	74			131
West Virginia	193	11		38	67			77
North Carolina	155	7	1	44	58		2	43
South Carolina	126	8	1	43	49			25
Georgia	190	8		42	86	3		51
Florida	188	2		42	41			103
Alabama	181	4	1	45	62			69
Mississippi	82	5		16	34			27
Louisiana	113	3		16	53			41
Texas	1,215	43		141	570	4		457
Arkansas	150	1		39	55			55
Kentucky	249	10	1	37	110	2	1	88
Tennessee	215	7		36	94	2	1	75
Total Southern States	3,310	128	5	567	1,353	11	4	1,242
Ohio	701	30	1	112	328		2	228
Indiana	439	13		98	204		1	123
Illinois	935	17		227	295	2		394
Michigan	323	11	3	77	154		3	75
Wisconsin	275	9		54	115			97
Minnesota	495	8		116	192			179
Iowa	549	4		204	242	2		97
Missouri	295	11	1	58	147	2	1	75
Total Middle Western States	4,012	103	5	946	1,677	6	7	1,268
North Dakota	259	3		100	118			38
South Dakota	220	12		93	81			34
Nebraska	405	1		83	198			123
Kansas	447	6		76	196			169
Montana	196	3		76	76			41
Wyoming	63			12	26			25
Colorado	220	5		55	84			76
New Mexico	88			25	36			27
Oklahoma	746	12		84	453			197
Total Western States	2,644	42		604	1,268			730

TABLE No. 2.—*Total number of national banks organized, consolidated and merged under Act Nov. 7, 1918, as amended, insolvent, in voluntary liquidation, converted into and merged or consolidated with State banks under Public Law 706 (12 U.S.C. 214), and in existence Dec. 31, 1958*—Continued

Location	Organized	Consolidated and merged under Act Nov. 7, 1918, as amended		Insolvent	In liquidation	Public Law 706 (12 U.S.C. 214)		In existence
		Consolidations under secs. 1, 2, and 3	Mergers under secs. 4 and 5			Converted to State banks	Merged or consolidated with State banks	
Washington	228	18	2	51	132	--------	---------	25
Oregon	148	2	1	31	102	--------	---------	11
California	530	19	6	65	382	1	11	46
Idaho	110	--------	---------	35	65	--------	1	9
Utah	38	4	---------	6	19	1	1	7
Nevada	17	1	---------	4	8	--------	1	3
Arizona	31	1	---------	6	21	--------	---------	3
Total Pacific States	1,102	45	9	198	729	2	15	104
Alaska	8	--------	---------	--------	1	--------	---------	7
The Territory of Hawaii	6	1	---------	--------	4	--------	---------	1
Puerto Rico	1	--------	---------	--------	1	--------	---------	
Virgin Islands of the United States	1	--------	---------	--------	--------	--------	---------	1
Total possessions	16	1	---------	--------	6	--------	---------	9
Total United States and possessions	[1] 14,848	594	62	[2] 2,812	[3] 6,643	23	133	4,581

[1] Includes 456 organized under Act Feb. 25, 1863; 9,401 under Act June 3, 1864, as amended; 10 under Gold Currency Act of July 12, 1870; and 4,981 under Act Mar. 14, 1900.
[2] Exclusive of those restored to solvency.
[3] Includes 208 passed into liquidation upon expiration of corporate existence.

TABLE No. 3.—*National banks chartered during the year ended Dec. 31, 1958*

Charter No.	Title and location of bank	Capital stock
	COLORADO	
14826	First National Bank in Walsenburg	$100,000
14833	First National Bank, Cortez	150,000
	Total (2 banks)	250,000
	FLORIDA	
14827	Springs National Bank of Tampa [1]	350,000
14838	First National Bank of Stuart [1]	100,000
14844	National Bank of Sarasota	500,000
14845	First National Bank of Melbourne	400,000
14848	Coral Ridge National Bank of Fort Lauderdale	500,000
	Total (5 banks)	1,850,000
	ILLINOIS	
14839	First National Bank of Morton [1]	200,000
	IOWA	
14832	South Des Moines National Bank, Des Moines	200,000
	KENTUCKY	
14840	Citizens Union National Bank & Trust Company, Lexington [1]	1,000,000
	MARYLAND	
14846	National Bank of Maryland, Silver Spring	500,000
	MASSACHUSETTS	
14831	Pilgrim National Bank of Boston [1]	1,500,000
14834	First National Bank of Natick	300,000
	Total (2 banks)	1,800,000
	MICHIGAN	
14843	Security National Bank of Manistee	200,000
	MINNESOTA	
14825	First National Bank of Hoyt Lakes	125,000
	NEW HAMPSHIRE	
14835	Hampton National Bank, Hampton	100,000
	NEW MEXICO	
14836	First National Bank of Grants	200,000
	TENNESSEE	
14828	National Bank of Newport	200,000
	TEXAS	
14830	Chimney Rock National Bank of Houston	250,000
14837	Northeast National Bank of Houston	100,000
14842	First National Bank of Fort Stockton	125,000
14847	The Brooks Field National Bank of San Antonio	200,000
	Total (4 banks)	675,000
	WISCONSIN	
14829	Southgate National Bank of Milwaukee	300,000
	WYOMING	
14841	First National Bank in Worland [1]	50,000
	Total United States (24 banks)	7,650,000

[1] Conversion of State-chartered bank.

TABLE No. 4.—*National banks chartered which were conversions of State banks during the year ended Dec. 31, 1958*

Charter No.	Title and location of bank	State	Effective date of charter	Authorized capital	Approximate surplus and undivided profits	Approximate assets
14827	Springs National Bank of Tampa_____	Fla_____	Feb. 28	$350,000	$296,520	$11,739,555
14831	Pilgrim National Bank of Boston_____	Mass_____	Apr. 18	1,500,000	2,422,713	37,713,865
14838	First National Bank of Stuart_____	Fla_____	Aug. 30	100,000	517,433	13,524,898
14839	First National Bank of Morton_____	Ill_____	___do_____	200,000	505,855	9,604,099
14840	Citizens Union National Bank & Trust Co., Lexington.	Ky_____	___do_____	1,000,000	1,294,134	23,484,545
14841	First National Bank in Worland_____	Wyo_____	Sept. 12	50,000	670,190	6,484,560
	Total (6 banks)_____			3,200,000	5,706,845	102,551,522

TABLE No. 5.—*National banks reported in voluntary liquidation during the year ended Dec. 31, 1958, the names of succeeding banks in cases of succession, with date of liquidation and capital stock*

Title and location of bank	Date of liquidation	Capital stock
The First National Bank of Whitney Point, N.Y. (7679), absorbed by First-City National Bank of Binghamton, N.Y_____	Feb. 7, 1958	$100,000
The First National Bank of South Fork, Pa. (6573), absorbed by First National Bank in Indiana, Pa_____	Mar. 8, 1958	50,000
The First National Bank of Cody, Wyo. (7319), absorbed by the Shoshone National Bank of Cody which changed its title to "Shoshone-First National Bank"_____	May 3, 1958	25,000
The National Metropolitan Bank of Washington, D.C.[1] (1069), absorbed by American Security & Trust Company, Washington, D.C_____	May 20, 1958	1,500,000
The First National Bank in Parkton, Md. (13867), absorbed by The Second National Bank of Towson, Md_____	May 12, 1958	50,000
The First National Bank in Wellington, Tex. (13249), absorbed by Wellington State Bank, Wellington_____	May 19, 1958	100,000
Pilgrim National Bank of Boston, Mass. (14831), absorbed by The Merchants National Bank of Boston_____	Apr. 30, 1958	1,500,000
The First National Bank of Trevorton, Pa. (7722), absorbed by National-Dime National Bank of Shamokin, Pa_____	May 28, 1958	50,000
The Second National Bank of Towson, Md.[2] (8381), absorbed by The First National Bank of Baltimore, Md_____	June 17, 1958	300,000
The First National Bank of Smithfield, Slatersville, R.I. (1035), absorbed by Industrial National Bank of Providence, R.I_____	June 11, 1958	100,000
The National Bank of Wray, Colo. (9676), absorbed by The First National Bank of Wray_____	Aug. 2, 1958	50,000
The Loveland National Bank, Loveland, Ohio (6779), absorbed by The Milford National Bank, Milford, Ohio_____	Aug. 30, 1958	75,000
The Prospect National Bank of Trenton, N.J.[3] (12949), absorbed by Trenton Trust Co., Trenton_____	Aug. 29, 1958	300,000
The First National Bank of Elysburg, Pa. (10837), absorbed by The Guarantee Trust & Safe Deposit Co. of Shamokin, Pa_____	Oct. 10, 1958	45,000
The Union National Bank of Minersville, Pa. (6131), absorbed by The Miners National Bank of Pottsville, Pa_____	July 31, 1958	100,000
First National Bank of Palmdale, Calif. (14812), absorbed by California Bank, Los Angeles, Calif_____	Oct. 3, 1958	250,000
The St. Michael National Bank, St. Michael, Pa. (12588), absorbed by Windber Trust Co., Windber, Pa_____	Oct. 31, 1958	50,000
First National Bank in Fairbury, Ill. (14413), absorbed by Farmers National Bank of Fairbury_____	Dec. 31, 1958	50,000
Sun Valley National Bank of Los Angeles, Calif.[4] (14671), absorbed by Security-First National Bank, Los Angeles_____	Dec. 18, 1958	400,000
Total (19 banks)_____		5,095,000
NONNATIONAL BANK IN DISTRICT OF COLUMBIA		
The Munsey Trust Co., Washington, D.C., absorbed by Union Trust Co. of the District of Columbia_____	Dec. 26, 1958	1,250,000

[1] With 2 local branches.
[2] With 1 local branch and 1 each in Parkton and White Hall.
[3] With 1 local branch.
[4] With 1 local branch.

TABLE No. 6.—*National banks merged or consolidated with and into State banks under the provisions of Public Law 706 (12 U.S.C. 214), approved Aug. 17, 1950, and the laws of the States where the banks are located, during the year ended Dec. 31, 1958, with the effective date and the capital stock*

Title and location of bank	Effective date	Capital stock
Springfield National Bank, Springfield, Mass.[1] (4907), merged with and into Union Trust Co. of Springfield, and under the title "Valley Bank & Trust Company"	Jan. 17, 1958	$1,300,000
The Ansonia National Bank, Ansonia, Conn. (1093), merged with and into The Union & New Haven Trust Co., New Haven, Conn.	Feb. 10, 1958	200,000
National Bank & Trust Company of Skaneateles, N.Y. (5360), merged with and into First Trust & Deposit Co., Syracuse, N.Y.	Feb. 11, 1958	100,000
The First National Bank & Trust Co. of New Canaan, Conn.[2] (1249), merged with and into The Fairfield County Trust Co., Stamford, Conn.	Feb. 28, 1958	750,000
The First National Bank of Springfield, Ky. (1767), merged with and into Peoples Deposit Bank, Springfield, and under the title "First & Peoples Bank, Springfield, Ky."	Apr. 2, 1958	50,000
The Union National Bank of Friendship, N.Y. (11055), merged with and into The First Trust Co. of Allegany County, Wellsville, N.Y.	Apr. 18, 1958	100,000
Upper Darby National Bank, Upper Darby, Pa.[3] (13196), merged with and into Girard Trust Corn Exchange Bank, Philadelphia, Pa.	Apr. 25, 1958	1,050,000
The Security National Bank Savings & Trust Co. of St. Louis, Mo. (12066), merged with and into Mutual Bank & Trust Co., St. Louis, and under the title "Security-Mutual Bank & Trust Co."	May 29, 1958	750,000
The Lynbrook National Bank & Trust Company, Lynbrook, N.Y. (8923), merged with and into Central Bank & Trust Co., Great Neck, N.Y.	June 6, 1958	350,000
Passaic-Clifton National Bank & Trust Co., Clifton, N.J.[4] (12205), merged with and into County Bank & Trust Co., Paterson, N.J., and under the title "New Jersey Bank & Trust Co.," Clifton, N.J.	June 20, 1958	3,000,000
Peoples National Bank of Grand Rapids, Mich.[5] (13799), merged with and into Old Kent Bank & Michigan Trust Co., Grand Rapids, Mich., and under the title "Old Kent Bank & Trust Co."	July 31, 1958	1,050,000
The Citizens National Bank of Waverly, N.Y. (12954), merged with and into Marine Midland Trust Co. of Southern New York, Elmira, N.Y.	Sept. 29, 1958	100,000
The National Bank of Pottstown, Pa.[6] (608), merged with and into Montgomery County Bank & Trust Co., Norristown, Pa.	Oct. 17, 1958	1,000,000
The First National Bank of Gaithersburg, Md. (4608), merged with and into The Germantown Bank, Germantown, Md., and under the title "The Maryland State Bank of Montgomery County," Gaithersburg	Oct. 14, 1958	100,000
The Farmers National Bank & Trust Co. of Rome, N.Y.[7] (2410), and The First National Bank of Herkimer, N.Y.[8] (3183), merged with and into First Bank & Trust Co. of Utica, N.Y., and under the title "Marine Midland Trust Co. of the Mohawk Valley"	Dec. 26, 1958	{ 475,000 475,000
The First National Bank of Harrisville, N.Y. (10767), merged with and into State Bank of Edwards and Star Lake, Edwards, N.Y., and under the title "United Bank," Star Lake	Nov. 28, 1958	25,000
Total (17 banks)		10,875,000

[1] With 4 local branches and 1 each in Indian Orchard, Longmeadow, and Agawam.
[2] With 1 local branch and 1 in Wilton.
[3] With 4 local branches and 1 each in Havertown, Yeadon, Broomall, Newtown Square, Pilgrim Gardens, Manoa, and Marple Township.
[4] With 2 local branches and 2 in Passaic.
[5] With 5 local branches and 1 in Rogers Heights.
[6] With 1 local branch and 1 in Stowe.
[7] With 1 local branch and 1 in Ramsen.
[8] With 1 branch in Middleville.

TABLE No. 7.—*National banks converted into State banks under the provisions of Public Law 706 (12 U.S.C. 214), approved Aug. 17, 1950, and the laws of the States where the banks are located, during the year ended Dec. 31, 1958, with the effective date and the capital stock*

Title and location of bank	Effective date	Capital stock
American National Bank of Houston, Tex. (14679), converted into American Bank & Trust Co., Houston	June 30, 1958	$200,000
The First National Bank of Shellman, Ga. (8417), converted into First State Bank, Shellman	Dec. 31, 1958	25,000
The First National Bank of Italy, Tex. (5663), converted into First State Bank, Italy	____do____	50,000
Total (3 banks)		275,000

TABLE No. 8.—*Purchases of State banks by national banks reported during the year ended Dec. 31, 1958, with title, location, and capital stock of the State banks and effective dates of purchase*

Title and location of bank	Effective date	Capital stock
First National Bank in Walsenburg, Colo. (14826), purchased The First State Bank of Walsenburg	Jan. 25	$100,000
The Rushville National Bank, Rushville, Ind. (1456), purchased Citizens State Bank, Manilla, Ind.	Feb. 1	25,000
The Clinton County National Bank & Trust Co. of Wilmington, Ohio (1997), purchased The New Vienna Bank, New Vienna, Ohio	Feb. 21	60,000
Central-Penn National Bank of Philadelphia, Pa. (723), purchased Newtown Bank & Trust Co., Newtown, Pa.	Apr. 25	150,000
The Pauls Valley National Bank, Pauls Valley, Okla. (7892), purchased Bank of Paoli, Okla.	May 2	10,000
First National Bank, Cortez, Colo. (14833), purchased J. J. Harris & Co., Bankers, Dolores, Colo.	June 2	100,000
The Second National Bank of Towson, Md. (8381), purchased White Hall Bank, White Hall, Md.	June 13	50,000
The National Bank of Commerce of Seattle, Wash. (4375), purchased Farmers & Merchants Bank, Deer Park, Wash.	June 27	30,000
Plainfield Trust State National Bank, Plainfield, N.J. (13474), purchased The State Trust Co., Plainfield	___do___	550,000
The Miners National Bank of Pottsville, Pa. (649), purchased Williamstown Bank, Williamstown, Pa.	July 11	50,000
The Philadelphia National Bank, Philadelphia, Pa. (539), purchased Gimbel Bros. Bank & Trust Co., Philadelphia	___do___	200,000
The American National Bank & Trust Co. of Bowling Green, Ky. (9365), purchased The Deposit Bank of Smiths Grove, Ky.	July 31	25,000
Vermont-Peoples National Bank of Brattleboro, Vt. (1430), purchased Vermont Savings Bank, Brattleboro	June 30	None
Seattle-First National Bank, Seattle, Wash. (11280), purchased North Western Bank, Spokane, Wash.	Aug. 8	120,000
Society National Bank of Cleveland, Ohio (14761), purchased Society for Savings in the City of Cleveland	Dec. 31	None
Total (15 banks)		1,470,000

TABLE No. 9.—*Consolidations of national banks, or national and State banks, during the year ended Dec. 31, 1958, under sec. 1, 2, and 3 of the act of Nov. 7, 1918, as amended*

	Capital stock	Surplus	Undivided profits	Total assets
The National Bank of Andes, N.Y. (11243), with	$40,000	$60,000	$58,566	$1,546,738
and The First National Bank & Trust Co. of Walton, N.Y. (4495), which had	150,000	200,000	209,890	6,113,085
consolidated Jan. 31, 1958, under charter of the latter bank (4495), and title "The National Bank of Delaware County, Walton." The consolidated bank at date of consolidation had	190,000	260,000	268,456	7,659,823
Haywood County Bank, Canton, N.C.,[1] with	100,000	100,000	223,295	4,246,004
and First National Bank & Trust Co. in Asheville, N.C. (13721), which had	585,000	1,415,000	667,412	38,669,537
consolidated Feb. 14, 1958, under charter and title of the latter bank (13721). The consolidated bank at date of consolidation had	665,000	1,535,000	890,708	42,608,484
The Greenwich Trust Co., Greenwich, Conn.,[2] with	1,450,440	2,600,000	227,149	68,305,301
and The First-Stamford National Bank & Trust Co., Stamford, Conn. (4), which had	1,375,000	1,375,000	974,456	46,957,645
consolidated Mar. 1, 1958, under charter of the latter bank (4), and title "The National Bank & Trust Co. of Fairfield County." The consolidated bank at date of consolidation had	2,904,750	4,400,000	697,295	115,262,946
The Fort Neck National Bank of Seaford, N.Y.[3] (12963), with	1,448,545	1,448,545	413,344	47,098,626
and Security National Bank of Huntington, N.Y. (6587), which had	2,871,110	5,678,890	685,127	138,460,239
consolidated May 23, 1958, under charter of the latter bank (6587), and title "Security National Bank of Long Island." The consolidated bank at date of consolidation had	4,589,080	6,858,010	850,827	185,713,043
The First National Bank of Warwick, N.Y. (314), with	100,000	300,000	184,178	5,724,954
and County National Bank, Middletown, N.Y. (13956), which had	650,000	1,000,000	247,937	29,903,198
consolidated May 26, 1958, under charter and title of the latter bank (13956). The consolidated bank at date of consolidation had	850,000	1,150,000	450,115	35,627,102
The Grange Trust Co., Huntingdon, Pa., with	125,000	250,000	79,230	4,422,711
and The First National Bank of Huntingdon Pa. (31), which had	150,000	450,000	191,409	8,180,453
consolidated May 31, 1958, under charter of the latter bank (31), and title "First-Grange National Bank Bank of Huntingdon." The consolidated bank at date of consolidation had	330,500	700,000	215,139	12,603,164
The Market Exchange Bank Co., Columbus, Ohio, with	600,000	600,000	1,101,781	34,482,897
and The Huntington National Bank of Columbus, Ohio, (7745), which had	6,000,000	7,000,000	2,277,731	177,633,751
consolidated May 29, 1958, under charter and title of the latter bank (7745). The consolidated bank at date of consolidation had	7,200,000	7,800,000	3,224,589	211,530,278
The Plainfield Trust Co., Plainfield, N.J.,[4] with	1,500,000	2,000,000	1,178,420	55,834,703
and the Plainfield National Bank, Plainfield, N.J. (13174), which had	350,000	350,000	447,808	19,997,764
consolidated June 27, 1958, under charter of the latter bank (13174), and title "Plainfield Trust State National Bank." The consolidated bank at date of consolidation had	1,600,325	2,350,000	1,654,556	75,384,407
Potter-Matlock Bank & Trust Co. of Bowling Green, Ky., with	100,000	100,000	78,115	4,011,753
and The American National Bank of Bowling Green, Ky. (9365), which had	100,000	350,000	127,766	9,338,404
consolidated June 30, 1958, under charter of the latter bank (9365), and title "The American National Bank & Trust Co. of Bowling Green." The consolidated bank at date of consolidation had	200,000	450,000	205,882	13,350,157
Hutchings-Sealy National Bank of Galveston, Tex. (12434), with	750,000	480,000	652,974	29,966,736
and The First National Bank of Galveston, Tex. (1566), which had	300,000	500,000	512,325	16,647,427
consolidated June 27, 1958, under charter of the latter bank (1566), and title "First Hutchings-Sealy National Bank of Galveston." The consolidated bank at date of consolidation had	1,250,000	1,250,000	698,253	46,087,716

See footnotes at end of table, p. 54

TABLE NO. 9.—*Consolidations of national banks, or national and State banks, during the year ended Dec. 31, 1958, under sec. 1, 2, and 3 of the act of Nov. 7, 1918, as amended*—Continued

	Capital stock	Surplus	Undivided profits	Total assets
Warwick National Bank, Warwick, Va. (14795), with.	$200,000	$50,000	$71,588	$4,094,076
and The First National Bank of Newport News, Va. (4635), which had	500,000	1,000,000	1,448,757	42,107,363
consolidated July 1, 1958, under charter of the latter bank (4635), and title "First National Bank of Newport News." The consolidated bank at date of consolidation had	600,000	1,000,000	1,670,345	45,044,222
First National Bank & Trust Co. in Asheville, N.C.[5] (13721), with	665,000	1,535,000	542,517	45,656,594
and The Union National Bank of Charlotte, N.C. (9164), which had	1,200,000	5,300,000	638,106	75,079,110
consolidated July 18, 1958, under charter of the latter bank (9164), and title "First Union National Bank of North Carolina." The consolidated bank at date of consolidation had	2,165,000	6,835,000	880,623	116,294,194
The International Trust Co., Denver, Colo., with	1,350,000	2,500,000	2,501,277	78,713,822
and The First National Bank of Denver, Colo. (1016), which had	4,000,000	7,000,000	1,743,665	242,667,939
consolidated Aug. 8, 1958, under charter and title of the latter bank (1016). The consolidated bank at date of consolidation had	7,500,000	9,500,000	2,094,941	306,611,469
The Central Islip National Bank, Central Islip, N.Y. (12379), with	200,000	200,000	251,075	10,302,643
and The Franklin National Bank of Long Island, Franklin Square, N.Y. (12997), which had	14,077,000	15,923,000	3,895,416	563,647,730
consolidated Aug. 22, 1958, under charter and title of the latter bank (12997). The consolidated bank at date of consolidation had	14,302,000	16,000,000	4,244,491	573,950,373
The Trenton Banking Co., Trenton, N.J.,[6] with	1,875,000	1,625,000	1,688,703	61,982,483
and The First-Mechanics National Bank of Trenton, N.J. (1327), which had	2,500,000	3,000,000	2,382,393	120,527,667
consolidated Aug. 29, 1958, under charter of the latter bank (1327), and title "First Trenton National Bank." The consolidated bank at date of consolidation had	4,000,000	6,000,000	3,105,662	182,530,745
The National Bank of Newburgh, N.Y. (468), with	200,000	300,000	251,890	8,913,626
and County National Bank, Middletown, N.Y. (13956), which had	850,000	1,150,000	444,356	42,149,421
consolidated Sept. 26, 1958, under charter and title of the latter bank (13956). The consolidated bank at date of consolidation had	1,130,000	1,370,000	698,943	51,071,445
The City Savings Bank & Trust Co., Alliance, Ohio, with	200,000	400,000	217,451	9,074,648
and Alliance First National Bank, Alliance, Ohio (3721), which had	750,000	750,000	1,032,221	28,644,997
consolidated Sept. 30, 1958, under charter of the latter bank (3721), and title "First National City Bank of Alliance." The consolidated bank at date of consolidation had	1,000,000	1,150,000	1,199,672	37,719,645
The Liberty Bank, Ada, Ohio, with	50,000	150,000	58,042	2,707,748
and The First National Bank of Ada, Ohio (5425), which had	75,000	75,000	130,790	2,041,170
consolidated Sept. 30, 1958, under charter of the latter bank (5425), and title "The Liberty National Bank of Ada." The consolidated bank at date of consolidation had	200,000	200,000	138,831	4,748,918
Rome Trust Co., Rome, N.Y.,[7] with	300,000	1,400,000	579,142	20,320,952
and The Oneida National Bank & Trust Co. of Utica, N.Y., (1392), which had	1,453,820	3,750,000	1,698,999	88,982,816
consolidated Oct. 3, 1958, under charter and title of the latter bank (1392). The consolidated bank at date of consolidation had	1,963,820	6,000,000	1,218,140	109,303,768
Citizens National Bank of Bradford, Pa. (14358), with	200,000	200,000	577,776	9,000,464
and The Bradford National Bank, Bradford, Pa. (2428), which had	600,000	1,400,000	465,793	24,026,740
consolidated Oct. 31, 1958, under charter and title of the latter bank (2428). The consolidated bank at date of consolidation had	1,020,000	1,730,000	712,495	33,052,993

See footnotes at end of table, p. 54.

TABLE No. 9.—*Consolidations of national banks, or national and State banks, during the year ended Dec. 31, 1958, under secs. 1, 2, and 3 of the act of Nov. 7, 1918, as amended*—Continued

	Capital stock	Surplus	Undivided profits	Total assets
The American National Bank of Ebensburg, Pa. (6209), with_____	$100,000	$150,000	$159,203	$3,401,332
and The First National Bank of Carrolltown, Pa. (5855), which had_____	50,000	200,000	262,524	6,795,932
consolidated Nov. 1, 1958, under charter of the latter bank (5855), and title "The Carrolltown American National Bank." The consolidated bank at date of consolidation had_____	375,000	300,000	246,727	10,197,264
The First National Bank of Stewartstown, Pa. (4665), with_____	50,000	150,000	41,572	1,822,322
and First National Bank & Trust Co. of Red Lion, Pa. (5184), which had_____	225,000	775,000	270,657	15,955,275
consolidated Nov. 1, 1958, under charter and title of the latter bank (5184). The consolidated bank at date of consolidation had_____	267,500	932,500	312,229	17,777,597
The Lincoln National Bank of Washington, D.C.[8] (4247), with_____	1,000,000	1,200,000	639,746	44,545,254
and The Riggs National Bank of Washington, D.C., (5046), which had_____	8,000,000	15,000,000	8,289,321	486,993,817
consolidated Nov. 10, 1958, under charter and title of the latter bank (5046). The consolidated bank at date of consolidation had_____	8,850,000	16,200,000	9,079,068	531,539,071
The Machinists National Bank of Taunton, Mass.,[9] (947) with_____	200,000	200,000	269,603	9,929,001
and The First National Bank of Easton, North Easton, Mass. (416), which had_____	150,000	150,000	161,198	2,680,234
consolidated Nov. 28, 1958, under charter of the latter bank (416), and title "The First-Machinists National Bank of Taunton." The consolidated bank at date of consolidation had_____	350,000	400,000	380,801	12,609,235
The Union National Bank of Indiana Harbor at East Chicago, Ind. (13532), with_____	200,000	1,400,000	204,968	32,967,169
and The First National Bank in East Chicago, Ind. (13531), which had_____	200,000	1,200,000	315,226	32,158,410
consolidated Nov. 28, 1958, under charter of the latter bank (13531), and title "First National Bank of East Chicago, Indiana." The consolidated bank at date of consolidation had_____	1,000,000	2,000,000	520,193	65,125,578
French Lick State Bank, French Lick, Ind., with____	50,000	50,000	71,535	2,224,231
and The West Baden National Bank, West Baden Springs, Ind. (6388), which had_____	50,000	60,000	120,949	3,001,379
consolidated Dec. 31, 1958, under charter of the latter bank (6388), and title "The Springs Valley National Bank," French Lick. The consolidated bank at date of consolidation had_____	125,000	125,000	151,789	5,224,915
The United States National Bank of Denver, Colo. (7408), with_____	3,300,000	4,700,000	1,795,774	141,201,766
and The Denver National Bank, Denver, Colo. (3269), which had_____	3,500,000	5,000,000	3,713,966	160,264,710
consolidated Dec. 31, 1958, under charter of the latter bank (3269), and title "Denver United States National Bank." The consolidated bank at date of consolidation had_____	8,000,000	10,000,000	4,009,740	301,466,476

[1] With 1 branch in Clyde.
[2] With 1 branch each in Greenwich, Cos Cob, Byram, Stamford, and Old Greenwich.
[3] With 1 branch each in Wantagh, North Bellmore, Massapequa Park, South Plainedge, and 2 in Massapequa.
[4] With 1 branch in Fanwood.
[5] With 1 branch each in Hendersonville, East Asheville, Waynesville, Brevard, Canton, and Clyde, and 2 local branches.
[6] With 2 local branches and 2 in Pennington.
[7] With 1 branch in Rome.
[8] With 2 local branches.
[9] With 1 branch in Norton.

TABLE No. 10.—*Mergers of national banks, or national and State banks, during the year ended Dec. 31, 1958, under secs. 4 and 5 of the act of Nov. 7, 1918, as amended*

	Capital stock	Surplus	Undivided ‡profits	Total assets
Woodlawn Trust Co., Aliquippa, Pa.,[1] with	$375,000	$375,000	$353,714	$22,393,061
and Mellon National Bank & Trust Co., Pittsburgh, Pa. (6301), which had	60,100,000	180,000,000	23,919,759	1,949,044,971
merged Jan. 31, 1958, under charter and title of the latter bank (6301). The merged bank at date of merger had	60,475,000	180,375,000	24,116,858	1,971,563,604
Madison County Trust Co., Oneida, N.Y., with	200,000	300,000	90,800	7,199,406
and Lincoln National Bank & Trust Co. of Syracuse, N.Y. (13393), which had	1,895,000	3,470,000	1,157,568	104,379,595
merged Jan. 31, 1958, under charter and title of the latter bank (13393). The merged bank at date of merger had	2,000,000	3,365,000	891,987	111,602,620
National Bank of Commerce of Portland, Maine[2] (13710), with	550,000	1,000,000	218,863	20,348,056
and First Portland National Bank, Portland, Maine (4128), which had	1,250,000	1,750,000	658,417	39,721,134
merged Jan. 31, 1958, under charter and title of the latter bank (4128). The merged bank at date of merger had	2,250,000	2,250,000	700,382	60,132,292
The City National Bank of South Norwalk, Conn.[3] (2643), with	300,000	450,000	109,352	14,577,507
and The Connecticut National Bank, Bridgeport, Conn. (335), which had	4,780,000	6,640,000	951,340	158,660,027
merged Mar. 7, 1958, under charter and title of the latter bank (335). The merged bank at date of merger had	5,230,000	6,940,000	1,060,692	173,237,534
Union National Bank in Mount Wolf, Pa. (14121), with	50,000	150,000	113,716	2,204,451
and The York National Bank & Trust Co., York, Pa. (604), which had	1,250,000	2,750,000	969,436	45,097,231
merged Mar. 27, 1958, under charter and title of the latter bank (604). The merged bank at date of merger had	1,335,000	2,900,000	1,048,152	47,301,682
Barclay-Westmoreland Trust Co., Greensburg, Pa.,[4] with	400,000	4,000,000	60,607	32,648,212
and Mellon National Bank & Trust Co., Pittsburgh, Pa. (6301), which had	61,684,500	180,375,000	24,615,674	1,970,848,895
merged Apr. 11, 1958, under charter and title of the latter bank (6301). The merged bank at date of merger had	62,704,500	183,755,000	24,492,960	2,001,243,904
The Luzerne-Hadley Bank, Luzerne (P.O. Lake Luzerne), N.Y., with	[5] 26,750	40,000	39,111	1,248,977
and The Emerson National Bank of Warrensburgh, Warrensburg, N.Y. (9135), which had	100,000	250,000	248,715	5,194,447
merged Apr. 11, 1958, under charter and title of the latter bank (9135). The merged bank at date of merger had	100,000	250,000	238,704	6,443,369
The Peoples National Bank of Lemasters, Pa. (10950), with	25,000	50,000	7,061	959,189
and The Valley National Bank of Chambersburg, Pa. (4272), which had	350,000	800,000	129,373	11,556,251
merged Apr. 26, 1958, under charter and title of the latter bank (4272). The merged bank at date of merger had	380,000	850,000	131,434	12,515,440
The First National Bank of Camden, S.C.[6] (9083), with	160,000	112,000	117,765	5,194,375
and The South Carolina National Bank of Charleston, S.C. (2044), which had	3,650,000	8,350,000	3,572,528	228,414,729
merged May 9, 1958, under charter and title of the latter bank (2044). The merged bank at date of merger had	3,734,000	8,766,000	3,455,952	233,609,104
The First National Bank of Owego, N.Y. (1019), with	150,000	250,000	181,931	7,889,428
and First-City National Bank of Binghamton, N.Y. (202), which had	2,500,000	2,500,000	1,698,347	78,738,209
merged May 16, 1958, under charter and title of the latter bank (202). The merged bank at date of merger had	2,800,000	2,800,000	1,680,278	86,627,637
The National Bank of Wappingers Falls, N.Y. (9326), with	50,000	100,000	110,810	3,264,645
and The First National Bank of Poughkeepsie, N.Y. (465), which had	924,000	1,876,000	773,384	45,820,969
merged June 6, 1958, under charter and title of the latter bank (465). The merged bank at date of merger had	1,004,000	1,996,000	834,193	49,085,614

See footnotes at end of table, p. 57.

TABLE NO. 10.—*Mergers of national banks, or national and State banks, during the year ended Dec. 31, 1958, under secs. 4 and 5 of the act of Nov. 7, 1918, as amended*—Continued

	Capital stock	Surplus	Undivided profits	Total assets
The Hartwick National Bank, Hartwick, N.Y. (11657), with_____	$50,000	$50,000	$60,019	$1,632,856
and The National Commercial Bank & Trust Co. of Albany, N.Y. (1301), which had_____	5,532,975	9,467,025	3,926,914	283,553,486
merged July 11, 1958, under charter and title of the latter bank (1301). The merged bank at date of merger had_____	5,562,975	9,467,025	4,056,933	285,186,341
The National Bank of Gordonsville, Va. (10287), with_	25,000	105,000	47,187	1,890,681
and The Peoples National Bank of Charlottesville, Va. (2594), which had_____	1,718,960	3,281,040	1,740,648	65,737,282
merged July 25, 1958, under charter and title of the latter bank (2594). The merged bank at date of merger had_____	1,778,960	3,351,040	1,787,834	67,627,964
Markle Banking & Trust Co., Hazleton, Pa.,[7] with___	600,000	1,200,000	753,012	15,562,486
Wilkes-Barre Deposit & Savings Bank, Wilkes-Barre, Pa., with_____	500,000	750,000	415,906	16,343,495
and The First National Bank & Trust Co. of Scranton, Pa. (77), which had_____	4,500,000	5,500,000	1,853,389	121,539,449
merged July 31, 1958, under charter of the last-named bank (77), and title "Northeastern Pennsylvania National Bank and Trust Company." The merged bank at date of merger had_____	5,454,000	5,546,000	2,836,365	150,918,793
The National Bank of Cockeysville, Md. (4496), with_	100,000	150,000	39,433	4,229,915
and Fidelity-Baltimore National Bank, Baltimore, Md. (13745), which had_____	3,600,000	11,400,000	3,726,228	284,609,667
merged Aug. 15, 1958, under charter and title of the latter bank (13745). The merged bank at date of merger had_____	3,725,000	12,275,000	3,015,661	288,839,582
The Peoples National Bank & Trust Co., Langhorne, Pa.[8] (3063), with_____	300,000	500,000	395,332	17,486,203
and Central-Penn National Bank of Philadelphia, Pa. (723), which had_____	5,000,000	15,000,000	3,254,634	253,096,680
merged Sept. 5, 1958, under charter and title of the latter bank (723). The merged bank at date of merger had_____	5,360,000	15,500,000	3,549,005	266,131,849
State Bank of Norwood, N.Y., with_____	100,000	100,000	159,536	2,528,966
and The St. Lawrence County National Bank of Canton, N.Y. (8531), which had_____	200,000	400,000	143,394	6,869,226
merged Sept. 30, 1958, under charter and title of the latter bank (8531). The merged bank at date of merger had_____	200,000	400,000	202,931	9,398,192
Peoples Bank & Trust Co., Westfield, N.J., with_____	400,000	700,000	553,728	19,930,541
and "The National State Bank, Elizabeth, N.J.," Elizabeth, N.J. (1436), which had_____	1,875,000	2,125,000	425,268	77,699,579
merged Oct. 3, 1958, under charter and title of the latter bank (1436). The merged bank at date of merger had_____	1,875,000	2,125,000	231,741	98,475,934
Federal Trust Co., Newark, N.J.,[9] with_____	1,622,500	1,622,500	2,764,817	85,539,146
and The National State Bank of Newark, N.J. (1452), which had_____	5,700,000	15,000,000	4,003,849	327,346,968
merged Oct. 10, 1958, under charter and title of the latter bank (1452). The merged bank at date of merger had_____	5,700,000	15,000,000	1,738,916	413,119,886
The Torrington National Bank & Trust Co., Torrington, Conn. (5235), with_____	600,000	600,000	1,332,815	27,666,005
and Hartford National Bank & Trust Co., Hartford, Conn. (1338), which had_____	11,000,000	15,000,000	7,990,698	416,169,812
merged Oct. 31, 1958, under charter and title of the latter bank (1338). The merged bank at date of merger had_____	11,900,000	15,600,000	9,023,513	443,835,818
The New Augusta State Bank, New Augusta, Ind.,[10] with_____	100,000	150,000	123,476	5,387,851
and The Indiana National Bank of Indianapolis, Ind. (984), which had_____	12,500,000	22,500,000	7,319,419	488,994,083
merged Oct. 31, 1958, under charter and title of the latter bank (984). The merged bank at date of merger had_____	12,760,000	24,740,000	5,138,009	492,895,355
The First National Bank of Cato, N.Y. (9857), with__	68,750	137,500	96,513	2,884,134
and Lincoln National Bank & Trust Co. of Syracuse, N.Y. (13393), which had_____	2,000,000	3,365,000	1,179,859	122,281,840
merged Nov. 21, 1958, under charter and title of the latter bank (13393). The merged bank at date of merger had_____	2,096,250	3,475,000	1,276,372	125,162,274

See footnotes at end of table, p. 57.

TABLE NO. 10.—*Mergers of national banks, or national and State banks, during the year ended Dec. 31, 1958, under secs. 4 and 5 of the act of Nov. 7, 1918, as amended*—Continued

	Capital stock	Surplus	Undivided profits	Total assets
The Union National Bank of Lenoir, N.C. (13523), with_____	$150,000	$450,000	$129,561	$6,917,684
Bank of Lenoir, N.C.,[11] with_____	200,000	600,000	229,091	7,209,819
and First Union National Bank of North Carolina, Charlotte, N.C. (9164), which had_____	2,165,000	6,835,000	1,111,224	132,214,605
merged Nov. 28, 1958, under charter and title of the last-named bank (9164). The merged bank at date of merger had_____	2,515,000	7,485,000	1,782,759	144,714,075
Allegheny Trust Co., Pittsburgh, Pa., with_____	700,000	700,000	229,477	11,160,438
and The Union National Bank of Pittsburgh, Pa. (705), which had_____	2,500,000	7,500,000	2,595,216	114,175,962
merged Dec. 31, 1958, under charter and title of the latter bank (705). The merged bank at date of merger had_____	2,850,000	10,000,000	1,374,693	125,336,400

[1] With 2 local branches.
[2] With 1 local branch and 1 in South Portland.
[3] With 1 local branch.
[4] With 1 local branch.
[5] Includes $1,750 preferred capital stock.
[6] With 1 branch in Bethune.
[7] With 1 local branch.
[8] With 1 branch each in Penndel, Feasterville, and Levittown.
[9] With 2 local branches.
[10] With 1 branch in Indianapolis.
[11] With 1 branch in Whitnel.

TABLE No. 11.—*Number of domestic branches of national banks authorized during the year ended Dec. 31, 1958*

Charter No.	Title and location of bank	Branches authorized under act of Feb. 25, 1927, as amended		
		Local	Other than local	Total
	ALABAMA			
14590	First National Bank of Columbiana		1	1
3981	The First National Bank of Florence	1		1
1853	The First National Bank of Tuskaloosa	1		1
	ALASKA			
14651	National Bank of Alaska in Anchorage	1		1
14747	Alaska National Bank of Fairbanks		1	1
5117	The First National Bank of Juneau		1	1
	ARIZONA			
3728	First National Bank of Arizona, Phoenix	1	3	4
14324	The Valley National Bank of Phoenix	4	4	8
	ARKANSAS			
2832	The Arkansas National Bank of Hot Springs		1	1
13958	Union National Bank of Little Rock		1	1
6680	The Simmons National Bank of Pine Bluff		2	2
	CALIFORNIA			
14670	Community National Bank of Buttonwillow		1	1
14725	First National Bank of Saratoga and Cupertino, Cupertino		1	1
5927	Citizens National Trust & Savings Bank of Los Angeles	1	2	3
2491	Security-First National Bank, Los Angeles	5	16	21
6919	Central Valley National Bank, Oakland	1	3	4
6268	The First National Bank of Ontario		1	1
13044	Bank of America National Trust & Savings Association, San Francisco	1	20	21
9655	The Bank of California, National Association, San Francisco		1	1
1741	Crocker-Anglo National Bank, San Francisco		7	7
12640	First National Bank in San Rafael		1	1
2456	County National Bank & Trust Co. of Santa Barbara		1	1
	CONNECTICUT			
335	The Connecticut National Bank, Bridgeport		3	3
943	Danbury National Bank, Danbury	1		1
1338	Hartford National Bank & Trust Co., Hartford		2	2
2	The First New Haven National Bank, New Haven		1	1
4	The National Bank & Trust Co. of Fairfield County, Stamford	1	8	9
780	The Waterbury National Bank, Waterbury	1	1	2
	DELAWARE			
795	The First National Bank of Seaford		1	1
	DISTRICT OF COLUMBIA [1]			
3425	The National Bank of Washington	1		1
5046	The Riggs National Bank of Washington, D.C.	1		1
	GEORGIA			
9617	The Fulton National Bank of Atlanta	1		1
4691	The Fourth National Bank of Columbus	1		1
10270	The First National Bank & Trust Co. in Macon	1		1
13068	The Citizens & Southern National Bank, Savannah	1		1
	HAWAII			
5550	Bishop National Bank of Hawaii, Honolulu		2	2
	IDAHO			
14444	First Security Bank of Idaho, National Association, Boise		1	1

[1] Four branches also authorized for 2 nonnational banks in the District of Columbia.

TABLE No. 11.—*Number of domestic branches of national banks authorized during the year ended Dec. 31, 1958*—Continued

Charter No.	Title and location of bank	Branches authorized under act of Feb. 25, 1927, as amended		
		Local	Other than local	Total
	INDIANA			
1066	The First National Bank of Columbus	1		1
13531	First National Bank of East Chicago, Indiana	1		1
12132	The National City Bank of Evansville	1		1
12444	Old National Bank in Evansville	1		1
6388	The Springs Valley National Bank, French Lick		1	1
14468	Gary National Bank, Gary	1		1
13759	American Fletcher National Bank & Trust Co., Indianapolis		1	1
984	The Indiana National Bank of Indianapolis	2	1	3
869	Merchants National Bank & Trust Co. of Indianapolis		1	1
14519	First National Bank, Kokomo	1		1
14175	Lafayette National Bank, Lafayette	1		1
11148	Purdue National Bank of Lafayette	1		1
2234	The Merchants National Bank of Muncie		1	1
1456	The Rushville National Bank, Rushville		1	1
	KANSAS			
3819	The First National Bank of Chanute	1		1
13990	The Garden National Bank of Garden City	1		1
13801	Security National Bank of Kansas City	1		1
3078	The First National Bank of Topeka	1		1
8399	The National Bank of Commerce of Wellington	1		1
	KENTUCKY			
3944	The Second National Bank of Ashland	1		1
9365	The American National Bank & Trust Co. of Bowling Green	1	1	2
14840	Citizens Union National Bank & Trust Co., Lexington	1		1
	LOUISIANA			
13737	City National Bank of Baton Rouge	1		1
14462	Fidelity National Bank of Baton Rouge		1	1
13732	The First National Bank of Jefferson Parish at Gretna	1		1
14503	Citizens National Bank & Trust Co. of Houma	1		1
5023	The First National Bank of Lafayette		1	1
14228	The Calcasieu-Marine National Bank of Lake Charles	1		1
13655	The Ouachita National Bank in Monroe	1		1
3069	Whitney National Bank of New Orleans	1		1
	MAINE			
4128	First Portland National Bank, Portland	1		1
941	The Canal National Bank of Portland	1		1
13768	Northern National Bank of Presque Isle	1	1	2
	MARYLAND			
1244	The Farmers National Bank of Annapolis		1	1
1413	The First National Bank of Baltimore		4	4
13745	Fidelity-Baltimore National Bank, Baltimore		1	1
4049	The Second National Bank of Hagerstown	1		1
8381	The Second National Bank of Towson		2	2
	MASSACHUSETTS			
2232	The First National Bank of Attleboro		1	1
475	The Merchants National Bank of Boston	1		1
2152	The Home National Bank of Brockton		1	1
2504	National Bank of Plymouth County, Brockton		1	1
614	Middlesex County National Bank, Everett		1	1
528	The Framingham National Bank, Framingham		1	1
1129	Merrimack Valley National Bank, Haverhill	1	1	2
1939	Holyoke National Bank, Holyoke	1		1
6077	Union National Bank of Lowell	1		1
736	The First National Bank of Provincetown		1	1
726	Merchants-Warren National Bank of Salem		1	1
11388	The Peoples National Bank of Southbridge		1	1
14816	Security National Bank of Springfield	1		1
308	The Third National Bank & Trust Co. of Springfield	1		1
416	The First-Machinists National Bank of Taunton		1	1

TABLE No. 11.—*Number of domestic branches of national banks authorized during the year ended Dec. 31, 1958*—Continued

Charter No.	Title and location of bank	Branches authorized under act of Feb. 25, 1927, as amended		
		Local	Other than local	Total
	MICHIGAN			
13833	Farmers and Merchants National Bank in Benton Harbor		1	1
13738	Manufacturers National Bank of Detroit		3	3
13671	National Bank of Detroit		2	2
3761	The First National Bank of Escanaba	1		1
13741	The National Bank of Jackson	1		1
13820	The American National Bank & Trust Co. of Kalamazoo		1	1
191	The First National Bank & Trust Co. of Kalamazoo		1	1
390	The First National Bank & Trust Co. of Marquette	1		1
4840	The National Lumbermen's Bank of Muskegon		1	1
13739	Community National Bank of Pontiac		1	1
14729	St. Clair Shores National Bank, St. Clair Shores	1		1
3886	The First National Bank of St. Ignace		1	1
13874	The National Bank of Wyandotte		1	1
	MISSISSIPPI			
10738	First-Columbus National Bank, Columbus	1		1
10523	First National Bank of Jackson	1		1
	NEW JERSEY			
8800	The Boardwalk National Bank of Atlantic City		1	1
11658	Beach Haven National Bank & Trust Co., Beach Haven		1	1
1222	The Mechanics National Bank of Burlington		1	1
1209	First Camden National Bank & Trust Co., Camden		1	1
8394	Closter National Bank & Trust Co., Closter		1	1
1436	The National State Bank, Elizabeth, N.J.		1	1
12014	The City National Bank & Trust Co. of Hackensack		1	1
1113	The First National Iron Bank of Morristown	1	1	2
1452	The National State Bank of Newark	3		3
12195	The First National Bank of Park Ridge		1	1
13174	Plainfield Trust State National Bank, Plainfield	3	1	4
11759	Citizens First National Bank & Trust Co. of Ridgewood		1	1
12978	The First National Bank of Stone Harbor		1	1
2509	The First National Bank of Toms River, N.J.		1	1
1327	First Trenton National Bank, Trenton	3	2	5
12425	The Union Center National Bank, Union	1		1
3716	The Farmers & Mechanics National Bank of Woodbury	1		1
	NEW MEXICO			
6183	The First National Bank of Farmington	1	1	2
	NEW YORK			
1301	The National Commercial Bank & Trust Co. of Albany		1	1
10029	The First National Bank & Trust Co. of Bay Shore		1	1
202	First-City National Bank of Binghamton		2	2
8531	The St. Lawrence County National Bank of Canton		1	1
6587	Security National Bank of Long Island, Huntington		2	2
5816	The National Exchange Bank of Castleton on Hudson		1	1
11854	Peninsula National Bank of Cedarhurst		1	1
10109	The First National Bank of Central Square		1	1
11511	The Tinker National Bank of East Setauket		1	1
12997	The Franklin National Bank of Long Island, Franklin Square		2	2
13956	County National Bank, Middletown		2	2
14734	Tappan Zee National Bank of Nyack		1	1
465	The First National Bank of Poughkeepsie		1	1
11708	Scarsdale National Bank & Trust Co., Scarsdale		1	1
14763	The Eastern National Bank of Smithtown		1	1
5846	Rockland National Bank, Suffern		1	1
13393	Lincoln National Bank & Trust Co. of Syracuse		2	2
1342	The Merchants National Bank & Trust Co. of Syracuse	1	1	2
1392	The Oneida National Bank & Trust Co. of Utica		2	2
4495	The National Bank of Delaware County, Walton		1	1
9135	The Emerson National Bank of Warrensburgh		1	1
552	National Bank of Chester County & Trust Co., West Chester		1	1
13962	The National Bank of Windham		1	1
7703	The Meadow Brook National Bank of Nassau County, West Hempstead		1	1

TABLE No. 11.—*Number of domestic branches of national banks authorized during the year ended Dec. 31, 1958*—Continued

Charter No.	Title and location of bank	Branches authorized under act of Feb. 25, 1927, as amended		
		Local	Other than local	Total
	NORTH CAROLINA			
13721	First National Bank & Trust Co. in Asheville		2	2
9164	First Union National Bank of North Carolina, Charlotte		4	4
13761	Security National Bank of Greensboro		2	2
13636	First National Bank in Henderson	1		1
14147	The First National Bank of Winston-Salem	3		3
	NORTH DAKOTA			
8976	The First National Bank of Bowman		1	1
9590	The First National Bank of Linton		1	1
	OHIO			
5425	The Liberty National Bank of Ada	1		1
14579	First National Bank of Akron		1	1
3721	First National City Bank of Alliance	1		1
975	The Farmers National Bank & Trust Co. of Ashtabula		1	1
715	The First National Bank of Batavia		1	1
76	First National Bank of Canton	1		1
14724	The Southern Ohio National Bank of Cincinnati		1	1
4318	Central National Bank of Cleveland	1	1	2
14761	Society National Bank of Cleveland		2	2
7621	The City National Bank & Trust Co. of Columbus	1		1
7745	The Huntington National Bank of Columbus	1		1
13923	Coshocton National Bank, Coshocton		1	1
652	The Kent National Bank, Kent	1		1
11831	The National City Bank of Marion	1		1
3876	The First National Bank of Miamisburg		1	1
14565	First National Bank of Middletown		1	1
3234	The Milford National Bank, Milford		1	1
14203	The National Bank of Oak Harbor		1	1
14686	The Lake County National Bank of Painesville		1	1
1006	The Piqua National Bank & Trust Co., Piqua	1		1
14586	The National Bank of Toledo	1	1	2
3825	The First Troy National Bank & Trust Co., Troy	1		1
1997	The Clinton County National Bank & Trust Co. of Wilmington		1	1
7670	The Citizens National Bank of Wooster	1		1
2350	The Mahoning National Bank of Youngstown		1	1
13586	The Union National Bank of Youngstown		2	2
	OKLAHOMA			
12169	The First National Bank of Bethany	1		1
9952	The First National Bank of Elk City	1		1
12044	The Central National Bank of Enid	1		1
5753	The City National Bank of Lawton	1		1
12890	The Commercial National Bank in Muskogee	1		1
11001	The Central National Bank of Okmulgee	1		1
5206	The First National Bank of Stillwater	1		1
	OREGON			
1553	The First National Bank of Oregon, Portland		2	2
4514	The United States National Bank of Portland		2	2
	PENNSYLVANIA			
4894	The Farmers National Bank of Beaver Falls		1	1
14007	Bethlehem National Bank, Bethlehem	1		1
13868	Blairsville National Bank, Blairsville	1		1
2428	The Bradford National Bank, Bradford	2		2
5855	The Carrolltown American National Bank, Carrolltown		1	1
4272	The Valley National Bank of Chambersburg		1	1
13998	The County National Bank at Clearfield	1		1
9862	Peoples National Bank of Edwardsville	1		1
12	The First National Bank of Erie	1		1
870	The Marine National Bank of Erie		1	1
6220	The First National Bank of Everett		1	1

TABLE No. 11.—*Number of domestic branches of national banks authorized during the year ended Dec. 31, 1958*—Continued

Charter No.	Title and location of bank	Branches authorized under act of Feb. 25, 1927, as amended		
		Local	Other than local	Total
	PENNSYLVANIA—continued			
14098	First National Bank in Indiana		1	1
1579	The First National Bank of Lewistown		1	1
10506	The Russell National Bank of Lewistown		1	1
5773	The Farmers National Bank of Lititz		1	1
3147	The National Bank of Malvern		1	1
2222	Western Pennsylvania National Bank, McKeesport		1	1
14542	Cumberland County National Bank & Trust Co., New Cumberland		1	1
723	Central-Penn National Bank of Philadelphia	1	3	4
539	The Philadelphia National Bank, Philadelphia	1		1
213	Second National Bank of Philadelphia	1		1
6301	Mellon National Bank & Trust Co., Pittsburgh		5	5
252	Peoples First National Bank & Trust Co., Pittsburgh	1	2	3
705	The Union National Bank of Pittsburgh	1		1
649	The Miners National Bank of Pottsville		2	2
5184	First National Bank & Trust Co. of Red Lion		1	1
77	Northeastern Pennsylvania National Bank & Trust Co., Scranton		3	3
6942	National-Dime Bank of Shamokin	1	1	2
42	The First National Bank of Strasburg		1	1
3632	The First-Stroudsburg National Bank, Stroudsburg		1	1
5034	Gallatin National Bank, Uniontown		2	2
732	The Wyoming National Bank of Wilkes Barre, Wilkes-Barre		1	1
604	The York National Bank & Trust Co., York		1	1
	RHODE ISLAND			
1302	Industrial National Bank of Providence		4	4
	SOUTH CAROLINA			
14425	The Citizens & Southern National Bank of South Carolina, Charleston	1		1
2044	The South Carolina National Bank of Charleston		3	3
13720	The First National Bank of South Carolina of Columbia		2	2
14784	Carolina National Bank of Easley		1	1
10635	The Peoples National Bank of Greenville	1		1
10680	The First National Bank of Holly Hill		1	1
14448	Rock Hill National Bank, Rock Hill	1		1
14594	Piedmont National Bank of Spartanburg		1	1
	TENNESSEE			
13640	The First National Bank in Bristol		1	1
14611	American National Bank & Trust Co. of Chattanooga		1	1
7848	The Hamilton National Bank of Chattanooga		1	1
14710	First Farmers and Merchants National Bank of Columbia	1		1
13635	The Hamilton National Bank of Johnson City	1		1
10842	The First National Bank of Kingsport	1		1
336	The First National Bank of Memphis	1		1
13681	National Bank of Commerce in Memphis	1		1
14231	First National Bank & Trust Co. of Rockwood		1	1
10785	First National Bank of Shelbyville	1		1
	VERMONT			
1430	Vermont National & Savings Bank, Brattleboro	1	9	10
	VIRGINIA			
2594	The Peoples National Bank of Charlottesville	1	1	2
1522	The Lynchburg National Bank & Trust Co., Lynchburg	1		1
5032	The National Bank of Manassas	1		1
4635	First National Bank of Newport News	1		1
10194	The Seaboard Citizens National Bank of Norfolk	1		1
1111	First and Merchants National Bank of Richmond	1		1
2737	The First National Exchange Bank of Roanoke	1		1
11817	The Colonial-American National Bank of Roanoke	1		1
6123	Tazewell National Bank, Tazewell		1	1
6084	Farmers and Merchants National Bank, Winchester	1		1

TABLE No. 11.—*Number of domestic branches of national banks authorized during the year ended Dec. 31, 1958*—Continued

Charter No.	Title and location of bank	Branches authorized under act of Feb. 25, 1927, as amended		
		Local	Other than local	Total
	WASHINGTON			
4375	The National Bank of Commerce of Seattle	1	1	2
13230	The Pacific National Bank of Seattle	1	--------	1
14394	Peoples National Bank of Washington in Seattle	1	--------	1
11280	Seattle-First National Bank, Seattle	--------	1	1
4668	The Old National Bank of Spokane	--------	1	1
12292	The Puget Sound National Bank of Tacoma	1	--------	1
3956	The Baker-Boyer National Bank of Walla Walla	1	--------	1
	Total (259 banks)	139	270	409

TABLE No. 12.—*Number of domestic branches of national banks closed during the year ended Dec. 31, 1958*

Char-ter No.	Title and location of bank	Branches closed		
		Local	Other than local	Total
	CALIFORNIA			
2491	Security-First National Bank, Los Angeles	1	1	2
14671	Sun Valley National Bank of Los Angeles	1		1
1741	Crocker-Anglo National Bank, San Francisco		1	1
	CONNECTICUT			
1249	The First National Bank & Trust Co. of New Canaan	1	1	2
	DISTRICT OF COLUMBIA			
3425	The National Bank of Washington	1		1
1069	The National Metropolitan Bank of Washington	2		2
	MARYLAND			
13745	Fidelity-Baltimore National Bank, Baltimore	1	1	2
8381	The Second National Bank of Towson	1	2	3
	MASSACHUSETTS			
4907	Springfield National Bank, Springfield	5	2	7
	MICHIGAN			
13799	Peoples National Bank of Grand Rapids	5	1	6
	NEW JERSEY			
12205	Passaic-Clifton National Bank & Trust Co., Clifton	2	2	4
9339	Montclair National Bank & Trust Co., Montclair	1		1
12949	The Prospect National Bank of Trenton	1		1
	NEW YORK			
12997	The Franklin National Bank of Long Island, Franklin Square		1	1
3183	The First National Bank of Herkimer		1	1
2410	The Farmers National Bank & Trust Co. of Rome	1	1	2
13962	The National Bank of Windham		¹ 1	1
11059	The First National Bank of Woodridge	1		1
	NORTH CAROLINA			
9164	First Union National Bank of North Carolina, Charlotte		1	1
13761	Security National Bank of Greensboro	1		1
14147	The First National Bank of Winston-Salem	2		2
	NORTH DAKOTA			
9590	The First National Bank of Linton		1	1
	OHIO			
858	The First National Bank of Newark	1		1
	PENNSYLVANIA			
373	The First National Bank of Allentown	1		1
608	The National Bank of Pottstown	1	1	2
77	Northeastern Pennsylvania National Bank & Trust Co., Scranton	1		1
6942	National-Dime Bank of Shamokin	1		1
13196	Upper Darby National Bank, Upper Darby	4	7	11
	TENNESSEE			
13349	Union Planters National Bank of Memphis		1	1
	Total (29 banks)	36	26	62

¹ Seasonal agency.

Table No. 13.—*Principal items of assets and liabilities of national banks, by size of banks, according to deposits, Dec. 31, 1957 and 1958*

[In thousands of dollars]

	Number of banks	Loans and securities				Cash, balances with other banks, including reserve with Federal Reserve banks	Real estate assets	Total assets	Capital stock	Surplus, profits and reserves	Deposits		
		Total	Loans and discounts, including rediscounts and overdrafts	U.S. Government obligations direct and guaranteed	Other bonds and securities						Total	Demand	Time
1957													
Banks with deposits of—													
Less than $500,000	22	7,027	3,591	2,904	532	3,455	59	10,542	610	871	9,052	7,633	1,419
$500,000 to $750,000	47	25,429	12,429	10,845	2,155	8,802	171	34,431	1,322	2,967	30,055	25,113	4,942
$750,000 to $1,000,000	92	70,386	32,800	30,298	7,288	21,987	947	93,369	3,610	7,896	81,528	60,925	20,603
$1,000,000 to $2,000,000	606	804,876	357,557	362,705	84,614	226,374	9,048	1,041,110	31,316	78,935	926,623	644,292	282,331
$2,000,000 to $5,000,000	1,556	4,523,106	2,021,539	1,904,044	597,523	1,183,360	59,249	5,771,915	139,899	379,284	5,229,659	3,453,057	1,776,602
$5,000,000 to $10,000,000	1,043	6,336,908	2,880,865	2,574,830	871,213	1,610,475	92,517	8,049,341	171,764	470,449	7,361,201	4,724,637	2,636,564
$10,000,000 to $25,000,000	723	9,508,808	4,443,637	3,383,016	1,232,115	2,418,516	162,649	12,118,166	263,624	619,066	11,128,055	7,192,097	3,935,358
$25,000,000 to $50,000,000	259	7,575,676	3,600,621	3,082,457	892,598	1,939,949	132,253	9,679,072	208,558	441,725	8,932,517	5,965,278	2,967,239
$50,000,000 to $100,000,000	131	7,633,783	3,927,966	2,857,726	848,091	2,217,152	120,651	10,008,030	225,938	456,294	9,206,507	6,651,787	2,554,720
$100,000,000 to $500,000,000	125	22,082,023	12,622,529	7,402,229	2,057,265	7,631,036	368,021	30,236,888	662,220	1,429,248	27,708,777	21,546,723	6,162,054
$500,000,000 or more	23	32,915,964	20,588,743	9,276,952	3,050,239	9,604,028	394,216	43,479,776	1,097,352	2,400,269	38,822,337	27,608,823	11,213,514
Total	4,627	91,483,986	50,502,277	31,338,076	9,643,633	26,865,134	1,339,781	120,522,640	2,806,213	6,287,004	109,436,311	77,880,965	31,555,346
1958													
Banks with deposits of—													
Less than $500,000	15	4,659	2,423	1,840	396	2,441	48	7,148	410	622	6,108	5,390	718
$500,000 to $750,000	42	22,713	12,694	8,608	1,411	7,721	235	30,699	1,547	2,458	26,600	22,699	3,901
$750,000 to $1,000,000	62	48,717	22,967	20,997	4,753	13,678	402	62,894	2,823	5,197	54,664	39,595	15,069
$1,000,000 to $2,000,000	541	722,358	331,378	316,074	74,706	195,885	8,015	927,081	26,703	70,691	826,438	575,101	251,337
$2,000,000 to $5,000,000	1,507	4,475,787	2,035,419	1,855,122	585,246	1,096,121	58,813	5,636,484	132,067	372,173	5,109,428	3,350,678	1,758,750
$5,000,000 to $10,000,000	1,087	6,710,526	3,085,562	2,688,154	936,810	1,588,515	100,099	8,410,205	179,345	496,638	7,680,911	4,819,924	2,860,987
$10,000,000 to $25,000,000	771	10,275,106	4,743,251	4,178,086	1,353,769	2,456,472	179,407	12,938,037	275,065	675,592	11,867,728	7,526,335	4,341,393
$25,000,000 to $50,000,000	261	7,783,487	3,645,557	3,194,661	943,269	1,835,512	139,436	9,791,073	212,991	455,689	9,017,834	5,849,927	3,167,907
$50,000,000 to $100,000,000	138	8,748,622	3,983,955	3,112,522	952,145	2,051,355	129,957	10,270,746	229,496	477,545	9,441,587	6,494,498	2,947,089
$100,000,000 to $500,000,000	137	24,394,926	13,423,288	8,620,047	2,351,591	7,804,300	417,713	32,801,364	712,396	1,581,059	30,039,958	23,116,333	6,923,625
$500,000,000 or more	26	37,097,547	21,509,730	11,828,449	3,759,368	9,812,820	452,877	47,921,235	1,178,436	2,579,858	43,014,872	29,551,319	13,463,553
Total	4,585	99,584,448	52,796,224	35,824,760	10,963,464	26,864,820	1,487,002	128,796,966	2,951,279	6,717,522	117,086,128	81,351,799	35,734,329

TABLE No. 14.—*Number of national banks in United States and possessions with surplus fund equal to or exceeding common capital stock, and the number with surplus fund less than common capital stock 1942 to 1958*

	Number of banks	Banks with surplus equal to or exceeding common capital stock		Banks with surplus less than common capital stock	
		Number	Percent	Number	Percent
June 30, 1942	5,107	2,115	41.41	2,992	58.59
Dec. 31, 1942	5,087	2,205	43.35	2,882	56.65
June 30, 1943	5,066	2,275	44.91	2,791	55.09
Dec. 31, 1943	5,046	2,434	48.24	2,612	51.76
June 30, 1944	5,042	2,576	51.09	2,466	48.91
Dec. 30, 1944	5,031	2,749	54.64	2,282	45.36
June 30, 1945	5,021	2,946	58.67	2,075	41.33
Dec. 31, 1945	5,023	3,180	63.31	1,843	36.69
June 29, 1946	5,018	3,318	66.12	1,700	33.88
Dec. 31, 1946	5,013	3,531	70.44	1,482	29.56
June 30, 1947	5,018	3,637	72.48	1,381	27.52
Dec. 31, 1947	5,011	3,773	75.29	1,238	24.71
June 30, 1948	5,004	3,820	76.34	1,184	23.66
Dec. 31, 1948	4,997	3,963	79.31	1,034	20.69
June 30, 1949	4,993	4,003	80.17	990	19.83
Dec. 31, 1949	4,981	4,132	82.96	849	17.04
June 30, 1950	4,977	4,148	83.34	829	16.66
Dec. 30, 1950	4,965	4,236	85.32	729	14.68
June 30, 1951	4,953	4,242	85.65	711	14.35
Dec. 31, 1951	4,946	4,324	87.42	622	12.58
June 30, 1952	4,932	4,327	87.73	605	12.27
Dec. 31, 1952	4,916	4,398	89.46	518	10.54
June 30, 1953	4,881	4,368	89.49	513	10.51
Dec. 31, 1953	4,864	4,406	90.58	458	9.42
June 30, 1954	4,842	4,400	90.87	442	9.13
Dec. 31, 1954	4,796	4,417	92.10	379	7.90
June 30, 1955	4,751	4,378	92.15	373	7.85
Dec. 31, 1955	4,700	4,363	92.83	337	7.17
June 30, 1956	4,675	4,330	92.62	345	7.38
Dec. 31, 1956	4,659	4,337	93.09	322	6.91
June 6, 1957	4,654	4,316	92.74	338	7.26
Dec. 31, 1957	4,627	4,316	93.28	311	6.72
June 23, 1958	4,606	4,299	93.33	307	6.67
Dec. 31, 1958	4,585	4,308	93.96	277	6.04

TABLE No. 15.—*Dates of reports of condition of national banks, 1914 to 1958*

[For dates of previous calls see report for 1920, vol. 2, table No. 42, p. 150]

Year	Jan.	Feb.	Mar.	Apr.	May	June	July	Aug.	Sept.	Oct.	Nov.	Dec.
1914	13		4			30			12	31		31
1915			4		1	23			2		10	31
1916			7		1	30			12		17	27
1917			5		1	20			11		20	31
1918			4		10	29		31			1	31
1919			4		12	30			12		17	31
1920		28			4	30			8		15	29
1921		21		28		30			6			31
1922			10		5	30			15			29
1923				3		30			14			31
1924			31			30				10		31
1925				6		30			28			31
1926				12		30						31
1927			23			30				10		31
1928		28				30				3		31
1929			27			29				4		31
1930			27			30			24			31
1931			25			30			29			31
1932						30			30			31
1933						30				25		30
1934			5			30				17		31
1935			4			29					1	31
1936			4			30						31
1937			31			30						31
1938			7			30			28			31
1939			29			30				2		30
1940			26			29						31
1941				4		30			24			31
1942				4		30						31
1943						30				18		30
1944				13		30						31
1945			20			30						31
1946						29			30			31
1947						30				6		31
1948				12		30						31
1949				11		30					1	31
1950				24		30				4		30
1951				9		30				10		31
1952			31			30			5			31
1953				20		30			30			31
1954				15		30				7		31
1955				11		30				5		31
1956				10		30			26			31
1957			14			6					11	31
1958			4			23			24			31

NOTES

Act of Feb. 25, 1863, provided for reports of condition on the first of each quarter, before commencement of business.

Act of June 3, 1864—First Monday of January, April, July, and October, before commencement of business, on form prescribed by Comptroller (in addition to reports on first Tuesday of each month showing condition at commencement of business in respect to certain items; i.e., loans, specie, deposits, and circulation).

Act of Mar. 3, 1869, not less than 5 reports per year, on form prescribed by Comptroller, at close of business on any past date by him specified.

Act of Dec. 28, 1922, minimum number of calls reduced from 5 to 3 per year.

Act of Feb. 25, 1927, authorized a vice president or an assistant cashier designated by the board of directors to verify reports of condition in absence of president and cashier.

Act of June 16, 1933, requires each national bank to furnish and publish not less than 3 reports each year of affiliates other than member banks, as of dates identical with those for which the Comptroller shall during such year require reports of condition of the bank. The report of each affiliate shall contain such information as in the judgment of the Comptroller shall be necessary to disclose fully the relations between the affiliate and the bank and to enable the Comptroller to inform himself as to the effect of such relations upon the affairs of the bank.

Sec. 21(a) of the Banking Act of 1933 provided, in part, that after June 16, 1934, it would be unlawful for any private bank not under State supervision to continue the transaction of business unless it submitted to periodic examination by the Comptroller of the Currency or the Federal Reserve bank of the district, and made and published periodic reports of condition the same as required of national banks under section 5211, U.S.R.S. Sec. 21(a) of the Banking Act of 1933, however, was amended by sec. 303 of the Banking Act of 1935, approved Aug. 23, 1935, under the provisions of which private banks are no longer required to submit to examination by the Comptroller or Federal Reserve bank, nor are they required to make to the Comptroller and publish periodic reports of condition. (5 calls for reports of condition of private banks were made by the Comptroller, the first one for June 30, 1934, and the last one for June 29, 1935.)

TABLE NO. 16

ASSETS AND LIABILITIES OF NATIONAL BANKS ON MARCH 4, JUNE 23, SEPTEMBER 24, AND DECEMBER 31, 1958, BY STATES AND TERRITORIES

Assets and liabilities of national banks, by States, at date of each call during year ended Dec. 31, 1958

ALABAMA

[In thousands of dollars]

	Mar. 4, 1958	June 23, 1958	Sept. 24, 1958	Dec. 31, 1958
	69 banks	69 banks	69 banks	69 banks
ASSETS				
Loans and discounts (including overdrafts)	541, 603	566, 006	573, 771	598, 936
U.S. Government securities, direct obligations	335, 521	360, 250	384, 980	400, 045
Obligations guaranteed by U. S. Government				
Obligations of States and political subdivisions	123, 202	134, 643	136, 081	142, 664
Other bonds, notes, and debentures	28, 409	29, 602	28, 558	27, 351
Corporate stocks, including stock of Federal Reserve bank	2, 536	2, 548	2, 564	2, 582
Reserve with Federal Reserve bank	131, 500	140, 680	119, 692	130, 060
Currency and coin	24, 266	28, 437	33, 134	31, 654
Balances with other banks, and cash items in process of collection	167, 772	153, 447	153, 701	181, 206
Bank premises owned, furniture and fixtures	14, 501	14, 743	15, 260	15, 587
Real estate owned other than bank premises	871	899	424	433
Investments and other assets indirectly representing bank premises or other real estate	1, 970	2, 321	2, 332	2, 437
Customers' liability on acceptances outstanding	25	194	128	155
Income earned or accrued but not collected	3, 025	2, 953	3, 074	} 4, 999
Other assets	1, 332	1, 647	1, 756	
Total assets	1, 376, 533	1, 438, 370	1, 455, 455	1, 538, 109
LIABILITIES				
Demand deposits of individuals, partnerships, and corporations	701, 715	720, 648	734, 542	786, 510
Time deposits of individuals, partnerships, and corporations	318, 705	337, 606	346, 593	349, 768
Postal savings deposits	10	10	10	10
Deposits of U.S. Government	21, 437	46, 882	31, 657	28, 993
Deposits of States and political subdivisions	107, 411	110, 851	105, 157	134, 328
Deposits of banks	91, 068	80, 179	91, 252	93, 121
Other deposits (certified and cashiers' checks, etc.)	11, 333	12, 134	12, 129	12, 809
Total deposits	*1, 251, 679*	*1, 308, 310*	*1, 321, 340*	*1, 405, 539*
Demand deposits	*926, 163*	*961, 200*	*962, 278*	*1, 043, 830*
Time deposits	*325, 516*	*347, 110*	*359, 062*	*361, 709*
Bills payable, rediscounts, and other liabilities for borrowed money	90	1, 700	350	100
Acceptances executed by or for account of reporting banks and outstanding	25	194	128	155
Income collected but not earned	6, 963	7, 403	7, 618	} 16, 491
Expenses accrued and unpaid	7, 290	5, 283	7, 640	
Other liabilities	1, 801	1, 967	1, 935	
Total liabilities	1, 267, 848	1, 324, 857	1, 339, 011	1, 422, 285
CAPITAL ACCOUNTS				
Capital stock: Common stock	33, 270	33, 570	33, 970	34, 020
Surplus	50, 730	51, 129	51, 725	53, 180
Undivided profits	20, 020	22, 740	24, 314	21, 750
Reserves	4, 665	6, 074	6, 435	6, 874
Total capital accounts	108, 685	113, 513	116, 444	115, 824
Total liabilities and capital accounts	1, 376, 533	1, 438, 370	1, 455, 455	1, 538, 109
MEMORANDUM				
Assets pledged or assigned to secure liabilities and for other purposes	184, 874	218, 229	225, 766	226, 672

Assets and liabilities of national banks, by States, at date of each call during year ended Dec. 31, 1958—Continued

ALASKA

[In thousands of dollars]

	Mar. 4, 1958	June 23, 1958	Sept. 24, 1958	Dec. 31, 1958
	7 banks	7 banks	7 banks	7 banks
ASSETS				
Loans and discounts (including overdrafts)	46,093	49,670	51,954	52,402
U.S. Government securities, direct obligations	45,437	46,735	49,536	55,944
Obligations guaranteed by U.S. Government				
Obligations of States and political subdivisions	5,619	6,465	6,409	6,869
Other bonds, notes, and debentures	4,540	5,955	7,095	3,784
Corporate stocks, including stock of Federal Reserve bank	13		37	37
Reserve with Federal Reserve bank and approved national banking associations	14,122	14,408	17,994	15,242
Currency and coin	6,412	7,062	8,376	6,082
Balances with other banks, and cash items in process of collection	4,536	5,282	5,560	5,618
Bank premises owned, furniture and fixtures	2,178	2,425	2,448	2,413
Real estate owned other than bank premises	145	165	209	186
Investments and other assets indirectly representing bank premises or other real estate	330	371	344	339
Income earned or accrued but not collected	15	11	10	168
Other assets	183	192	212	
Total assets	129,623	138,778	150,184	149,084
LIABILITIES				
Demand deposits of individuals, partnerships, and corporations	53,686	54,501	65,106	64,192
Time deposits of individuals, partnerships, and corporations	30,836	31,433	32,845	34,341
Postal savings deposits	10	10	10	10
Deposits of U.S. Government	22,198	23,791	22,470	21,692
Deposits of States and political subdivisions	11,897	18,051	17,961	17,279
Deposits of banks	1,604	1,437	1,790	2,288
Other deposits (certified and cashiers' checks, etc.)	1,268	1,219	1,311	1,227
Total deposits	*121,499*	*130,442*	*141,493*	*141,029*
Demand deposits	*74,850*	*78,923*	*88,917*	*86,906*
Time deposits	*46,649*	*51,519*	*52,576*	*54,123*
Bills payable, rediscounts, and other liabilities for borrowed money				
Income collected but not earned	392	457	505	
Expenses accrued and unpaid	159	182	131	648
Other liabilities	14	3	3	
Total liabilities	122,064	131,084	142,132	141,677
CAPITAL ACCOUNTS				
Capital stock: Common stock	2,350	2,350	2,750	2,750
Surplus	2,420	2,420	2,445	2,670
Undivided profits	2,343	2,514	2,447	1,547
Reserves	446	410	410	440
Total capital accounts	7,559	7,694	8,052	7,407
Total liabilities and capital accounts	129,623	138,778	150,184	149,084
MEMORANDUM				
Assets pledged or assigned to secure liabilities and for other purposes	36,278	35,881	36,197	37,391

Assets and liabilities of national banks, by States, at date of each call during year ended Dec. 31, 1958—Continued

ARIZONA

[In thousands of dollars]

	Mar. 4, 1958	June 23, 1958	Sept. 24, 1958	Dec. 31, 1958
	3 banks	3 banks	3 banks	3 banks
ASSETS				
Loans and discounts (including overdrafts)	428, 075	434, 324	421, 889	452, 965
U.S. Government securities, direct obligations	141, 424	160, 026	153, 194	166, 055
Obligations guaranteed by U.S. Government	11	11	4	11
Obligations of States and political subdivisions	37, 545	39, 248	43, 767	43, 114
Other bonds, notes, and debentures	11, 651	17, 363	14, 893	11, 523
Corporate stocks, including stock of Federal Reserve bank	1, 334	1, 364	1, 363	1, 483
Reserve with Federal Reserve bank	42, 774	55, 544	57, 971	59, 648
Currency and coin	11, 744	12, 691	13, 995	15, 562
Balances with other banks, and cash items in process of collection	68, 318	63, 329	57, 289	88, 161
Bank premises owned, furniture and fixtures	15, 194	16, 256	16, 545	16, 938
Real estate owned other than bank premises	12	17	17	12
Investments and other assets indirectly representing bank premises or other real estate	5, 161	5, 161	5, 161	5, 160
Customers' liability on acceptances outstanding	20	152	192	154
Income earned or accrued but not collected	2, 760	2, 440	2, 384	} 5, 564
Other assets	2, 077	3, 049	1, 557	
Total assets	768, 100	810, 975	790, 221	866, 350
LIABILITIES				
Demand deposits of individuals, partnerships, and corporations	400, 354	403, 499	395, 812	451, 154
Time deposits of individuals, partnerships, and corporations	188, 241	210, 208	217, 295	215, 569
Postal savings deposits	27	27	27	27
Deposits of U.S. Government	8, 231	19, 160	12, 730	11, 001
Deposits of States and political subdivisions	74, 779	76, 605	61, 528	78, 050
Deposits of banks	16, 802	23, 304	18, 979	23, 120
Other deposits (certified and cashiers' checks, etc.)	11, 698	10, 303	7, 757	14, 153
Total deposits	*700, 132*	*743, 106*	*714, 128*	*793, 074*
Demand deposits	*489, 450*	*510, 230*	*471, 683*	*554, 723*
Time deposits	*210, 682*	*232, 876*	*242, 445*	*238, 351*
Bills payable, rediscounts, and other liabilities for borrowed money			7, 500	
Acceptances executed by or for account of reporting banks and outstanding	20	152	192	154
Income collected but not earned	8, 448	9, 059	9, 245	} 16, 109
Expenses accrued and unpaid	5, 194	5, 246	5, 731	
Other liabilities	1, 699	1, 301	910	
Total liabilities	715, 493	758, 864	737, 706	809, 337
CAPITAL ACCOUNTS				
Capital stock: Common stock	16, 970	16, 970	16, 970	17, 480
Surplus	27, 680	27, 680	27, 680	31, 170
Undivided profits	7, 952	7, 456	7, 856	8, 353
Reserves	5	5	9	10
Total capital accounts	52, 607	52, 111	52, 515	57, 013
Total liabilities and capital accounts	768, 100	810, 975	790, 221	866, 350
MEMORANDUM				
Assets pledged or assigned to secure liabilities and for other purposes	129, 680	148, 062	129, 915	**144, 711**

Assets and liabilities of national banks, by States, at date of each call during year ended Dec. 31, 1958—Continued

ARKANSAS

[In thousands of dollars]

	Mar. 4, 1958	June 23, 1958	Sept. 24, 1958	Dec. 31, 1958
	55 banks	55 banks	55 banks	55 banks
ASSETS				
Loans and discounts (including overdrafts)	203, 030	209, 468	209, 758	224, 438
U.S. Government securities, direct obligations	153, 199	149, 434	162, 197	171, 099
Obligations guaranteed by U.S. Government			11	
Obligations of States and political subdivisions	60, 161	66, 593	69, 675	72, 849
Other bonds, notes, and debentures	12, 479	9, 317	8, 899	7, 787
Corporate stocks, including stock of Federal Reserve bank	1, 085	1, 125	1, 149	1, 155
Reserve with Federal Reserve bank	54, 437	48, 917	54, 554	50, 223
Currency and coin	8, 631	10, 355	10, 959	11, 469
Balances with other banks, and cash items in process of collection	72, 096	74, 512	76, 452	99, 075
Bank premises owned, furniture and fixtures	7, 585	7, 993	8, 198	8, 183
Real estate owned other than bank premises	218	211	256	269
Investments and other assets indirectly representing bank premises or other real estate	45	46	47	40
Income earned or accrued but not collected	966	1, 084	1, 143	} 1, 693
Other assets	340	352	449	
Total assets	574, 272	579, 407	603, 747	648, 280
LIABILITIES				
Demand deposits of individuals, partnerships, and corporations	309, 548	303, 007	309, 014	352, 259
Time deposits of individuals, partnerships, and corporations	109, 506	116, 461	120, 307	122, 190
Postal savings deposits	24	24	24	24
Deposits of U.S. Government	7, 001	11, 240	8, 450	8, 847
Deposits of States and political subdivisions	39, 597	38, 187	50, 373	35, 853
Deposits of banks	50, 845	50, 315	54, 877	66, 754
Other deposits (certified and cashiers' checks, etc.)	3, 293	4, 503	4, 042	6, 379
Total deposits	*519, 814*	*523, 737*	*547, 087*	*592, 306*
Demand deposits	*408, 637*	*404, 954*	*424, 408*	*468, 148*
Time deposits	*111, 177*	*118, 783*	*122, 679*	*124, 158*
Bills payable, rediscounts, and other liabilities for borrowed money		50	50	
Income collected but not earned	2, 239	2, 287	2, 382	}
Expenses accrued and unpaid	1, 887	1, 702	2, 262	4, 602
Other liabilities	8	343	109	}
Total liabilities	523, 948	528, 119	551, 890	596, 908
CAPITAL ACCOUNTS				
Capital stock: Common stock	15, 655	16, 355	16, 605	16, 655
Surplus	20, 605	21, 165	21, 690	22, 203
Undivided profits	12, 477	12, 378	12, 085	10, 800
Reserves	1, 587	1, 390	1, 477	1, 714
Total capital accounts	50, 324	51, 288	51, 857	51, 372
Total liabilities and capital accounts	574, 272	579, 407	603, 747	648, 280
MEMORANDUM				
Assets pledged or assigned to secure liabilities and for other purposes	37, 822	40, 534	41, 600	43, 689

Assets and liabilities of national banks, by States, at date of each call during year ended Dec. 31, 1958—Continued

CALIFORNIA

[In thousands of dollars]

	Mar. 4, 1958	June 23, 1958	Sept. 24, 1958	Dec. 31, 1958
	48 banks	48 banks	48 banks	46 banks
ASSETS				
Loans and discounts (including overdrafts)	8, 153, 912	8, 105, 710	8, 228, 685	8, 512, 791
U.S. Government securities, direct obligations	4, 149, 561	4, 550, 633	4, 556, 357	4, 676, 473
Obligations guaranteed by U.S. Government	557	719	585	672
Obligations of States and political subdivisions	973, 723	1, 213, 350	1, 210, 441	1, 205, 110
Other bonds, notes, and debentures	239, 378	308, 432	293, 996	264, 886
Corporate stocks, including stock of Federal Reserve bank	63, 175	63, 256	63, 819	65, 325
Reserve with Federal Reserve bank	1, 445, 297	1, 430, 653	1, 555, 172	1, 583, 724
Currency and coin	110, 843	133, 681	138, 513	149, 912
Balances with other banks, and cash items in process of collection	1, 075, 245	981, 490	993, 661	1, 291, 974
Bank premises owned, furniture and fixtures	166, 830	173, 515	175, 625	181, 392
Real estate owned other than bank premises	2, 673	3, 031	3, 330	2, 908
Investments and other assets indirectly representing bank premises or other real estate	39, 496	39, 899	40, 198	41, 697
Customers' liability on acceptances outstanding	181, 322	144, 615	96, 500	115, 052
Income earned or accrued but not collected	53, 325	43, 493	47, 104	} 101, 640
Other assets	27, 874	29, 420	25, 908	
Total assets	16, 683, 211	17, 221, 897	17, 429, 894	18, 193, 556
LIABILITIES				
Demand deposits of individuals, partnerships, and corporations	6, 325, 761	6, 216, 171	6, 587, 742	7, 132, 566
Time deposits of individuals, partnerships, and corporations	6, 195, 229	6, 502, 599	6, 607, 267	6, 777, 253
Postal savings deposits	202	202	202	202
Deposits of U.S. Government	264, 664	466, 538	289, 689	269, 825
Deposits of States and political subdivisions	1, 177, 151	1, 304, 291	1, 172, 045	1, 405, 902
Deposits of banks	726, 917	705, 810	687, 677	702, 505
Other deposits (certified and cashiers' checks, etc.)	243, 858	234, 791	281, 372	364, 233
Total deposits	*14, 933, 782*	*15, 430, 402*	*15, 625, 994*	*16, 652, 486*
Demand deposits	*7, 660, 154*	*7, 752, 264*	*7, 948, 950*	*8, 751, 100*
Time deposits	*7, 273, 628*	*7, 678, 138*	*7, 677, 044*	*7, 901, 386*
Bills payable, rediscounts, and other liabilities for borrowed money	168, 408	101, 000	243, 429	----------
Acceptances executed by or for account of reporting banks and outstanding	183, 644	147, 691	98, 735	116, 708
Income collected but not earned	104, 985	104, 381	112, 941	} 337, 407
Expenses accrued and unpaid	131, 443	128, 373	132, 064	
Other liabilities	128, 674	253, 406	154, 519	
Total liabilities	15, 650, 936	16, 165, 253	16, 367, 682	17, 106, 601
CAPITAL ACCOUNTS				
Capital stock: Common stock	319, 458	320, 642	331, 025	330, 784
Surplus	465, 464	466, 866	475, 088	525, 830
Undivided profits	240, 629	262, 220	249, 032	223, 601
Reserves	6, 724	6, 916	7, 067	6, 740
Total capital accounts	1, 032, 275	1, 056, 644	1, 062, 212	1, 086, 955
Total liabilities and capital accounts	16, 683, 211	17, 221, 897	17, 429, 894	18, 193, 556
MEMORANDUM				
Assets pledged or assigned to secure liabilities and for other purposes	2, 470, 439	2, 774, 017	2, 695, 032	2, 604, 958

Assets and liabilities of national banks, by States, at date of each call during year ended Dec. 31, 1958—Continued

COLORADO

[In thousands of dollars]

	Mar. 4, 1958	June 23, 1958	Sept. 24, 1958	Dec. 31, 1958
	77 banks	78 banks	77 banks	77 banks
ASSETS				
Loans and discounts (including overdrafts)	502,176	515,701	577,952	611,535
U.S. Government securities, direct obligations	365,317	385,545	430,880	413,575
Obligations guaranteed by U.S. Government			9	
Obligations of States and political subdivisions	53,769	54,360	56,392	56,124
Other bonds, notes, and debentures	11,394	9,623	8,433	7,153
Corporate stocks, including stock of Federal Reserve bank	2,125	2,139	2,336	2,359
Reserve with Federal Reserve bank	121,585	113,239	126,077	137,145
Currency and coin	13,146	15,638	17,724	17,276
Balances with other banks, and cash items in process of collection	165,305	149,002	194,777	199,740
Bank premises owned, furniture and fixtures	8,157	9,372	11,296	10,949
Real estate owned other than bank premises	290	313	297	227
Investments and other assets indirectly representing bank premises or other real estate	1,065	987	938	1,142
Income earned or accrued but not collected	2,440	2,625	3,300	} 5,339
Other assets	2,117	1,093	1,478	
Total assets	1,248,886	1,259,637	1,431,889	1,462,564
LIABILITIES				
Demand deposits of individuals, partnerships, and corporations	668,646	650,951	756,839	800,201
Time deposits of individuals, partnerships, and corporations	279,499	293,764	328,313	334,765
Postal savings deposits	10	10	10	10
Deposits of U.S. Government	21,272	40,974	30,541	30,288
Deposits of States and political subdivisions	74,671	75,464	85,606	70,921
Deposits of banks	87,097	79,722	97,359	98,150
Other deposits (certified and cashiers' checks, etc.)	12,711	9,916	11,171	13,633
Total deposits	*1,143,906*	*1,150,801*	*1,309,839*	*1,347,968*
Demand deposits	*841,075*	*836,647*	*953,440*	*988,779*
Time deposits	*302,831*	*314,154*	*356,399*	*359,189*
Bills payable, rediscounts, and other liabilities for borrowed money	200	3,900	6,500	-----------
Mortgages or other liens on bank premises and other real estate	13	30	30	30
Income collected but not earned	4,742	5,194	5,398	} 11,650
Expenses accrued and unpaid	7,225	4,716	6,793	
Other liabilities	568	1,171	1,654	
Total liabilities	1,156,654	1,165,812	1,330,214	1,359,648
CAPITAL ACCOUNTS				
Capital stock: Common stock	29,080	29,280	32,905	32,930
Surplus	41,069	41,399	44,249	45,302
Undivided profits	20,254	21,523	22,379	22,441
Reserves	1,829	1,623	2,142	2,243
Total capital accounts	92,232	93,825	101,675	102,916
Total liabilities and capital accounts	1,248,886	1,259,637	1,431,889	1,462,564
MEMORANDUM				
Assets pledged or assigned to secure liabilities and for other purposes	136,504	149,995	174,077	164,175

Assets and liabilities of national banks, by States, at date of each call during year ended Dec. 31, 1958—Continued

CONNECTICUT

[In thousands of dollars]

	Mar. 4, 1958	June 23, 1958	Sept. 24, 1958	Dec. 31, 1958
	32 banks	31 banks	31 banks	30 banks
ASSETS				
Loans and discounts (including overdrafts)	492, 069	533, 245	515, 904	537, 957
U.S. Government securities, direct obligations	291, 631	301, 368	315, 581	317, 407
Obligations guaranteed by U.S. Government				12
Obligations of States and political subdivisions	108, 871	109, 053	117, 079	119, 255
Other bonds, notes, and debentures	12, 092	11, 713	9, 205	9, 533
Corporate stocks, including stock of Federal Reserve bank	3, 722	3, 778	3, 487	3, 638
Reserve with Federal Reserve bank	99, 712	105, 647	83, 822	84, 929
Currency and coin	27, 668	27, 572	31, 159	31, 346
Balances with other banks, and cash items in process of collection	117, 689	117, 097	99, 657	139, 095
Bank premises owned, furniture and fixtures	14, 857	15, 159	15, 950	17, 392
Real estate owned other than bank premises	61	348	281	928
Investments and other assets indirectly representing bank premises or other real estate	844	818	805	342
Customers' liability on acceptances outstanding	69	96	87	59
Income earned or accrued but not collected	1, 733	2, 034	1, 930	5, 840
Other assets	3, 606	4, 338	3, 572	
Total assets	1, 174, 624	1, 232, 266	1, 198, 519	1, 267, 733
LIABILITIES				
Demand deposits of individuals, partnerships, and corporations	673, 486	690, 858	664, 996	741, 014
Time deposits of individuals, partnerships, and corporations	258, 594	265, 405	272, 443	268, 832
Postal savings deposits				
Deposits of U.S. Government	28, 498	51, 078	35, 467	34, 790
Deposits of States and political subdivisions	39, 090	49, 366	51, 033	44, 090
Deposits of banks	28, 931	27, 117	25, 346	28, 509
Other deposits (certified and cashiers' checks, etc.)	33, 798	35, 072	35, 613	34, 442
Total deposits	*1, 062, 597*	*1, 118, 896*	*1, 084, 898*	*1, 151, 677*
Demand deposits	*801, 604*	*851, 013*	*809, 741*	*880, 293*
Time deposits	*260, 793*	*267, 883*	*275, 157*	*271, 384*
Bills payable, rediscounts, and other liabilities for borrowed money	1, 230	800	50	1, 500
Mortgages or other liens on bank premises and other real estate				203
Acceptances executed by or for account of reporting banks and outstanding	69	96	87	59
Income collected but not earned	7, 399	7, 559	7, 976	17, 062
Expenses accrued and unpaid	6, 909	4, 865	7, 088	
Other liabilities	1, 557	2, 669	1, 486	
Total liabilities	1, 079, 561	1, 134, 885	1, 101, 585	1, 170, 501
CAPITAL ACCOUNTS				
Capital stock: Common stock	32, 788	32, 963	32, 963	33, 323
Surplus	43, 974	43, 905	43, 934	46, 532
Undivided profits	17, 082	19, 307	18, 674	15, 598
Reserves	1, 219	1, 206	1, 363	1, 779
Total capital accounts	95, 063	97, 381	96, 934	97, 232
Total liabilities and capital accounts	1, 174, 624	1, 232, 266	1, 198, 519	1, 267, 733
MEMORANDUM				
Assets pledged or assigned to secure liabilities and for other purposes	95, 579	90, 580	105, 763	106, 424

Assets and liabilities of national banks, by States, at date of each call during year ended Dec. 31, 1958—Continued

DELAWARE

[In thousands of dollars]

	Mar. 4, 1958	June 23, 1958	Sept. 24, 1958	Dec. 31, 1958
	7 banks	7 banks	7 banks	7 banks
ASSETS				
Loans and discounts (including overdrafts)	12,872	13,465	13,727	14,189
U.S. Government securities, direct obligations	10,413	10,544	11,022	12,117
Obligations guaranteed by U.S. Government				
Obligations of States and political subdivisions	2,216	2,223	2,719	2,696
Other bonds, notes, and debentures	753	751	648	643
Corporate stocks, including stock of Federal Reserve bank	91	91	94	94
Reserve with Federal Reserve bank	2,923	2,567	2,996	2,961
Currency and coin	658	772	794	725
Balances with other banks, and cash items in process of collection	2,209	2,215	2,343	1,942
Bank premises owned, furniture and fixtures	525	518	524	558
Income earned or accrued but not collected	1		3	} 22
Other assets	17	44	65	
Total assets	32,678	33,190	34,935	35,947
LIABILITIES				
Demand deposits of individuals, partnerships, and corporations	14,912	14,232	15,886	16,632
Time deposits of individuals, partnerships, and corporations	12,967	13,517	13,933	14,096
Postal savings deposits				
Deposits of U.S. Government	193	653	235	355
Deposits of States and political subdivisions	246	235	448	342
Deposits of banks				
Other deposits (certified and cashiers' checks, etc.)	398	421	287	395
Total deposits	*28,716*	*29,058*	*30,789*	*31,820*
Demand deposits	*15,651*	*15,435*	*16,715*	*17,582*
Time deposits	*13,065*	*13,623*	*14,074*	*14,238*
Bills payable, rediscounts, and other liabilities for borrowed money				
Income collected but not earned	2	27	38	} 85
Expenses accrued and unpaid	4	3		
Other liabilities	2	34	4	
Total liabilities	28,724	29,122	30,831	31,905
CAPITAL ACCOUNTS				
Capital stock: Common stock	775	775	775	775
Surplus	2,275	2,275	2,375	2,400
Undivided profits	837	950	887	793
Reserves	67	68	67	74
Total capital accounts	3,954	4,068	4,104	4,042
Total liabilities and capital accounts	32,678	33,190	34,935	35,947
MEMORANDUM				
Assets pledged or assigned to secure liabilities and for other purposes	984	1,514	2,013	2,080

Assets and liabilities of national banks, by States, at date of each call during year ended Dec. 31, 1958—Continued

DISTRICT OF COLUMBIA

[In thousands of dollars]

	Mar. 4, 1958	June 23, 1958	Sept. 24, 1958	Dec. 31, 1958
	7 banks	6 banks	6 banks	5 banks
ASSETS				
Loans and discounts (including overdrafts)	378, 691	358, 553	362, 539	376, 878
U.S. Government securities, direct obligations	307, 832	314, 415	307, 229	304, 462
Obligations guaranteed by U.S. Government				
Obligations of States and political subdivisions	24, 138	27, 497	27, 690	28, 141
Other bonds, notes, and debentures	15, 411	17, 313	18, 862	15, 951
Corporate stocks, including stock of Federal Reserve bank	1, 631	1, 541	1, 541	1, 536
Reserve with Federal Reserve bank	116, 947	110, 068	108, 099	90, 700
Currency and coin	15, 144	15, 820	16, 302	16, 011
Balances with other banks, and cash items in process of collection	88, 797	72, 924	66, 282	72, 045
Bank premises owned, furniture and fixtures	15, 739	14, 471	15, 064	15, 476
Real estate owned other than bank premises	192	144	139	137
Customers' liability on acceptances outstanding		41	141	
Income earned or accrued but not collected	1, 268	1, 117	1, 570	} 2, 088
Other assets	811	745	815	
Total assets	966, 601	934, 649	926, 273	923, 425
LIABILITIES				
Demand deposits of individuals, partnerships, and corporations	600, 802	554, 186	556, 362	571, 858
Time deposits of individuals, partnerships, and corporations	191, 750	202, 762	191, 207	190, 851
Postal savings deposits	754	729	656	656
Deposits of U.S. Government	25, 193	33, 576	27, 309	24, 692
Deposits of States and political subdivisions	81	72	57	104
Deposits of banks	60, 435	46, 986	49, 443	53, 339
Other deposits (certified and cashiers' checks, etc.)	13, 007	21, 238	13, 652	10, 788
Total deposits	*892, 022*	*859, 549*	*838, 686*	*852, 288*
Demand deposits	*690, 543*	*647, 363*	*637, 502*	*651, 460*
Time deposits	*201, 479*	*212, 186*	*201, 184*	*200, 828*
Bills payable, rediscounts, and other liabilities for borrowed money		5, 000	16, 500	
Acceptances executed by or for account of reporting banks and outstanding		41	141	
Income collected but not earned	1, 163	1, 278	1, 317	} 7, 534
Expenses accrued and unpaid	5, 761	2, 924	4, 236	
Other liabilities	1, 643	2, 099	1, 022	
Total liabilities	900, 589	870, 891	861, 902	859, 822
CAPITAL ACCOUNTS				
Capital stock: Common stock	19, 750	18, 250	18, 250	18, 100
Surplus	34, 600	33, 100	33, 100	33, 100
Undivided profits	9, 512	10, 433	11, 003	9, 981
Reserves	2, 150	1, 975	2, 018	2, 422
Total capital accounts	66, 012	63, 758	64, 371	63, 603
Total liabilities and capital accounts	966, 601	934, 649	926, 273	923, 425
MEMORANDUM				
Assets pledged or assigned to secure liabilities and for other purposes	58, 808	53, 176	67, 235	44, 258

Assets and liabilities of national banks, by States, at date of each call during year ended Dec. 31, 1958—Continued

FLORIDA

[In thousands of dollars]

	Mar. 4, 1958	June 23, 1958	Sept. 24, 1958	Dec. 31, 1958
	99 banks	99 banks	100 banks	103 banks
ASSETS				
Loans and discounts (including overdrafts)	976,141	985,751	992,259	1,103,148
U.S. Government securities, direct obligations	869,957	954,109	953,834	970,387
Obligations guaranteed by U.S. Government	13	28		14
Obligations of States and political subdivisions	178,339	192,936	203,809	208,915
Other bonds, notes, and debentures	40,838	33,109	31,626	34,242
Corporate stocks, including stock of Federal Reserve bank	4,530	4,716	4,874	5,038
Reserve with Federal Reserve bank	231,563	234,626	247,212	233,962
Currency and coin	44,415	45,460	45,078	53,655
Balances with other banks, and cash items in process of collection	443,386	400,613	347,177	526,558
Bank premises owned, furniture and fixtures	37,711	39,471	41,034	42,883
Real estate owned other than bank premises	2,179	1,489	1,625	1,273
Investments and other assets indirectly representing bank premises or other real estate	8,201	9,818	11,372	13,566
Customers' liability on acceptances outstanding	84	191	58	138
Income earned or accrued but not collected	7,494	6,476	6,114	} 11,852
Other assets	4,010	4,489	4,179	
Total assets	2,848,861	2,913,282	2,890,251	3,205,631
LIABILITIES				
Demand deposits of individuals, partnerships, and corporations	1,447,863	1,457,431	1,449,361	1,569,990
Time deposits of individuals, partnerships, and corporations	556,735	608,479	634,608	646,849
Postal savings deposits	66	66	66	61
Deposits of U.S. Government	36,413	75,671	46,103	46,962
Deposits of States and political subdivisions	289,444	261,515	229,149	340,580
Deposits of banks	268,969	244,943	238,604	320,263
Other deposits (certified and cashiers' checks, etc.)	22,076	22,449	20,551	27,402
Total deposits	*2,621,566*	*2,670,554*	*2,618,442*	*2,952,107*
Demand deposits	*1,993,071*	*1,960,166*	*1,912,236*	*2,237,000*
Time deposits	*628,495*	*710,388*	*706,206*	*715,107*
Bills payable, rediscounts, and other liabilities for borrowed money	2,000	6,650	25,700	3,475
Mortgages or other liens on bank premises and other real estate	32	31	156	31
Acceptances executed by or for account of reporting banks and outstanding	87	205	75	145
Income collected but not earned	18,793	20,348	21,347	} 36,780
Expenses accrued and unpaid	13,079	12,287	14,273	
Other liabilities	1,378	1,630	1,009	
Total liabilities	2,656,935	2,711,705	2,681,002	2,992,538
CAPITAL ACCOUNTS				
Capital stock:				
Preferred stock	200	200	200	200
Common stock	69,425	72,400	74,100	76,510
Total capital stock	*69,625*	*72,600*	*74,300*	*76,710*
Surplus	80,006	82,670	88,125	93,559
Undivided profits	29,582	33,133	32,981	27,754
Reserves and retirement account for preferred stock	12,713	13,174	13,843	15,070
Total capital accounts	191,926	201,577	209,249	213,093
Total liabilities and capital accounts	2,848,861	2,913,282	2,890,251	3,205,631
MEMORANDUM				
Assets pledged or assigned to secure liabilities and for other purposes	590,320	668,875	663,309	731,666

Assets and liabilities of national banks, by States, at date of each call during year ended Dec. 31, 1958—Continued

GEORGIA

[In thousands of dollars]

	Mar. 4, 1958	June 23, 1958	Sept. 24, 1958	Dec. 31, 1958
	52 banks	52 banks	52 banks	52 banks
ASSETS				
Loans and discounts (including overdrafts)	629,610	666,590	674,593	696,092
U.S. Government securities, direct obligations	318,753	347,215	393,963	417,141
Obligations guaranteed by U.S. Government				
Obligations of States and political subdivisions	79,038	88,340	91,874	84,094
Other bonds, notes, and debentures	22,346	24,038	26,635	20,071
Corporate stocks, including stock of Federal Reserve bank	2,614	2,722	2,738	2,743
Reserve with Federal Reserve bank	154,799	164,591	163,498	120,547
Currency and coin	16,548	18,344	19,834	20,359
Balances with other banks, and cash items in process of collection	172,202	166,840	189,221	228,499
Bank premises owned, furniture and fixtures	20,615	21,335	21,895	22,409
Real estate owned other than bank premises	1,311	1,092	833	870
Investments and other assets indirectly representing bank premises or other real estate		10	1	
Customers' liability on acceptances outstanding	395			
Income earned or accrued but not collected	2,131	2,161	2,410	3,925
Other assets	2,645	1,900	1,995	
Total assets	1,423,007	1,505,178	1,589,490	1,616,750
LIABILITIES				
Demand deposits of individuals, partnerships, and corporations	726,187	740,558	768,143	802,452
Time deposits of individuals, partnerships, and corporations	242,270	259,820	261,980	266,973
Postal savings deposits	761	761	756	756
Deposits of U.S. Government	25,468	74,321	39,672	34,704
Deposits of States and political subdivisions	94,021	110,794	116,655	122,807
Deposits of banks	176,642	164,128	207,419	217,048
Other deposits (certified and cashiers' checks, etc.)	7,666	7,911	8,639	24,373
Total deposits	*1,273,015*	*1,358,293*	*1,403,264*	*1,469,113*
Demand deposits	*1,024,529*	*1,090,018*	*1,130,973*	*1,191,699*
Time deposits	*248,486*	*268,275*	*272,291*	*277,414*
Bills payable, rediscounts, and other liabilities for borrowed money	10,965	1,390	36,900	850
Mortgages or other liens on bank premises and other real estate	8			
Acceptances executed by or for account of reporting banks and outstanding	395		1	
Income collected but not earned	14,950	15,776	16,317	
Expenses accrued and unpaid	8,268	6,514	7,623	24,286
Other liabilities	979	935	715	
Total liabilities	1,308,580	1,382,908	1,464,820	1,494,249
CAPITAL ACCOUNTS				
Capital stock: Common stock	31,932	33,632	33,957	33,957
Surplus	54,372	56,148	56,398	57,352
Undivided profits	16,256	19,618	20,480	16,596
Reserves	11,867	12,872	13,835	14,596
Total capital accounts	114,427	122,270	124,670	122,501
Total liabilities and capital accounts	1,423,007	1,505,178	1,589,490	1,616,750
MEMORANDUM				
Assets pledged or assigned to secure liabilities and for other purposes	219,989	261,290	236,960	208,601

Assets and liabilities of national banks, by States, at date of each call during year ended Dec. 31, 1958—Continued

THE TERRITORY OF HAWAII

[In thousands of dollars]

	Mar. 4, 1958	June 23, 1958	Sept. 24, 1958	Dec. 31, 1958
	1 bank	1 bank	1 bank	1 bank
ASSETS				
Loans and discounts (including overdrafts)	105,366	112,337	113,243	120,745
U.S. Government securities, direct obligations	54,550	59,985	68,346	57,717
Obligations guaranteed by U.S. Government				
Obligations of States and political subdivisions	11,968	11,762	14,662	14,580
Other bonds, notes, and debentures	4,474	4,474	2,273	2,273
Reserve with approved national banking associations	20,024	18,056	20,642	26,272
Currency and coin	10,414	13,529	14,309	10,649
Balances with other banks, and cash items in process of collection	11,452	11,569	9,658	20,762
Bank premises owned, furniture and fixtures	3,209	3,499	5,452	5,232
Customers' liability on acceptances outstanding	14	5	6	8
Income earned or accrued but not collected	915	840	1,005	} 1,136
Other assets	1,833	1,847	251	
Total assets	224,219	237,903	249,847	259,374
LIABILITIES				
Demand deposits of individuals, partnerships, and corporations	79,549	78,571	83,601	98,692
Time deposits of individuals, partnerships, and corporations	78,525	78,969	81,182	77,796
Postal savings deposits	10	10	10	10
Deposits of U.S. Government	14,511	20,021	18,544	17,584
Deposits of States and political subdivisions	26,885	29,029	33,492	37,490
Deposits of banks	4,126	9,761	10,199	5,060
Other deposits (certified and cashiers' checks, etc.)	1,931	1,950	1,630	1,913
Total deposits	*205,537*	*218,311*	*228,658*	*238,545*
Demand deposits	*108,498*	*119,173*	*121,786*	*133,149*
Time deposits	*97,039*	*99,138*	*106,872*	*105,396*
Bills payable, rediscounts, and other liabilities for borrowed money				
Acceptances executed by or for account of reporting banks and outstanding	14	5	6	8
Income collected but not earned	539	658	839	} 2,037
Expenses accrued and unpaid	1,077	1,387	1,077	
Other liabilities	470	93	287	
Total liabilities	207,637	220,454	230,867	240,590
CAPITAL ACCOUNTS				
Capital stock: Common stock	4,000	4,000	6,000	6,000
Surplus	7,000	7,000	7,750	9,000
Undivided profits	3,406	4,274	3,055	1,608
Reserves	2,176	2,175	2,175	2,176
Total capital accounts	16,582	17,449	18,980	18,784
Total liabilities and capital accounts	224,219	237,903	249,847	259,374
MEMORANDUM				
Assets pledged or assigned to secure liabilities and for other purposes	63,122	70,753	74,877	74,127

Assets and liabilities of national banks, by States, at date of each call during year ended Dec. 31, 1958—Continued

IDAHO

[In thousands of dollars]

	Mar. 4, 1958	June 23, 1958	Sept. 24, 1958	Dec. 31, 1958
	9 banks	9 banks	9 banks	9 banks
ASSETS				
Loans and discounts (including overdrafts)	185,754	195,902	208,624	213,865
U.S. Government securities, direct obligations	168,878	170,818	168,567	180,694
Obligations guaranteed by U.S. Government				
Obligations of States and political subdivisions	20,373	24,589	26,607	34,877
Other bonds, notes, and debentures	2,289	2,295	130	75
Corporate stocks, including stock of Federal Reserve bank	672	676	683	684
Reserve with Federal Reserve bank	40,771	30,856	33,410	34,950
Currency and coin	4,614	6,414	6,028	5,974
Balances with other banks, and cash items in process of collection	23,452	25,087	26,731	38,562
Bank premises owned, furniture and fixtures	6,234	6,490	6,798	6,902
Real estate owned other than bank premises	55	56	63	59
Investments and other assets indirectly representing bank premises or other real estate	35	35	34	34
Income earned or accrued but not collected	37	175	59	} 294
Other assets	355	243	328	
Total assets	453,519	463,636	478,062	516,970
LIABILITIES				
Demand deposits of individuals, partnerships, and corporations	211,547	203,485	224,556	236,374
Time deposits of individuals, partnerships, and corporations	154,512	160,405	167,175	171,294
Postal savings deposits	11	11	11	11
Deposits of U.S. Government	4,928	9,235	8,260	7,089
Deposits of States and political subdivisions	46,707	47,234	37,088	61,003
Deposits of banks	2,004	2,865	2,722	2,244
Other deposits (certified and cashiers' checks, etc.)	2,994	2,691	3,365	3,950
Total deposits	*422,703*	*425,926*	*443,177*	*481,965*
Demand deposits	*267,194*	*264,524*	*275,005*	*309,279*
Time deposits	*155,509*	*161,402*	*168,172*	*172,686*
Bills payable, rediscounts, and other liabilities for borrowed money		4,000		
Acceptances executed by or for account of reporting banks and outstanding	995			
Income collected but not earned	1,547	1,723	1,793	} 4,227
Expenses accrued and unpaid	2,602	2,638	2,581	
Other liabilities	33	71	21	
Total liabilities	427,880	434,358	447,572	486,192
CAPITAL ACCOUNTS				
Capital stock: Common stock	11,325	11,325	11,525	11,525
Surplus	11,164	11,214	11,294	12,045
Undivided profits	3,049	5,407	5,770	4,029
Reserves	101	1,332	1,901	3,179
Total capital accounts	25,639	29,278	30,490	30,778
Total liabilities and capital accounts	453,519	463,636	478,062	516,970
MEMORANDUM				
Assets pledged or assigned to secure liabilities and for other purposes	100,872	96,942	88,438	97,638

Assets and liabilities of national banks, by States, at date of each call during year ended Dec. 31, 1958—Continued

ILLINOIS

[In thousands of dollars]

	Mar. 4, 1958	June 23, 1958	Sept. 24, 1958	Dec. 31, 1958
	394 banks	394 banks	395 banks	395 banks
ASSETS				
Loans and discounts (including overdrafts)	4,483,280	4,656,481	4,475,767	4,778,748
U.S. Government securities, direct obligations	3,890,742	4,289,286	4,301,354	4,264,729
Obligations guaranteed by U.S. Government	91	83	79	79
Obligations of States and political subdivisions	741,402	784,353	784,075	787,219
Other bonds, notes, and debentures	248,016	261,685	244,524	236,667
Corporate stocks, including stock of Federal Reserve bank	22,502	23,300	23,503	23,719
Reserve with Federal Reserve bank	1,410,785	1,428,647	1,314,785	1,303,403
Currency and coin	98,552	107,572	109,632	118,399
Balances with other banks, and cash items in process of collection	1,022,557	1,019,353	1,079,183	1,351,720
Bank premises owned, furniture and fixtures	45,597	47,278	48,282	49,236
Real estate owned other than bank premises	2,029	2,255	2,032	2,055
Investments and other assets indirectly representing bank premises or other real estate	3,004	3,307	3,482	3,584
Customers' liability on acceptances outstanding	7,857	8,650	10,592	10,195
Income earned or accrued but not collected	32,975	27,189	29,758	} 55,260
Other assets	21,606	25,067	23,377	
Total assets	12,030,995	12,684,506	12,450,425	12,985,013
LIABILITIES				
Demand deposits of individuals, partnerships, and corporations	5,861,181	5,724,070	5,866,026	6,562,286
Time deposits of individuals, partnerships, and corporations	2,748,959	2,847,528	2,863,855	2,915,636
Postal savings deposits	1,004	1,004	999	1,004
Deposits of U.S. Government	231,241	715,655	287,109	286,436
Deposits of States and political subdivisions	650,200	862,361	831,134	626,714
Deposits of banks	1,192,069	1,236,299	1,305,147	1,329,752
Other deposits (certified and cashiers' checks, etc.)	101,791	107,623	103,376	122,858
Total deposits	*10,786,445*	*11,494,540*	*11,257,646*	*11,844,686*
Demand deposits	*7,843,701*	*8,451,362*	*8,190,619*	*8,746,108*
Time deposits	*2,942,744*	*3,043,178*	*3,067,027*	*3,098,578*
Bills payable, rediscounts, and other liabilities for borrowed money	162,006	85,077	63,300	375
Mortgages or other liens on bank premises and other real estate	99	94	211	155
Acceptances executed by or for account of reporting banks and outstanding	7,866	9,534	12,328	10,383
Income collected but not earned	37,293	38,586	38,528	} 142,625
Expenses accrued and unpaid	74,590	64,975	68,279	
Other liabilities	30,658	31,395	34,522	
Total liabilities	11,098,957	11,724,201	11,474,814	11,998,224
CAPITAL ACCOUNTS				
Capital stock:				
Preferred stock	1,500	1,500	1,500	1,500
Common stock	318,558	319,698	347,573	349,773
Total capital stock	*320,058*	*321,198*	*349,073*	*351,273*
Surplus	421,953	447,340	425,803	430,872
Undivided profits	137,141	136,357	143,882	145,584
Reserves and retirement account for preferred stock	52,886	55,410	56,853	59,060
Total capital accounts	932,038	960,305	975,611	986,789
Total liabilities and capital accounts	12,030,995	12,684,506	12,450,425	12,985,013
MEMORANDUM				
Assets pledged or assigned to secure liabilities and for other purposes	1,114,539	1,596,415	1,240,413	1,201,782

Assets and liabilities of national banks, by States, at date of each call during year ended Dec. 31, 1958—Continued

INDIANA

[In thousands of dollars]

	Mar. 4, 1958	June 23, 1958	Sept. 24, 1958	Dec. 31, 1958
	124 banks	124 banks	124 banks	123 banks
ASSETS				
Loans and discounts (including overdrafts)	957, 608	982, 516	989, 153	1, 022, 380
U.S. Government securities, direct obligations	936, 259	987, 417	984, 249	1, 002, 634
Obligations guaranteed by U.S. Government	15	‼10	18	18
Obligations of States and political subdivisions	141, 612	144, 384	150, 974	151, 042
Other bonds, notes, and debentures	39, 447	39, 656	36, 931	36, 866
Corporate stocks, including stock of Federal Reserve bank	4, 414	4, 551	4, 575	4, 833
Reserve with Federal Reserve bank	243, 214	259, 495	240, 977	255, 419
Currency and coin	47, 251	51, 710	54, 410	56, 557
Balances with other banks, and cash items in process of collection	254, 813	261, 934	240, 710	341, 444
Bank premises owned, furniture and fixtures	27, 276	28, 299	28, 084	28, 692
Real estate owned other than bank premises	366	283	311	374
Investments and other assets indirectly representing bank premises or other real estate	68	194	327	325
Customers' liability on acceptances outstanding	65	124	-----------	9
Income earned or accrued but not collected	4, 706	4, 475	4, 870	} 8, 938
Other assets	4, 111	4, 311	4, 557	
Total assets	2, 661, 225	2, 769, 353	2, 740, 146	2, 909, 531
LIABILITIES				
Demand deposits of individuals, partnerships, and corporations	1, 297, 775	1, 253, 912	1, 297, 484	1, 429, 199
Time deposits of individuals, partnerships, and corporations	694, 835	712, 615	725, 471	730, 522
Postal savings deposits	1, 607	1, 607	1, 478	1, 478
Deposits of U. S. Government	47, 938	90, 242	58, 733	54, 187
Deposits of States and political subdivisions	231, 733	298, 919	241, 531	270, 759
Deposits of banks	124, 477	124, 633	131, 520	133, 378
Other deposits (certified and cashiers' checks, etc.)	30, 211	48, 798	37, 185	46, 655
Total deposits	*2, 428, 576*	*2, 530, 726*	*2, 493, 402*	*2, 666, 178*
Demand deposits	*1, 697, 455*	*1, 781, 164*	*1, 730, 777*	*1, 894, 044*
Time deposits	*731, 121*	*749, 562*	*762, 625*	*772, 134*
Bills payable, rediscounts, and other liabilities for borrowed money	1, 000	100	3, 050	-----------
Mortgages or other liens on bank premises and other real estate	20	55	55	55
Acceptances executed by or for account of reporting banks and outstanding	65	124	-----------	9
Income collected but not earned	15, 152	15, 983	16, 457	} 29, 959
Expenses accrued and unpaid	12, 241	8, 238	10, 614	
Other liabilities	1, 146	1, 742	1, 277	
Total liabilities	2, 458, 200	2, 556, 968	2, 524, 855	2, 696, 201
CAPITAL ACCOUNTS				
Capital stock:				
Preferred stock	25	25	25	25
Common stock	54, 163	55, 043	55, 193	56, 378
Total capital stock	*54, 188*	*55, 068*	*55, 218*	*56, 403*
Surplus	92, 831	96, 672	97, 281	105, 608
Undivided profits	47, 422	52, 475	54, 143	42, 072
Reserves and retirement account for preferred stock	8, 584	8, 170	8, 649	9, 247
Total capital accounts	203, 025	212, 385	215, 291	213, 330
Total liabilities and capital accounts	2, 661, 225	2, 769, 353	2, 740, 146	2, 909, 531
MEMORANDUM				
Assets pledged or assigned to secure liabilities and for other purposes	182, 264	200, 669	209, 134	216, 384

Assets and liabilities of national banks, by States, at date of each call during year ended Dec. 31, 1958—Continued

IOWA

[In thousands of dollars]

	Mar. 4, 1958	June 23, 1958	Sept. 24, 1958	Dec. 31, 1958
	96 banks	97 banks	97 banks	97 banks
ASSETS				
Loans and discounts (including overdrafts)	363,430	365,228	376,627	405,921
U.S. Government securities, direct obligations	278,766	314,328	349,705	329,175
Obligations guaranteed by U.S. Government				
Obligations of States and political subdivisions	80,720	84,122	88,460	86,907
Other bonds, notes, and debentures	15,224	17,450	16,344	15,826
Corporate stocks, including stock of Federal Reserve bank	1,493	1,516	1,522	1,537
Reserve with Federal Reserve bank	85,976	87,209	76,674	73,765
Currency and coin	12,773	14,252	15,108	15,831
Balances with other banks, and cash items in process of collection	132,701	138,112	137,870	168,416
Bank premises owned, furniture and fixtures	6,269	6,432	6,562	6,567
Real estate owned other than bank premises	365	1,238	1,175	946
Investments and other assets indirectly representing bank premises or other real estate	1,356	1,356	1,356	1,357
Customers' liability on acceptances outstanding	58	43	33	60
Income earned or accrued but not collected	1,720	1,897	2,100	} 2,965
Other assets	758	870	838	
Total assets	981,609	1,034,053	1,074,374	1,109,273
LIABILITIES				
Demand deposits of individuals, partnerships, and corporations	471,389	469,170	496,236	547,825
Time deposits of individuals, partnerships, and corporations	216,587	227,309	232,367	231,465
Postal savings deposits	53	53	53	53
Deposits of U.S. Government	14,910	31,416	18,814	20,671
Deposits of States and political subdivisions	72,511	84,949	86,949	70,575
Deposits of banks	107,667	121,922	139,604	141,868
Other deposits (certified and cashiers' checks, etc.)	6,880	16,079	10,218	11,765
Total deposits	*889,997*	*950,898*	*984,241*	*1,024,222*
Demand deposits	*672,129*	*722,235*	*750,200*	*790,518*
Time deposits	*217,868*	*228,663*	*234,041*	*233,704*
Bills payable, rediscounts, and other liabilities for borrowed money	12,203		5,000	200
Mortgages or other liens on bank premises and other real estate	78	78	52	52
Acceptances executed by or for account of reporting banks and outstanding	58	43	33	60
Income collected but not earned	2,196	2,361	2,466	} 5,501
Expenses accrued and unpaid	2,262	2,362	2,850	
Other liabilities	30	165	153	
Total liabilities	906,824	955,907	994,795	1,030,035
CAPITAL ACCOUNTS				
Capital stock: Common stock	18,758	19,158	19,158	19,298
Surplus	31,008	31,463	31,773	34,649
Undivided profits	22,238	24,898	25,719	22,287
Reserves	2,781	2,627	2,929	3,004
Total capital accounts	74,785	78,146	79,579	79,238
Total liabilities and capital accounts	981,609	1,034,053	1,074,374	1,109,273
MEMORANDUM				
Assets pledged or assigned to secure liabilities and for other purposes	68,928	69,348	69,443	67,637

Assets and liabilities of national banks, by States, at date of each call during year ended Dec. 31, 1958—Continued

KANSAS

[In thousands of dollars]

	Mar. 4, 1958	June 23, 1958	Sept. 24, 1958	Dec. 31, 1958
	169 banks	169 banks	169 banks	169 banks
ASSETS				
Loans and discounts (including overdrafts)	398, 544	421, 876	445, 504	467, 350
U.S. Government securities, direct obligations	379, 478	379, 152	396, 956	400, 165
Obligations guaranteed by U.S. Government	53	53	37	37
Obligations of States and political subdivisions	113, 129	116, 967	119, 831	123, 123
Other bonds, notes, and debentures	32, 035	34, 541	32, 784	30, 511
Corporate stocks, including stock of Federal Reserve bank	2, 100	2, 139	2, 194	2, 310
Reserve with Federal Reserve bank	120, 825	109, 114	119, 493	125, 784
Currency and coin	13, 147	17, 204	16, 658	16, 418
Balances with other banks, and cash items in process of collection	134, 374	143, 458	128, 826	158, 179
Bank premises owned, furniture and fixtures	12, 052	12, 917	13, 585	13, 761
Real estate owned other than bank premises	808	866	598	659
Investments and other assets indirectly representing bank premises or other real estate	194	188	178	181
Customers' liability on acceptances outstanding	48	68	127	
Income earned or accrued but not collected	1, 683	1, 863	1, 822	} 2, 717
Other assets	778	730	727	
Total assets	1, 209, 248	1, 241, 136	1, 279, 320	1, 341, 195
LIABILITIES				
Demand deposits of individuals, partnerships, and corporations	611, 470	630, 234	681, 026	694, 482
Time deposits of individuals, partnerships, and corporations	176, 311	190, 206	194, 192	193, 942
Postal savings deposits	39	39	39	39
Deposits of U.S. Government	23, 579	38, 547	28, 387	27, 434
Deposits of States and political subdivisions	195, 473	180, 268	163, 116	204, 979
Deposits of banks	81, 128	81, 229	90, 659	96, 931
Other deposits (certified and cashiers' checks, etc.)	14, 556	8, 525	6, 514	11, 261
Total deposits	*1, 102, 556*	*1, 129, 048*	*1, 163, 933*	*1, 229, 068*
Demand deposits	*899, 934*	*911, 979*	*942, 969*	*1, 008, 323*
Time deposits	*202, 622*	*217, 069*	*220, 964*	*220, 745*
Bills payable, rediscounts, and other liabilities for borrowed money	2, 304	4, 227	3, 430	225
Mortgages or other liens on bank premises and other real estate	10	10	58	58
Acceptances executed by or for account of reporting banks and outstanding	48	68	127	
Income collected but not earned	3, 413	3, 700	3, 827	} 8, 208
Expenses accrued and unpaid	4, 464	3, 733	4, 462	
Other liabilities	259	503	329	
Total liabilities	1, 113, 054	1, 141, 289	1, 176, 166	1, 237, 559
CAPITAL ACCOUNTS				
Capital stock: Common stock	26, 602	26, 722	28, 185	29, 625
Surplus	43, 198	44, 548	46, 026	48, 205
Undivided profits	24, 564	26, 748	26, 802	23, 709
Reserves	1, 830	1, 829	2, 141	2, 097
Total capital accounts	96, 194	99, 847	103, 154	103, 636
Total liabilities and capital accounts	1, 209, 248	1, 241, 136	1, 279, 320	1, 341, 195
MEMORANDUM				
Assets pledged or assigned to secure liabilities and for other purposes	264, 916	262, 653	274, 146	283, 437

Assets and liabilities of national banks, by States, at date of each call during year ended Dec. 31, 1958—Continued

KENTUCKY

[In thousands of dollars]

	Mar. 4, 1958	June 23, 1958	Sept. 24, 1958	Dec. 31, 1958
	88 banks	87 banks	88 banks	88 banks
ASSETS				
Loans and discounts (including overdrafts)	295, 245	304, 258	327, 384	334, 116
U.S. Government securities, direct obligations	283, 352	278, 673	277, 685	308, 858
Obligations guaranteed by U.S. Government	9	9	4	4
Obligations of States and political subdivisions	46, 315	49, 462	52, 247	51, 668
Other bonds, notes, and debentures	19, 354	20, 352	17, 335	16, 966
Corporate stocks, including stock of Federal Reserve bank	1, 659	1, 664	1, 774	1, 804
Reserve with Federal Reserve bank	84, 236	76, 898	75, 596	90, 081
Currency and coin	13, 905	17, 185	18, 488	19, 379
Balances with other banks, and cash items in process of collections	87, 970	75, 841	76, 252	124, 597
Bank premises owned, furniture and fixtures	7, 577	7, 836	8, 267	8, 141
Real estate owned other than bank premises	145	116	125	49
Investments and other assets indirectly representing bank premises or other real estate	182	189	182	182
Customers' liability on acceptances outstanding	59	51	49	39
Income earned or accrued but not collected	1, 385	1, 417	1, 551	} 2, 235
Other assets	840	757	694	
Total assets	842, 233	834, 708	857, 633	958, 119
LIABILITIES				
Demand deposits of individuals, partnerships, and corporations	496, 983	482, 218	491, 553	573, 643
Time deposits of individuals, partnerships, and corporations	159, 234	165, 948	174, 843	175, 566
Postal savings deposits	15	15	15	15
Deposits of U.S. Government	13, 631	27, 929	16, 218	18, 814
Deposits of States and political subdivisions	45, 969	36, 615	40, 761	42, 318
Deposits of banks	40, 539	32, 276	31, 722	55, 232
Other deposits (certified and cashiers' checks, etc.)	4, 905	5, 614	5, 600	6, 610
Total deposits	*761, 276*	*750, 615*	*760, 712*	*872, 198*
Demand deposits	*590, 654*	*574, 941*	*575, 794*	*685, 716*
Time deposits	*170, 622*	*175, 674*	*184, 918*	*186, 482*
Bills payable, rediscounts, and other liabilities for borrowed money	800	2, 800	10, 800	-----------
Acceptances executed by or for account of reporting banks and outstanding	59	51	49	39
Income collected but not earned	3, 311	3, 472	3, 682	} 7, 381
Expenses accrued and unpaid	3, 214	2, 463	2, 892	
Other liabilities	438	577	607	
Total liabilities	769, 098	759, 978	778, 742	879, 618
CAPITAL ACCOUNTS				
Capital stock: Common stock	21, 575	21, 525	22, 675	23, 175
Surplus	33, 974	33, 824	36, 354	37, 295
Undivided profits	15, 713	17, 794	17, 865	15, 890
Reserves	1, 873	1, 587	1, 997	2, 141
Total capital accounts	73, 135	74, 730	78, 891	78, 501
Total liabilities and capital accounts	842, 233	834, 708	857, 633	958, 119
MEMORANDUM				
Assets pledged or assigned to secure liabilities and for other purposes	77, 862	94, 624	97, 613	90, 911

Assets and liabilities of national banks, by States, at date of each call during year ended Dec. 31, 1958—Continued

LOUISIANA

[In thousands of dollars]

	Mar. 4, 1958	June 23, 1958	Sept. 24, 1958	Dec. 31, 1958
	41 banks	41 banks	41 banks	41 banks
ASSETS				
Loans and discounts (including overdrafts)	698, 821	703, 707	675, 302	723, 383
U.S. Government securities, direct obligations	560, 500	585, 449	591, 816	576, 141
Obligations guaranteed by U.S. Government				
Obligations of States and political subdivisions	118, 713	125, 068	126, 555	127, 256
Other bonds, notes, and debentures	22, 968	19, 054	18, 098	17, 297
Corporate stocks, including stock of Federal Reserve bank	3, 705	3, 725	3, 924	3, 910
Reserve with Federal Reserve bank	184, 609	194, 677	178, 417	172, 457
Currency and coin	22, 394	26, 022	28, 054	28, 064
Balances with other banks, and cash items in process of collection	232, 317	240, 369	214, 452	297, 921
Bank premises owned, furniture and fixtures	17, 804	18, 492	19, 017	19, 416
Real estate owned other than bank premises	727	682	716	297
Investments and other assets indirectly representing bank premises or other real estate	3, 204	2, 140	2, 310	2, 825
Customers' liability on acceptances outstanding	5, 161	2, 106	3, 170	3, 416
Income earned or accrued but not collected	4, 940	4, 895	4, 437	} 8, 254
Other assets	2, 332	2, 505	1, 894	
Total assets	1, 878, 195	1, 928, 891	1, 868, 162	1, 980, 637
LIABILITIES				
Demand deposits of individuals, partnerships, and corporations	918, 055	957, 422	949, 113	1, 008, 982
Time deposits of individuals, partnerships, and corporations	321, 050	337, 176	344, 865	347, 605
Postal savings deposits	51	51	51	51
Deposits of U.S. Government	23, 116	51, 129	28, 449	26, 116
Deposits of States and political subdivisions	238, 237	210, 198	178, 486	178, 097
Deposits of banks	202, 286	196, 425	188, 680	238, 583
Other deposits (certified and cashiers' checks, etc.)	16, 618	15, 475	14, 876	18, 754
Total deposits	*1,719,413*	*1,767,876*	*1,704,520*	*1,818,188*
Demand deposits	*1,392,173*	*1,418,628*	*1,351,165*	*1,461,248*
Time deposits	*327,240*	*349,248*	*353,355*	*356,940*
Bills payable, rediscounts, and other liabilities for borrowed money	1, 800	3, 800	3, 200	1, 040
Acceptances executed by or for account of reporting banks and outstanding	5, 581	2, 281	3, 285	3, 575
Income collected but not earned	4, 104	4, 274	4, 240	} 15, 984
Expenses accrued and unpaid	10, 804	9, 493	9, 367	
Other liabilities	699	1, 143	730	
Total liabilities	1, 742, 401	1, 788, 867	1, 725, 342	1, 838, 787
CAPITAL ACCOUNTS				
Capital stock: Common stock	37, 113	37, 438	37, 938	37, 938
Surplus	72, 622	73, 722	79, 897	80, 623
Undivided profits	25, 631	28, 487	24, 522	22, 603
Reserves	428	377	463	686
Total capital accounts	135. 794	140, 024	142, 820	141, 850
Total liabilities and capital accounts	1, 878, 195	1, 928, 891	1, 868, 162	1, 980, 637
MEMORANDUM				
Assets pledged or assigned to secure liabilities and for other purposes	368, 015	384, 186	395, 950	347, 412

Assets and liabilities of national banks, by States, at date of each call during year ended Dec. 31, 1958—Continued

MAINE

[In thousands of dollars]

	Mar. 4, 1958	June 23, 1958	Sept. 24, 1958	Dec. 31, 1958
	29 banks	29 banks	29 banks	29 banks
ASSETS				
Loans and discounts (including overdrafts)	146, 365	154, 818	153, 617	154, 124
U.S. Government securities, direct obligations	76, 452	83, 648	92, 960	95, 880
Obligations guaranteed by U.S. Government	9	9	9	14
Obligations of States and political subdivisions	14, 205	15, 554	15, 981	13, 776
Other bonds, notes, and debentures	7, 307	8, 739	8, 405	8, 092
Corporate stocks, including stock of Federal Reserve bank	691	691	695	711
Reserve with Federal Reserve bank	24, 980	23, 088	24, 103	25, 223
Currency and coin	6, 031	7, 865	8, 600	8, 125
Balances with other banks, and cash items in process of collection	21, 352	25, 528	24, 382	28, 035
Bank premises owned, furniture and fixtures	5, 090	5, 337	5, 455	5, 457
Real estate owned other than bank premises	273	259	246	289
Investments and other assets indirectly representing bank premises or other real estate	278	267	281	258
Income earned or accrued but not collected	558	773	769	} 1, 213
Other assets	431	663	449	
Total assets	304, 022	327, 239	335, 952	341, 197
LIABILITIES				
Demand deposits of individuals, partnerships, and corporations	132, 919	143, 348	149, 365	154, 795
Time deposits of individuals, partnerships, and corporations	106, 268	111, 658	117, 584	118, 525
Postal savings deposits	7	7	7	7
Deposits of U.S. Government	4, 968	11, 544	7, 061	6, 343
Deposits of States and political subdivisions	13, 304	11, 944	14, 215	14, 654
Deposits of banks	7, 329	8, 300	8, 024	7, 675
Other deposits (certified and cashiers' checks, etc.)	3, 603	3, 975	3, 946	4, 076
Total deposits	*268, 398*	*290, 776*	*300, 202*	*306, 075*
Demand deposits	*160, 630*	*175, 847*	*180, 410*	*185, 339*
Time deposits	*107, 768*	*114, 929*	*119, 792*	*120, 736*
Bills payable, rediscounts, and other liabilities for borrowed money	1, 300	1, 550	200	
Income collected but not earned	2, 153	2, 300	2, 390	} 3, 898
Expenses accrued and unpaid	1, 380	1, 178	1, 375	
Other liabilities	165	194	201	
Total liabilities	273, 396	295, 998	304, 368	309, 973
CAPITAL ACCOUNTS				
Capital stock: Common stock	11, 225	11, 225	11, 250	11, 250
Surplus	11, 822	11, 824	11, 959	12, 476
Undivided profits	6, 508	7, 221	7, 261	6, 369
Reserves	1, 071	971	1, 114	1, 129
Total capital accounts	30, 626	31, 241	31, 584	31, 224
Total liabilities and capital accounts	304, 022	327, 239	335, 952	341, 197
MEMORANDUM				
Assets pledged or assigned to secure liabilities and for other purposes	21, 697	21, 733	23, 245	21, 422

Assets and liabilities of national banks, by States, at date of each call during year ended Dec. 31, 1958—Continued

MARYLAND

[In thousands of dollars]

	Mar. 4, 1958	June 23, 1958	Sept. 24, 1958	Dec. 31, 1958
	56 banks	55 banks	53 banks	53 banks
ASSETS				
Loans and discounts (including overdrafts)	347,900	377,640	352,252	359,941
U.S. Government securities, direct obligations	335,680	344,652	359,733	349,751
Obligations guaranteed by U.S. Government				
Obligations of States and political subdivisions	73,377	76,472	76,948	77,463
Other bonds, notes, and debentures	22,480	21,189	22,286	20,516
Corporate stocks, including stock of Federal Reserve bank	1,823	1,834	1,843	1,858
Reserve with Federal Reserve bank	106,744	105,212	101,762	89,693
Currency and coin	19,057	19,406	20,008	20,386
Balances with other banks, and cash items in process of collection	108,968	117,700	100,774	132,517
Bank premises owned, furniture and fixtures	11,456	11,630	11,808	11,829
Real estate owned other than bank premises	240	389	324	360
Investments and other assets indirectly representing bank premises or other real estate	357	353	353	363
Customers' liability on acceptances outstanding	116	88	160	199
Income earned or accrued but not collected	2,270	2,111	2,517	} 3,390
Other assets	1,661	1,458	2,283	
Total assets	1,032,129	1,080,134	1,053,051	1,068,266
LIABILITIES				
Demand deposits of individuals, partnerships, and corporations	510,340	522,406	508,006	550,592
Time deposits of individuals, partnerships, and corporations	224,840	232,994	237,621	237,096
Postal savings deposits				
Deposits of U.S. Government	31,900	55,560	39,331	31,220
Deposits of States and political subdivisions	98,729	107,769	103,950	85,639
Deposits of banks	72,657	64,557	63,902	68,714
Other deposits (certified and cashiers' checks, etc.)	5,491	6,688	3,573	4,256
Total deposits	*943,957*	*989,974*	*956,383*	*977,517*
Demand deposits	*710,022*	*740,184*	*700,404*	*733,114*
Time deposits	*233,935*	*249,790*	*255,979*	*244,403*
Bills payable, rediscounts, and other liabilities for borrowed money	800	600	6,900	500
Acceptances executed by or for account of reporting banks and outstanding	116	88	160	199
Income collected but not earned	3,486	3,524	3,836	} 8,199
Expenses accrued and unpaid	3,162	2,307	2,950	
Other liabilities	768	1,129	811	
Total liabilities	952,289	997,622	971,040	986,415
CAPITAL ACCOUNTS				
Capital stock: Common stock	17,465	17,690	17,415	17,815
Surplus	43,235	43,510	44,065	44,485
Undivided profits	13,708	15,762	14,532	13,580
Reserves	5,432	5,550	5,999	5,971
Total capital accounts	79,840	82,512	82,011	81,851
Total liabilities and capital accounts	1,032,129	1,080,134	1,053,051	1,068,266
MEMORANDUM				
Assets pledged or assigned to secure liabilities and for other purposes	178,681	191,984	207,405	159,674

Assets and liabilities of national banks, by States, at date of each call during year ended Dec. 31, 1958—Continued

MASSACHUSETTS

[In thousands of dollars]

	Mar. 4, 1958	June 23, 1958	Sept. 24, 1958	Dec. 31, 1958
	107 banks	107 banks	108 banks	107 banks
ASSETS				
Loans and discounts (including overdrafts)	1,718,582	1,764,242	1,756,007	1,808,323
U.S. Government securities, direct obligations	792,276	898,065	920,746	931,298
Obligations guaranteed by U.S. Government	609	609	1,170	1,170
Obligations of States and political subdivisions	174,948	215,767	230,572	192,294
Other bonds, notes, and debentures	30,672	30,709	28,935	29,298
Corporate stocks, including stock of Federal Reserve bank	9,583	9,626	9,654	9,683
Reserve with Federal Reserve bank	398,089	417,740	373,410	416,083
Currency and coin	46,083	53,235	53,262	53,932
Balances with other banks, and cash items in process of collection	299,376	317,542	307,824	411,865
Bank premises owned, furniture and fixtures	35,517	36,718	36,889	36,739
Real estate owned other than bank premises	392	511	494	307
Investments and other assets indirectly representing bank premises or other real estate	409	505	583	658
Customers' liability on acceptances outstanding	41,160	43,042	42,014	28,462
Income earned or accrued but not collected	9,373	11,509	10,732	} 16,581
Other assets	5,456	8,180	4,901	
Total assets	3,562,525	3,808,000	3,777,193	3,936,693
LIABILITIES				
Demand deposits of individuals, partnerships, and corporations	2,011,747	2,072,337	2,118,790	2,229,277
Time deposits of individuals, partnerships, and corporations	432,753	449,076	460,198	452,076
Postal savings deposits	1,150	1,150	1,041	1,041
Deposits of U.S. Government	80,293	208,192	98,063	97,565
Deposits of States and political subdivisions	133,117	170,728	157,141	233,100
Deposits of banks	380,102	382,904	394,038	414,477
Other deposits (certified and cashiers' checks, etc.)	50,771	64,486	59,288	66,500
Total deposits	*3,089,933*	*3,348,873*	*3,288,559*	*3,494,036*
Demand deposits	*2,616,015*	*2,854,629*	*2,775,195*	*2,990,938*
Time deposits	*473,918*	*494,244*	*513,364*	*503,098*
Bills payable, rediscounts, and other liabilities for borrowed money	18,005	5,050	29,100	
Acceptances executed by or for account of reporting banks and outstanding	42,312	44,652	43,344	29,564
Income collected but not earned	17,870	18,575	19,240	} 57,913
Expenses accrued and unpaid	30,297	21,537	26,524	
Other liabilities	17,114	15,377	14,854	
Total liabilities	3,215,531	3,454,064	3,421,621	3,581,513
CAPITAL ACCOUNTS				
Capital stock: Common stock	82,796	83,238	83,588	83,688
Surplus	188,961	189,777	190,468	191,614
Undivided profits	55,883	60,350	63,010	62,326
Reserves	19,354	20,571	18,506	17,552
Total capital accounts	346,994	353,936	355,572	355,180
Total liabilities and capital accounts	3,562,525	3,808,000	3,777,193	3,936,693
MEMORANDUM				
Assets pledged or assigned to secure liabilities and for other purposes	214,773	302,596	292,939	241,461

Assets and liabilities of national banks, by States, at date of each call during year ended Dec. 31, 1958—Continued

MICHIGAN

[In thousands of dollars]

	Mar. 4, 1958	June 23, 1958	Sept. 24, 1958	Dec. 31, 1958
	75 banks	75 banks	74 banks	75 banks
ASSETS				
Loans and discounts (including overdrafts)	1,621,601	1,637,093	1,647,028	1,716,712
U.S. Government securities, direct obligations	1,378,909	1,534,539	1,423,697	1,419,605
Obligations guaranteed by U.S. Government	21	21	15	15
Obligations of States and political subdivisions	319,209	356,472	375,628	379,078
Other bonds, notes, and debentures	23,511	26,586	24,352	23,051
Corporate stocks, including stock of Federal Reserve bank	7,210	7,236	7,180	7,202
Reserve with Federal Reserve bank	407,914	393,028	366,807	331,415
Currency and coin	59,322	63,740	65,145	63,817
Balances with other banks, and cash items in process of collections	299,690	293,553	287,981	373,785
Bank premises owned, furniture and fixtures	36,772	37,202	36,955	37,664
Real estate owned other than bank premises	1,099	1,285	1,361	987
Investments and other assets indirectly representing bank premises or other real estate	6,531	6,525	6,424	6,434
Customers' liability on acceptances outstanding	93	118	106	70
Income earned or accrued but not collected	13,708	12,341	14,861	} 18,481
Other assets	5,342	4,490	4,275	
Total assets	4,180,932	4,374,229	4,261,815	4,378,316
LIABILITIES				
Demand deposits of individuals, partnerships, and corporations	1,795,955	1,861,572	1,826,725	2,014,593
Time deposits of individuals, partnerships, and corporations	1,322,583	1,365,258	1,372,219	1,370,837
Postal savings deposits	35	35	29	29
Deposits of U.S. Government	139,952	280,181	110,896	131,466
Deposits of States and political subdivisions	303,655	270,073	295,048	261,573
Deposits of banks	190,442	179,184	173,717	186,994
Other deposits (certified and cashiers' checks, etc.)	27,131	29,183	26,965	33,181
Total deposits	*3,779,753*	*3,985,486*	*3,805,599*	*3,998,673*
Demand deposits	*2,372,025*	*2,524,045*	*2,319,141*	*2,530,339*
Time deposits	*1,407,728*	*1,461,441*	*1,486,458*	*1,468,334*
Bills payable, rediscounts, and other liabilities for borrowed money	38,950	23,600	82,550	
Mortgages or other liens on bank premises and other real estate	37	10	10	10
Acceptances executed by or for account of reporting banks and outstanding	93	118	106	70
Income collected but not earned	35,953	36,612	37,702	} 76,205
Expenses accrued and unpaid	32,556	27,420	33,520	
Other liabilities	2,089	2,236	1,843	
Total liabilities	3,889,431	4,075,482	3,961,330	4,074,958
CAPITAL ACCOUNTS				
Capital stock: Common stock	77,681	77,786	76,786	77,236
Surplus	153,433	154,127	153,209	158,682
Undivided profits	55,872	62,377	65,383	62,232
Reserves	4,515	4,457	5,107	5,208
Total capital accounts	291,501	298,747	300,485	303,358
Total liabilities and capital accounts	4,180,932	4,374,229	4,261,815	4,378,316
MEMORANDUM				
Assets pledged or assigned to secure liabilities and for other purposes	372,727	473,249	415,957	359,842

Assets and liabilities of national banks, by States, at date of each call during year ended Dec. 31, 1958—Continued

MINNESOTA

[In thousands of dollars]

	Mar. 4, 1958	June 23, 1958	Sept. 24, 1958	Dec. 31, 1958
	179 banks	179 banks	179 banks	179 banks
ASSETS				
Loans and discounts (including overdrafts)	1, 146, 876	1, 216, 002	1, 243, 617	1, 219, 272
U.S. Government securities, direct obligations	660, 160	741, 441	750, 727	757, 534
Obligations guaranteed by U.S. Government		18	18	21
Obligations of States and political subdivisions	170, 818	184, 531	179, 951	185, 051
Other bonds, notes, and debentures	60, 333	73, 105	68, 644	65, 687
Corporate stocks, including stock of Federal Reserve bank	4, 592	5, 048	5, 086	5, 143
Reserve with Federal Reserve bank	265, 141	244, 325	233, 541	246, 763
Currency and coin	22, 485	27, 143	29, 124	28, 027
Balances with other banks, and cash items in process of collection	313, 287	347, 861	329, 638	441, 834
Bank premises owned, furniture and fixtures	22, 059	23, 556	24, 240	25, 297
Real estate owned other than bank premises	1, 031	1, 640	1, 334	1, 315
Investments and other assets indirectly representing bank premises or other real estate	6, 550	6, 560	6, 555	6, 506
Customers' liability on acceptances outstanding	608	845	609	946
Income earned or accrued but not collected	6, 685	7, 775	7, 738	} 13, 322
Other assets	2, 633	4, 099	6, 096	
Total assets	2, 683, 258	2, 883, 949	2, 886, 918	2, 996, 718
LIABILITIES				
Demand deposits of individuals, partnerships, and corporations	1, 145, 584	1, 154, 019	1, 206, 748	1, 337, 133
Time deposits of individuals, partnerships, and corporations	694, 359	718, 795	739, 800	753, 620
Postal savings deposits	68	68	68	68
Deposits of U.S. Government	46, 737	145, 046	66, 784	64, 863
Deposits of States and political subdivisions	172, 498	239, 260	138, 387	157, 711
Deposits of banks	340, 316	330, 294	399, 314	381, 977
Other deposits (certified and cashiers' checks, etc.)	19, 850	24, 720	23, 927	26, 918
Total deposits	*2, 419, 412*	*2, 612, 202*	*2, 575, 028*	*2, 722, 290*
Demand deposits	*1, 712, 906*	*1, 879, 418*	*1, 820, 163*	*1, 954, 127*
Time deposits	*706, 506*	*732, 784*	*754, 865*	*768, 163*
Bills payable, rediscounts, and other liabilities for borrowed money	11, 300	6, 015	38, 750	
Mortgages or other liens on bank premises and other real estate	161	161	133	133
Acceptances executed by or for account of reporting banks and outstanding	608	845	609	946
Income collected but not earned	19, 004	19, 676	20, 789	} 42, 840
Expenses accrued and unpaid	18, 961	15, 839	18, 964	
Other liabilities	4, 246	4, 046	3, 479	
Total liabilities	2, 473, 692	2, 658, 784	2, 657, 752	2, 766, 209
CAPITAL ACCOUNTS				
Capital stock: Common stock	63, 751	71, 251	71, 801	72, 281
Surplus	89, 052	96, 935	97, 817	99, 862
Undivided profits	46, 808	47, 356	49, 843	48, 582
Reserves	9, 955	9, 623	9, 705	9, 784
Total capital accounts	209, 566	225, 165	229, 166	230, 509
Total liabilities and capital accounts	2, 683, 258	2, 883, 949	2, 886, 918	2, 996, 718
MEMORANDUM				
Assets pledged or assigned to secure liabilities and for other purposes	377, 184	510, 300	445, 102	448, 741

Assets and liabilities of national banks, by States, at date of each call during year ended Dec. 31, 1958—Continued

MISSISSIPPI

[In thousands of dollars]

	Mar. 4, 1958	June 23, 1958	Sept. 24, 1958	Dec. 31, 1958
	27 banks	27 banks	27 banks	27 banks
ASSETS				
Loans and discounts (including overdrafts)	115, 353	128, 154	130, 996	133, 769
U.S. Government securities, direct obligations	82, 977	89, 245	92, 051	98, 534
Obligations guaranteed by U.S. Government				
Obligations of States and political subdivisions	36, 918	40, 307	40, 554	41, 253
Other bonds, notes, and debentures	3, 106	3, 492	3, 402	3, 259
Corporate stocks, including stock of Federal Reserve bank	680	722	724	732
Reserve with Federal Reserve bank	29, 485	28, 248	28, 614	32, 288
Currency and coin	6, 136	8, 044	8, 084	8, 082
Balances with other banks, and cash items in process of collection	47, 817	44, 481	49, 708	54, 212
Bank premises owned, furniture and fixtures	4, 639	4, 855	4, 855	4, 673
Real estate owned other than bank premises	170	156	28	10
Investments and other assets indirectly representing bank premises or other real estate	500	500	500	500
Customers' liability on acceptances outstanding		15	25	
Income earned or accrued but not collected	419	517	549	} 977
Other assets	259	235	447	
Total assets	328, 459	348, 971	360, 537	378, 289
LIABILITIES				
Demand deposits of individuals, partnerships, and corporations	155, 443	153, 839	158, 298	175, 485
Time deposits of individuals, partnerships, and corporations	67, 820	74, 400	76, 638	78, 248
Postal savings deposits				
Deposits of U.S. Government	6, 894	10, 771	7, 025	7, 366
Deposits of States and political subdivisions	45, 573	52, 802	53, 072	45, 784
Deposits of banks	26, 241	27, 719	35, 338	41, 674
Other deposits (certified and cashiers' checks, etc.)	731	840	820	1, 517
Total deposits	*302, 702*	*320, 371*	*331, 191*	*350, 074*
Demand deposits	*232, 796*	*237, 474*	*242, 361*	*261, 754*
Time deposits	*69, 906*	*82, 897*	*88, 830*	*88, 320*
Bills payable, rediscounts, and other liabilities for borrowed money				
Acceptances executed by or for account of reporting banks and outstanding		16	28	
Income collected but not earned	1, 042	1, 193	1, 308	}
Expenses accrued and unpaid	862	1, 172	1, 296	} 2, 577
Other liabilities	3	216	29	}
Total liabilities	304, 609	322, 968	333, 852	352, 651
CAPITAL ACCOUNTS				
Capital stock: Common stock	6, 630	6, 993	6, 993	7, 093
Surplus	16, 139	17, 077	17, 229	18, 029
Undivided profits	859	1, 791	2, 217	287
Reserves	222	142	246	229
Total capital accounts	23, 850	26, 003	26, 685	25, 638
Total liabilities and capital accounts	328, 459	348, 971	360, 537	378, 289
MEMORANDUM				
Assets pledged or assigned to secure liabilities and for other purposes	62, 226	64, 998	63, 791	69, 038

Assets and liabilities of national banks, by States, at date of each call during year ended Dec. 31, 1958—Continued

MISSOURI

[In thousands of dollars]

	Mar. 4, 1958	June 23, 1958	Sept. 24, 1958	Dec. 31, 1958
	76 banks	75 banks	75 banks	75 banks
ASSETS				
Loans and discounts (including overdrafts)	861, 207	922, 940	886, 776	911, 841
U.S. Government securities, direct obligations	638, 708	660, 352	680, 453	708, 356
Obligations guaranteed by U.S. Government	29	29	109	102
Obligations of States and political subdivisions	101, 406	122, 119	122, 688	128, 411
Other bonds, notes, and debentures	27, 704	28, 426	26, 992	24, 039
Corporate stocks, including stock of Federal Reserve bank	4, 737	4, 770	4, 528	4, 068
Reserve with Federal Reserve bank	248, 095	248, 492	219, 990	262, 173
Currency and coin	18, 710	20, 372	22, 762	23, 124
Balances with other banks, and cash items in process of collection	274, 715	263, 893	296, 589	366, 834
Bank premises owned, furniture and fixtures	10, 954	10, 636	10, 853	13, 220
Real estate owned other than bank premises	1, 122	1, 201	1, 086	1, 023
Investments and other assets indirectly representing bank premises or other real estate	1, 037	1, 022	1, 018	1, 148
Customers' liability on acceptances outstanding	995	67	187	518
Income earned or accrued but not collected	4, 591	5, 245	4, 904	} 8, 038
Other assets	2, 327	2, 164	2, 113	
Total assets	2, 196, 337	2, 291, 728	2, 281, 048	2, 452, 895
LIABILITIES				
Demand deposits of individuals, partnerships, and corporations	1, 137, 906	1, 157, 245	1, 165, 440	1, 264, 135
Time deposits of individuals, partnerships, and corporations	324, 138	340, 546	341, 249	338, 870
Postal savings deposits	487	28	28	28
Deposits of U.S. Government	38, 072	104, 419	53, 545	50, 078
Deposits of States and political subdivisions	79, 002	93, 751	87, 066	137, 905
Deposits of banks	411, 489	398, 204	430, 416	455, 512
Other deposits (certified and cashiers' checks, etc.)	10, 038	11, 935	11, 239	15, 603
Total deposits	*2, 001, 132*	*2, 106, 128*	*2, 088, 983*	*2, 262, 131*
Demand deposits	*1, 655, 614*	*1, 722, 325*	*1, 707, 946*	*1, 895, 924*
Time deposits	*345, 518*	*383, 803*	*381, 037*	*366, 207*
Bills payable, rediscounts, and other liabilities for borrowed money	7, 100	1, 300	2, 550	
Acceptances executed by or for account of reporting banks and outstanding	995	67	187	532
Income collected but not earned	6, 528	6, 627	6, 875	} 18, 529
Expenses accrued and unpaid	11, 285	8, 113	9, 907	
Other liabilities	1, 067	1, 919	1, 506	
Total liabilities	2, 028, 107	2, 124, 154	2, 110, 008	2, 281, 192
CAPITAL ACCOUNTS				
Capital stock: Common stock	50, 583	49, 983	50, 008	52, 603
Surplus	72, 877	74, 327	74, 883	81, 016
Undivided profits	40, 355	40, 610	42, 705	34, 300
Reserves	4, 415	2, 654	3, 444	3, 784
Total capital accounts	168, 230	167, 574	171, 040	171, 703
Total liabilities and capital accounts	2, 196, 337	2, 291, 728	2, 281, 048	2, 452, 895
MEMORANDUM				
Assets pledged or assigned to secure liabilities and for other purposes	223, 814	301, 377	259, 627	295, 031

Assets and liabilities of national banks, by States, at date of each call during year ended Dec. 31, 1958—Continued

MONTANA

[In thousands of dollars]

	Mar. 4, 1958	June 23, 1958	Sept. 24, 1958	Dec. 31, 1958
	41 banks	41 banks	41 banks	41 banks
ASSETS				
Loans and discounts (including overdrafts)	147,183	153,713	156,460	156,849
U.S. Government securities, direct obligations	130,086	127,332	131,567	156,773
Obligations guaranteed by U.S. Government				
Obligations of States and political subdivisions	19,064	19,611	21,402	23,901
Other bonds, notes, and debentures	10,356	9,890	10,644	12,981
Corporate stocks, including stock of Federal Reserve bank	501	548	558	563
Reserve with Federal Reserve bank	29,968	30,814	32,411	33,686
Currency and coin	3,733	4,907	5,253	5,125
Balances with other banks, and cash items in process of collection	37,318	38,800	44,491	41,212
Bank premises owned, furniture and fixtures	5,046	5,158	5,466	5,584
Real estate owned other than bank premises	191	201	243	232
Investments and other assets indirectly representing bank premises or other real estate	5	5	5	23
Customers' liability on acceptances outstanding	26	14	15	9
Income earned or accrued but not collected	934	985	1,043	} 1,531
Other assets	104	179	153	
Total assets	384,515	392,157	409,711	438,469
LIABILITIES				
Demand deposits of individuals, partnerships, and corporations	202,267	196,246	217,194	228,601
Time deposits of individuals, partnerships, and corporations	100,891	104,132	106,639	111,101
Postal savings deposits				
Deposits of U.S. Government	6,142	8,422	6,253	6,850
Deposits of States and political subdivisions	33,794	38,684	28,346	39,845
Deposits of banks	12,076	11,591	14,732	15,283
Other deposits (certified and cashiers' checks, etc.)	3,255	3,136	5,227	4,534
Total deposits	*358,425*	*362,211*	*378,391*	*406,214*
Demand deposits	*252,031*	*252,126*	*266,093*	*289,727*
Time deposits	*106,394*	*110,085*	*112,298*	*116,487*
Bills payable, rediscounts, and other liabilities for borrowed money	50			450
Acceptances executed by or for account of reporting banks and outstanding	26	14	15	9
Income collected but not earned	3,000	3,544	3,698	} 6,614
Expenses accrued and unpaid	1,207	2,265	2,717	
Other liabilities	123	157	162	
Total liabilities	362,831	368,191	384,983	413,287
CAPITAL ACCOUNTS				
Capital stock: Common stock	8,213	9,288	9,333	9,408
Surplus	8,840	9,275	9,285	9,442
Undivided profits	4,482	5,257	5,965	6,059
Reserves	149	146	145	273
Total capital accounts	21,684	23,966	24,728	25,182
Total liabilities and capital accounts	384,515	392,157	409,711	438,469
MEMORANDUM				
Assets pledged or assigned to secure liabilities and for other purposes	62,352	62,592	63,556	69,255

Assets and liabilities of national banks, by States, at date of each call during year ended Dec. 31, 1958—Continued

NEBRASKA

[In thousands of dollars]

	Mar. 4, 1958	June 23, 1958	Sept. 24, 1958	Dec. 31, 1958
	123 banks	123 banks	123 banks	123 banks
ASSETS				
Loans and discounts (including overdrafts)	413, 475	437, 749	443, 653	487, 435
U.S. Government securities, direct obligations	330, 990	333, 195	345, 305	346, 559
Obligations guaranteed by U.S. Government				
Obligations of States and political subdivisions	80, 086	84, 535	87, 392	90, 100
Other bonds, notes, and debentures	14, 483	14, 054	16, 770	14, 813
Corporate stocks, including stock of Federal Reserve bank	1, 924	1, 937	1, 948	1, 975
Reserve with Federal Reserve bank	118, 245	111, 750	124, 194	111, 564
Currency and coin	9, 816	12, 729	12, 755	12, 290
Balances with other banks, and cash items in process of collection	136, 266	146, 164	150, 096	197, 804
Bank premises owned, furniture and fixtures	8, 523	8, 572	8, 672	8, 604
Real estate owned other than bank premises	108	106	101	81
Investments and other assets indirectly representing bank premises or other real estate	1, 007	1, 011	1, 000	1, 000
Customers' liability on acceptances outstanding			26	55
Income earned or accrued but not collected	2, 441	2, 412	2, 604	} 3, 453
Other assets	496	618	704	
Total assets	1, 117, 860	1, 154, 832	1, 195, 220	1, 275, 733
LIABILITIES				
Demand deposits of individuals, partnerships, and corporations	647, 818	646, 410	683, 159	773, 741
Time deposits of individuals, partnerships, and corporations	111, 437	115, 588	118, 036	118, 928
Postal savings deposits	29	29	29	29
Deposits of U.S. Government	26, 687	41, 378	30, 548	26, 967
Deposits of States and political subdivisions	83, 523	86, 376	81, 438	74, 202
Deposits of banks	132, 544	130, 810	165, 373	160, 579
Other deposits (certified and cashiers' checks, etc.)	8, 360	10, 358	7, 033	10, 770
Total deposits	*1, 010, 398*	*1, 030, 949*	*1, 085, 616*	*1, 165, 216*
Demand deposits	*898, 527*	*914, 030*	*966, 122*	*1, 044, 804*
Time deposits	*111, 871*	*116, 919*	*119, 494*	*120, 412*
Bills payable, rediscounts, and other liabilities for borrowed money	9, 160	23, 045	5, 998	7, 010
Acceptances executed by or for account of reporting banks and outstanding			26	55
Income collected but not earned	3, 201	3, 577	3, 679	} 7, 787
Expenses accrued and unpaid	3, 694	2, 980	3, 727	
Other liabilities	352	256	240	
Total liabilities	1, 026, 805	1, 060, 807	1, 099, 286	1, 180, 068
CAPITAL ACCOUNTS				
Capital stock: Common stock	26, 475	26, 475	26, 490	26, 815
Surplus	36, 688	37, 191	37, 680	38, 427
Undivided profits	22, 499	25, 466	26, 554	25, 395
Reserves	5, 393	4, 893	5, 210	5, 028
Total capital accounts	91, 055	94, 025	95, 934	95, 665
Total liabilities and capital accounts	1, 117, 860	1, 154, 832	1, 195, 220	1, 275, 733
MEMORANDUM				
Assets pledged or assigned to secure liabilities and for other purposes	177, 106	193, 629	192, 795	186, 726

Assets and liabilities of national banks, by States, at date of each call during year ended Dec. 31, 1958—Continued

NEVADA

[In thousands of dollars]

	Mar. 4, 1958	June 23, 1958	Sept. 24, 1958	Dec. 31, 1958
	3 banks	3 banks	3 banks	3 banks
ASSETS				
Loans and discounts (including overdrafts)	102,993	116,110	106,511	110,804
U.S. Government securities, direct obligations	85,515	83,227	102,710	87,539
Obligations guaranteed by U.S. Government				
Obligations of States and political subdivisions	18,006	19,617	32,381	37,813
Other bonds, notes, and debentures	9,719	9,658	8,236	8,390
Corporate stocks, including stock of Federal Reserve bank	330	330	330	330
Reserve with Federal Reserve bank	20,662	18,936	19,377	20,300
Currency and coin	2,665	4,341	3,750	4,468
Balances with other banks, and cash items in process of collection	12,548	8,956	11,116	9,654
Bank premises owned, furniture and fixtures	4,513	4,533	4,312	4,307
Real estate owned other than bank premises	11	11	11	10
Investments and other assets indirectly representing bank premises or other real estate			225	220
Income earned or accrued but not collected	971	623	749	} 2,085
Other assets	402	459	355	
Total assets	258,335	266,801	290,063	285,920
LIABILITIES				
Demand deposits of individuals, partnerships, and corporations	103,367	103,606	116,361	114,308
Time deposits of individuals, partnerships, and corporations	85,630	88,417	93,869	96,024
Postal savings deposits				
Deposits of U.S. Government	4,752	7,701	9,298	7,260
Deposits of States and political subdivisions	42,162	43,307	47,710	46,582
Deposits of banks	1,142	1,034	1,909	289
Other deposits (certified and cashiers' checks, etc.)	2,337	2,252	2,035	2,807
Total deposits	239,390	246,317	271,182	267,270
Demand deposits	147,354	147,093	167,171	160,464
Time deposits	92,036	99,224	104,011	106,806
Bills payable, rediscounts, and other liabilities for borrowed money				
Income collected but not earned	1,339	1,570	1,537	} 2,612
Expenses accrued and unpaid	1,953	2,126	1,722	
Other liabilities	262	1,326	14	
Total liabilities	242,944	251,339	274,455	269,882
CAPITAL ACCOUNTS				
Capital stock: Common stock	5,450	5,450	5,450	5,450
Surplus	5,550	5,550	5,550	5,550
Undivided profits	4,332	4,411	4,484	4,981
Reserves	59	51	124	57
Total capital accounts	15,391	15,462	15,608	16,038
Total liabilities and capital accounts	258,335	266,801	290,063	285,920
MEMORANDUM				
Assets pledged or assigned to secure liabilities and for other purposes	53,891	58,243	57,095	58,669

Assets and liabilities of national banks, by States, at date of each call during year ended Dec. 31, 1958—Continued

NEW HAMPSHIRE

In thousands of dollars]

	Mar. 4, 1958	June 23, 1958	Sept. 24, 1958	Dec. 31, 1958
	50 banks	50 banks	51 banks	51 banks
ASSETS				
Loans and discounts (including overdrafts)	122,545	128,175	129,175	132,459
U.S. Government securities, direct obligations	60,519	59,710	73,286	74,494
Obligations guaranteed by U.S. Government	21	21	18	18
Obligations of States and political subdivisions	15,341	17,531	18,408	15,766
Other bonds, notes, and debentures	5,634	4,594	3,659	3,253
Corporate stocks, including stock of Federal Reserve bank	612	626	632	636
Reserve with Federal Reserve bank	22,992	21,657	24,514	20,153
Currency and coin	6,590	8,543	7,897	7,810
Balances with other banks, and cash items in process of collection	26,633	28,497	30,076	38,840
Bank premises owned, furniture and fixtures	3,141	3,330	3,287	3,925
Real estate owned other than bank premises	671	814	989	205
Investments and other assets indirectly representing bank premises or other real estate	57	53	53	56
Income earned or accrued but not collected	12	29	5	} 525
Other assets	181	325	230	
Total assets	264,949	273,905	292,229	298,140
LIABILITIES				
Demand deposits of individuals, partnerships, and corporations	144,833	143,299	157,075	161,569
Time deposits of individuals, partnerships, and corporations	47,591	49,583	53,673	52,851
Postal savings deposits	15	15	15	10
Deposits of U.S. Government	6,955	13,218	8,509	8,108
Deposits of States and political subdivisions	17,589	14,517	18,812	22,454
Deposits of banks	9,746	9,955	10,696	11,621
Other deposits (certified and cashiers' checks, etc.)	6,416	9,985	9,020	8,941
Total deposits	*233,145*	*240,572*	*257,800*	*265,554*
Demand deposits	*184,729*	*190,356*	*203,101*	*211,561*
Time deposits	*48,416*	*50,216*	*54,699*	*53,993*
Bills payable, rediscounts, and other liabilities for borrowed money	1,370	1,640	1,900	200
Income collected but not earned	923	1,122	1,216	} 1,985
Expenses accrued and unpaid	458	370	522	
Other liabilities	47	147	102	
Total liabilities	235,943	243,851	261,540	267,739
CAPITAL ACCOUNTS				
Capital stock: Common stock	6,369	6,369	6,469	6,469
Surplus	14,023	14,493	14,616	15,080
Undivided profits	6,877	8,237	8,403	7,440
Reserves	1,737	955	1,201	1,412
Total capital accounts	29,006	30,054	30,689	30,401
Total liabilities and capital accounts	264,949	273,905	292,229	298,140
MEMORANDUM				
Assets pledged or assigned to secure liabilities and for other purposes	18,092	21,343	24,111	22,939

Assets and liabilities of national banks, by States, at date of each call during year ended Dec. 31, 1958—Continued

NEW JERSEY

[In thousands of dollars]

	Mar. 4, 1958	June 23, 1958	Sept. 24, 1958	Dec. 31, 1958
	169 banks	168 banks	167 banks	167 banks
ASSETS				
Loans and discounts (including overdrafts)	1,487,568	1,465,262	1,532,095	1,618,820
U.S. Government securities, direct obligations	1,036,081	1,034,234	1,148,531	1,214,153
Obligations guaranteed by U.S. Government	338	308	308	413
Obligations of States and political subdivisions	418,001	438,540	469,730	497,840
Other bonds, notes, and debentures	90,355	89,657	99,434	90,323
Corporate stocks, including stock of Federal Reserve bank	6,346	6,237	7,388	7,476
Reserve with Federal Reserve bank	277,606	263,075	286,587	261,357
Currency and coin	69,619	73,831	77,475	80,115
Balances with other banks, and cash items in process of collection	244,125	239,264	209,117	302,530
Bank premises owned, furniture and fixtures	48,645	47,384	49,688	50,880
Real estate owned other than bank premises	787	693	1,099	807
Investments and other assets indirectly representing bank premises or other real estate	585	585	577	603
Customers' liability on acceptances outstanding	83	44	55	134
Income earned or accrued but not collected	9,290	8,758	8,921	} 14,686
Other assets	4,084	3,825	4,727	
Total assets	3,693,513	3,671,697	3,895,732	4,140,137
LIABILITIES				
Demand deposits of individuals, partnerships, and corporations	1,496,318	1,477,870	1,577,819	1,771,205
Time deposits of individuals, partnerships, and corporations	1,473,430	1,458,852	1,554,182	1,597,474
Postal savings deposits				
Deposits of U.S. Government	62,046	106,646	67,752	72,990
Deposits of States and political subdivisions	253,963	227,017	282,774	269,784
Deposits of banks	49,161	36,117	37,353	42,624
Other deposits (certified and cashiers' checks, etc.)	49,550	55,882	51,976	68,224
Total deposits	*3,384,468*	*3,362,584*	*3,571,856*	*3,822,301*
Demand deposits	*1,888,486*	*1,865,061*	*1,976,086*	*2,187,403*
Time deposits	*1,495,982*	*1,497,323*	*1,595,770*	*1,634,898*
Bills payable, rediscounts, and other liabilities for borrowed money	11,275	10,250	7,575	1,942
Mortgages or other liens on bank premises and other real estate	50	50	50	
Acceptances executed by or for account of reporting banks and outstanding	83	44	55	134
Income collected but not earned	20,108	18,963	20,944	} 38,397
Expenses accrued and unpaid	12,712	12,339	14,521	
Other liabilities	2,729	4,336	3,703	
Total liabilities	3,431,425	3,408,366	3,618,704	3,862,774
CAPITAL ACCOUNTS				
Capital stock:				
Class A preferred stock	629 }	689	638	638
Class B preferred dtock	60			
Common stock	84,005	82,018	84,726	85,921
Total capital stock	*84,694*	*82,707*	*85,364*	*86,559*
Surplus	125,871	125,273	132,091	134,965
Undivided profits	44,794	48,647	51,617	46,667
Reserves and retirement account for preferred stock	6,729	6,704	7,956	9,172
Total capital accounts	262,088	263,331	277,028	277,363
Total liabilities and capital accounts	3,693,513	3,671,697	3,895,732	4,140,137
MEMORANDUM				
Assets pledged or assigned to secure liabilities and for other purposes	234,269	251,825	284,001	257,924

Assets and liabilities of national banks, by States, at date of each call during year ended Dec. 31, 1958—Continued

NEW MEXICO

[In thousands of dollars]

	Mar. 4, 1958	June 23, 1958	Sept. 24, 1958	Dec. 31, 1958
	26 banks	26 banks	27 banks	27 banks
ASSETS				
Loans and discounts (including overdrafts)	156,993	163,326	176,048	191,348
U.S. Government securities, direct obligations	148,037	151,169	156,025	167,774
Obligations guaranteed by U.S. Government				
Obligations of States and political subdivisions	15,990	16,002	17,572	19,303
Other bonds, notes, and debentures	3,585	3,584	2,569	2,469
Corporate stocks, including stock of Federal Reserve bank	513	513	587	594
Reserve with Federal Reserve bank	43,734	40,904	34,740	40,368
Currency and coin	5,944	7,790	8,074	7,723
Balances with other banks, and cash items in process of collection	54,714	54,876	42,806	66,647
Bank premises owned, furniture and fixtures	6,066	6,271	6,334	6,316
Real estate owned other than bank premises	225	138	69	62
Investments and other assets indirectly representing bank premises or other real estate	100	100	100	100
Income earned or accrued but not collected	402	386	398	} 716
Other assets	218	224	190	
Total assets	436,521	445,283	445,512	503,420
LIABILITIES				
Demand deposits of individuals, partnerships, and corporations	217,567	214,151	222,825	258,884
Time deposits of individuals, partnerships, and corporations	78,896	84,027	86,517	89,704
Postal savings deposits	11	11	11	11
Deposits of U.S. Government	10,260	18,090	14,046	17,869
Deposits of States and political subdivisions	78,621	81,827	75,404	84,505
Deposits of banks	16,152	12,869	11,910	16,527
Other deposits (certified and cashiers' checks, etc.)	3,422	5,009	2,940	4,751
Total deposits	*404,929*	*415,984*	*413,653*	*472,251*
Demand deposits	*312,812*	*317,520*	*313,943*	*367,329*
Time deposits	*92,117*	*98,464*	*99,710*	*104,922*
Bills payable, rediscounts, and other liabilities for borrowed money	3,000	100		
Income collected but not earned	2,121	2,302	2,466	} 3,961
Expenses accrued and unpaid	877	467	887	
Other liabilities	455	604	589	
Total liabilities	411,382	419,457	417,595	476,212
CAPITAL ACCOUNTS				
Capital stock: Common stock	8,500	8,500	9,500	9,850
Surplus	8,585	9,010	10,140	10,780
Undivided profits	3,799	4,940	5,434	3,149
Reserves	4,255	3,376	2,843	3,429
Total capital accounts	25,139	25,826	27,917	27,208
Total liabilities and capital accounts	436,521	445,283	445,512	503,420
MEMORANDUM				
Assets pledged or assigned to secure liabilities and for other purposes	107,065	106,782	112,707	114,208

Assets and liabilities of national banks, by States, at date of each call during year ended Dec. 31, 1958—Continued

NEW YORK

[In thousands of dollars]

	Mar. 4, 1958	June 23, 1958	Sept. 24, 1958	Dec. 31, 1958
	272 banks	266 banks	264 banks	258 banks
ASSETS				
Loans and discounts (including overdrafts)	5, 563, 738	5, 747, 732	5, 342, 928	5, 639, 091
U.S. Government securities, direct obligations	2, 359, 411	2, 724, 200	2, 862, 643	2, 791, 327
Obligations guaranteed by U.S. Government	165	200	187	257
Obligations of States and political subdivisions	807, 685	843, 386	914, 131	961, 533
Other bonds, notes, and debentures	174, 436	185, 145	165, 149	149, 958
Corporate stocks, including stock of Federal Reserve bank	35, 055	35, 063	35, 162	35, 115
Reserve with Federal Reserve bank	1, 142, 624	1, 164, 696	1, 061, 681	1, 101, 297
Currency and coin	91, 691	110, 267	105, 307	106, 613
Balances with other banks, and cash items in process of collection	799, 864	1, 024, 701	662, 221	1, 069, 520
Bank premises owned, furniture and fixtures	93, 111	96, 676	102, 109	107, 061
Real estate owned other than bank premises	2, 075	2, 226	1, 865	1, 675
Investments and other assets indirectly representing bank premises or other real estate	3, 496	3, 604	3, 776	3, 778
Customers' liability on acceptances outstanding	122, 338	99, 185	90, 745	86, 387
Income earned or accrued but not collected	29, 433	26, 009	25, 026	} 99, 687
Other assets	65, 693	74, 887	65, 643	
Total assets	11, 290, 815	12, 137, 977	11, 438, 573	12, 153, 299
LIABILITIES				
Demand deposits of individuals, partnerships, and corporations	5, 152, 940	5, 202, 907	5, 139, 531	5, 712, 460
Time deposits of individuals, partnerships, and corporations	2, 436, 691	2, 582, 386	2, 684, 942	2, 716, 364
Postal savings deposits				
Deposits of U.S. Government	201, 674	682, 292	232, 006	275, 032
Deposits of States and political subdivisions	543, 432	558, 638	555, 927	452, 096
Deposits of banks	1, 088, 886	1, 150, 277	1, 031, 470	1, 180, 999
Other deposits (certified and cashiers' checks, etc.)	317, 066	424, 389	244, 157	351, 282
Total deposits	9, 740, 689	10, 600, 889	9, 888, 033	10, 688, 233
Demand deposits	6, 839, 132	7, 441, 101	6, 678, 778	7, 492, 190
Time deposits	2, 901, 557	3, 159, 788	3, 209, 255	3, 196, 043
Bills payable, rediscounts, and other liabilities for borrowed money	51, 465	89, 115	93, 702	6, 882
Mortgages or other liens on bank premises and other real estate	10	10	10	97
Acceptances executed by or for account of reporting banks and outstanding	126, 849	103, 292	94, 942	89, 435
Income collected but not earned	58, 768	67, 341	69, 706	} 296, 177
Expenses accrued and unpaid	83, 725	70, 570	68, 962	
Other liabilities	176, 425	151, 723	162, 619	
Total liabilities	10, 237, 931	11, 082, 940	10, 377, 974	11, 080, 824
CAPITAL ACCOUNTS				
Capital stock:				
Class A preferred stock	164 }	229	229	229
Class B preferred stock	65 }			
Common stock	352, 443	352, 892	353, 388	353, 815
Total capital stock	*352, 672*	*353, 121*	*353, 617*	*354, 044*
Surplus	541, 441	541, 457	544, 292	547, 286
Undivided profits	148, 075	149, 216	151, 127	159, 262
Reserves and retirement account for preferred stock	10, 696	11, 243	11, 563	11, 883
Total capital accounts	1, 052, 884	1, 055, 037	1, 060, 599	1, 072, 475
Total liabilities and capital accounts	11, 290, 815	12, 137, 977	11, 438, 573	12, 153, 299
MEMORANDUM				
Assets pledged or assigned to secure liabilities and for other purposes	1, 073, 156	1, 440, 325	1, 320, 640	1, 104, 406

Assets and liabilities of national banks, by States, at date of each call during year ended Dec. 31, 1958—Continued

NORTH CAROLINA

[In thousands of dollars]

	Mar. 4, 1958	June 23, 1958	Sept. 24, 1958	Dec. 31, 1958
	45 banks	45 banks	44 banks	43 banks
ASSETS				
Loans and discounts (including overdrafts)	269, 347	286, 645	287, 553	305, 057
U.S. Government securities, direct obligations	161, 447	164, 803	174, 889	197, 978
Obligations guaranteed by U.S. Government				
Obligations of States and political subdivisions	41, 625	41, 159	42, 558	49, 050
Other bonds, notes, and debentures	11, 696	12, 970	14, 883	15, 875
Corporate stocks, including stock of Federal Reserve bank	1, 393	1, 400	1, 457	1, 481
Reserve with Federal Reserve bank	55, 086	54, 219	42, 931	54, 079
Currency and coin	14, 662	15, 958	19, 864	20, 589
Balances with other banks, and cash items in process of collection	79, 173	84, 890	99, 165	108, 021
Bank premises owned, furniture and fixtures	9, 088	9, 410	9, 481	9, 624
Real estate owned other than bank premises	105	101	96	76
Investments and other assets indirectly representing bank premises or other real estate	493	359	363	432
Customers' liability on acceptances outstanding				150
Income earned or accrued but not collected	774	987	1, 017	} 2, 069
Other assets	870	663	748	
Total assets	645, 759	673, 564	695, 005	764, 481
LIABILITIES				
Demand deposits of individuals, partnerships, and corporations	353, 643	343, 774	371, 888	433, 858
Time deposits of individuals, partnerships, and corporations	122, 623	132, 445	137, 850	137, 141
Postal savings deposits				
Deposits of U.S. Government	14, 044	32, 318	19, 252	19, 217
Deposits of States and political subdivisions	56, 027	56, 461	57, 589	63, 010
Deposits of banks	17, 238	16, 873	20, 095	25, 106
Other deposits (certified and cashiers' checks, etc.)	11, 840	20, 571	17, 694	14, 298
Total deposits	*575, 415*	*602, 442*	*624, 368*	*692, 630*
Demand deposits	*429, 629*	*439, 190*	*458, 584*	*528, 675*
Time deposits	*145, 786*	*163, 252*	*165, 784*	*163, 955*
Bills payable, rediscounts, and other liabilities for borrowed money	2, 250	2, 825	630	200
Acceptances executed by or for account of reporting banks and outstanding				150
Income collected but not earned	4, 668	4, 898	5, 338	} 10, 332
Expenses accrued and unpaid	3, 671	2, 034	2, 358	
Other liabilities	873	1, 284	1, 171	
Total liabilities	586, 877	613, 483	633, 865	703, 312
CAPITAL ACCOUNTS				
Capital stock: Common stock	14, 540	14, 690	15, 190	15, 515
Surplus	31, 884	32, 161	33, 468	34, 615
Undivided profits	10, 678	11, 754	10, 932	9, 388
Reserves	1, 780	1, 476	1, 550	1, 651
Total capital accounts	58, 882	60, 081	61, 140	61, 169
Total liabilities and capital accounts	645, 759	673, 564	695, 005	764, 481
MEMORANDUM				
Assets pledged or assigned to secure liabilities and for other purposes	98, 849	118, 761	112, 514	112, 269

Assets and liabilities of national banks, by States, at date of each call during year ended Dec. 31, 1958—Continued

NORTH DAKOTA

[In thousands of dollars]

	Mar. 4, 1958	June 23, 1958	Sept. 24, 1958	Dec. 31, 1958
	38 banks	38 banks	38 banks	38 banks
ASSETS				
Loans and discounts (including overdrafts)	129, 588	127, 859	135, 769	134, 902
U.S. Government securities, direct obligations	115, 604	120, 272	125, 021	135, 622
Obligations guaranteed by U.S. Government	10	10	5	5
Obligations of States and political subdivisions	17, 883	18, 569	20, 575	24, 041
Other bonds, notes, and debentures	14, 178	12, 947	14, 331	15, 168
Corporate stocks, including stock of Federal Reserve bank	454	458	485	532
Reserve with Federal Reserve bank	30, 052	26, 912	27, 640	30, 098
Currency and coin	3, 287	3, 877	3, 961	4, 000
Balances with other banks, and cash items in process of collection	25, 993	22, 142	28, 505	26, 932
Bank premises owned, furniture and fixtures	3, 813	3, 850	3, 878	4, 159
Real estate owned other than bank premises	401	419	290	280
Investments and other assets indirectly representing bank premises or other real estate	250	255	250	250
Income earned or accrued but not collected	1, 072	1, 011	956	} 1, 871
Other assets	389	465	668	
Total assets	342, 974	339, 046	362, 334	377, 860
LIABILITIES				
Demand deposits of individuals, partnerships, and corporations	170, 845	164, 539	187, 085	198, 216
Time deposits of individuals, partnerships, and corporations	101, 708	106, 520	110, 562	114, 305
Postal savings deposits	6	6	6	6
Deposits of U.S. Government	5, 451	6, 091	3, 790	6, 676
Deposits of States and political subdivisions	24, 316	21, 489	18, 709	16, 174
Deposits of banks	10, 886	10, 511	11, 519	10, 720
Other deposits (certified and cashiers' checks, etc.)	3, 591	2, 071	2, 257	2, 942
Total deposits	*316, 803*	*311, 227*	*333, 928*	*349, 039*
Demand deposits	*211, 687*	*200, 106*	*219, 054*	*231, 149*
Time deposits	*105, 116*	*111, 121*	*114, 874*	*117, 890*
Bills payable, rediscounts, and other liabilities for borrowed money		1, 000		
Income collected but not earned	2, 139	2, 281	2, 342	} 5, 110
Expenses accrued and unpaid	2, 187	1, 571	2, 003	
Other liabilities	4	69	120	
Total liabilities	321, 133	316, 148	338, 393	354, 149
CAPITAL ACCOUNTS				
Capital stock: Common stock	5, 985	6, 010	6, 760	6, 960
Surplus	9, 336	9, 737	9, 937	10, 815
Undivided profits	5, 751	6, 239	6, 302	5, 267
Reserves	769	912	942	669
Total capital accounts	21, 841	22, 898	23, 941	23, 711
Total liabilities and capital accounts	342, 974	339, 046	362, 334	377, 860
MEMORANDUM				
Assets pledged or assigned to secure liabilities and for other purposes	47, 159	49, 707	49, 138	52, 850

Assets and liabilities of national banks, by States, at date of each call during year ended Dec. 31, 1958—Continued

OHIO

[In thousands of dollars]

	Mar. 4, 1958	June 23, 1958	Sept. 24, 1958	Dec. 31, 1958
	229 banks	229 banks	228 banks	228 banks
ASSETS				
Loans and discounts (including overdrafts)	2,116,080	2,157,617	2,164,607	2,224,974
U.S. Government securities, direct obligations	1,707,260	1,882,982	1,811,936	1,913,334
Obligations guaranteed by U.S. Government	326	326	311	308
Obligations of States and political subdivisions	336,756	366,290	370,420	366,035
Other bonds, notes, and debentures	68,902	69,553	62,594	56,175
Corporate stocks, including stock of Federal Reserve bank	10,474	10,632	10,649	10,812
Reserve with Federal Reserve bank	523,867	510,175	560,273	509,415
Currency and coin	80,168	88,115	95,948	96,375
Balances with other banks, and cash items in process of collection	470,603	475,032	435,951	562,244
Bank premises owned, furniture and fixtures	58,793	61,551	61,830	63,321
Real estate owned other than bank premises	1,009	822	796	805
Investments and other assets indirectly representing bank premises or other real estate	3,480	3,491	3,416	3,301
Customers' liability on acceptances outstanding	80	197	205	374
Income earned or accrued but not collected	10,914	10,993	11,992	} 17,898
Other assets	5,964	5,881	6,869	
Total assets	5,394,676	5,643,657	5,597,797	5,825,371
LIABILITIES				
Demand deposits of individuals, partnerships, and corporations	2,570,414	2,604,968	2,592,176	2,863,024
Time deposits of individuals, partnerships, and corporations	1,430,133	1,469,049	1,490,142	1,513,061
Postal savings deposits	190	190	190	190
Deposits of U.S. Government	103,962	203,260	139,637	131,943
Deposits of States and political subdivisions	433,418	507,098	517,750	456,334
Deposits of banks	261,295	233,391	239,789	267,463
Other deposits (certified and cashiers' checks, etc.)	68,231	85,388	73,881	80,311
Total deposits	*4,867,643*	*5,103,344*	*5,053,565*	*5,312,326*
Demand deposits	*3,357,241*	*3,534,715*	*3,458,243*	*3,705,415*
Time deposits	*1,510,402*	*1,568,629*	*1,595,322*	*1,606,911*
Bills payable, rediscounts, and other liabilities for borrowed money	31,874	33,453	35,371	1,711
Mortgages or other liens on bank premises and other real estate	31	29	29	27
Acceptances executed by or for account of reporting banks and outstanding	80	197	205	374
Income collected but not earned	29,647	30,459	31,325	} 67,413
Expenses accrued and unpaid	35,970	31,666	30,514	
Other liabilities	5,322	6,568	4,324	
Total liabilities	4,970,567	5,205,716	5,155,333	5,381,851
CAPITAL ACCOUNTS				
Capital stock: Common stock	136,303	137,696	137,646	138,121
Surplus	213,024	216,806	217,810	223,643
Undivided profits	70,061	79,327	82,651	78,192
Reserves	4,721	4,112	4,357	3,564
Total capital accounts	424,109	437,941	442,464	443,520
Total liabilities and capital accounts	5,394,676	5,643,657	5,597,797	5,825,371
MEMORANDUM				
Assets pledged or assigned to secure liabilities and for other purposes	839,335	978,320	968,964	948,071

Assets and liabilities of national banks, by States, at date of each call during year ended Dec. 31, 1958—Continued

OKLAHOMA

[In thousands of dollars]

	Mar. 4, 1958	June 23, 1958	Sept. 24, 1958	Dec. 31, 1958
	197 banks	197 banks	197 banks	197 banks
ASSETS				
Loans and discounts (including overdrafts)	726,374	730,894	764,949	787,896
U.S. Government securities, direct obligations	520,526	568,163	580,952	614,274
Obligations guaranteed by U.S. Government	17	17	17	23
Obligations of States and political subdivisions	147,959	152,636	155,745	163,901
Other bonds, notes, and debentures	30,127	37,918	32,253	33,702
Corporate stocks, including stock of Federal Reserve bank	3,705	3,695	3,736	3,788
Reserve with Federal Reserve bank	188,356	197,101	189,227	165,426
Currency and coin	20,250	25,064	26,609	26,943
Balances with other banks, and cash items in process of collection	311,047	357,974	311,924	439,991
Bank premises owned, furniture and fixtures	19,003	19,626	20,068	27,432
Real estate owned other than bank premises	782	841	454	384
Investments and other assets indirectly representing bank premises or other real estate	7,539	8,576	10,177	6,999
Customers' liability on acceptances outstanding	1,023	325	447	875
Income earned or accrued but not collected	2,487	2,765	2,559	} 5,214
Other assets	1,281	1,229	2,114	
Total assets	1,980,476	2,106,824	2,101,231	2,276,848
LIABILITIES				
Demand deposits of individuals, partnerships, and corporations	1,085,512	1,149,836	1,176,706	1,305,497
Time deposits of individuals, partnerships, and corporations	278,870	297,611	314,791	305,783
Postal savings deposits	97	97	97	97
Deposits of U.S. Government	39,986	68,139	41,132	48,561
Deposits of States and political subdivisions	168,147	153,029	139,827	166,951
Deposits of banks	206,008	233,089	219,025	222,625
Other deposits (certified and cashiers' checks, etc.)	12,389	13,970	11,855	20,697
Total deposits	*1,791,009*	*1,915,771*	*1,903,433*	*2,070,211*
Demand deposits	*1,503,941*	*1,608,740*	*1,575,956*	*1,755,214*
Time deposits	*287,068*	*307,031*	*327,477*	*314,997*
Bills payable, rediscounts, and other liabilities for borrowed money	----------	----------	1,075	10,000
Mortgages or other liens on bank premises and other real estate	7	7	7	7
Acceptances executed by or for account of reporting banks and outstanding	1,023	325	447	875
Income collected but not earned	2,982	3,137	3,243	} 12,572
Expenses accrued and unpaid	8,350	5,926	7,881	
Other liabilities	1,125	1,044	723	
Total liabilities	1,804,496	1,926,210	1,916,809	2,093,665
CAPITAL ACCOUNTS				
Capital stock: Common stock	49,762	50,107	50,282	50,777
Surplus	72,147	72,672	73,922	74,850
Undivided profits	48,600	52,915	55,040	51,898
Reserves	5,471	4,920	5,178	5,658
Total capital accounts	175,980	180,614	184,422	183,183
Total liabilities and capital accounts	1,980,476	2,106,824	2,101,231	2,276,848
MEMORANDUM				
Assets pledged or assigned to secure liabilities and for other purposes	344,107	367,632	364,247	380,077

Assets and liabilities of national banks, by States, at date of each call during year ended Dec. 31, 1958—Continued

OREGON

[In thousands of dollars]

	Mar. 4, 1958	June 23, 1958	Sept. 24, 1958	Dec. 31, 1958
	12 banks	11 banks	11 banks	11 banks
ASSETS				
Loans and discounts (including overdrafts)	743,358	750,461	770,472	770,727
U.S. Government securities, direct obligations	502,909	511,134	500,970	534,110
Obligations guaranteed by U.S. Government				
Obligations of States and political subdivisions	146,204	188,639	204,115	196,094
Other bonds, notes, and debentures	27,493	17,636	17,308	16,660
Corporate stocks, including stock of Federal Reserve bank	2,789	2,788	2,796	2,796
Reserve with Federal Reserve bank	170,183	159,700	163,535	193,983
Currency and coin	10,762	13,646	13,655	14,255
Balances with other banks, and cash items in process of collection	101,391	113,308	113,728	132,533
Bank premises owned, furniture and fixtures	25,070	25,835	26,131	26,382
Real estate owned other than bank premises	141	62	158	278
Investments and other assets indirectly representing bank premises or other real estate	20			58
Customers' liability on acceptances outstanding	31	16	14	8
Income earned or accrued but not collected	7,336	5,863	5,771	} 8,967
Other assets	1,409	1,094	1,060	
Total assets	1,739,096	1,790,182	1,819,713	1,896,851
LIABILITIES				
Demand deposits of individuals, partnerships, and corporations	721,951	719,153	782,603	810,691
Time deposits of individuals, partnerships, and corporations	597,027	634,126	640,807	649,512
Postal savings deposits	14	14	14	14
Deposits of U.S. Government	22,952	48,905	17,685	19,442
Deposits of States and political subdivisions	182,761	156,886	126,468	185,254
Deposits of banks	24,728	25,650	29,800	27,037
Other deposits (certified and cashiers' checks, etc.)	21,487	33,518	30,478	33,443
Total deposits	*1,570,920*	*1,618,252*	*1,627,855*	*1,725,393*
Demand deposits	*913,916*	*923,633*	*941,577*	*1,030,407*
Time deposits	*657,004*	*694,619*	*686,278*	*694,986*
Bills payable, rediscounts, and other liabilities for borrowed money		200	20,000	
Mortgages or other liens on bank premises and other real estate	183	159	200	197
Acceptances executed by or for account of reporting banks and outstanding	31	16	14	8
Income collected but not earned	8,653	9,545	10,269	} 30,101
Expenses accrued and unpaid	11,845	12,433	10,682	
Other liabilities	12,819	11,271	12,602	
Total liabilities	1,604,451	1,651,876	1,681,622	1,755,699
CAPITAL ACCOUNTS				
Capital stock: Common stock	40,865	40,840	40,840	40,840
Surplus	52,315	52,295	52,345	52,435
Undivided profits	41,355	45,150	44,850	47,756
Reserves	110	21	56	121
Total capital accounts	134,645	138,306	138,091	141,152
Total liabilities and capital accounts	1,739,096	1,790,182	1,819,713	1,896,851
MEMORANDUM				
Assets pledged or assigned to secure liabilities and for other purposes	458,446	490,227	443,203	468,506

Assets and liabilities of national banks, by States, at date of each call during year ended Dec. 31, 1958—Continued

PENNSYLVANIA

[In thousands of dollars]

	Mar. 4, 1958	June 23, 1958	Sept. 24, 1958	Dec. 31, 1958
	498 banks	493 banks	492 banks	485 banks
ASSETS				
Loans and discounts (including overdrafts)	3,648,001	3,748,673	3,709,839	3,735,515
U. S. Government securities, direct obligations	2,163,259	2,356,882	2,406,616	2,378,080
Obligations guaranteed by U. S. Government	42	35	224	102
Obligations of States and political subdivisions	689,773	722,714	758,123	768,291
Other bonds, notes, and debentures	157,853	169,217	160,859	152,132
Corporate stocks, including stock of Federal Reserve bank	21,479	21,625	21,867	22,150
Reserve with Federal Reserve bank	789,158	747,863	749,741	739,491
Currency and coin	123,428	135,664	142,366	145,828
Balances with other banks, and cash items in process of collection	574,732	605,891	554,049	725,890
Bank premises owned, furniture and fixtures	97,891	100,376	104,912	105,278
Real estate owned other than bank premises	2,224	2,201	2,372	2,378
Investments and other assets indirectly representing bank premises or other real estate	3,506	3,723	3,581	3,349
Customers' liability on acceptances outstanding	8,301	5,565	5,784	5,824
Income earned or accrued but not collected	15,834	18,484	17,262	} 28,503
Other assets	12,380	15,378	10,373	
Total assets	8,307,861	8,654,291	8,647,968	8,812,811
LIABILITIES				
Demand deposits of individuals, partnerships, and corporations	3,793,208	3,777,355	3,777,867	4,068,341
Time deposits of individuals, partnerships, and corporations	2,562,442	2,656,302	2,760,616	2,750,093
Postal savings deposits	672	682	682	684
Deposits of U. S. Government	135,313	417,625	159,589	168,741
Deposits of States and political subdivisions	332,089	344,738	368,021	305,789
Deposits of banks	407,436	392,848	404,964	437,406
Other deposits (certified and cashiers' checks, etc.)	81,212	77,581	76,654	91,327
Total deposits	*7,312,372*	*7,667,131*	*7,548,393*	*7,822,381*
Demand deposits	*4,673,810*	*4,902,746*	*4,681,370*	*4,995,872*
Time deposits	*2,638,562*	*2,764,385*	*2,867,023*	*2,826,509*
Bills payable, rediscounts, and other liabilities for borrowed money	29,010	17,280	111,255	4,850
Mortgages or other liens on bank premises and other real estate	32	87	155	155
Acceptances executed by or for account of reporting banks and outstanding	9,643	6,119	6,398	6,210
Income collected but not earned	36,999	38,354	39,382	} 101,020
Expenses accrued and unpaid	53,849	44,569	51,941	
Other liabilities	11,685	10,100	8,168	
Total liabilities	7,453,590	7,783,640	7,765,692	7,934,616
CAPITAL ACCOUNTS				
Capital stock:				
Preferred stock	50	50	50	50
Common stock	224,466	225,853	226,917	227,031
Total capital stock	*224,516*	*225,903*	*226,967*	*227,081*
Surplus	489,011	492,696	498,145	509,073
Undivided profits	128,281	141,731	145,233	128,803
Reserves and retirement account for preferred stock	12,463	10,321	11,931	13,238
Total capital accounts	854,271	870,651	882,276	878,195
Total liabilities and capital accounts	8,307,861	8,654,291	8,647,968	8,812,811
MEMORANDUM				
Assets pledged or assigned to secure liabilities and for other purposes	896,131	1,141,530	1,013,227	973,452

Assets and liabilities of national banks, by States, at date of each call during year ended Dec. 31, 1958—Continued

RHODE ISLAND

[In thousands of dollars]

	Mar. 4, 1958	June 23, 1958	Sept. 24, 1958	Dec. 31, 1958
	5 banks	5 banks	4 banks	4 banks
ASSETS				
Loans and discounts (including overdrafts)	268,541	267,470	266,248	271,327
U.S. Government securities, direct obligations	108,915	136,608	136,052	137,110
Obligations guaranteed by U.S. Government			11	12
Obligations of States and political subdivisions	44,855	40,799	43,591	43,560
Other bonds, notes, and debentures	4,018	3,321	3,263	2,588
Corporate stocks, including stock of Federal Reserve bank	1,399	1,399	1,393	1,272
Reserve with Federal Reserve bank	39,413	41,627	47,827	41,821
Currency and coin	9,303	9,480	9,887	10,252
Balances with other banks, and cash items in process of collection	17,227	21,840	16,633	22,600
Bank premises owned, furniture and fixtures	7,695	7,686	7,697	7,821
Real estate owned other than bank premises	28	139	97	107
Customers' liability on acceptances outstanding	2,822	31	1,092	4,279
Income earned or accrued but not collected	1,404	1,027	893	⎱ 2,096
Other assets	896	574	551	⎰
Total assets	506,516	532,001	535,235	544,845
LIABILITIES				
Demand deposits of individuals, partnerships, and corporations	193,284	196,942	189,641	211,150
Time deposits of individuals, partnerships, and corporations	217,595	229,043	234,282	232,695
Postal savings deposits	24	24	24	24
Deposits of U.S. Government	7,610	12,965	8,553	8,097
Deposits of States and political subdivisions	22,230	28,247	25,497	22,721
Deposits of banks	3,710	4,446	4,288	4,082
Other deposits (certified and cashiers' checks, etc.)	7,941	10,480	8,622	10,221
Total deposits	*452,394*	*482,147*	*470,907*	*488,990*
Demand deposits	*233,893*	*252,249*	*235,261*	*255,163*
Time deposits	*218,501*	*229,898*	*235,646*	*233,827*
Bills payable, rediscounts, and other liabilities for borrowed money			11,500	
Acceptances executed by or for account of reporting banks and outstanding	2,822	31	1,092	4,279
Income collected but not earned	3,037	3,411	3,454	⎱ 8,229
Expenses accrued and unpaid	4,556	2,853	4,665	⎰
Other liabilities	532	639	584	
Total liabilities	463,341	489,081	492,202	501,498
CAPITAL ACCOUNTS				
Capital stock: Common stock	12,745	12,745	12,645	12,645
Surplus	25,340	25,350	25,280	25,292
Undivided profits	5,035	4,814	5,080	5,365
Reserves	55	11	28	45
Total capital accounts	43,175	42,920	43,033	43,347
Total liabilities and capital accounts	506,516	532,001	535,235	544,845
MEMORANDUM				
Assets pledged or assigned to secure liabilities and for other purposes	27,435	27,541	32,620	30,565

Assets and liabilities of national banks, by States, at date of each call during year ended Dec. 31, 1958—Continued

SOUTH CAROLINA

[In thousands of dollars]

	Mar. 4, 1958	June 23, 1958	Sept. 24, 1958	Dec. 31, 1958
	26 banks	25 banks	25 banks	25 banks
ASSETS				
Loans and discounts (including overdrafts)	231,337	268,084	249,662	254,381
U.S. Government securities, direct obligations	165,891	170,928	184,068	181,184
Obligations guaranteed by U.S. Government				
Obligations of States and political subdivisions	37,151	35,627	37,230	37,603
Other bonds, notes, and debentures	10,661	8,703	10,495	9,852
Corporate stocks, including stock of Federal Reserve bank	1,036	1,046	1,048	1,086
Reserve with Federal Reserve bank	49,350	51,473	49,604	56,182
Currency and coin	13,667	16,239	16,579	16,687
Balances with other banks, and cash items in process of collection	60,891	61,111	66,621	89,144
Bank premises owned, furniture and fixtures	7,826	8,166	8,155	8,448
Real estate owned other than bank premises	285	366	333	174
Customers' liability on acceptances outstanding	18		3	1
Income earned or accrued but not collected	726	973	807	} 2,674
Other assets	555	627	855	
Total assets	579,394	623,343	625,460	657,416
LIABILITIES				
Demand deposits of individuals, partnerships, and corporations	342,087	345,942	371,443	396,697
Time deposits of individuals, partnerships, and corporations	83,616	89,008	93,856	89,561
Postal savings deposits	7	2	2	2
Deposits of U.S. Government	15,916	29,827	21,715	19,011
Deposits of States and political subdivisions	62,204	80,772	56,990	69,942
Deposits of banks	14,765	13,808	17,283	15,133
Other deposits (certified and cashiers' checks, etc.)	9,596	11,360	11,142	13,292
Total deposits	*528,191*	*570,719*	*572,431*	*603,638*
Demand deposits	*433,047*	*469,679*	*465,739*	*500,478*
Time deposits	*95,144*	*101,040*	*106,692*	*103,160*
Bills payable, rediscounts, and other liabilities for borrowed money	838	500		
Acceptances executed by or for account of reporting banks and outstanding	18		3	1
Income collected but not earned	2,203	2,347	2,450	} 8,505
Expenses accrued and unpaid	2,210	2,796	3,572	
Other liabilities	1,909	1,374	885	
Total liabilities	535,369	577,736	579,341	612,144
CAPITAL ACCOUNTS				
Capital stock: Common stock	11,860	11,909	11,909	12,059
Surplus	22,705	23,053	23,084	24,584
Undivided profits	7,887	8,444	8,643	6,911
Reserves	1,573	2,201	2,483	1,718
Total capital accounts	44,025	45,607	46,119	45,272
Total liabilities and capital accounts	579,394	623,343	625,460	657,416
MEMORANDUM				
Assets pledged or assigned to secure liabilities and for other purposes	99,365	99,007	93,661	106,064

Assets and liabilities of national banks, by States, at date of each call during year ended Dec. 31, 1958—Continued

SOUTH DAKOTA

[In thousands of dollars]

	Mar. 4, 1958	June 23, 1958	Sept. 24, 1958	Dec. 31, 1958
	34 banks	34 banks	34 banks	34 banks
ASSETS				
Loans and discounts (including overdrafts)	143,082	153,752	153,732	159,161
U.S. Government securities, direct obligations	112,261	110,907	128,285	138,756
Obligations guaranteed by U.S. Government				
Obligations of States and political subdivisions	18,041	18,886	20,300	22,713
Other bonds, notes, and debentures	8,726	8,135	12,149	10,177
Corporate stocks, including stock of Federal Reserve bank	573	598	607	631
Reserve with Federal Reserve bank	30,026	26,928	31,296	28,644
Currency and coin	3,148	4,423	4,311	4,140
Balances with other banks, and cash items in process of collection	24,669	24,228	29,984	32,011
Bank premises owned, furniture and fixtures	3,245	3,505	3,600	4,444
Real estate owned other than bank premises	544	536	536	348
Investments and other assets indirectly representing bank premises or other real estate	238	238	238	238
Income earned or accrued but not collected	1,188	1,256	1,151	} 2,731
Other assets	835	1,115	1,442	
Total assets	346,576	354,507	387,631	403,994
LIABILITIES				
Demand deposits of individuals, partnerships, and corporations	169,791	163,529	192,643	206,399
Time deposits of individuals, partnerships, and corporations	95,031	100,148	106,202	111,922
Postal savings deposits				
Deposits of U.S. Government	6,399	7,974	6,653	6,140
Deposits of States and political subdivisions	35,363	41,361	37,655	37,412
Deposits of banks	8,646	10,388	11,909	9,786
Other deposits (certified and cashiers' checks, etc.)	2,405	2,235	3,470	2,681
Total deposits	*317,635*	*325,635*	*358,532*	*374,340*
Demand deposits	*216,344*	*217,156*	*242,897*	*253,029*
Time deposits	*101,291*	*108,479*	*115,635*	*121,311*
Bills payable, rediscounts, and other liabilities for borrowed money	1,000	1,000		
Income collected but not earned	1,873	2,209	2,467	} 4,981
Expenses accrued and unpaid	2,520	1,703	1,942	
Other liabilities	3	22	14	
Total liabilities	323,031	330,569	362,955	379,321
CAPITAL ACCOUNTS				
Capital stock: Common stock	6,548	6,798	6,923	6,998
Surplus	10,660	10,920	11,120	11,795
Undivided profits	5,661	5,573	5,961	5,285
Reserves	676	647	672	595
Total capital accounts	23,545	23,938	24,676	24,673
Total liabilities and capital accounts	346,576	354,507	387,631	403,994
MEMORANDUM				
Assets pledged or assigned to secure liabilities and for other purposes	63,300	61,805	63,162	72,710

Assets and liabilities of national banks, by States, at date of each call during year ended Dec. 31, 1958—Continued

TENNESSEE

[In thousands of dollars]

	Mar. 4, 1958	June 23, 1958	Sept. 24, 1958	Dec. 31, 1958
	74 banks	75 banks	75 banks	75 banks
ASSETS				
Loans and discounts (including overdrafts)	893,766	887,925	903,279	959,678
U.S. Government securities, direct obligations	504,109	552,840	562,025	573,264
Obligations guaranteed by U.S. Government	3	232	232	82
Obligations of States and political subdivisions	113,018	125,847	124,077	136,809
Other bonds, notes, and debentures	26,153	33,542	28,734	25,529
Corporate stocks, including stock of Federal Reserve bank	3,833	3,864	4,095	4,062
Reserve with Federal Reserve bank	194,139	198,619	202,838	187,024
Currency and coin	30,069	36,415	37,264	41,317
Balances with other banks, and cash items in process of collection	266,559	256,602	244,893	353,709
Bank premises owned, furniture and fixtures	23,180	23,886	24,252	23,976
Real estate owned other than bank premises	325	215	211	209
Customers' liability on acceptances outstanding	11,450	4,114	3,596	11,852
Income earned or accrued but not collected	2,944	3,608	3,520	} 5,475
Other assets	2,138	2,210	1,512	
Total assets	2,071,686	2,129,919	2,140,528	2,322,986
LIABILITIES				
Demand deposits of individuals, partnerships, and corporations	855,467	848,316	876,764	990,651
Time deposits of individuals, partnerships, and corporations	502,642	527,841	550,792	559,037
Postal savings deposits	164	164	164	165
Deposits of U.S. Government	31,170	77,464	41,391	35,619
Deposits of States and political subdivisions	160,338	178,671	160,517	143,983
Deposits of banks	320,973	283,250	293,495	381,233
Other deposits (certified and cashiers' checks, etc.)	11,852	17,906	12,398	13,662
Total deposits	*1,882,606*	*1,933,612*	*1,935,521*	*2,124,350*
Demand deposits	*1,353,868*	*1,376,341*	*1,349,588*	*1,533,298*
Time deposits	*528,738*	*557,271*	*585,933*	*591,052*
Bills payable, rediscounts, and other liabilities for borrowed money	-----------	10,400	13,840	-----------
Mortgages or other liens on bank premises and other real estate	45	45	45	53
Acceptances executed by or for account of reporting banks and outstanding	11,450	4,114	3,596	11,852
Income collected but not earned	11,180	11,502	11,798	} 22,430
Expenses accrued and unpaid	10,365	9,205	10,504	
Other liabilities	942	1,103	1,532	
Total liabilities	1,916,588	1,969,981	1,976,836	2,158,685
CAPITAL ACCOUNTS				
Capital stock: Common stock	45,155	45,355	47,480	47,530
Surplus	77,555	78,332	83,922	84,246
Undivided profits	28,847	32,970	28,734	28,396
Reserves	3,541	3,281	3,556	4,129
Total capital accounts	155,098	159,938	163,692	164,301
Total liabilities and capital accounts	2,071,686	2,129,919	2,140,528	2,322,986
MEMORANDUM				
Assets pledged or assigned to secure liabilities and for other purposes	240,822	269,856	261,790	234,267

Assets and liabilities of national banks, by States, at date of each call during year ended Dec. 31, 1958—Continued

TEXAS

[In thousands of dollars]

	Mar. 4, 1958	June 23, 1958	Sept. 24, 1958	Dec. 31, 1958
	457 banks	457 banks	456 banks	458 banks
ASSETS				
Loans and discounts (including overdrafts)	3,561,223	3,633,059	3,670,998	3,934,359
U.S. Government securities, direct obligations	1,920,931	2,206,695	2,237,516	2,285,940
Obligations guaranteed by U.S. Government		6	6	
Obligations of States and political subdivisions	398,668	448,285	474,958	511,789
Other bonds, notes, and debentures	125,056	142,310	137,286	140,498
Corporate stocks, including stock of Federal Reserve bank	16,998	17,235	17,367	17,905
Reserve with Federal Reserve bank	806,795	816,148	816,176	831,870
Currency and coin	95,532	100,707	112,551	112,699
Balances with other banks, and cash items in process of collection	1,310,192	1,402,179	1,358,574	1,802,492
Bank premises owned, furniture and fixtures	145,883	150,113	157,216	158,630
Real estate owned other than bank premises	9,016	8,847	9,123	6,876
Investments and other assets indirectly representing bank premises or other real estate	8,683	8,616	8,585	8,525
Customers' liability on acceptances outstanding	52,337	24,210	30,876	51,066
Income earned or accrued but not collected	13,309	15,338	15,048	} 25,088
Other assets	6,950	8,029	7,733	
Total assets	8,471,573	8,981,777	9,054,013	9,887,737
LIABILITIES				
Demand deposits of individuals, partnerships, and corporations	4,565,482	4,645,923	4,775,114	5,187,184
Time deposits of individuals, partnerships, and corporations	1,160,308	1,367,846	1,424,217	1,412,093
Postal savings deposits	1,143	1,143	1,143	1,143
Deposits of U.S. Government	127,128	242,462	148,938	149,959
Deposits of States and political subdivisions	708,286	726,253	629,428	772,457
Deposits of banks	1,010,301	1,113,142	1,167,149	1,378,441
Other deposits (certified and cashiers' checks, etc.)	70,420	81,069	71,094	148,305
Total deposits	*7,643,068*	*8,177,838*	*8,217,083*	*9,049,680*
Demand deposits	*6,186,696*	*6,446,446*	*6,445,998*	*7,307,786*
Time deposits	*1,456,372*	*1,731,392*	*1,771,085*	*1,741,794*
Bills payable, rediscounts, and other liabilities for borrowed money	16,591	3,400	17,500	
Mortgages or other liens on bank premises and other real estate	123	124	198	269
Acceptances executed by or for account of reporting banks and outstanding	52,975	24,222	31,488	53,270
Income collected but not earned	15,192	16,299	17,170	
Expenses accrued and unpaid	40,394	35,930	39,664	} 57,003
Other liabilities	2,021	5,438	4,437	
Total liabilities	7,770,364	8,263,251	8,327,540	9,160,122
CAPITAL ACCOUNTS				
Capital stock: Common stock	260,316	263,546	264,506	267,826
Surplus	306,174	310,586	313,896	329,906
Undivided profits	111,280	123,608	125,488	101,062
Reserves	23,439	20,786	22,583	28,821
Total capital accounts	701,209	718,526	726,473	727,615
Total liabilities and capital accounts	8,471,573	8,981,777	9,054,013	9,887,737
MEMORANDUM				
Assets pledged or assigned to secure liabilities and for other purposes	1,269,079	1,394,763	1,334,338	1,400,760

Assets and liabilities of national banks, by States, at date of each call during year ended Dec. 31, 1958—Continued

UTAH

(In thousands of dollars)

	Mar. 4, 1958	June 23, 1958	Sept. 24, 1958	Dec. 31, 1958
	7 banks	7 banks	7 banks	7 banks
ASSETS				
Loans and discounts (including overdrafts)	205, 876	210, 066	221, 495	229, 704
U. S. Government securities, direct obligations	96, 261	106, 012	109, 365	111, 984
Obligations guaranteed by U. S. Government				
Obligations of States and political subdivisions	31, 827	31, 486	38, 463	36, 478
Other bonds, notes, and debentures	5, 815	8, 112	4, 444	3, 659
Corporate stocks, including stock of Federal Reserve bank	779	781	783	843
Reserve with Federal Reserve bank	48, 522	36, 579	39, 016	38, 692
Currency and coin	4, 129	4, 816	5, 235	5, 148
Balances with other banks, and cash items in process of collection	28, 524	31, 586	31, 159	43, 414
Bank premises owned, furniture and fixtures	1, 308	1, 328	1, 312	1, 255
Real estate owned other than bank premises	22	72	22	22
Investments and other assets indirectly representing bank premises or other real estate	5, 850	6, 000	6, 000	6, 000
Customers' liability on acceptances outstanding	80	80		
Income earned or accrued but not collected	49	113	79	} 405
Other assets	539	287	228	
Total assets	429, 581	437, 318	457, 601	477, 604
LIABILITIES				
Demand deposits of individuals, partnerships, and corporations	171, 157	173, 024	187, 808	194, 176
Time deposits of individuals, partnerships, and corporations	144, 150	153, 486	163, 011	166, 203
Postal savings deposits	744	744	670	670
Deposits of U. S. Government	12, 573	11, 884	8, 712	8, 124
Deposits of States and political subdivisions	43, 626	35, 402	31, 871	46, 790
Deposits of banks	14, 145	13, 000	15, 563	15, 717
Other deposits (certified and cashiers' checks, etc.)	3, 505	2, 903	3, 292	5, 147
Total deposits	*389, 900*	*390, 443*	*410, 927*	*436, 827*
Demand deposits	*228, 849*	*219, 830*	*230, 256*	*252, 102*
Time deposits	*161, 051*	*170, 613*	*180, 671*	*184, 725*
Bills payable, rediscounts, and other liabilities for borrowed money		7, 000	6, 000	
Acceptances executed by or for account of reporting banks and outstanding	80	80		
Income collected but not earned	3, 277	3, 424	3, 482	} 6, 633
Expenses accrued and unpaid	3, 890	2, 526	2, 669	
Other liabilities	712	353	521	
Total liabilities	397, 859	403, 826	423, 599	443, 460
CAPITAL ACCOUNTS				
Capital stock: Common stock	9, 950	9, 950	9, 950	9, 950
Surplus	15, 430	15, 430	15, 490	17, 500
Undivided profits	5, 629	6, 870	6, 922	5, 058
Reserves	713	1, 242	1, 640	1, 636
Total capital accounts	31, 722	33, 492	34, 002	34, 144
Total liabilities and capital accounts	429, 581	437, 318	457, 601	477, 604
MEMORANDUM				
Assets pledged or assigned to secure liabilities and for other purposes	19, 467	23, 682	22, 294	20, 437

Assets and liabilities of national banks, by States, at date of each call during year ended Dec. 31, 1958—Continued

VERMONT

[In thousands of dollars]

	Mar. 4, 1958	June 23, 1958	Sept. 24, 1958	Dec. 31, 1958
	32 banks	32 banks	32 banks	32 banks
ASSETS				
Loans and discounts (including overdrafts)	81,561	87,169	107,232	107,652
U. S. Government securities, direct obligations	49,099	46,714	58,038	58,550
Obligations guaranteed by U. S. Government	5	5	5	16
Obligations of States and political subdivisions	10,594	12,632	13,554	11,945
Other bonds, notes, and debentures	3,249	3,226	3,258	3,775
Corporate stocks, including stock of Federal Reserve bank	351	358	417	417
Reserve with Federal Reserve bank	12,699	11,160	15,117	15,055
Currency and coin	3,104	3,407	3,998	3,719
Balances with other banks, and cash items in process of collection	13,273	13,605	13,538	15,592
Bank premises owned, furniture and fixtures	1,999	2,181	2,398	2,364
Real estate owned other than bank premises	139	137	86	81
Investments and other assets indirectly representing bank premises or other real estate	508	508	602	598
Income earned or accrued but not collected	213	171	370}	489
Other assets	148	112	130}	
Total assets	176,942	181,385	218,743	220,253
LIABILITIES				
Demand deposits of individuals, partnerships, and corporations	59,574	59,749	65,195	64,327
Time deposits of individuals, partnerships, and corporations	87,017	89,262	118,686	119,416
Postal savings deposits	3	3	3	3
Deposits of U. S. Government	2,005	2,966	2,262	2,371
Deposits of States and political subdivisions	5,412	3,916	5,801	8,044
Deposits of banks	1,722	2,098	1,425	1,262
Other deposits (certified and cashiers' checks, etc.)	1,889	2,394	2,524	2,597
Total deposits	*157,622*	*160,388*	*195,896*	*198,020*
Demand deposits	*70,062*	*70,670*	*76,553*	*77,766*
Time deposits	*87,560*	*89,718*	*119,343*	*120,254*
Bills payable, rediscounts, and other liabilities for borrowed money	250	510	200	----------
Income collected but not earned	1,095	1,211	1,295}	
Expenses accrued and unpaid	527	279	668}	2,900
Other liabilities	531	1,220	951}	
Total liabilities	160,025	163,608	199,010	200,920
CAPITAL ACCOUNTS				
Capital stock:				
Preferred stock	----------	----------	800	800
Common stock	5,195	5,295	5,945	5,945
Total capital stock	*5,195*	*5,295*	*6,745*	*6,745*
Surplus	6,617	6,648	7,162	7,237
Undivided profits	3,926	4,562	4,480	3,973
Reserves and retirement account for preferred stock	1,179	1,272	1,346	1,378
Total capital accounts	16,917	17,777	19,733	19,333
Total liabilities and capital accounts	176,942	181,385	218,743	220,253
MEMORANDUM				
Assets pledged or assigned to secure liabilities and for other purposes	7,967	8,860	9,938	8,708

Assets and liabilities of national banks, by States, at date of each call during year ended Dec. 31, 1958—Continued

VIRGINIA

[In thousands of dollars]

	Mar. 4, 1958	June 23, 1958	Sept. 24, 1958	Dec. 31, 1958
	133 banks	133 banks	131 banks	131 banks
ASSETS				
Loans and discounts (including overdrafts)	757,674	799,695	804,476	817,199
U. S. Government securities, direct obligations	473,327	504,789	511,098	544,628
Obligations guaranteed by U. S. Government	36	37	23	23
Obligations of States and political subdivisions	113,216	117,346	122,683	125,022
Other bonds, notes, and debentures	41,805	37,393	45,249	43,982
Corporate stocks, including stock of Federal Reserve bank	3,494	3,522	3,586	3,642
Reserve with Federal Reserve bank	158,730	173,830	136,144	143,370
Currency and coin	32,425	37,258	37,804	37,863
Balances with other banks, and cash items in process of collection	168,778	181,983	177,987	228,500
Bank premises owned, furniture and fixtures	23,565	24,305	25,029	24,796
Real estate owned other than bank premises	743	787	713	847
Investments and other assets indirectly representing bank premises or other real estate	1,453	1,547	1,547	1,620
Customers' liability on acceptances outstanding	144	104	260	238
Income earned or accrued but not collected	2,084	1,920	2,081	} 3,976
Other assets	1,968	1,888	1,776	
Total assets	1,779,442	1,886,404	1,870,456	1,975,706
LIABILITIES				
Demand deposits of individuals, partnerships, and corporations	795,149	788,538	822,909	854,611
Time deposits of individuals, partnerships, and corporations	540,296	558,682	585,214	597,001
Postal savings deposits	110	111	110	111
Deposits of U. S. Government	38,853	82,880	51,548	53,089
Deposits of States and political subdivisions	105,667	147,337	105,384	124,029
Deposits of banks	105,926	104,214	100,829	140,616
Other deposits (certified and cashiers' checks, etc.)	16,905	33,608	21,822	33,679
Total deposits	*1,602,906*	*1,715,370*	*1,687,816*	*1,803,136*
Demand deposits	*1,013,714*	*1,097,442*	*1,040,475*	*1,143,161*
Time deposits	*589,192*	*617,928*	*647,341*	*659,975*
Bills payable, rediscounts, and other liabilities for borrowed money	9,390	3,125	9,350	875
Mortgages or other liens on bank premises and other real estate	39	34	34	52
Acceptances executed by or for account of reporting banks and outstanding	144	104	260	238
Income collected but not earned	7,335	7,850	8,018	} 16,815
Expenses accrued and unpaid	9,911	5,515	7,653	
Other liabilities	179	1,616	608	
Total liabilities	1,629,904	1,733,614	1,713,739	1,821,116
CAPITAL ACCOUNTS				
Capital stock: Common stock	42,198	42,404	43,371	43,571
Surplus	74,330	75,229	76,391	78,967
Undivided profits	28,994	31,451	32,964	27,538
Reserves	4,016	3,706	3,991	4,514
Total capital accounts	149,538	152,790	156,717	154,590
Total liabilities and capital accounts	1,779,442	1,886,404	1,870,456	1,975,706
MEMORANDUM				
Assets pledged or assigned to secure liabilities and for other purposes	271,492	309,360	304,413	315,125

Assets and liabilities of national banks, by States, at date of each call during year ended Dec. 31, 1958—Continued

VIRGIN ISLANDS OF THE UNITED STATES

[In thousands of dollars]

	Mar. 4, 1958	June 23, 1958	Sept. 24, 1958	Dec. 31, 1958
	1 bank	1 bank	1 bank	1 bank
ASSETS				
Loans and discounts (including overdrafts)	3,868	4,232	4,557	4,914
U. S. Government securities, direct obligations	7,048	6,448	5,328	6,011
Obligations guaranteed by U. S. Government				
Obligations of States and political subdivisions				947
Other bonds, notes, and debentures	2	2	761	2
Corporate stocks, including stock of Federal Reserve bank	13	13	13	13
Reserve with Federal Reserve bank	953	900	872	1,106
Currency and coin	564	416	439	534
Balances with other banks, and cash items in process of collection	1,091	485	500	1,167
Bank premises owned, furniture and fixtures	11	11	9	25
Real estate owned other than bank premises	15	15	41	41
Income earned or accrued but not collected	18	2	11	161
Other assets	13	20	22	
Total assets	13,596	12,544	12,553	14,921
LIABILITIES				
Demand deposits of individuals, partnerships, and corporations	3,449	2,964	3,023	3,501
Time deposits of individuals, partnerships, and corporations	4,955	5,201	5,333	5,434
Postal savings deposits				
Deposits of U. S. Government	130	101	153	155
Deposits of States and political subdivisions	4,183	3,345	3,089	4,826
Deposits of banks	30	58	39	32
Other deposits (certified and cashiers' checks, etc.)	73	53	42	67
Total deposits	*12,820*	*11,722*	*11,679*	*14,015*
Demand deposits	*5,437*	*4,582*	*4,460*	*6,693*
Time deposits	*7,383*	*7,140*	*7,219*	*7,322*
Bills payable, rediscounts, and other liabilities for borrowed money				
Income collected but not earned	55	54	57	197
Expenses accrued and unpaid	50	8	58	
Other liabilities	56	87	124	
Total liabilities	12,981	11,871	11,918	14,212
CAPITAL ACCOUNTS				
Capital stock: Common stock	225	225	225	250
Surplus	225	225	225	250
Undivided profits	115	173	105	129
Reserves	50	50	80	80
Total capital accounts	615	673	635	709
Total liabilities and capital accounts	13,596	12,544	12,553	14,921
MEMORANDUM				
Assets pledged or assigned to secure liabilities and for other purposes	4,629	3,835	3,789	5,316

Assets and liabilities of national banks, by States, at date of each call during year ended Dec. 31, 1958—Continued

WASHINGTON

[In thousands of dollars]

	Mar. 4, 1958	June 23, 1958	Sept. 24, 1958	Dec. 31, 1958
	25 banks	25 banks	25 banks	25 banks
ASSETS				
Loans and discounts (including overdrafts)	1,022,388	1,064,640	1,082,033	1,090,842
U. S. Government securities, direct obligations	571,191	628,839	672,365	685,593
Obligations guaranteed by U. S. Government	6	5	10	
Obligations of States and political subdivisions	158,747	177,942	182,175	185,653
Other bonds, notes, and debentures	60,170	41,892	36,789	34,947
Corporate stocks, including stock of Federal Reserve bank	3,914	3,917	3,959	3,961
Reserve with Federal Reserve bank	247,263	226,901	244,210	232,160
Currency and coin	23,732	29,902	30,965	30,985
Balances with other banks, and cash items in process of collection	206,804	201,860	206,870	235,272
Bank premises owned, furniture and fixtures	33,405	34,186	36,546	35,812
Real estate owned other than bank premises	823	836	741	720
Investments and other assets indirectly representing bank premises or other real estate	497	486	508	480
Customers' liability on acceptances outstanding	707	496	992	1,062
Income earned or accrued but not collected	6,264	7,568	7,673	} 10,108
Other assets	1,848	3,175	2,120	
Total assets	2,337,759	2,422,645	2,507,956	2,547,595
LIABILITIES				
Demand deposits of individuals, partnerships, and corporations	1,163,058	1,165,884	1,231,000	1,312,007
Time deposits of individuals, partnerships, and corporations	672,127	693,222	717,007	731,500
Postal savings deposits	10	10	10	10
Deposits of U. S. Government	43,072	83,327	56,227	44,070
Deposits of States and political subdivisions	160,002	161,240	142,653	153,199
Deposits of banks	68,513	76,375	82,004	77,689
Other deposits (certified and cashiers' checks, etc.)	22,508	17,701	18,909	17,487
Total deposits	*2,129,290*	*2,197,759*	*2,247,810*	*2,335,962*
Demand deposits	*1,447,780*	*1,495,048*	*1,519,965*	*1,592,586*
Time deposits	*681,510*	*702,711*	*727,845*	*743,376*
Bills payable, rediscounts, and other liabilities for borrowed money	200	12,000	46,276	
Mortgages or other liens on bank premises and other real estate	24	16	16	16
Acceptances executed by or for account of reporting banks and outstanding	707	496	992	1,062
Income collected but not earned	13,776	14,497	15,392	} 30,739
Expenses accrued and unpaid	17,533	16,669	15,620	
Other liabilities	4,157	3,220	3,227	
Total liabilities	2,165,687	2,244,657	2,329,333	2,367,779
CAPITAL ACCOUNTS				
Capital stock: Common stock	52,450	53,500	53,500	53,500
Surplus	78,005	78,155	78,475	78,525
Undivided profits	40,681	45,250	45,182	46,092
Reserves	936	1,083	1,466	1,699
Total capital accounts	172,072	177,988	178,623	179,816
Total liabilities and capital accounts	2,337,759	2,422,645	2,507,956	2,547,595
MEMORANDUM				
Assets pledged or assigned to secure liabilities and for other purposes	384,735	424,191	400,540	412,453

Assets and liabilities of national banks, by States, at date of each call during year ended Dec. 31, 1958—Continued

WEST VIRGINIA

[In thousands of dollars]

	Mar. 4, 1958	June 23, 1958	Sept. 24, 1958	Dec. 31, 1958
	77 banks	77 banks	77 banks	77 banks
ASSETS				
Loans and discounts (including overdrafts)	229, 405	232, 703	235, 426	240, 504
U. S. Government securities, direct obligations	261, 686	272, 570	267, 067	272, 902
Obligations guaranteed by U. S. Government				
Obligations of States and political subdivisions	31, 307	33, 087	34, 374	36, 134
Other bonds, notes, and debentures	10, 961	8, 988	8, 515	8, 464
Corporate stocks, including stock of Federal Reserve bank	1, 477	1, 478	1, 481	1, 500
Reserve with Federal Reserve bank	60, 148	52, 441	56, 599	61, 172
Currency and coin	14, 583	18, 437	18, 943	17, 707
Balances with other banks, and cash items in process of collection	72, 301	67, 695	64, 329	81, 348
Bank premises owned, furniture and fixtures	7, 144	7, 417	7, 562	7, 442
Real estate owned other than bank premises	370	365	120	119
Investments and other assets indirectly representing bank premises or other real estate			367	367
Income earned or accrued but not collected	360	285	265	} 2, 347
Other assets	1, 220	1, 464	1, 695	
Total assets	690, 962	696, 930	696, 743	730, 006
LIABILITIES				
Demand deposits of individuals, partnerships, and corporations	329, 098	326, 041	327, 847	347, 766
Time deposits of individuals, partnerships, and corporations	186, 250	191, 341	193, 350	193, 611
Postal savings deposits	171	171	171	171
Deposits of U. S. Government	13, 323	23, 144	11, 919	12, 650
Deposits of States and political subdivisions	54, 448	51, 538	53, 344	60, 284
Deposits of banks	30, 546	24, 796	25, 607	35, 435
Other deposits (certified and cashiers' checks, etc.)	7, 650	6, 765	8, 723	9, 109
Total deposits	*621, 486*	*623, 796*	*620, 961*	*659, 026*
Demand deposits	*433, 330*	*430, 405*	*425, 419*	*463, 399*
Time deposits	*188, 156*	*193, 391*	*195, 542*	*195, 627*
Bills payable, rediscounts, and other liabilities for borrowed money	450	3, 250	3, 960	250
Income collected but not earned	1, 570	1, 822	2, 076	} 4, 293
Expenses accrued and unpaid	2, 543	1, 464	1, 721	
Other liabilities	379	733	349	
Total liabilities	626, 428	631, 065	629, 067	663, 569
CAPITAL ACCOUNTS				
Capital stock: Common stock	17, 296	17, 346	17, 346	17, 346
Surplus	31, 607	31, 572	31, 940	32, 965
Undivided profits	12, 855	14, 199	15, 473	12, 755
Reserves	2, 776	2, 748	2, 917	3, 371
Total capital accounts	64, 534	65, 865	67, 676	66, 437
Total liabilities and capital accounts	690, 962	696, 930	696, 743	730, 006
MEMORANDUM				
Assets pledged or assigned to secure liabilities and for other purposes	105, 983	119, 392	120, 606	123, 145

Assets and liabilities of national banks, by States, at date of each call during year ended Dec. 31, 1958—Continued

WISCONSIN

[In thousands of dollars]

	Mar. 4, 1958	June 23, 1958	Sept. 24, 1958	Dec. 31, 1958
	96 banks	97 banks	97 banks	97 banks
ASSETS				
Loans and discounts (including overdrafts)	755, 719	793, 264	732, 244	769, 994
U. S. Government securities, direct obligations	602, 949	649, 683	719, 221	718, 644
Obligations guaranteed by U. S. Government	7	12	5	5
Obligations of States and political subdivisions	91, 089	94, 869	99, 662	105, 153
Other bonds, notes, and debentures	49, 287	48, 728	43, 415	42, 164
Corporate stocks, including stock of Federal Reserve bank	3, 145	3, 161	3, 178	3, 232
Reserve with Federal Reserve bank	165, 806	169, 822	184, 388	201, 783
Currency and coin	20, 725	25, 225	25, 633	27, 347
Balances with other banks, and cash items in process of collection	205, 673	203, 435	180, 890	236, 312
Bank premises owned, furniture and fixtures	15, 770	17, 703	18, 355	18, 003
Real estate owned other than bank premises	388	625	622	689
Investments and other assets indirectly representing bank premises or other real estate	37	37		
Customers' liability on acceptances outstanding	57	57	99	58
Income earned or accrued but not collected	4, 288	3, 947	4, 756	} 8, 250
Other assets	4, 542	3, 800	2, 970	
Total assets	1, 919, 482	2, 014, 368	2, 015, 438	2, 131, 634
LIABILITIES				
Demand deposits of individuals, partnerships, and corporations	848, 088	861, 623	872, 724	1, 002, 206
Time deposits of individuals, partnerships, and corporations	588, 223	622, 118	641, 850	653, 073
Postal savings deposits	957	957	957	957
Deposits of U. S. Government	37, 471	104, 556	54, 774	50, 866
Deposits of States and political subdivisions	109, 991	87, 773	84, 496	79, 689
Deposits of banks	169, 667	144, 062	151, 822	151, 450
Other deposits (certified and cashiers' checks, etc.)	14, 916	28, 626	22, 557	36, 943
Total deposits	*1, 769, 313*	*1, 849, 715*	*1, 829, 180*	*1, 975, 184*
Demand deposits	*1, 171, 876*	*1, 209, 371*	*1, 167, 709*	*1, 309, 170*
Time deposits	*597, 437*	*640, 344*	*661, 471*	*666, 014*
Bills payable, rediscounts, and other liabilities for borrowed money	300	11, 000	26, 250	
Mortgages or other liens on bank premises and other real estate	32	32	26	26
Acceptances executed by or for account of reporting banks and outstanding	57	57	99	58
Income collected but not earned	6, 260	6, 491	6, 916	} 18, 386
Expenses accrued and unpaid	9, 669	7, 105	10, 304	
Other liabilities	2, 501	3, 037	2, 291	
Total liabilities	1, 788, 132	1, 877, 437	1, 875, 066	1, 993, 654
CAPITAL ACCOUNTS				
Capital stock:				
Preferred stock	50	50	50	50
Common stock	35, 880	36, 180	36, 355	36, 705
Total capital stock	*35, 930*	*36, 230*	*36, 405*	*36, 755*
Surplus	68, 575	68, 850	69, 700	72, 070
Undivided profits	22, 806	28, 305	29, 933	24, 033
Reserves and retirement account for preferred stock	4, 039	3, 546	4, 334	5, 122
Total capital accounts	131, 350	136, 931	140, 372	137, 980
Total liabilities and capital accounts	1, 919, 482	2, 014, 368	2, 015, 438	2, 131, 634
MEMORANDUM				
Assets pledged or assigned to secure liabilities and for other purposes	136, 086	175, 384	199, 101	150, 254

Assets and liabilities of national banks, by States, at date of each call during year ended Dec. 31, 1958—Continued

WYOMING

[In thousands of dollars]

	Mar. 4, 1958	June 23, 1958	Sept. 24, 1958	Dec. 31, 1958
	25 banks	24 banks	25 banks	25 banks
ASSETS				
Loans and discounts (including overdrafts)	96,970	104,487	108,403	108,811
U.S. Government securities, direct obligations	93,830	91,532	92,947	108,968
Obligations guaranteed by U.S. Government				
Obligations of States and political subdivisions	11,821	12,224	13,514	14,219
Other bonds, notes, and debentures	4,887	5,103	5,150	5,640
Corporate stocks, including stock of Federal Reserve bank	404	399	420	423
Reserve with Federal Reserve bank	23,274	20,831	23,550	24,567
Currency and coin	3,442	4,265	4,934	4,480
Balances with other banks, and cash items in process of collection	27,106	25,967	32,854	41,445
Bank premises owned, furniture and fixtures	2,076	3,157	3,295	3,457
Real estate owned other than bank premises	184	637	172	96
Income earned or accrued but not collected	489	382	422	} 908
Other assets	1,493	409	372	
Total assets	265,976	269,393	286,033	313,014
LIABILITIES				
Demand deposits of individuals, partnerships, and corporations	126,572	123,016	135,307	147,831
Time deposits of individuals, partnerships, and corporations	65,549	68,519	72,558	76,235
Postal savings deposits	18	18	18	18
Deposits of U.S. Government	4,795	7,086	5,216	5,844
Deposits of States and political subdivisions	34,832	34,729	35,631	41,850
Deposits of banks	9,904	9,996	11,785	14,863
Other deposits (certified and cashiers' checks, etc.)	1,428	1,870	1,775	2,147
Total deposits	*243,098*	*245,234*	*262,290*	*288,788*
Demand deposits	*171,995*	*169,418*	*182,325*	*205,518*
Time deposits	*71,103*	*75,816*	*79,965*	*83,270*
Bills payable, rediscounts, and other liabilities for borrowed money	1,085	1,800	100	400
Income collected but not earned	1,566	1,761	1,873	} 2,831
Expenses accrued and unpaid	1,025	998	965	
Other liabilities	18	54	51	
Total liabilities	246,792	249,847	265,279	292,019
CAPITAL ACCOUNTS				
Capital stock: Common stock	3,288	3,413	3,463	3,528
Surplus	9,727	9,402	10,052	10,402
Undivided profits	5,132	5,912	6,415	5,909
Reserves	1,037	819	824	1,156
Total capital accounts	19,184	19,546	20,754	20,995
Total liabilities and capital accounts	265,976	269,393	286,033	313,014
MEMORANDUM				
Assets pledged or assigned to secure liabilities and for other purposes	56,288	57,100	56,222	58,695

TABLE No. 17.—*Fiduciary activities of national banks as of Dec. 31, 1958*

	Banks with capital stock of—						
	$25,000	$25,001 to $50,000	$50,001 to $100,000	$100,001 to $200,000	$200,001 to $500,000	$500,001 and over	Total
Number of national banks with trust powers but not administering trusts	6	34	75	68	54	11	248
Number of national banks with trust powers administering trusts	6	33	169	340	412	517	1,477
Total number of national banks authorized to exercise trust powers	12	67	244	408	466	528	¹1,725
Total assets of national banks with trust powers but not administering trusts	$10,865,409	$109,558,488	$353,387,923	$615,539,521	$788,212,748	$1,375,294,130	$3,252,858,219
Total assets of national banks with trust powers administering trusts	11,710,916	108,089,058	1,073,342,846	2,988,207,613	7,173,910,315	95,744,782,295	107,100,043,043
Total assets of national banks authorized to exercise trust powers	22,576,325	217,647,546	1,426,730,769	3,603,747,134	7,962,123,063	97,120,076,425	110,352,901,262
TRUST DEPARTMENT ASSETS							
Investments	119,478	3,235,271	49,568,014	242,721,274	933,324,250	31,551,005,004	32,779,973,291
Time deposits	15,160	206,002	1,714,761	9,040,582	25,047,681	656,463,109	692,487,295
Demand deposits	20,205	357,633	5,942,600	29,125,201	77,281,946	1,025,777,537	1,138,505,122
Other assets		50,004	2,524,700	20,650,478	135,028,897	12,012,403,169	12,170,657,248
Total	154,843	3,848,910	59,750,075	301,537,535	1,170,682,774	45,245,648,819	46,781,622,956
TRUST DEPARTMENT LIABILITIES							
Private trusts	51,659	443,493	12,314,659	79,500,842	432,277,863	11,218,722,787	11,743,311,303
Court trusts	103,079	2,516,190	36,419,513	150,771,833	420,379,508	5,584,120,583	6,194,310,701
Other liabilities:							
Agency, escrow, custodian, etc., accounts		634,231	7,179,612	48,342,569	259,449,976	24,663,193,976	24,978,800,364
Corporate accounts		247,198	2,739,593	20,525,478	41,896,318	3,559,744,401	3,625,152,988
Miscellaneous	105	7,798	1,096,698	2,396,813	16,679,114	219,867,072	240,047,600
Total	154,843	3,848,910	59,750,075	301,537,535	1,170,682,774	45,245,648,819	46,781,622,956
Total volume of bond issues outstanding for which banks are acting as trustee	46,000	1,319,500	11,653,676	242,062,737	273,585,419	24,224,068,199	24,762,735,531

¹ Includes 27 banks which have been granted only certain specific fiduciary powers.

TABLE No. 17.—*Fiduciary activities of national banks as of Dec. 31, 1958*—Continued

	Banks with capital stock of—						
	$25,000	$25,001 to $50,000	$50,001 to $100,000	$100,001 to $200,000	$200,001 to $500,000	$500,001 and over	Total
TRUST DEPARTMENT LIABILITIES—continued							
Number of national banks administering personal accounts:							
Voluntary, private or living trusts	4	15	123	283	373	505	1,303
Court accounts	5	29	143	298	370	504	1,349
Agencies, escrows, custodianships, etc		5	49	155	276	479	964
Number of national banks administering corporate accounts:							
Bond or debenture issues	1	4	37	112	176	394	724
Paying agencies		2	10	23	93	320	448
Depositories and other miscellaneous corporate accounts			11	17	57	224	309
Number of national banks acting as transfer agent			2	11	38	255	306
Number of national banks acting as registrar			6	16	54	249	325
Number of personal accounts being administered:							
Voluntary, private or living trusts	6	51	845	3,564	14,325	131,305	150,096
Court accounts	13	154	2,160	7,883	17,404	93,079	120,693
Agencies, escrows, custodianships, etc		7	365	1,231	6,047	79,943	87,093
Total	19	212	3,370	12,678	37,776	304,327	358,382
Number of corporate accounts being administered:							
Bond or debenture issues	2	4	62	600	643	8,308	9,619
Paying agencies		2	19	147	398	24,532	25,098
Depositories and other miscellaneous corporate accounts			21	34	188	5,620	5,863
Total	2	6	102	781	1,229	38,460	40,580
Number of accounts for which national banks are acting as transfer agent			2	18	57	3,497	3,574
Number of accounts for which national banks are acting as registrar			6	23	87	3,259	3,375
Total number of accounts being administered	21	218	3,480	13,500	33,149	349,543	405,911

TABLE No. 18.—*Fiduciary activities of national banks by Federal Reserve districts as of Dec. 31, 1958*

Federal Reserve districts	Number of banks exercising fiduciary powers	Number with authority but not exercising fiduciary powers	Total number authorized to exercise fiduciary powers	Total banking assets of banks authorized to exercise fiduciary powers	Personal account liabilities — Living trusts	Personal account liabilities — Court accounts	Personal account liabilities — Agency, escrow, custodian, etc.	All other liabilities	Total liabilities
Boston	138	28	166	$5,903,219,439	$671,041,282	$723,959,740	$2,068,789,281	$131,179,347	$3,594,969,650
New York	164	22	186	14,374,074,966	648,704,951	544,988,551	1,386,508,475	416,714,442	2,996,916,419
Philadelphia	191	4	195	4,755,822,688	311,325,249	405,943,479	509,530,352	98,120,952	1,325,920,032
Cleveland	100	13	113	8,510,754,157	2,599,685,050	1,075,550,090	2,450,507,247	792,213,514	6,917,955,901
Richmond	136	26	162	5,233,009,597	513,111,880	425,200,907	1,213,102,129	90,439,559	2,241,854,475
Atlanta	121	26	147	8,118,823,915	690,898,602	504,497,813	1,609,468,310	274,032,404	3,078,897,129
Chicago	228	31	259	17,784,143,284	2,565,671,481	711,677,400	9,819,284,450	749,267,159	13,845,900,490
St. Louis	108	22	130	3,895,445,157	189,659,466	120,768,097	190,063,906	130,671,752	631,163,221
Minneapolis	49	14	63	2,894,032,065	270,235,986	184,348,933	1,565,414,553	397,207,649	2,417,207,121
Kansas City	105	33	138	5,830,665,861	613,863,782	218,929,831	1,725,456,153	214,618,810	2,772,868,576
Dallas	95	24	119	8,498,755,297	949,821,917	106,520,305	305,746,414	129,139,206	1,491,227,842
San Francisco	42	5	47	24,554,154,836	1,719,291,657	1,170,925,555	2,134,929,094	441,595,794	5,466,742,100
Total	1,477	248	[1] 1,725	110,352,901,262	11,743,311,303	6,194,310,701	24,978,800,364	3,865,200,558	46,781,622,956

Federal Reserve districts	Number of personal accounts — Living trusts	Number of personal accounts — Court accounts	Number of personal accounts — Agency, escrow, custodian, etc.	Number of corporate trust bond issue accounts being administered	Number of all other accounts being administered [2]	Total number of accounts being administered	Bond and debenture issues outstanding where bank acts as trustee	Common trust funds — Number of funds	Common trust funds — Ledger value of assets in cash	Trust department gross earnings for year ended Dec. 31, 1958
Boston	7,160	8,203	5,780	285	1,250	22,678	$727,280,446	13	$47,225,457	$11,006,000
New York	4,674	9,816	6,537	366	4,694	26,087	4,842,351,913	26	9,953,205	11,969,000
Philadelphia	9,294	17,556	2,451	595	521	30,417	448,645,657	46	36,478,130	4,882,000
Cleveland	12,330	14,783	5,988	1,118	2,647	36,866	3,000,059,680	17	85,488,785	17,161,000
Richmond	8,437	11,430	5,226	422	907	26,422	907,177,101	22	47,962,415	7,265,000
Atlanta	9,230	7,459	6,337	1,007	4,364	28,397	1,606,405,709	26	37,332,760	8,988,000
Chicago	56,060	16,676	21,115	1,951	9,899	105,701	6,973,612,164	15	38,675,068	31,279,000
St. Louis	3,207	4,251	1,342	1,738	1,842	12,380	856,965,914	4	6,550,286	2,498,000
Minneapolis	4,208	5,013	6,127	418	430	16,196	420,989,475	8	13,067,693	4,959,000
Kansas City	8,750	4,424	14,867	760	4,386	33,187	1,248,563,715	13	42,552,402	6,439,000
Dallas	8,505	3,161	2,165	437	4,356	18,624	967,304,637	10	28,218,445	7,509,000
San Francisco	18,241	17,921	9,658	522	2,614	48,956	2,753,406,120	18	125,230,216	27,518,000
Total	150,096	120,693	87,593	9,619	37,910	405,911	24,752,735,531	[3] 218	518,734,862	141,473,000

[1] Includes 27 banks which have been granted only certain specific fiduciary powers.
[2] Corporate paying agency, depository, registrar, transfer agency, etc.
[3] Includes 53 funds operated under Section 17(b) of Regulation F of the Board of Governors of the Federal Reserve System, with assets of $1,388,882.

TABLE No. 19.—*Classification of investments under administration by the active national bank trust departments, Dec. 31, 1958*

Trust department investments classified according to capital stock of banks administering trusts	Bonds	Per cent	Stocks	Per cent	Real-estate mortgages	Per cent	Real estate	Per cent	Miscellaneous	Per cent	Total investments
Banks with capital stock of $25,000	$89,148	74.61	$15,730	13.17			$600	0.50	$14,000	11.72	$119,478
Banks with capital stock of $25,001 to $50,000	1,296,407	40.07	1,131,478	34.97	$39,603	1.22	741,369	22.92	26,414	.82	3,235,271
Banks with capital stock of $50,001 to $100,000	17,489,917	35.29	20,825,190	42.01	4,288,416	8.65	4,963,321	10.01	2,001,170	4.04	49,568,014
Banks with capital stock of $100,001 to $200,000	85,172,339	35.09	100,612,865	41.45	26,009,909	10.72	22,546,660	9.29	8,379,501	3.45	242,721,274
Banks with capital stock of $200,001 to $500,000	277,604,280	29.74	461,240,654	49.42	74,675,771	8.00	67,651,951	7.25	52,151,594	5.59	933,324,250
Banks with capital stock of $500,001 and over	19,382,629,335	61.43	8,574,175,037	27.18	1,377,316,821	4.36	1,131,781,044	3.59	1,085,102,767	3.44	31,551,005,004
Total	19,764,281,426	60.29	9,158,000,954	27.94	1,482,330,520	4.52	1,227,684,945	3.75	1,147,675,446	3.50	32,779,973,291

TABLE No. 20.—*Fiduciary activities of national banks by States as of Dec. 31, 1958*

Location	Number of banks exercising fiduciary powers	Number with authority but not exercising fiduciary powers	Total number authorized to exercise fiduciary powers	Total banking assets of banks authorized to exercise fiduciary powers	Personal account liabilities			All other liabilities
					Living trusts	Court accounts	Agency, escrow, custodian, etc.	
Alabama	25	9	34	$1,284,768,324	$199,929,027	$63,627,381	$182,904,870	$28,548,589
Alaska	4		4	122,434,226	1,433,911	1,387,030		165,887
Arizona	2		2	886,493,334	(1)	(1)	(1)	(1)
Arkansas	20	3	23	506,486,021	51,868,171	14,235,852	11,155,591	8,640,539
California	13		13	17,722,206,869	1,138,406,280	992,845,672	1,592,772,246	368,757,141
Colorado	19	11	30	1,152,219,271	186,188,685	59,944,762	350,456,928	48,812,044
Connecticut	17	1	18	1,218,528,135	287,397,605	326,665,559	453,166,157	5,273,537
Delaware	4		4	26,214,595	437,352	2,651,107	60,423	5,273,684
District of Columbia	3		3	876,353,405	118,329,589	13,738,131	223,775,167	2,546,038
Florida	37	2	39	2,322,700,223	223,404,312	201,842,385	587,301,134	56,845,789
Georgia	17	6	23	1,495,176,640	116,549,257	149,220,298	307,038,734	126,717,673
Hawaii	3	1	4	259,374,298				204,037
Idaho	3	1	4	495,865,867	8,440,425	5,896,573	778,782	472,793,612
Illinois	103	16	119	10,119,126,616	1,712,429,344	167,853,418	8,330,009,749	95,146,803
Indiana	88	6	94	2,792,619,857	254,342,265	232,343,568	348,839,544	2,194,214
Iowa	35	15	50	937,683,731	38,561,456	46,499,401	39,626,591	5,073,304
Kansas	28	7	35	896,826,794	49,344,164	38,861,238	190,536,063	7,199,090
Kentucky	49	6	55	823,184,136	29,433,828	50,477,956	15,670,126	54,000,346
Louisiana	17	3	20	1,824,211,947	64,726,502	19,966,135	356,516,012	9,180,833
Maine	23	1	24	319,361,457	33,550,720	43,219,721	91,299,071	

Maryland	15	4	19	862,239,753	143,033,366	36,413,270	240,381,069	43,775,992
Massachusetts	63	15	78	3,785,674,637	313,417,251	267,469,331	1,421,455,692	112,964,183
Michigan	20	4	24	3,924,449,132	486,021,265	190,226,596	849,668,139	171,800,103
Minnesota	19	5	24	2,097,441,319	246,671,188	157,104,729	1,539,494,133	305,388,141
Mississippi	16	2	18	333,676,034	12,222,101	8,445,230	3,327,009	324,167
Missouri	24	7	31	2,120,334,087	206,994,458	44,787,218	586,698,048	91,861,348
Montana	8	2	10	249,356,295	5,937,540	1,887,243	6,753,080	1,255,983
Nebraska	9	7	16	817,901,899	52,633,519	48,123,073	251,260,089	10,927,946
Nevada	3	----	3	285,920,377	[2]92,444,071	[2]68,128,938	[2]196,228,562	[2]14,051,012
New Hampshire	21	10	31	248,441,080	13,515,307	21,618,010	24,597,649	418,403
New Jersey	96	14	110	3,657,896,623	143,001,386	279,809,874	1,018,431,848	37,035,275
New Mexico	6	4	10	375,782,445	23,862,631	6,935,100	18,468,821	2,785,678
New York	103	9	112	11,235,261,794	480,468,755	276,628,778	646,178,108	384,357,499
North Carolina	23	4	27	659,542,853	34,019,105	53,916,502	36,999,877	7,386,319
North Dakota	5	2	7	119,367,087	6,222,102	9,034,827	11,391,330	165,793
Ohio	42	6	48	4,570,036,080	849,330,092	409,733,728	883,213,838	383,290,285
Oklahoma	21	6	27	1,545,236,145	113,811,259	21,802,853	422,147,815	69,065,155
Oregon	3	1	4	1,862,300,345	153,127,969	36,015,101	198,056,733	6,233,996
Pennsylvania	175	5	180	7,423,373,512	2,017,248,034	976,154,003	1,776,532,894	499,697,813
Rhode Island	2	----	2	518,754,286	(3)	(3)	(3)	(3)
South Carolina	11	4	15	606,349,313	54,886,384	47,130,988	54,144,733	11,065,256
South Dakota	7	2	9	271,309,768	7,732,025	10,317,494	6,817,335	293,331
Tennessee	25	6	31	2,099,967,406	154,766,603	123,014,976	214,735,233	102,388,017
Texas	91	17	108	8,068,604,653	923,186,566	95,646,864	280,733,764	128,741,189
Utah	2	1	3	459,837,749	(1)	(1)	(1)	(1)
Vermont	17	1	18	176,285,244	[4]477,499,594	[4]226,160,244	[4]146,073,975	[4]4,305,683
Virginia	64	9	73	1,717,670,424	128,481,118	66,652,241	638,525,860	23,271,585
Washington	13	----	13	2,489,721,771	325,439,001	53,480,030	148,092,771	52,183,721
West Virginia	23	5	28	538,663,858	36,380,330	101,118,935	20,015,700	2,449,928
Wisconsin	31	6	37	926,790,398	116,431,754		272,999,832	15,040,743
Wyoming	13	1	14	252,878,549	9,753,686	5,014,130	24,468,639	575,884
Total	1,477	248	[5]1,725	110,352,901,262	11,743,311,303	6,194,310,701	24,978,800,364	3,865,200,588

See footnotes at end of table.

Table No. 20—*Fiduciary activities of national banks by States as of Dec. 31, 1958*—Continued

Location	Total liabilities	Number of personal accounts			Number of corporate trust bond issue accounts being administered	Number of all other accounts being administered [6]	Total number of accounts being administered	Bond and debenture issues outstanding where bank acts as trustee	Trust Department gross earnings for year ended Dec. 31, 1958
		Living trusts	Court accounts	Agency, escrow, custodian, etc.					
Alabama	$475,009,867	2,166	702	888	397	1,157	5,310	$223,848,510	$1,658,000
Alaska	2,986,828	24	25		10	4	63	1,092,680	48,000
Arizona	(1)	(1)	(1)	(1)	(1)	(1)	(1)	(1)	(1)
Arkansas	85,900,153	444	1,069	134	378	352	3,377	245,080,288	317,000
California	4,092,781,339	9,903	13,244	6,009	308	1,705	31,169	2,546,706,295	21,508,000
Colorado	645,402,419	2,735	2,138	2,139	297	392	7,701	245,399,660	2,012,000
Connecticut	1,072,502,858	2,414	4,100	2,604	40	476	9,634	78,214,437	4,378,000
Delaware	3,149,566	18	89	3			110		26,000
District of Columbia	358,408,925	1,348	180	675	36	105	2,344	231,114,800	995,000
Florida	1,069,393,620	2,931	2,557	2,073	175	380	8,116	536,328,019	3,354,000
Georgia	699,525,962	1,536	2,098	1,110	145	1,087	5,976	408,944,305	2,127,000
Hawaii	15,319,817	199	721	38	28	9	995	12,628,800	114,000
Idaho									
Illinois	10,683,086,123	47,395	7,650	13,554	1,139	8,560	78,298	6,016,698,337	21,396,000
Indiana	930,672,180	3,771	4,739	2,618	323	362	11,813	529,915,521	3,101,000
Iowa	126,881,662	866	856	697	62	55	2,536	15,362,716	750,000
Kansas	283,814,769	1,101	496	5,279	107	64	7,047	122,643,062	712,000
Kentucky	102,781,000	655	2,124	330	66	145	3,320	20,662,625	647,000
Louisiana	495,208,995	923	932	1,470	156	1,511	4,992	276,076,025	662,000
Maine	177,250,345	495	843	430	63	196	2,027	122,449,837	602,000
Maryland	463,603,697	1,687	925	949	44	157	3,762	215,327,940	1,335,000
Massachusetts	2,115,306,457	3,603	2,577	2,549	150	430	9,309	502,782,813	5,420,000
Michigan	1,697,716,103	3,252	2,391	2,845	97	771	9,356	327,095,380	4,987,000
Minnesota	2,338,638,141	3,431	3,809	5,404	337	396	13,377	310,935,649	4,620,000
Mississippi	24,318,507	379	247	48	15	39	728	3,021,850	118,000
Missouri	930,341,072	3,029	481	2,137	153	1,172	6,972	450,818,529	2,115,000
Montana	15,834,446	152	64	529	7	7	774	14,872,775	33,000
Nebraska	362,944,627	965	571	1,500	109	47	3,192	230,046,686	790,000
Nevada	[2] 369,852,583	[2] 1,525	[2] 1,602	[2] 1,297	[2] 53	[2] 422	[2] 4,899	[2] 44,930,727	[2] 1,468,000
New Hampshire	60,149,369	303	286	148	8	21	766	3,357,470	221,000
New Jersey	1,478,278,383	2,405	4,334	2,699	94	579	10,111	167,417,007	4,016,000
New Mexico	52,052,230	410	182	492	2	93	1,179	200,000	208,000
New York	1,787,633,140	2,445	6,130	3,640	295	4,188	16,698	4,712,556,922	7,849,000
North Carolina	132,321,803	831	2,359	265	212	47	3,714	170,113,917	702,000
North Dakota	26,814,052	334	393	58	41	6	832	92,678,801	107,000
Ohio	2,475,567,943	5,573	4,509	4,118	766	2,009	16,975	905,256,619	6,936,000
Oklahoma	626,827,082	944	376	1,774	151	2,781	6,026	601,653,695	1,203,000
Oregon	393,433,799	2,675	763	808	36	134	4,416	23,839,639	1,770,000
Pennsylvania	5,269,632,744	14,990	25,197	3,708	888	1,028	45,811	2,502,648,402	14,029,000
Rhode Island	(3)	(3)	(3)	(3)	(3)	(3)	(3)	(3)	(3)

South Carolina	167, 227, 361	904	898	560	26	254	2, 642	52, 829, 060	728, 000
South Dakota	25, 160, 185	196	464	113	9	13	795	849, 000	142, 000
Tennessee	594, 904, 829	2, 339	1, 769	1, 274	328	1, 513	7, 223	341, 151, 950	1, 928, 000
Texas	1, 438, 308, 383	8, 212	2, 911	1, 987	432	4, 134	17, 676	965, 015, 337	7, 312, 000
Utah	(1)	(1)	(1)	(1)	(1)	(1)	(1)	(1)	(1)
Vermont	4 348, 039, 496	4 889	4 1, 219	4 718	4 32	4 160	4 3, 018	4 21, 798, 489	4 1, 192, 000
Virignia	1, 016, 522, 771	2, 650	5, 201	2, 505	86	327	10, 769	227, 381, 533	2, 961, 000
Washington	592, 367, 734	3, 915	1, 566	1, 506	87	340	7, 414	124, 207, 979	2, 610, 000
West Virginia	112, 325, 988	1, 059	1, 974	281	19	17	3, 350	10, 551, 051	586, 000
Wisconsin	505, 591, 264	1, 829	2, 579	1, 788	388	256	6, 840	95, 003, 744	1, 561, 000
Wyoming	39, 812, 339	246	353	1, 842	9	9	2, 459	1, 226, 650	119, 000
Total	46, 781, 622, 956	150, 096	120, 693	87, 593	9, 619	37, 910	405, 911	24, 752, 735, 531	141, 473, 000

[1] Included with figures for the State of Nevada.
[2] Includes figures for 2 banks in Arizona and 2 banks in Utah.
[3] Included with figures for the State of Vermont.
[4] Includes figures for 2 banks in Rhode Island.
[5] Includes 27 banks which have been granted only certain specific fiduciary powers.
[6] Corporate paying agency, depository, registrar, transfer agency, etc.

TABLE No. 21.—*General comparative figures of fiduciary activities*

December 31—	Number of banks exercising trust powers	Aggregate trust department liabilities	Outstanding bonds and debentures	Gross trust department earnings	Common trust funds		Number of accounts			
					Number	Amount	Fiduciary	Agency, etc.	Corporate trust, bond and debenture issues	Other accounts
1928	1, 585	$3, 297, 310, 000	$7, 978, 389, 000	$16, 165, 000	---	---	1 53, 853	(2)	9, 923	(2)
1951	1, 512	36, 136, 628, 000	14, 550, 564, 000	75, 130, 000	(2)	(2)	171, 589	78, 171	(2)	(2)
1952	1, 513	39, 665, 972, 000	16, 051, 953, 000	80, 627, 000	60	$187, 392, 016	184, 125	72, 725	7, 217	33, 893
1953	1, 513	43, 150, 202, 000	17, 625, 838, 000	85, 990, 000	71	213, 929, 020	194, 231	77, 473	7, 611	37, 370
1954	1, 503	47, 938, 669, 000	19, 485, 675, 000	100, 761, 000	88	276, 970, 954	207, 157	82, 032	8, 011	38, 396
1955	1, 480	37, 187, 831, 000	17, 358, 441, 000	103, 033, 000	105	320, 954, 835	214, 383	74, 832	8, 056	34, 543
1956	1, 486	39, 000, 150, 658	19, 200, 708, 415	116, 845, 000	130	382, 397, 189	231, 991	79, 327	8, 381	35, 103
1957	1, 476	42, 578, 976, 765	22, 044, 165, 180	129, 433, 000	165	432, 822, 133	248, 048	82, 916	8, 839	36, 860
1958	1, 477	46, 781, 622, 956	24, 752, 735, 531	141, 473, 000	218	518, 734, 862	270, 789	87, 593	9, 619	37, 910

[1] Includes agency accounts in 1928.
[2] These figures were not developed at that time.

TABLE No. 22.—*National banks administering employee benefit trusts and agencies during 1958 by Federal Reserve districts*

Federal Reserve districts	With investment responsibility		Investments directed by others		Held as agent only		Number of fully insured plans with no bank investment responsibility
	Number of plans	Market value	Number of plans	Market value	Number of plans	Amount	
Boston	261	$103,497,830	68	$12,988,727	28	$34,238,187	90
New York	250	232,634,494	154	209,502,531	82	62,710,911	60
Philadelphia	160	34,595,008	182	33,011,666	29	222,996,744	53
Cleveland	1,097	1,275,442,535	327	162,190,439	36	889,707,845	392
Richmond	283	25,921,858	175	38,797,587	8	14,578,972	72
Atlanta	341	76,716,232	209	41,637,380	31	136,506,218	171
Chicago	1,637	1,451,969,344	494	185,536,743	194	265,495,890	263
St. Louis	117	17,693,070	39	15,559,634	10	68,972,316	32
Minneapolis	488	139,063,706	62	15,479,667	16	2,735,561	123
Kansas City	218	42,346,514	191	27,468,871	23	9,971,842	118
Dallas	212	55,606,883	196	111,532,698	41	13,830,472	18
San Francisco	440	209,382,080	724	172,904,749	46	25,840,910	217
Total for national banks	5,504	3,664,869,554	2,821	1,026,910,692	544	1,747,583,868	1,609
Nonnational banks located in the District of Columbia	14	4,143,919	10	3,070,838	13	99,016,152	7
Total	5,518	3,669,013,473	2,831	1,029,981,530	557	1,846,600,020	1,616

TABLE No. 23.—*National banks administering employee benefit trusts and agencies during 1958 by States*

Location	With investment responsibility		Investments directed by others		Held as agent only		Number of fully insured plans with no bank investment responsibility
	Number of plans	Market value	Number of plans	Market value	Number of plans	Amount	
Alabama	121	$36,945,853	46	$9,595,925	7	$6,188,399	18
Alaska	2	83,140	6	157,763			
Arizona	20	1,144,948	10	476,222	1	170,668	2
Arkansas	6	934,295	3	380,274			2
California	317	175,362,530	626	157,779,866	18	16,832,484	152
Colorado	18	1,687,175	9	1,650,922	5	131,385	6
Connecticut	112	57,535,119	20	8,087,298	15	7,443,208	41
Delaware							
Florida	38	7,751,019	48	15,600,762	4	8,204,964	29
Georgia	111	20,497,882	57	6,954,829	14	118,761,057	48

State							
Hawaii	802	948,462,441	131	90,603,428	153	170,035,577	1
Idaho	265	44,269,207	91	17,934,314	14	4,928,683	68
Illinois	30	7,446,596	23	2,432,207	2	269,762	39
Indiana	20	2,201,342	30	3,159,785	2	154,400	10
Iowa	10	803,526	9	6,878,824	2	50,675	22
Kansas	27	5,588,464	30	8,522,551	1	474,129	4
Kentucky	10	536,167	2	20,226	16	619	31
Louisiana	107	24,424,705	48	8,234,266	10	6,992,493	5
Maine	16	4,726,566	50	7,937,112	16	62,585,855	28
Massachusetts	460	427,514,902	194	46,420,024	16	2,733,561	17
Maryland	464	137,861,612	47	14,972,517	1	63,118,663	106
Michigan	11	896,902	3	61,433	1	628,091	85
Minnesota	132	21,793,241	57	8,257,921	17	34,091	10
Mississippi	4	239,916	6	255,832	59	217,771,766	51
Missouri	7	3,210,432	60	7,210,951	14	56,984,991	5
Montana	2	14,604	5	412,955	4	5,523,100	44
Nebraska	6	407,780	3	120,980	4	2,969,970	10
Nevada	88	7,480,929	79	11,635,667	45	3,268,103	28
New Hampshire	12	472,153	9	79,704	5	891,048,121	2
New Jersey	187	225,480,408	108	197,500,024	9	23,804,623	38
New Mexico	41	1,856,620	17	1,389,131	40	15,139,837	17
New York	12	211,233	7	238,101	3	13,440,224	23
North Carolina	785	218,019,400	169	93,700,673	23	10,659,880	324
North Dakota	42	16,066,990	29	12,125,885	16	5,569,655	9
Ohio	28	7,988,076	10	2,838,347	5	27,745,742	6
Oklahoma	424	1,089,479,283	296	98,135,458		3,919,092	109
Oregon	42	22,610,463	1	24,830			7
Pennsylvania	21	3,025,791	16	811,825			6
Rhode Island	7	742,857	45	7,102,563			8
South Carolina	91	14,799,114	189	108,396,497			40
South Dakota	195	52,175,939	16	4,121,698			17
Tennessee	15	9,573,713	1	84,596			5
Texas	4	67,896	55	15,571,035			4
Utah	133	13,054,752	51	7,117,898			14
Vermont	56	15,215,069	20	2,418,300			51
Virginia	19	609,328	66	28,496,272			2
Washington	125	30,899,679	6	332,817			47
West Virginia	6	60,696	17	10,670,184			2
Wisconsin	53	2,648,801					16
Wyoming							
District of Columbia							
Total for national banks	5,504	3,664,869,554	2,821	1,026,910,692	544	1,747,583,868	1,609
Nonnational banks located in the District of Columbia	14	4,143,919	10	3,070,838	13	99,016,152	7
Total	5,518	3,669,013,473	2,831	1,029,981,530	557	1,846,600,020	1,616

TABLE No. 24.—Earnings, expenses, and dividends of national banks for the year ended Dec. 31, 1958

[In thousands of dollars]

Location	Number of banks[1]	Earnings from current operations								
		Interest and dividends on securities		Interest and discount on loans	Service charges and other fees on banks' loans	Service charges on deposit accounts	Other service charges, commissions, fees, and collection and exchange charges	Trust department	Other current earnings	Total earnings from current operations
		U.S. Government obligations	Other securities							
Maine	29	2,088	585	9,212	81	811	231	602	281	13,891
New Hampshire	51	1,610	563	7,636	56	1,249	251	221	265	11,851
Vermont	32	1,349	363	5,747	52	588	106	132	178	8,515
Massachusetts	107	22,285	5,305	90,333	1,217	9,103	6,057	5,420	7,522	147,242
Rhode Island	4	3,471	1,133	14,026	146	1,379	358	1,060	994	22,667
Connecticut	30	7,524	2,559	28,784	434	3,535	1,139	4,378	1,406	49,759
Total New England States	253	38,327	10,508	155,738	1,986	16,665	8,142	11,813	10,646	253,825
New York	258	66,143	26,974	273,047	6,620	21,605	7,729	7,849	23,574	433,541
New Jersey	167	27,286	13,813	84,792	794	10,760	1,772	4,016	3,299	146,532
Pennsylvania	485	55,652	24,034	192,791	2,414	10,848	4,127	14,029	7,650	311,545
Delaware	7	280	76	756	14	43	10	26	13	1,218
Maryland	53	8,330	2,283	18,295	227	2,009	417	1,335	1,237	34,133
District of Columbia	5	7,405	1,022	17,070	165	1,928	455	995	744	29,784
Total Eastern States	975	165,096	68,202	586,751	10,234	47,193	14,510	28,250	36,517	956,753
Virginia	131	12,159	4,406	46,024	545	4,036	1,077	2,961	1,526	72,734
West Virginia	77	6,874	1,055	14,201	152	977	363	586	890	25,098
North Carolina	43	4,610	1,255	16,752	421	2,176	717	702	596	27,229
South Carolina	25	4,164	1,156	13,837	38	2,131	832	728	364	23,250
Georgia	52	8,649	2,853	39,318	459	4,678	1,990	2,127	1,658	61,732
Florida	103	22,162	5,844	59,026	1,504	7,723	2,263	3,354	4,074	105,950
Alabama	69	9,085	4,081	34,110	462	3,270	995	1,658	1,673	55,334
Mississippi	27	2,285	1,138	7,612	13	1,033	583	118	884	13,666
Louisiana	41	14,403	3,646	37,300	347	3,843	1,363	662	2,774	64,338
Texas	458	54,061	17,652	197,785	2,880	13,279	4,523	7,312	17,885	315,377
Arkansas	55	4,072	2,130	12,231	38	1,357	545	317	673	21,363
Kentucky	88	7,586	2,130	18,117	321	1,568	248	647	711	31,328
Tennessee	75	13,480	4,350	51,169	311	3,396	1,715	1,928	2,239	78,588
Total Southern States	1,244	163,590	51,696	547,482	7,491	49,467	17,214	23,100	35,947	895,987

Ohio	228	44,543	11,669	114,054	1,320	11,097	2,551	6,936	7,298	199,468
Indiana	123	23,264	4,546	56,332	711	4,987	1,314	3,101	3,637	97,892
Illinois	395	100,338	26,832	219,521	3,298	15,955	3,979	21,396	10,715	402,334
Michigan	75	36,211	9,927	92,774	1,966	7,832	2,483	4,987	2,973	159,153
Wisconsin	97	15,548	3,691	37,351	474	3,009	906	1,561	1,981	64,521
Minnesota	179	17,747	6,812	65,458	819	6,532	3,947	4,620	2,814	108,749
Iowa	97	7,982	2,284	19,742	139	2,091	789	750	911	34,688
Missouri	75	16,207	3,880	43,361	253	2,536	543	2,115	1,376	70,271
Total Middle Western States	1,269	261,840	69,641	648,893	8,980	54,039	16,512	45,466	31,705	1,137,076
North Dakota	38	3,380	942	7,864	114	987	762	107	349	14,505
South Dakota	34	3,275	810	9,463	125	1,113	834	142	269	16,031
Nebraska	123	8,183	2,306	24,397	59	2,430	667	790	1,266	40,098
Kansas	169	10,477	3,639	23,689	194	3,271	599	712	1,659	44,240
Montana	41	3,751	961	9,776	198	1,306	499	33	703	17,227
Wyoming	25	2,405	493	6,500	163	787	378	119	282	11,127
Colorado	77	9,848	1,786	30,145	347	3,991	691	2,012	1,035	49,855
New Mexico	27	3,639	492	10,751	266	1,379	564	208	443	17,742
Oklahoma	197	13,944	4,638	43,581	263	4,568	867	1,203	3,175	72,239
Total Western States	731	58,902	16,067	166,166	1,729	19,832	5,861	5,326	9,181	283,064
Washington	25	16,121	6,098	61,928	1,453	10,407	2,658	2,610	2,312	103,887
Oregon	11	12,098	4,654	42,348	924	6,491	1,325	1,770	1,278	70,888
California	46	107,252	35,608	463,583	14,601	57,653	10,867	21,508	19,781	730,853
Idaho	9	4,310	751	11,835	314	1,890	465	114	462	20,141
Utah	7	2,590	1,252	11,846	812	1,267	439	303	166	18,675
Nevada	3	2,173	874	6,244	269	623	364	382	248	11,177
Arizona	3	3,952	1,514	26,281	1,450	3,081	985	783	2,117	40,163
Total Pacific States	104	148,496	50,751	624,065	19,823	81,412	17,103	27,470	26,364	995,484
Total United States (exclusive of possessions)	4,576	836,251	266,865	2,729,095	50,243	268,608	79,342	141,425	150,360	4,522,189
Alaska (member and nonmember banks)	7	1,183	281	3,778	371	521	584	48	120	6,886
The Territory of Hawaii (nonmember bank)	1	1,518	433	6,097	321	466	199	----	286	9,320
Virgin Islands of the United States (member bank)	1	193	4	265	10	11	60	----	5	848
Total possessions	9	2,894	718	10,140	702	998	843	48	411	16,754
Total United States and possessions	4,585	839,145	267,583	2,739,235	50,945	269,606	80,185	141,473	150,771	4,538,943
New York City (Central Reserve city)	2	35,154	14,076	148,949	3,060	4,879	3,983	5,591	20,118	235,810
Chicago (Central Reserve city)	11	48,198	12,234	131,085	1,643	2,219	997	18,443	6,536	221,355
Other Reserve cities	181	348,319	110,416	1,254,736	27,384	119,699	34,885	75,137	68,329	2,038,905
Country banks (member banks) [2]	4,384	404,853	130,152	1,194,791	18,220	141,875	39,551	42,254	55,390	2,027,086
Possessions (nonmember banks)	7	2,621	705	9,674	638	934	769	48	398	15,787

[1] Number of banks as of end of year, but figures of earnings, expenses, etc., include those banks which were in operation a part of the year but were inactive at the close of the year.

[2] Includes 1 member bank in Alaska and 1 member bank in the Virgin Islands of the United States.

TABLE No. 24.—*Earnings, expenses, and dividends of national banks for the year ended Dec. 31, 1958*—Continued

[In thousands of dollars]

Location	Salaries and wages				Current operating expenses							Net earnings from current operations
	Officers		Employees other than officers		Fees paid to directors and members of executive, discount and advisory committees	Interest on time deposits (including savings deposits)	Interest and discount on borrowed money	Taxes other than on net income	Recurring depreciation on banking house, furniture and fixtures	Other current operating expenses	Total current operating expenses	
	Amount	Number [1]	Amount	Number [2]								
Maine	1,534	204	2,768	925	140	2,709	19	415	432	2,563	10,580	3,311
New Hampshire	1,564	231	2,115	742	163	1,206	38	275	302	2,663	8,326	3,525
Vermont	906	148	1,451	552	110	2,676	9	116	227	1,393	6,888	1,627
Massachusetts	12,650	1,270	30,624	9,054	681	8,694	395	3,653	3,272	25,204	85,173	62,059
Rhode Island	1,474	170	3,790	1,307	95	6,088	37	887	515	3,412	16,309	6,258
Connecticut	5,557	526	11,729	3,535	297	5,652	154	1,037	1,133	10,100	35,659	14,100
Total New England States	23,685	2,549	52,477	16,115	1,486	27,025	652	6,383	5,881	45,346	162,935	90,890
New York	30,096	2,779	76,259	20,160	1,509	76,076	2,040	6,704	7,809	73,237	273,730	159,811
New Jersey	13,528	1,506	29,880	8,982	1,297	31,777	330	5,004	4,369	24,442	110,627	35,905
Pennsylvania	27,298	3,274	53,374	15,961	2,771	55,375	760	8,221	7,463	43,738	199,000	112,545
Delaware	139	27	151	59	25	292	---	25	41	151	824	394
Maryland	3,127	373	6,417	2,064	261	5,333	96	1,185	596	5,599	22,614	11,519
District of Columbia	3,097	252	6,129	1,691	202	4,221	116	1,094	773	4,153	19,785	9,999
Total Eastern States	77,285	8,211	172,210	48,917	6,065	173,074	3,342	22,233	21,051	151,320	626,580	330,173
Virginia	7,642	971	12,130	4,107	600	14,382	121	2,037	1,921	10,739	49,572	23,162
West Virginia	2,780	365	3,920	1,271	304	3,738	29	572	667	3,969	15,979	9,119
North Carolina	3,537	427	5,348	1,864	158	3,428	58	513	777	4,970	18,779	8,450
South Carolina	2,837	344	5,158	1,818	144	1,965	11	278	650	4,928	15,971	7,279
Georgia	6,217	637	12,455	3,869	326	6,719	305	2,721	1,564	13,141	43,448	18,284
Florida	9,750	1,108	20,656	6,811	608	16,246	312	2,254	3,602	18,785	72,213	33,737
Alabama	5,951	649	9,941	3,234	289	8,300	50	496	1,002	9,663	35,692	19,642
Mississippi	1,660	212	2,413	839	144	1,849	2	516	351	3,102	10,037	3,629
Louisiana	6,160	584	12,314	3,766	379	8,663	254	3,646	1,189	10,659	43,264	21,074
Texas	34,073	3,740	47,425	14,793	1,712	36,274	865	16,150	7,945	52,061	196,485	118,892
Arkansas	2,926	374	3,509	1,247	259	2,565	20	576	635	4,128	14,618	6,745
Kentucky	3,753	562	5,171	1,860	310	3,630	53	1,182	669	5,107	19,875	11,453
Tennessee	7,532	871	13,051	4,423	316	14,035	230	2,675	1,586	13,580	53,005	25,583
Total Southern States	94,818	10,844	153,491	49,902	5,549	121,794	2,310	33,616	22,558	154,802	588,938	307,049

Ohio	17,368	1,775	35,888	10,273	1,157	26,936	489	10,309	4,116	31,638	127,901	71,567
Indiana	9,816	1,062	19,188	5,824	599	12,777	75	4,145	2,099	16,748	65,447	32,445
Illinois	33,129	3,119	72,043	19,365	1,931	51,410	1,379	9,852	5,350	60,606	235,700	166,634
Michigan	11,222	925	34,260	8,889	1,540	25,383	791	5,373	2,836	25,463	105,868	53,285
Wisconsin	6,917	697	11,922	3,992	406	13,491	96	1,047	1,496	10,210	45,585	18,936
Minnesota	11,256	1,283	20,265	6,165	597	15,894	421	1,483	1,799	19,990	71,705	37,044
Iowa	4,740	554	5,358	1,827	243	5,029	115	829	622	6,443	23,379	11,309
Missouri	6,762	706	13,113	4,053	409	6,679	111	1,213	1,062	12,507	41,856	28,415
Total Middle Western States	101,210	10,121	212,037	60,388	5,882	157,599	3,477	34,251	19,380	183,605	717,441	419,635
North Dakota	1,640	214	2,115	775	88	2,644	5	241	323	2,342	9,398	5,107
South Dakota	2,136	283	2,208	823	74	2,605	11	212	371	2,707	10,324	5,707
Nebraska	6,047	687	6,683	2,225	372	1,563	256	963	724	7,771	24,379	15,719
Kansas	6,495	858	6,716	2,305	415	4,414	74	1,290	1,142	7,686	28,232	16,008
Montana	1,881	237	2,795	862	78	2,438	14	908	419	3,096	11,629	5,598
Wyoming	1,393	163	1,755	517	95	1,887	20	266	317	1,478	7,211	3,916
Colorado	5,433	649	9,161	2,992	405	8,184	74	559	816	8,329	32,961	16,894
New Mexico	1,981	230	3,620	1,198	80	2,138	6	556	631	3,147	12,159	5,583
Oklahoma	9,460	1,218	11,190	3,593	412	7,328	235	916	1,827	12,905	44,273	27,966
Total Western States	36,466	4,539	46,243	15,290	2,019	33,201	695	5,911	6,570	49,461	180,566	102,498
Washington	10,199	1,110	21,990	6,116	215	16,257	225	1,927	2,788	15,775	69,376	34,211
Oregon	7,663	951	13,847	3,770	115	15,736	106	1,367	1,449	9,144	49,427	21,461
California	51,060	5,740	136,422	35,657	532	198,087	1,951	18,483	8,608	85,833	500,976	229,877
Idaho	2,189	246	3,200	1,070	56	4,491	26	261	558	2,689	13,470	6,671
Utah	1,397	175	2,888	956	85	4,467	22	147	262	2,891	12,159	6,516
Nevada	1,242	160	2,044	604	13	2,514	---	328	224	1,347	7,712	3,465
Arizona	4,178	455	8,367	2,605	43	4,985	24	634	1,191	8,533	27,955	12,208
Total Pacific States	77,928	8,837	188,758	50,778	1,059	246,537	2,354	23,147	15,080	126,212	681,075	314,409
Total United States (exclusive of possessions)	411,392	45,101	825,216	241,390	22,060	759,230	12,880	125,541	90,520	710,746	2,957,535	1,564,654
Alaska (member and nonmember banks)	935	73	1,729	414	19	830	---	132	297	1,351	5,293	1,593
The Territory of Hawaii (nonmember bank)	763	76	1,589	474	27	2,087	5	196	363	1,946	6,976	2,344
Virgin Islands of the United States (member bank)	40	4	109	34	2	172	---	3	7	58	391	157
Total possessions	1,738	153	3,427	922	48	3,089	5	331	667	3,355	12,660	4,094
Total United States and possessions	413,130	45,254	828,643	242,312	22,108	762,319	12,835	125,872	91,187	714,101	2,970,195	1,568,748
New York City (Central Reserve city)	11,597	623	40,939	9,366	134	28,782	1,638	3,167	2,687	39,285	128,229	107,581
Chicago (Central Reserve city)	11,841	744	39,336	9,400	241	19,675	1,177	5,191	1,254	29,536	108,251	113,104
Other Reserve cities	152,585	14,455	388,783	106,734	3,601	349,461	7,438	59,848	31,812	298,281	1,291,809	747,096
Country banks (member banks)3	235,498	29,291	356,376	115,951	18,086	361,560	2,577	57,347	54,803	343,840	1,430,087	596,999
Possessions (nonmember banks)	1,609	141	3,209	861	46	2,841	5	319	631	3,159	11,819	3,968

1 Number at end of period.
2 Number of full-time employees at end of period.
3 Includes 1 member bank in Alaska and 1 member bank in the Virgin Islands of the United States.

TABLE No. 24.—*Earnings, expenses, and dividends of national banks for the year ended Dec. 31, 1958*—Continued

[In thousands of dollars]

Location	Recoveries, transfers from valuation reserves, and profits [1]							Losses, charge-offs, and transfers to valuation reserves					
	On securities			On loans		All other	Total recoveries, transfers from valuation reserves and profits	On securities		On loans		All other	Total losses, charge-offs, and transfers to valuation reserves [2]
	Recoveries	Transfers from valuation reserves	Profits on securities sold or redeemed	Recoveries	Transfers from valuation reserves			Losses and charge-offs	Transfers to valuation reserves	Losses and charge-offs	Transfers to valuation reserves		
Maine	10		827	62	10	132	1,079	367	172	38	389	1,184	2,150
New Hampshire	290	38	908	41	13	89	1,341	424	260	100	356	154	1,294
Vermont		38	350	41	3	49	481	70	44	12	161	144	431
Massachusetts	251	802	16,307	220	7,288	1,159	26,027	1,234	9,310	444	11,485	1,972	24,445
Rhode Island			2,084	6		78	2,168	21	1,544	70	360	251	2,246
Connecticut	14	96	2,621	45	142	332	3,250	604	671	48	2,309	654	4,286
Total New England States	565	974	23,097	415	7,456	1,839	34,346	2,720	12,001	712	15,060	4,359	34,852
New York	130	1,635	14,301	427	9,956	880	27,329	3,629	12,948	395	25,476	3,551	45,999
New Jersey	562	81	8,955	1,280	79	8,149	19,106	1,937	2,272	315	5,904	10,246	20,674
Pennsylvania	355	5,789	34,468	690	994	758	43,054	3,759	26,191	527	8,162	5,116	43,755
Delaware			58	2		6	66	14				1	16
Maryland	19		2,441	87	2	95	2,644	290	232	85	532	1,194	2,333
District of Columbia			906	25		106	1,037	341		53	820	203	1,417
Total Eastern States	1,066	7,505	61,129	2,511	11,031	9,994	93,236	9,970	41,643	1,376	40,894	20,311	114,194
Virginia		34	6,322	108	1,092	364	7,920	916	3,297	143	2,494	449	7,299
West Virginia	3		1,660	73	166	40	1,942	236	379	96	562	88	1,361
North Carolina	15	34	978	33	3	560	1,623	127	118	104	1,124	129	1,602
South Carolina			1,931	5		50	1,986	186		9	417	240	852
Georgia	21	1	7,241	67	142	1,053	8,525	762	1,600	24	1,446	559	4,391
Florida	40	426	7,062	155	81	650	8,414	1,112	714	213	4,253	879	7,171
Alabama	203	1	5,567	241	77	181	6,270	417	176	240	2,327	1,535	4,695
Mississippi	5	62	373	83	11	179	713	163	245	75	758	161	402
Louisiana	7	200	5,224	139	306	104	5,980	291	2,124	148	1,450	903	4,916
Texas	152	383	9,822	2,637	501	1,447	14,942	3,041	2,394	2,582	12,130	4,390	24,537
Arkansas	2	100	1,324	138	703	26	2,293	380	441	253	620	299	1,993
Kentucky		266	2,175	73	26	112	2,652	323	997	117	551	748	2,736
Tennessee	60	1,252	6,966	34	806	220	9,338	969	3,979	113	1,830	1,664	8,555
Total Southern States	508	2,759	56,645	3,786	3,237	5,663	72,598	8,923	16,464	4,117	29,962	12,044	71,510

Ohio	40	3,160	20,820	559	620	771	25,970	1,609	14,216	565	6,850	1,457	24,697
Indiana	94	1,407	11,779	97	510	421	14,308	2,001	3,526	182	2,504	3,199	11,412
Illinois	2,204	4,350	62,023	399	838	2,166	71,980	9,289	25,280	1,526	13,755	5,927	55,777
Michigan	320	4,266	9,693	42	1,062	2,801	18,184	2,812	8,438	58	3,306	5,604	20,218
Wisconsin	53	2	8,568	39	213	329	9,204	897	2,961	34	1,342	900	6,134
Minnesota	105	25	9,867	341	638	1,292	12,268	1,051	708	309	1,913	786	4,767
Iowa	234		3,086	40	67	103	3,530	739	81	81	893	495	2,289
Missouri	32	116	6,642	54	125	191	7,160	1,552	3,244	68	1,125	500	6,489
Total Middle Western States	3,082	13,326	132,478	1,571	4,073	8,074	162,604	19,950	58,454	2,823	31,688	18,868	131,783
North Dakota	10	26	1,482	16	5	96	1,635	546	67	22	415	108	1,158
South Dakota	8		812	54	6	87	967	499		49	770	96	1,414
Nebraska	83	299	2,911	140	172	171	3,776	557	1,294	267	1,565	966	4,649
Kansas	79	154	2,879	430	65	152	3,759	1,509	146	406	1,262	727	4,050
Montana	49	1,766	1,191	273	60	125	3,464	197	156	260	449	132	1,194
Wyoming	1		697	47	3	68	816	136		79	152	117	484
Colorado	36	150	2,444	267	14	1,619	4,530	1,376	651	144	1,563	1,462	5,196
New Mexico		75	957	194		47	1,273	26	363	178	1,473	219	2,259
Oklahoma	13	30	4,318	568	39	160	5,128	636	730	704	2,230	582	4,882
Total Western States	279	2,500	17,691	1,989	364	2,525	25,348	5,482	3,407	2,109	9,879	4,409	25,286
Washington	4	40	5,149	54	14	266	5,527	2,533	1,571	32	1,826	821	6,783
Oregon	17	1	2,352	40		226	2,636	468	1,154	2	172	475	2,271
California	5	5,717	45,806	773	1,379	1,590	55,270	3,700	22,168	147	25,832	4,635	56,482
Idaho			3,685	15		72	3,772	211		49	43	43	346
Utah			1,375	16		25	1,416	31			227	32	290
Nevada		256	916	1		6	1,179	500	644	6	160	66	1,376
Arizona			2,635	4		196	2,835	15	2,207	82	1,532	426	4,262
Total Pacific States	26	6,014	61,918	903	1,393	2,381	72,635	7,458	27,744	318	29,792	6,498	71,810
Total United States (exclusive of possessions)	5,526	33,078	352,958	11,175	27,554	30,476	460,767	54,503	159,713	11,455	157,275	66,489	449,435
Alaska (member and nonmember banks)			55	96		38	189	307		128	298	40	773
The Territory of Hawaii (nonmember bank)			59	2		47	108	13			100	78	191
Virgin Islands of the United States (member bank)						5	5	22				5	27
Total possessions			114	98		90	302	342		128	398	123	991
Total United States and possessions	5,526	33,078	353,072	11.273	27,554	30,566	461,069	54,845	159,713	11,583	157,673	66,612	450,426
New York City (Central Reserve city)		1,465	3,439	1	9,489		14,394	1,014	12,228		11,306	1,466	26,014
Chicago (Central Reserve city)	1,923	3,342	36,152	162	12	1,285	42,876	4,575	19,286	1,167	7,099	2,829	34,956
Other Reserve cities	658	22,963	178,182	1,872	14,246	11,371	229,292	20,014	98,665	897	65,124	25,254	209,954
Country banks (member banks) [3]	2,945	5,308	135,204	9,174	3,807	17,825	174,263	28,922	29,534	9,408	73,746	36,945	178,555
Possessions (nonmember banks)			95	64		85	244	320		111	398	118	947

[1] Not including recoveries credited to valuation reserves.
[2] Not including losses charged to valuation reserves.
[3] Includes 1 member bank in Alaska and 1 member bank in the Virgin Islands of the United States.

TABLE No. 24.—Earnings, expenses, and dividends of national banks for the year ended Dec. 31, 1958—Continued

[In thousands of dollars]

Location	Profits before income taxes	Taxes on net income		Net profits before dividends	Cash dividends declared			Capital accounts [1]	Ratios	
		Federal	State		On preferred stock	On common stock	Total cash dividends declared		Net profits before dividends to capital accounts	Expenses to gross earnings
									Percent	Percent
Maine	2,240	1,255		985		994	994	30,984	3.18	76.16
New Hampshire	3,572	864		2,708		816	816	29,570	9.16	70.26
Vermont	1,677	467	49	1,161	21	489	510	18,046	6.43	80.89
Massachusetts	63,651	28,615	5,415	29,621		15,602	15,602	351,504	8.43	57.85
Rhode Island	6,180	2,564	418	3,198		2,164	2,164	42,952	7.45	72.27
Connecticut	13,064	4,768	669	7,627		4,510	4,510	95,258	8.01	71.66
Total New England States	90,384	38,533	6,551	45,300	21	24,575	24,596	568,314	7.97	64.19
New York	141,141	61,770	6,890	72,481	9	48,987	48,996	1,058,737	6.85	63.14
New Jersey	34,337	9,491		24,846	36	9,531	9,567	266,193	9.33	75.50
Pennsylvania	111,844	49,625		62,219	2	31,984	31,986	864,160	7.20	63.87
Delaware	444	115	1	328		143	143	3,989	8.22	67.65
Maryland	11,830	4,507		7,323		3,202	3,202	80,833	9.06	66.25
District of Columbia	9,619	4,787		4,832		2,899	2,899	64,289	7.52	66.43
Total Eastern States	309,215	130,295	6,891	172,029	47	96,746	96,793	2,338,201	7.36	65.49
Virginia	23,783	9,605		14,178		5,814	5,814	150,477	9.42	68.16
West Virginia	9,700	4,256		5,444		2,031	2,031	64,946	8.38	63.67
North Carolina	8,471	3,505	136	4,830		2,255	2,255	59,421	8.13	68.97
South Carolina	8,413	3,711	216	4,486		2,121	2,121	44,554	10.07	68.69
Georgia	22,418	8,649		13,769		4,870	4,870	118,674	11.60	70.38
Florida	34,980	13,917		21,063	10	5,747	5,757	199,904	10.54	68.16
Alabama	21,217	7,290	704	13,223		4,389	4,389	111,695	11.84	64.50
Mississippi	2,940	687		2,253		887	887	24,942	9.03	73.44
Louisiana	22,138	9,537		12,601		3,639	3,639	137,408	9.17	67.24
Texas	109,297	44,174		65,123		30,083	30,083	709,289	9.18	62.30
Arkansas	7,045	2,211		4,834		2,447	2,447	50,485	9.58	68.43
Kentucky	11,369	4,584		6,785		2,458	2,458	74,750	9.08	63.44
Tennessee	26,366	11,874		14,492		5,253	5,253	158,870	9.12	67.45
Total Southern States	308,137	124,000	1,056	183,081	10	71,994	72,004	1,905,415	9.61	65.73
Ohio	72,840	33,516		39,324		16,206	16,206	432,590	9.09	64.12
Indiana	35,341	14,701		20,640	1	6,323	6,324	207,608	9.94	66.86
Illinois	182,837	80,926		101,911	68	32,197	32,265	953,862	10.68	58.58

Michigan	51,251	21,906		29,345	20	11,813	11,833	297,178	9.87	66.52
Wisconsin	22,006	8,261	612	13,133	2	5,086	5,088	134,632	9.75	70.65
Minnesota	44,545	16,069	2,566	25,910		9,673	9,673	220,452	11.75	65.94
Iowa	12,550	4,206		8,344		2,346	2,346	76,789	10.87	67.40
Missouri	29,086	13,331	847	14,908		5,976	5,976	168,006	8.87	59.56
Total Middle Western States	450,456	192,916	4,025	253,515	91	89,620	89,711	2,491,117	10.18	63.10
North Dakota	5,584	2,088	106	3,390		1,221	1,221	22,617	14.99	64.79
South Dakota	5,260	2,055	157	3,048		1,227	1,227	23,821	12.80	64.40
Nebraska	14,846	5,706		9,140		3,572	3,572	93,102	9.82	60.80
Kansas	15,717	5,383		10,334		2,937	2,937	99,390	10.40	63.82
Montana	7,868	2,458		5,410		1,436	1,436	23,414	23.11	67.50
Wyoming	4,248	1,501		2,747		851	851	19,716	13.93	64.81
Colorado	16,228	5,699	499	10,030		3,925	3,925	95,575	10.49	66.11
New Mexico	4,597	2,119		2,478		880	880	25,648	9.66	68.53
Oklahoma	28,212	10,702	716	16,794		5,868	5,868	178,474	9.41	61.29
Total Western States	102,560	37,711	1,478	63,371		21,917	21,917	581,757	10.89	63.79
Washington	32,955	16,154	1,825	16,801		7,212	7,212	176,000	9.55	66.97
Oregon	21,826	8,143	8,815	11,858		6,242	6,242	138,356	8.57	69.73
California	228,665	96,674	360	123,176		66,652	66,652	1,057,260	11.65	68.55
Idaho	10,097	2,766	229	6,971		1,433	1,433	28,432	24.52	66.88
Utah	7,642	2,996		4,417		1,731	1,731	33,030	13.37	65.11
Nevada	3,268	1,301		1,967		1,212	1,212	15,595	12.61	69.00
Arizona	10,781	5,486	413	4,882		2,674	2,674	53,454	9.13	69.60
Total Pacific States	315,234	133,520	11,642	170,072		87,156	87,156	1,502,127	11.32	68.42
Total United States (exclusive of possessions)	1,575,986	656,975	31,643	887,368	169	392,008	392,177	9,386,931	9.45	65.40
Alaska (member and nonmember banks)	1,009	666	13	330	68	221	221	7,466	4.42	76.87
The Territory of Hawaii (nonmember bank)	2,261	917		1,344	10	570	570	17,498	7.68	74.85
Virgin Islands of the United States (member bank)	135	57		78	91	23	23	662	11.78	71.35
Total possessions	3,405	1,640	13	1,752	169	814	814	25,626	6.84	75.56
Total United States and possessions	1,579,391	658,615	31,656	889,120		392,822	392,991	9,412,557	9.45	65.44
New York City (Central Reserve city)	95,961	46,123	4,387	45,451		33,360	33,360	717,293	6.34	54.38
Chicago (Central Reserve city)	121,024	59,501		61,523		22,890	22,958	609,692	10.09	48.90
Other Reserve cities	766,434	339,674	18,256	408,504		191,945	191,955	4,077,814	10.02	63.36
Country banks (member banks)[2]	592,707	211,741	9,000	371,966		143,854	143,945	3,983,234	9.34	70.55
Possessions (nonmember banks)	3,265	1,576	13	1,676		773	773	24,524	6.83	74.87

[1] Represents aggregate book value of capital stock, surplus, undivided profits, reserves, and retirement fund for preferred stock. Figures are averages of amounts reported for the June and December call dates in the current year and the December call date in the previous year.

[2] Includes 1 member bank in Alaska and 1 member bank in the Virgin Islands of the United States.

TABLE No. 25.—*Earnings, expenses, and dividends of national banks, by Federal Reserve districts, for the year ended Dec. 31, 1958*

[In thousands of dollars]

	District No. 1	District No. 2[1]	District No. 3	District No. 4	District No. 5	District No. 6	District No. 7	District No. 8	District No. 9	District No. 10	District No. 11	District No. 12[2]	Non-member	Grand total
Earnings from current operations:														
Interest and dividends on:														
U.S. Government obligations	35,765	89,051	37,459	73,717	43,105	63,137	168,328	33,948	31,653	53,807	57,978	148,576	2,621	839,145
Other securities	9,701	38,580	16,304	23,331	11,119	19,254	43,279	10,417	10,542	14,737	18,854	50,760	705	267,583
Interest and discount on loans	147,248	345,184	127,944	210,497	125,184	198,044	395,717	93,047	100,363	151,272	210,795	624,266	9,674	2,739,235
Service charges and other fees on banks' loans	1,718	7,516	1,081	2,949	1,535	2,857	6,238	890	1,384	1,315	2,947	19,877	638	50,945
Service charges on deposit accounts	15,440	31,166	8,616	16,417	13,196	21,500	31,517	6,925	10,797	17,255	14,378	81,465	934	299,006
Other service charges, commissions, fees and collection and exchange charges	7,933	9,312	2,314	4,933	3,845	7,699	8,675	2,529	6,337	3,777	4,945	17,117	769	80,185
Trust department	11,006	11,969	4,882	17,161	7,265	8,988	31,279	2,498	4,959	6,439	7,509	27,470	48	141,473
Other current earnings	10,250	26,224	4,759	11,795	5,277	11,637	18,785	3,761	4,540	8,383	18,590	26,372	398	150,771
Total earnings from current operations	239,061	559,002	203,359	360,800	210,526	333,116	703,818	154,015	170,575	256,985	335,996	995,903	15,787	4,538,943
Current operating expenses:														
Salaries and wages:														
Officers	22,078	42,010	19,078	30,977	22,806	32,833	58,537	16,910	18,940	32,778	36,557	78,017	1,609	413,130
Employees other than officers[3]	49,039	102,690	35,855	62,863	38,869	62,679	135,023	25,910	29,303	43,455	50,881	188,867	3,209	828,643
Number of officers[3]	*2,385*	*3,986*	*2,648*	*3,205*	*2,704*	*3,603*	*5,372*	*2,110*	*2,867*	*3,951*	*4,037*	*8,845*	*141*	*45,254*
Number of employees other than officers[3]	*14,980*	*28,017*	*11,469*	*17,964*	*12,737*	*20,328*	*37,309*	*8,628*	*9,313*	*14,081*	*15,920*	*60,805*	*861*	*242,512*
Fees paid to directors and members of executive, discount, and advisory committees	1,403	2,409	2,744	1,891	1,640	1,877	2,912	1,430	1,028	1,827	1,842	1,059	46	22,108
Interest on time deposits (including savings deposits)	24,070	103,861	40,118	52,040	32,875	49,254	100,046	18,173	26,238	27,123	39,067	246,613	2,841	762,319
Interest and discount on borrowed money	626	2,320	348	994	430	1,018	2,406	286	459	713	876	2,354	5	12,835
Taxes other than on net income	6,116	10,712	5,656	14,764	5,633	10,581	19,091	4,595	3,192	4,907	17,150	23,156	319	125,872
Recurring depreciation on banking house, furniture, and fixtures	5,468	11,482	5,238	7,827	5,362	8,632	11,256	2,927	3,214	5,680	8,361	15,109	631	91,187
Other current operating expenses	42,399	94,782	31,380	52,370	34,063	60,026	110,223	27,818	30,677	45,043	55,811	126,350	3,159	714,101
Total current operating expenses	151,199	370,266	140,417	223,726	141,678	226,900	439,494	98,049	113,051	161,526	210,545	681,525	11,819	2,970,195
Net earnings from current operations	87,862	188,736	62,942	137,074	68,848	106,216	264,324	55,966	57,524	95,459	125,451	314,378	3,968	1,568,748

Recoveries, transfers from valuation reserves, and profits:														
On securities:														
Recoveries	565	686	353	50	35	318	2,888	31	179	233	162	26		5,526
Transfers from valuation reserves	899	1,791	262	8,688	68	1,423	9,573	1,240	1,817	720	583	6,014		33,078
Profits on securities sold or redeemed	21,755	22,206	9,982	48,551	14,222	28,807	89,167	12,837	14,675	16,743	12,095	61,937	95	353,072
On loans:														
Recoveries	401	1,675	509	822	330	658	500	359	702	1,578	2,738	937	64	11,273
Transfers from valuation reserves	7,456	10,001	97	1,568	1,263	1,377	2,506	211	761	374	547	1,393		27,554
All other	1,606	8,490	1,219	1,112	1,212	2,358	5,591	1,116	1,706	2,221	1,469	2,381	85	30,566
Total recoveries, transfers from valuation reserves, and profits	32,682	44,849	12,422	60,791	17,130	34,941	110,225	15,794	19,840	21,869	17,594	72,688	244	461,069
Losses, charge-offs, and transfers to valuation reserves:														
On securities:														
Losses and charge-offs	2,597	5,356	3,497	2,480	2,083	3,076	12,930	4,550	2,620	4,734	3,144	7,458	320	54,845
Transfers to valuation reserves	11,744	15,477	1,799	38,630	4,019	7,293	39,424	4,481	1,131	4,628	3,343	27,744		159,713
On loans:														
Losses and charge-offs	683	593	510	796	483	727	1,594	692	667	1,715	2,677	335	111	11,383
Transfers to valuation reserves	13,722	30,337	6,277	11,436	5,933	11,482	20,308	2,669	4,035	8,575	12,709	29,792	398	157,673
All other	4,113	13,489	3,823	3,811	2,292	4,438	15,395	2,413	1,234	4,233	4,755	6,498	118	66,612
Total losses, charge-offs, and transfers to valuation reserves	32,859	65,252	15,906	57,153	14,810	27,016	89,651	14,805	9,687	23,885	26,628	71,827	947	450,426
Profits before income taxes	87,685	168,333	59,458	140,712	71,168	114,141	284,898	56,955	67,677	93,443	116,417	315,239	3,265	1,579,391
Taxes on net income:														
Federal	37,781	69,411	20,970	66,836	30,053	44,572	122,984	23,655	23,963	36,176	47,111	133,527	1,576	658,615
State	6,335	7,106	1		352	704	582	568	2,859	1,484	10	11,642	13	31,656
Total taxes on net income	44,116	76,517	20,971	66,836	30,405	45,276	123,566	24,223	26,822	37,660	47,121	145,169	1,589	690,271
Net profits before dividends	43,569	91,816	38,487	73,876	40,763	68,865	161,332	32,732	40,855	55,783	69,296	170,070	1,676	889,120
Cash dividends declared:														
On preferred stock	21	43	4			10	91							169
On common stock	23,264	57,348	19,024	33,090	18,156	21,074	54,166	13,717	14,492	19,075	31,469	87,174	773	392,822
Total cash dividends declared	23,285	57,391	19,028	33,090	18,156	21,084	54,257	13,717	14,492	19,075	31,469	87,174	773	392,991

See footnotes at end of table.

TABLE No. 25.—*Earnings, expenses, and dividends of national banks, by Federal Reserve districts, for the year ended Dec. 31, 1958—Con.*

[In thousands of dollars]

	District No. 1	District No. 2 [2]	District No. 3	District No. 4	District No. 5	District No. 6	District No. 7	District No. 8	District No. 9	District No. 10	District No. 11	District No. 12 [2]	Non-member	Grand total
Memoranda items:														
Recoveries credited to valuation reserves (not included in recoveries above):														
On securities	1,484	751	18	938	380		133	2,340	1	457	224	141		6,876
On loans	3,003	4,937	1,515	2,135	960	1,523	9,027	914	1,175	3,705	3,383	6,452	203	38,932
Losses charged to valuation reserves (not included in losses above):														
On securities	36	2,868	16	3,420	216	172	1,521	348		23	108	3,882		12,610
On loans	4,375	10,796	3,232	4,258	2,401	5,569	18,005	2,115	1,748	4,486	6,893	12,577	340	76,795
Stock dividends (increases in capital stock)	1,510	3,738	1,623	3,347	3,124	7,557	46,124	2,337	7,222	8,553	9,453	12,518	1,400	108,506
Number of banks [3]	247	366	448	394	327	331	578	319	346	617	500	105	7	4,585
Loans, gross	2,865,902	7,121,914	2,388,385	4,189,844	2,330,674	3,498,723	8,253,727	1,794,621	1,798,378	2,773,151	3,993,211	11,234,821	163,088	52,406,439
Securities	1,867,188	5,041,439	2,135,675	3,892,049	2,213,237	3,330,766	8,588,021	1,717,456	1,628,955	2,761,644	2,971,714	8,050,239	133,790	44,352,173
Capital stock (par value)	143,434	425,409	135,720	257,994	121,216	199,595	484,213	101,465	98,652	162,246	276,755	461,568	6,850	2,875,117
Capital accounts	543,986	1,280,314	508,788	898,950	459,424	648,398	1,543,866	363,606	319,405	566,351	752,367	1,502,568	24,524	9,412,557
	Percent	*Percent*	*Percent*	*Percent*	*Percent*	*Percent*	*Percent*	*Percent*	*Percent*	*Percent*	*Percent*	*Percent*	*Percent*	*Percent*
Ratios:														
To gross earnings:														
Interest and dividends on securities	19.02	22.83	26.44	26.90	25.76	24.73	30.07	28.81	24.74	26.67	22.87	20.02	21.07	24.38
Interest and discount on loans	61.59	61.75	62.91	58.34	59.46	59.45	56.22	60.41	58.84	58.86	62.74	62.68	61.28	60.35
Service charges on deposit accounts	6.46	5.58	4.24	4.55	6.27	6.46	4.48	4.50	6.33	6.72	4.28	8.18	5.91	5.94
All other current earnings	12.93	9.84	6.41	10.21	8.51	9.36	9.23	6.28	10.09	7.75	10.11	9.12	11.74	9.33
Total gross earnings	100.00	100.00	100.00	100.00	100.00	100.00	100.00	100.00	100.00	100.00	100.00	100.00	100.00	100.00
Salaries, wages, and fees	30.34	26.32	28.36	26.54	30.07	29.24	27.92	28.73	28.89	30.38	26.57	26.90	30.81	27.85
Interest on time deposits	10.07	18.58	19.73	14.42	15.62	14.78	14.21	11.80	15.38	10.55	11.63	24.76	18.00	16.79
All other current expenses	22.84	21.34	20.96	21.05	21.61	24.09	20.31	23.13	22.01	21.92	24.46	16.77	26.06	20.80
Total current expenses	63.25	66.24	69.05	62.01	67.30	68.11	62.44	63.66	66.28	62.85	62.66	68.43	74.87	65.44
Net current earnings	36.75	33.76	30.95	37.99	32.70	31.89	37.56	36.34	33.72	37.15	37.34	31.57	25.13	34.56
To gross loans: Interest and discount on loans	5.14	4.85	5.36	5.02	5.37	5.66	4.79	5.18	5.58	5.45	5.28	5.56	5.93	5.23
To securities: Interest and dividends on securities	2.43	2.53	2.49	2.49	2.45	2.47	2.46	2.58	2.59	2.48	2.59	2.48	2.49	2.50

To capital stock (par value):														
Net current earnings	61.26	44.37	46.38	53.13	56.80	53.22	54.59	55.16	58.31	58.84	45.33	68.11	57.93	54.56
Net profits before dividends	30.38	21.58	28.36	28.63	33.63	34.50	33.32	32.26	41.41	34.38	25.04	36.85	24.47	30.92
Cash dividends	16.22	13.49	14.02	12.83	14.98	10.56	11.21	13.52	14.69	11.76	11.37	18.89	11.28	13.67
To capital accounts:														
Net current earnings	16.15	14.74	12.37	15.25	14.99	16.38	17.12	15.39	18.01	16.86	16.67	20.92	16.18	16.67
Net profits before dividends	8.01	7.17	7.56	8.22	8.87	10.62	10.45	9.00	12.79	9.85	9.21	11.32	6.83	9.45
Cash dividends	4.28	4.48	3.74	3.68	3.95	3.25	3.51	3.77	4.54	3.37	4.18	5.80	3.15	4.17

1 Includes 1 member bank in the Virgin Islands of the United States.
2 Includes 1 member bank in Alaska.
3 Number at end of year. Remaining figures include earnings, expenses, etc., of those banks which were in operation a part of the year but were inactive at the close of the year.

NOTE.—The figures of loans, securities, capital stock and capital accounts are averages of amounts reported for the June and December call dates in the current year and the December call date in the previous year.

TABLE No. 26.—*Earnings, expenses, and dividends of national banks, by size of banks, for the year ended Dec. 31, 1958*

TOTAL UNITED STATES AND POSSESSIONS

[In thousands of dollars]

	Banks operating throughout entire year with deposits on Dec. 31, 1958, of—											Total
	Less than $500,000	$500,000 to $750,000	$750,000 to $1,000,000	$1,000,000 to $2,000,000	$2,000,000 to $5,000,000	$5,000,000 to $10,000,000	$10,000,000 to $25,000,000	$25,000,000 to $50,000,000	$50,000,000 to $100,000,000	$100,000,000 to $500,000,000	$500,000,000 or more	
Number of banks	15	40	58	534	1,503	1,084	768	261	136	137	26	4,562
Total deposits	6,108	25,459	51,242	816,129	5,094,975	7,659,604	11,819,696	9,017,833	9,441,587	30,039,959	43,014,872	116,987,464
Capital stock (par value)	410	1,147	1,873	24,803	131,017	178,895	273,315	212,991	229,496	712,396	1,178,436	2,944,779
Capital accounts	1,032	3,473	6,546	94,246	501,896	674,070	946,731	668,681	707,041	2,293,455	3,758,294	9,655,465
Earnings from current operations:												
Interest and dividends on:												
U.S. Government obligations	45	193	463	7,776	45,473	64,957	97,518	74,367	72,470	197,534	274,234	835,030
Other securities	7	35	121	1,954	14,670	22,645	31,755	22,231	22,190	57,705	93,100	266,413
Interest and discount on loans	190	699	1,330	19,738	117,834	177,677	270,970	199,308	210,256	669,034	1,059,547	2,726,583
Service charges and other fees on banks' loans	1	3	4	84	752	1,846	3,506	2,816	3,219	12,461	26,087	50,779
Service charges on deposit accounts	13	59	99	1,791	12,023	20,899	36,297	25,183	24,357	60,876	86,181	267,778
Other service charges, commissions, fees, and collection and exchange charges	11	37	63	866	4,409	5,961	9,899	5,960	5,736	19,638	27,206	79,786
Trust department				6	345	1,720	7,364	9,192	11,020	50,375	61,380	141,402
Other current earnings	4	18	39	557	3,665	5,899	11,332	11,956	11,686	44,734	59,916	149,806
Total earnings from current operations	271	1,044	2,119	32,772	199,171	301,604	468,641	351,013	360,934	1,112,357	1,687,651	4,517,577
Current operating expenses:												
Salaries and wages:												
Officers	102	320	561	7,318	34,596	41,860	54,078	36,928	34,358	94,605	105,996	410,722
Employees other than officers	20	99	162	3,415	26,322	46,181	83,408	65,603	69,395	221,553	308,195	824,353
Fees paid to directors and members of executive, discount, and advisory committees	7	25	48	662	3,920	4,163	4,420	2,268	1,761	3,205	1,433	21,912
Interest on time deposits (including savings deposits)	14	70	295	4,961	35,114	57,105	86,139	62,066	56,746	147,770	307,939	758,219
Interest and discount on borrowed money			2	23	167	235	420	445	744	3,951	6,824	12,811
Taxes other than on net income	9	35	66	966	5,779	8,859	12,939	10,294	10,715	32,562	43,107	125,331
Recurring depreciation on banking house, furniture and fixtures	4	17	36	680	5,290	8,714	13,399	9,912	8,460	22,291	21,891	90,694

Item	1	2	3	4	5	6	7	8	9	10	11	Total
Other current operating expenses	50	189	307	5,036	30,034	47,382	80,170	61,987	65,840	198,927	220,146	710,068
Total current operating expenses	206	755	1,477	23,061	141,222	214,499	334,973	249,503	248,019	724,864	1,015,531	2,954,110
Net earnings from current operations	65	289	642	9,711	57,949	87,105	133,668	101,510	112,915	387,493	672,120	1,563,467
Recoveries, transfers from valuation reserves, and profits: On securities: Recoveries				47	289	381	827	294	419	1,185	2,083	5,525
Transfers from valuation reserves					48	258	1,609	1,904	1,801	6,004	21,442	33,066
Profits on securities sold or redeemed	3	53	24	373	5,086	14,506	31,762	32,705	31,994	93,891	141,601	351,945
On loans: Recoveries	17	3	76	830	2,415	2,011	1,622	456	344	2,344	1,053	11,221
Transfers from valuation reserves	1			2	235	591	1,666	476	902	4,471	19,171	27,514
All other			2	126	745	1,643	3,417	1,322	2,220	14,276	6,497	30,252
Total recoveries, transfers from valuation reserves and profits	21	56	102	1,378	8,818	19,390	40,903	37,157	37,680	122,171	191,847	459,523
Losses, charge-offs, and transfers to valuation reserves: On securities: Losses and charge-offs	1	4	23	281	3,024	5,356	7,396	5,025	5,634	13,601	13,705	54,050
Transfers to valuation reserves				1	467	1,856	5,392	5,431	10,245	33,322	102,945	159,659
On loans: Losses and charge-offs	12	75	71	1,072	3,125	2,239	1,742	661	244	492	1,611	11,344
Transfers to valuation reserves	1	3	12	713	4,633	9,610	15,278	13,544	13,762	34,246	65,302	157,103
All other		2	10	262	2,165	4,444	7,578	4,096	6,323	22,660	18,819	66,360
Total losses, charge-offs, and transfers to valuation reserves	14	84	116	2,329	13,414	23,505	37,386	28,757	36,208	104,321	202,382	448,516
Profits before income taxes	72	261	628	8,760	53,353	82,990	137,185	109,910	114,387	405,343	661,585	1,574,474
Taxes on net income: Federal	17	69	170	2,210	14,436	25,174	47,254	40,561	47,464	174,769	304,805	656,929
State	1	3	9	100	674	994	1,718	1,142	1,325	6,853	18,737	31,556
Total taxes on net income	18	72	179	2,310	15,110	26,168	48,972	41,703	48,789	181,622	323,542	688,485
Net profits before dividends	54	189	449	6,450	38,243	56,822	88,213	68,207	65,598	223,721	338,043	885,989
Cash dividends declared: On preferred stock					11	9	30	31		88		169
On common stock	27	84	172	2,563	14,686	20,301	29,852	22,161	24,919	91,683	185,159	391,607
Total cash dividends declared	27	84	172	2,563	14,697	20,310	29,882	22,192	24,919	91,771	185,159	391,776

TABLE No. 26.—*Earnings, expenses, and dividends of national banks, by size of banks, for the year ended Dec. 31, 1958*—Continued

TOTAL UNITED STATES AND POSSESSIONS
[In thousands of dollars]

	Banks operating throughout entire year with deposits on Dec. 31, 1958, of—											
	Less than $500,000	$500,000 to $750,000	$750,000 to $1,000,000	$1,000,000 to $2,000,000	$2,000,000 to $5,000,000	$5,000,000 to $10,000,000	$10,000,000 to $25,000,000	$25,000,000 to $50,000,000	$50,000,000 to $100,000,000	$100,000,000 to $500,000,000	$500,000,000 or more	Total
Memoranda items:												
Recoveries credited to valuation reserves (not included in recoveries above):												
On securities					12	274	111	371	179	5,403	519	6,869
On loans		1	3	333	2,115	3,316	4,553	2,744	2,687	7,470	15,505	38,727
Losses charged to valuation reserves (not included in losses above):												
On securities					9	120	160	99	495	2,178	9,548	12,609
On loans		6	5	493	3,584	6,775	9,172	5,829	7,246	15,974	27,370	76,454
Stock dividends (increases in capital stock)			25	145	3,396	5,802	10,543	9,711	7,543	21,827	49,366	108,358
Average per bank:												
Gross earnings from current operations	18	26	37	61	133	278	610	1,345	2,654	8,119	64,910	991
Current operating expenses	14	19	25	43	94	198	436	956	1,824	5,291	39,059	648
Net earnings from current operations	4	7	12	18	39	80	174	389	830	2,828	25,851	343
Net profits before dividends	4	5	8	13	25	52	115	261	482	1,633	13,002	194
Per $100 of deposits:												
Net earnings from current operations	1.06	1.14	1.25	1.19	1.14	1.14	1.13	1.13	1.20	1.29	1.56	1.34
Net profits before dividends	.88	.74	.88	.79	.75	.74	.75	.76	.69	.74	.79	.76
Per $100 of capital accounts:												
Net earnings from current operations	6.30	8.32	9.81	10.30	11.55	12.92	14.12	15.18	15.97	16.90	17.88	16.19
Net profits before dividends	5.23	5.44	6.86	6.84	7.62	8.43	9.32	10.20	9.28	9.75	8.99	9.18
Cash dividends	2.62	2.42	2.63	2.72	2.93	3.01	3.16	3.32	3.52	4.00	4.93	4.06
Number of officers at end of period	35	91	145	1,511	5,708	5,745	6,345	3,776	3,357	8,623	9,821	45,157
Number of employees other than officers at end of period	14	57	100	1,609	9,997	15,974	27,412	20,711	21,959	65,573	78,640	242,046

NOTE.—The deposits, capital stock, and capital accounts shown in this table are as of end of period. Capital accounts represents the aggregate book value of capital stock, surplus, undivided profits, reserves and retirement fund for preferred stock.

TABLE No. 27.—*Earnings, expenses, and dividends of national banks, years ended Dec. 31, 1956–58*

[In thousands of dollars]

	1956		1957		1958	
Number of banks [1]	4, 659		4, 627		4, 585	
Capital stock, par value [2]	2, 562, 055		2, 716, 931		2, 875, 117	
Capital accounts [2]	8, 220, 620		8, 769, 839		9, 412, 557	
	Amount	*Percent to total*	*Amount*	*Percent to total*	*Amount*	*Percent to total*
Earnings from current operations:						
Interest and dividends on:						
U.S. Government obligations	737, 465	19. 24	782, 135	18. 26	839, 145	18. 49
Other securities	202, 352	5. 28	225, 367	5. 26	267, 583	5. 89
Interest and discount on loans	2, 321, 685	60. 56	2, 631, 136	61. 42	2, 739, 235	60. 35
Service charges and other fees on banks' loans	38, 027	. 99	45, 186	1. 05	50, 945	1. 12
Service charges on deposit accounts	211, 596	5. 52	244, 066	5. 70	269, 606	5. 94
Other service charges, commissions, fees, and collection and exchange charges	70, 810	1. 85	79, 710	1. 86	80, 185	1. 77
Trust department	116, 845	3. 05	129, 433	3. 02	141, 473	3. 12
Other current earnings	134, 672	3. 51	146, 753	3. 43	150, 771	3. 32
Total earnings from current operations	3, 833, 452	100. 00	4, 283, 786	100. 00	4, 538, 943	100. 00
Current operating expenses:						
Salaries and wages:						
Officers	359, 438	15. 38	386, 237	14. 27	413, 130	13. 91
Employees other than officers	719, 694	30. 80	782, 470	28. 90	828, 643	27. 90
Number of officers [1]	*42, 050*		*43, 645*		*45, 254*	
Number of employees other than officers [1]	*229, 227*		*239, 172*		*242, 312*	
Fees paid to directors and members of executive, discount, and advisory committees	19, 295	. 83	20, 728	. 77	22, 108	. 74
Interest on time deposits (including savings deposits)	437, 199	18. 71	635, 777	23. 48	762, 319	25. 67
Interest and discount on borrowed money	25, 542	1. 09	27, 871	1. 03	12, 835	. 43
Taxes other than on net income	106, 483	4. 56	116, 309	4. 30	125, 872	4. 24
Recurring depreciation on banking house, furniture and fixtures	70, 314	3. 01	79, 470	2. 93	91, 187	3. 07
Other current operating expenses	598, 461	25. 62	658, 367	24. 32	714, 101	24. 04
Total current operating expenses	2, 336, 426	100. 00	2, 707, 229	100. 00	2, 970, 195	100. 00
Net earnings from current operations	1, 497, 026		1, 576, 557		1, 568, 748	
Recoveries, transfers from valuation reserves and profits:						
On securities:						
Recoveries	10, 082	8. 46	4, 218	4. 60	5, 526	1. 20
Transfers from valuation reserves	25, 462	21. 37	14, 266	15. 57	33, 078	7. 17
Profits on securities sold or redeemed	11, 417	9. 58	31, 085	33. 94	353, 072	76. 58
On loans:						
Recoveries	10, 542	8. 85	9, 484	10. 35	11, 273	2. 44
Transfers from valuation reserves	32, 953	27. 66	15, 129	16. 52	27, 554	5. 98
All other	28, 685	24. 08	17, 422	19. 02	30, 566	6. 63
Total recoveries, transfers from valuation reserves and profits	119, 141	100. 00	91, 604	100. 00	461, 069	100. 00
Losses, charge-offs, and transfers to valuation reserves:						
On securities:						
Losses and charge-offs	182, 827	34. 03	119, 005	30. 28	54, 845	12. 18
Transfers to valuation reserves	61, 319	11. 41	37, 937	9. 65	159, 713	35. 46
On loans:						
Losses and charge-offs	11, 171	2. 08	11, 715	2. 98	11, 583	2. 57
Transfers to valuation reserves	233, 651	43. 49	177, 226	45. 09	157, 673	35. 00
All other	48, 278	8. 99	47, 187	12. 00	66, 612	14. 79
Total losses, charge-offs, and transfers to valuation reserves	537, 246	100. 00	393, 070	100. 00	450, 426	100. 00
Profits before income taxes	1, 078, 921		1, 275, 091		1, 579, 391	

See footnotes at end of table.

TABLE No. 27.—*Earnings, expenses, and dividends of national banks, years ended Dec. 31, 1956–58*—Continued

[In thousands of dollars]

	1956		1957		1958	
	Amount	*Percent to total*	*Amount*	*Percent to total*	*Amount*	*Percent to total*
Taxes on net income:						
Federal	413, 053	-------	522, 705	-------	658, 615	-------
State	18, 727	-------	22, 529	-------	31, 656	-------
Total taxes on net income	431, 780	-------	545, 234	-------	690, 271	-------
Net profits before dividends	647, 141	-------	729, 857	-------	889, 120	-------
Cash dividends declared:						
On preferred stock	177	-------	[3] 171	-------	169	-------
On common stock	329, 777	-------	363, 699	-------	392, 822	-------
Total cash dividends declared	329, 954	-------	363, 870	-------	392, 991	-------
Memoranda items:						
Recoveries credited to valuation reserves (not included in recoveries above):						
On securities	2, 945	-------	1, 588	-------	6, 876	-------
On loans	26, 807	-------	29, 525	-------	38, 932	-------
Losses charged to valuation reserves (not included in losses above):						
On securities	56, 170	-------	32, 147	-------	12, 610	-------
On loans	67, 184	-------	62, 722	-------	76, 795	-------
Stock dividends (increases in capital stock)	84, 970	-------	64, 738	-------	108, 506	-------
		Percent		*Percent*		*Percent*
Ratios to gross earnings:						
Salaries, wages, and fees	-------	28. 65	-------	27. 77	-------	27. 85
Interest on time deposits	-------	11. 41	-------	14. 84	-------	16. 79
All other current expenses	-------	20. 89	-------	20. 59	-------	20. 80
Total current expenses	-------	60. 95	-------	63. 20	-------	65. 44
Net current earnings	-------	39. 05	-------	36. 80	-------	34. 56
Ratio of cash dividends to capital stock (par value)	-------	12. 88	-------	13. 41	-------	13. 67
Ratio of cash dividends to capital accounts	-------	4. 01	-------	4. 15	-------	4. 18

[1] Number at end of period. Remaining figures include earnings, expenses, etc., of those banks which were in operation a part of the year but were inactive at the close of the year.
[2] Figures are averages of amounts reported for the June and December call dates in the year indicated and the December call date in the previous year.
[3] Revised.

NOTE.—Earnings and dividends figures for 1869 to 1937 were published for the years ended August 31 or June 30 and appear in the table beginning on page 96 of the Comptroller's Annual Report for 1937. Similar figures for 1938 through 1941 appear in table 26 on page 136 of the 1941 report. Calendar year figures are available, beginning with the year 1917, and are published in the Comptroller's reports as follows: 1938, p. 100; 1940, p. 17; 1942, p. 34; 1943, p. 30; 1946, p. 98; 1949, p. 100; 1951, p. 118; 1954, p. 142; and 1957, p. 152.

TABLE No. 28.—*Number of national banks, capital stock, capital funds, net profits, dividends, and ratios, years ended Dec. 31, 1930-58*

[In thousands of dollars. Figures for previous years published in report for 1938, p. 115]

Year	Number of banks	Capital stock (par value)¹ Preferred	Capital stock (par value)¹ Common	Capital stock (par value)¹ Total	Capital accounts¹	Net profits before dividends	Cash dividends On preferred stock	Cash dividends On common stock	Ratio: Cash dividends on preferred stock to preferred capital (Percent)	Ratio: Cash dividends on common stock to common capital (Percent)	Ratio: Total cash dividends to capital accounts (Percent)	Ratio: Net profits before dividends to capital stock (Percent)	Ratio: Net profits before dividends to capital accounts (Percent)
1930	7,038		1,724,028	1,724,028	3,919,950	158,411		211,272		12.25	5.39	9.19	4.04
1931	6,373		1,680,780	1,680,780	3,753,412	²54,550		193,196		11.49	5.15	²3.25	²1.45
1932	6,016		1,597,037	1,597,037	3,323,536	²164,737		135,381		8.48	4.07	²10.32	²4.96
1933	³5,159	92,469	1,507,834	1,600,303	2,981,678	²286,116	558	71,106	.60	4.72	2.40	²17.88	²9.60
1934	³5,467	349,470	1,359,573	1,709,043	2,982,008	²153,451	10,103	80,915	2.89	5.95	3.05	²8.98	²5.15
1935	5,392	510,511	1,280,813	1,791,324	3,084,092	158,491	18,862	94,377	3.69	7.37	3.67	8.85	5.14
1936	5,331	447,501	1,259,027	1,706,528	3,143,029	313,826	18,166	101,850	4.06	8.09	3.82	18.39	9.98
1937	5,266	305,842	1,285,946	1,591,788	3,206,194	228,021	11,532	110,231	3.77	8.57	3.80	14.32	7.11
1938	5,230	267,495	1,310,243	1,577,738	3,281,819	198,649	9,378	113,347	3.51	8.65	3.74	12.59	6.05
1939	5,193	241,075	1,320,446	1,561,521	3,380,749	251,576	8,911	122,267	3.70	9.26	3.88	16.11	7.44
1940	5,150	204,244	1,328,071	1,532,315	3,463,862	241,465	8,175	125,174	4.00	9.43	3.85	15.76	6.97
1941	5,123	182,056	1,341,398	1,523,454	3,596,865	269,295	7,816	124,805	4.29	9.30	3.69	17.68	7.49
1942	5,087	156,739	1,354,384	1,511,123	3,684,882	243,343	6,683	121,177	4.26	8.95	3.47	16.10	6.60
1943	5,046	135,713	1,372,457	1,508,170	3,860,443	350,457	6,158	125,357	4.54	9.13	3.41	23.24	9.08
1944	5,031	110,597	1,440,519	1,551,116	4,114,972	411,844	5,296	139,012	4.79	9.65	3.51	26.55	10.01
1945	5,023	80,672	1,536,212	1,616,884	4,467,718	490,133	4,131	151,525	5.12	9.86	3.48	30.31	10.97
1946	5,013	53,202	1,646,631	1,699,833	4,893,038	494,898	2,427	167,702	4.56	10.18	3.48	29.11	10.11
1947	5,011	32,529	1,736,676	1,769,205	5,293,267	452,983	1,372	182,147	4.22	10.49	3.47	25.60	8.56
1948	4,997	25,128	1,779,362	1,804,490	5,545,993	423,757	1,304	192,603	5.19	10.82	3.50	23.48	7.64
1949	4,981	20,979	1,863,373	1,884,352	5,811,044	474,881	1,100	203,644	5.24	10.93	3.52	25.20	8.17
1950	4,965	16,079	1,949,898	1,965,977	6,152,799	537,610	712	228,792	4.43	11.73	3.73	27.35	8.74
1951	4,946	12,032	2,046,018	2,058,050	6,506,378	506,695	615	247,230	5.11	12.08	3.81	24.62	7.79
1952	4,916	6,862	2,171,026	2,177,888	6,875,134	561,481	400	258,663	5.83	11.91	3.77	25.78	8.17
1953	4,864	5,512	2,258,234	2,263,746	7,235,820	573,287	332	274,884	6.02	12.17	3.80	25.32	7.92
1954	4,796	4,797	2,381,429	2,386,226	7,739,553	741,065	264	299,841	5.50	12.59	3.88	31.06	9.58
1955	4,700	4,167	2,456,454	2,460,621	7,924,719	643,149	203	309,532	4.87	12.60	3.91	26.14	8.12
1956	4,659	3,944	2,558,111	2,562,055	8,220,620	647,141	177	329,777	4.49	12.89	4.01	25.26	7.87
1957	4,627	3,786	2,713,145	2,716,931	8,769,839	729,857	⁴171	363,699	⁴4.52	13.41	4.15	26.86	8.32
1958	4,585	3,332	2,871,785	2,875,117	9,412,557	889,120	169	392,822	5.07	13.68	4.18	30.92	9.45

¹ Averages of amounts from reports of condition made in each year.
² Deficit.
³ Licensed banks, i.e., those operating on an unrestricted basis.
⁴ Revised.

TABLE No. 29.—*Total loans of national banks, losses and recoveries on loans, and ratio of net losses or recoveries to loans, by calendar years, 1939–58*

[In thousands of dollars]

Year	Total loans end of year	Losses and charge-offs	Recoveries	Net losses or recoveries (+)	Ratio of losses (or recoveries+) to loans
					Percent
1939	9,043,632	67,171	39,927	27,244	0.30
1940	10,027,773	58,249	36,751	21,498	.21
1941	11,751,792	51,989	43,658	8,331	.07
1942	10,200,798	43,134	40,659	2,475	.02
1943	10,133,532	43,101	52,900	+9,799	+.10
1944	11,497,802	41,039	50,348	+9,309	+.08
1945	13,948,042	29,652	37,392	+7,740	+.06
1946	17,309,767	44,520	41,313	3,207	.02
1947	21,480,457	73,542	43,629	29,913	.14
1948	23,818,513	¹ 50,482	² 31,133	19,349	.08
1949	23,928,293	¹ 59,482	² 26,283	33,199	.14
1950	29,277,480	¹ ³ 45,970	² ³ 31,525	³ 14,445	.05
1951	32,423,777	¹ 53,940	² 31,832	22,108	.07
1952	36,119,673	¹ 52,322	² 32,996	19,326	.05
1953	37,944,146	¹ 68,533	² 36,332	32,201	.08
1954	39,827,678	¹ 67,198	² 41,524	25,674	.06
1955	43,559,726	¹ 68,951	² 39,473	29,478	.07
1956	48,248,332	¹ 78,355	² 37,349	41,006	.08
1957	50,502,277	¹ 74,437	² 39,009	35,428	.07
1958	52,796,224	¹ 88,378	² 50,205	38,173	.07
Average for 1939–58	26,691,986	58,022	39,212	18,810	.07

¹ Excludes transfers to valuation reserves.
² Excludes transfers from valuation reserves.
³ Revised.

NOTE.—For prior figures beginning with the year 1928 see Annual Report for 1947, p. 100.

TABLE No. 30.—*Total securities of national banks, losses and recoveries on securities and ratio of net losses or recoveries to securities, by calendar years, 1939–58*

[In thousands of dollars]

Year	Total securities end of year	Losses and charge-offs	Recoveries	Net losses or recoveries (+)	Ratio of losses (or recoveries+) to securities
					Percent
1939	12,811,576	109,378	33,631	75,747	0.59
1940	13,668,040	107,960	40,993	66,967	.49
1941	15,887,508	92,134	48,157	43,977	.28
1942	27,482,788	73,253	36,170	37,083	.13
1943	37,504,253	66,008	59,652	6,356	.02
1944	47,022,329	67,574	50,302	17,272	.04
1945	55,611,609	74,627	54,153	20,474	.04
1946	46,642,816	74,620	33,816	40,804	.09
1947	44,009,966	69,785	25,571	44,214	.10
1948	40,228,353	¹ 55,369	² 25,264	30,105	.07
1949	44,207,750	¹ 23,595	² 7,516	16,079	.04
1950	43,022,623	¹ 26,825	² 11,509	15,316	.04
1951	43,043,617	¹ 57,546	² 6,712	50,834	.12
1952	44,292,285	¹ 76,524	² 9,259	67,265	.15
1953	44,210,233	¹ 119,124	² 8,325	110,799	.25
1954	48,932,258	¹ 49,469	² 9,286	40,183	.08
1955	42,857,330	¹ 152,858	² 15,758	137,100	.32
1956	40,503,392	¹ 238,997	² 13,027	225,970	.56
1957	40,981,709	¹ 151,152	² 5,806	145,346	.35
1958	46,788,224	¹ 67,455	² 12,402	55,053	.12
Average for 1939–58	38,985,433	87,713	25,366	62,347	.16

¹ Excludes transfers to valuation reserves.
² Excludes transfers from valuation reserves.

NOTE.—For prior figures beginning with the year 1928 see Annual Report for 1947, p. 100.

TABLE No. 31.—*Foreign branches of American national banks, Dec. 31, 1958* [1]

BANK OF AMERICA NATIONAL TRUST AND SAVINGS ASSOCIATION, SAN FRANCISCO, CALIF.:

England:
London.
London (West End).

Guam:
Agana.

Japan:
Kobe.
Osaka.
Tokyo.
Yokohama.

Philippines:
Manila.

Thailand:
Bangkok.

FIRST NATIONAL BANK OF BOSTON, MASS.:

Argentina:
Avellaneda.
Buenos Aires.
Buenos Aires (Alsina).
Buenos Aires (Constitucion).
Buenos Aires (Once).
Rosario.

Brazil:
Rio de Janeiro.
Santos.
Sao Paulo.

Cuba:
Cienfuegos.
Havana.
Havana (Avenida de Italia).
Havana (Avenida Maximo Gomez).
Sancti Spiritus.
Santiago de Cuba.

FIRST NATIONAL CITY BANK OF NEW YORK, N. Y.:

Argentina:
Buenos Aires.
Buenos Aires (Flores).
Buenos Aires (Plaza Once).
Rosario.

Brazil:
Porto Alegre.
Recife (Pernambuco).
Rio de Janeiro.
Salvador.
Santos.
Sao Paulo (Praca Antonio Prado).
Sao Paulo (Avenida Ipiranga).

Canal Zone:
Balboa.
Cristobal.

Chile:
Santiago.
Valparaiso.

Colombia:
Barranquilla.
Bogota.
Cali.
Medellin.

FIRST NATIONAL CITY BANK OF NEW YORK, N. Y.—Continued

Cuba:
Caibarien.
Cardenas.
Havana.
Havana (Ave Rancho Boyeros).
Havana (Cuatro Caminos).
Havana (Galiano).
Havana (La Lonja).
Havana (Twenty-third Street Branch).
Manzanillo.
Matanzas.
Santiago de Cuba.

Egypt:
Cairo.

England:
London.
London (Berkley Square Branch).

France:
Paris.

Hong Kong:
Hong Kong.

India:
Bombay.
Calcutta.

Japan:
Nagoya.
Osaka.
Tokyo.
Yokohama.

Lebanon:
Beirut.

Mexico:
Mexico City (Isabel la Catolica).
Mexico City (Parque San Martin).
Mexico City (Republica).

Panama:
Panama City.
Panama City (La Exposicion).

Paraguay:
Asuncion.

Peru:
Lima.

Philippines:
Cebu City.
Clark Field.
Manila.
Manila (Port Area Branch).

Puerto Rico:
Arecibo.
Bayamon.
Caguas.
Mayaguez.
Mayaguez (Plaza de Colon).
Ponce.
San Juan.
San Juan (Hato Rey).
San Juan (Santurce).

Saudi Arabia:
Jeddah.

Singapore:
Singapore.

Uruguay:
Montevideo.

Venezuela:
Caracas.
Caracas (Miranda).
Maracaibo.
Valencia.

[1] Excludes banking facilities at military establishments.

NOTE.—Consolidated statement of the assets and liabilities of the above-named branches as of Dec. 31, 1958, appears in the following table.

TABLE NO. 32.—*Consolidated statement of assets and liabilities of foreign branches of national banks, Dec. 31, 1958* [1]

[In thousands of dollars]

Number of branches _____ 93

ASSETS

Loans and discounts, including overdrafts _____	743, 331
Securities _____	81, 344
Currency and coin _____	37, 477
Balances with other banks and cash items in process of collection ____	288, 405
Due from head office and branches _____	116, 611
Real estate, furniture, and fixtures _____	14, 923
Customers' liability on account of acceptances _____	101, 032
Other assets _____	21, 897
Total assets _____	1, 405, 020

LIABILITIES

Demand deposits of individuals, partnerships, and corporations _____	605, 110
Time deposits of individuals, partnerships, and corporations _____	310, 872
Deposits of U.S. Government _____	119, 710
State and municipal deposits _____	13, 690
Deposits of banks _____	180, 918
Other deposits (certified and cashiers' checks, etc.) _____	17, 030
Total deposits _____	1, 247, 330
Due to head office and branches _____	4, 963
Bills payable and rediscounts _____	4, 139
Acceptances executed by or for account of reporting branches and outstanding _____	103, 918
Other liabilities _____	44, 630
Total liabilities _____	1, 404, 980

CAPITAL ACCOUNTS

Undivided profits, including reserve accounts _____	40
Total liabilities and capital accounts _____	1, 405, 020

[1] Excludes figures for banking facilities at military establishments.

NOTE.—For location of foreign branches see preceding table.

TABLE NO. 33.—*Assets and liabilities of banks in the District of Columbia, by classes, Dec. 31, 1958*

[In thousands of dollars]

	Total all banks	National banks	Non-national banks
Number of banks	13	5	8
ASSETS			
Loans and discounts:			
Real estate loans:			
Secured by farm land	1,158	185	973
Secured by residential properties:			
Insured by Federal Housing Administration	11,929	6,299	5,630
Insured or guaranteed by Veterans' Administration	42,607	27,178	15,429
Not insured or guaranteed by FHA or VA	78,155	44,783	33,372
Secured by other properties	62,322	38,334	23,988
Loans to banks	1,399	1,399	
Loans to brokers and dealers in securities	12,474	3,534	8,940
Other loans for purchasing or carrying securities	3,313	2,914	399
Loans to farmers directly guaranteed by the Commodity Credit Corporation			
Other loans to farmers (excluding loans on real estate)	120	38	82
Commercial and industrial loans (including open market paper)	265,312	170,572	94,740
Other loans to individuals for personal expenditures:			
Passenger automobile installment loans	37,587	15,572	22,015
Other retail consumer installment loans	14,648	4,690	9,958
Residential repair and modernization installment loans	15,760	8,079	7,681
Other installment loans for personal expenditures	35,437	10,709	24,728
Single-payment loans for personal expenditures	61,664	31,785	29,879
All other loans	35,053	18,081	16,972
Overdrafts	152	104	48
Total gross loans	679,090	384,256	294,834
Less valuation reserves	8,884	7,378	1,506
Net loans	670,206	376,878	293,328
Securities:			
U.S. Government obligations, direct and guaranteed:			
Direct obligations:			
Treasury bills	21,899	3,136	18,763
Treasury certificates of indebtedness	39,818	23,743	16,075
Treasury notes	91,005	50,887	40,118
United States nonmarketable bonds (savings, investment series A–1965, B–1975–80, and depositary bonds)	16,301	7,818	8,483
Other bonds maturing in 5 years or less	209,195	119,812	89,383
Other bonds maturing in 5 to 10 years	113,168	73,117	40,051
Other bonds maturing in 10 to 20 years	32,991	25,260	7,731
Bonds maturing after 20 years	779	689	90
Total	525,156	304,462	220,694
Obligations guaranteed by U.S. Government (Federal Housing Administration debentures)	7		7
Total	525,163	304,462	220,701
Obligations of States and political subdivisions	40,502	28,141	12,361
Other bonds, notes, and debentures	26,971	15,951	11,020
Corporate stocks, including stock of Federal Reserve Bank	2,295	1,536	759
Total securities	594,931	350,090	244,841
Cash, balances with other banks, including reserve balances and cash items in process of collection:			
Cash items in process of collection, including exchanges for clearing house	85,470	45,731	39,739
Demand balances with banks in the United States (except private banks and American branches of foreign banks)	39,771	25,836	13,935
Other balances with banks in United States	215	89	126
Balances with banks in foreign countries	493	389	104
Currency and coin	28,841	16,011	12,830
Reserve with Federal Reserve Bank and approved reserve agencies	178,424	90,700	87,724
Total cash, balances with other banks, etc	333,214	178,756	154,458
Bank premises owned, furniture and fixtures	21,839	15,476	6,363
Real estate owned other than bank premises	137	137	
Investments and other assets indirectly representing bank premises or other real estate	4,560		4,560
Other assets	5,374	2,088	3,286
Total assets	1,630,261	923,425	706,836

TABLE No. 33.—*Assets and liabilities of banks in the District of Columbia, by classes, Dec. 31, 1958*—Continued

[In thousands of dollars]

	Total all banks	National banks	Non-national banks
LIABILITIES			
Demand deposits:			
Individuals, partnerships, and corporations	995, 385	571, 858	423, 527
U.S. Government	22, 630	15, 371	7, 259
States and political subdivisions	133	104	29
Banks in United States	70, 153	49, 029	21, 124
Banks in foreign countries	6, 400	4, 310	2, 090
Certified and cashiers' checks (including dividend checks), letters of credit and travelers' checks sold for cash, and amounts due to Federal Reserve Bank and agents (transit account)	25, 404	10, 788	14, 616
Total demand deposits	1, 120, 105	651, 460	468, 645
Time deposits:			
Individuals, partnerships, and corporations	363, 306	190, 851	172, 455
U.S. Government	18, 216	9, 321	8, 895
Postal savings	656	656	
States and political subdivisions			
Banks in United States			
Banks in foreign countries	1, 450		1, 450
Total time deposits	383, 628	200, 828	182, 800
Total deposits	1, 503, 733	852, 288	651, 445
Bills payable, rediscounts, and other liabilities for borrowed money			
Other liabilities	16, 495	7, 534	8, 961
Total liabilities	1, 520, 228	859, 822	660, 406
CAPITAL ACCOUNTS			
Capital stock: Common stock	29, 770	18, 100	11, 670
Surplus	59, 100	33, 100	26, 000
Undivided profits	16, 369	9, 981	6, 388
Reserves	4, 794	2, 422	2, 372
Total capital accounts	110, 033	63, 603	46, 430
Total liabilities and capital accounts	1, 630, 261	923, 425	706, 836
MEMORANDUM			
Assets pledged or assigned to secure liabilities and for other purposes (including notes and bills rediscounted and securities sold with agreement to repurchase)	99, 713	44, 258	55, 455

TABLE No. 34.—*Assets and liabilities of all banks in the District of Columbia at date of each call during the year ended Dec. 31, 1958*

[In thousands of dollars]

	Mar. 4, 1958	June 23, 1958	Sept. 24, 1958	Dec. 31, 1958
	16 banks	15 banks	15 banks	13 banks
ASSETS				
Loans and discounts (including overdrafts)	640,983	646,229	661,623	670,206
U. S. Government securities, direct obligations	468,658	508,474	521,700	525,156
Obligations guaranteed by U. S. Government	7	7	7	7
Obligations of States and political subdivisions	31,733	39,693	40,625	40,502
Other bonds, notes, and debentures	27,782	31,095	31,378	26,971
Corporate stocks, including stock of Federal Reserve bank	2,474	2,384	2,386	2,295
Reserve with Federal Reserve bank and approved reserve agencies	187,780	182,735	173,465	178,424
Currency and coin	25,600	28,624	28,475	28,841
Balances with other banks, and cash items in process of collection	124,272	114,116	104,468	125,949
Bank premises owned, furniture and fixtures	21,095	21,608	20,967	21,839
Real estate owned other than bank premises	192	144	139	137
Investments and other assets indirectly representing bank premises or other real estate	4,136	4,136	5,562	4,560
Customers' liability on acceptances outstanding	64	207	161	----------
Income earned or accrued but not collected	2,686	2,077	2,865	} 5,374
Other assets	2,829	2,633	2,538	
Total assets	1,540,291	1,584,162	1,596,359	1,630,261
LIABILITIES				
Demand deposits of individuals, partnerships, and corporations	930,906	927,027	948,113	995,385
Time deposits of individuals, partnerships, and corporations	341,263	370,648	363,848	363,306
Postal savings deposits	754	729	656	656
Deposits of U. S. Government	38,397	52,920	45,450	40,846
Deposits of States and political subdivisions	93	86	91	133
Deposits of banks	79,607	70,529	72,964	78,003
Other deposits (certified and cashiers' checks, etc.)	17,412	31,534	21,216	25,404
Total deposits	*1,408,432*	*1,453,473*	*1,452,338*	*1,503,733*
Demand deposits	*1,045,282*	*1,061,464*	*1,065,634*	*1,120,105*
Time deposits	*363,150*	*392,009*	*386,704*	*383,628*
Bills payable, rediscounts, and other liabilities for borrowed money	----------	5,500	16,500	----------
Acceptances executed by or for account of reporting banks and outstanding	68	207	161	----------
Income collected but not earned	5,307	6,005	6,189	} 16,495
Expenses accrued and unpaid	10,225	6,151	8,224	
Other liabilities	1,854	2,769	1,614	
Total liabilities	1,425,886	1,474,105	1,485,026	1,520,228
CAPITAL ACCOUNTS				
Capital stock: Common stock	31,870	30,370	30,370	29,770
Surplus	59,350	58,350	58,400	59,100
Undivided profits	17,730	17,031	18,219	16,369
Reserves	5,455	4,306	4,344	4,794
Total capital accounts	114,405	110,057	111,333	110,033
Total liabilities and capital accounts	1,540,291	1,584,162	1,596,359	1,630,261
MEMORANDUM				
Assets pledged or assigned to secure liabilities and for other purposes	97,877	108,131	124,820	99,713

TABLE 35.—*Assets and liabilities of nonnational banks in the District of Columbia at date of each call during the year ended Dec. 31, 1958*

[In thousands of dollars]

	Mar. 4, 1958	June 23, 1958	Sept. 24, 1958	Dec. 31, 1958
	9 banks	9 banks	9 banks	8 banks
ASSETS				
Loans and discounts (including overdrafts)	262,292	287,676	299,084	293,328
U.S. Government securities, direct obligations	160,826	194,059	214,471	220,694
Obligations guaranteed by U.S. Government	7	7	7	7
Obligations of States and political subdivisions	7,595	12,196	12,935	12,361
Other bonds, notes, and debentures	12,371	13,782	12,516	11,020
Corporate stocks, including stock of Federal Reserve bank	843	843	845	759
Reserve with Federal Reserve bank and approved reserve agencies	70,833	72,667	65,366	87,724
Currency and coin	10,456	12,804	12,173	12,830
Balances with other banks, and cash items in process of collection	35,475	41,192	38,186	53,904
Bank premises owned, furniture and fixtures	5,356	7,137	5,903	6,363
Investments and other assets indirectly representing bank premises or other real estate	4,136	4,136	5,562	4,560
Customers' liability on acceptances outstanding	64	166	20	------------
Income earned or accrued but not collected	1,418	960	1,295⎫	
Other assets	2,018	1,888	1,723⎭	3,286
Total assets	573,690	649,513	670,086	706,836
LIABILITIES				
Demand deposits of individuals, partnerships, and corporations	330,104	372,841	391,751	423,527
Time deposits of individuals, partnerships, and corporations	149,513	167,886	172,641	172,455
Postal savings deposits	----------	----------	----------	----------
Deposits of U.S. Government	13,204	19,344	18,141	16,154
Deposits of States and political subdivisions	12	14	34	29
Deposits of banks	19,172	23,543	23,521	24,664
Other deposits (certified and cashiers' checks, etc.)	4,405	10,296	7,564	14,616
Total deposits	*516,410*	*593,924*	*613,652*	*651,445*
Demand deposits	*354,739*	*414,101*	*428,132*	*468,645*
Time deposits	*161,671*	*179,823*	*185,520*	*182,800*
Bills payable, rediscounts, and other liabilities for borrowed money	------------	500	------------	
Acceptances executed by or for account of reporting banks and outstanding	68	166	20	------------
Income collected but not earned	4,144	4,727	4,872⎫	
Expenses accrued and unpaid	4,464	3,227	3,988⎬	8,961
Other liabilities	211	670	592⎭	
Total liabilities	525,297	603,214	623,124	660,406
CAPITAL ACCOUNTS				
Capital stock: Common stock	12,120	12,120	12,120	11,670
Surplus	24,750	25,250	25,300	26,000
Undivided profits	8,218	6,598	7,216	6,388
Reserves	3,305	2,331	2,326	2,372
Total capital accounts	48,393	46,299	46,962	46,430
Total liabilities and capital accounts	573,690	649,513	670,086	706,836
MEMORANDUM				
Assets pledged or assigned to secure liabilities and for other purposes	39,069	54,955	57,585	55,455

TABLE No. 36.—*Earnings, expenses, and dividends of banks in the District of Columbia, years ended Dec. 31, 1958 and 1957*

[In thousands of dollars]

	Years ended Dec. 31—					
	Total		National banks		Nonnational banks	
	1958	1957	1958	1957	1958	1957
Number of banks [1]	13	16	5	7	8	9
Capital stock, par value [2]	30,637	31,307	18,700	19,433	11,937	11,874
Capital accounts [2]	110,950	112,236	63,970	64,854	46,980	47,382
Earnings from current operations:						
Interest and dividends on:						
U.S. Government obligations	12,099	11,212	7,405	7,185	4,694	4,027
Other securities	1,970	1,577	1,022	904	948	673
Interest and discount on loans	31,682	30,613	17,070	17,427	14,612	13,186
Service charges and other fees on banks' loans	347	498	165	161	182	337
Service charges on deposit accounts	3,982	3,663	1,928	1,807	2,054	1,856
Other service charges, commissions, fees, and collection and exchange charges	1,204	1,391	455	419	749	972
Trust department	3,017	2,984	995	1,286	2,022	1,698
Other current earnings	1,473	1,244	744	604	729	640
Total earnings from current operations	55,774	53,182	29,784	29,793	25,990	23,389
Current operating expenses:						
Salaries and wages:						
Officers	5,577	5,383	3,097	3,126	2,480	2,257
Employees other than officers	11,844	11,286	6,129	5,971	5,715	5,315
Number of officers [1]	*489*	*475*	*252*	*265*	*237*	*210*
Number of employees other than officers [1]	*3,380*	*3,337*	*1,691*	*1,809*	*1,689*	*1,528*
Fees paid to directors and members of executive, discount, and advisory committees	412	408	202	223	210	185
Interest on time deposits (including savings deposits)	8,115	7,502	4,221	4,054	3,894	3,448
Interest and discount on borrowed money	158	206	116	147	42	59
Taxes other than on net income	2,145	2,142	1,094	1,162	1,051	980
Recurring depreciation on banking house, furniture and fixtures	1,139	1,189	773	759	366	430
Other current operating expenses	8,874	7,656	4,153	4,041	4,721	3,615
Total current operating expenses	38,264	35,772	19,785	19,483	18,479	16,289
Net earnings from current operations	17,510	17,410	9,999	10,310	7,511	7,100
Recoveries, transfers from valuation reserves, and profits:						
On securities:						
Recoveries		1		1		
Transfers from valuation reserves	107				107	
Profits on securities sold or redeemed	1,963	197	906	104	1,057	93
On loans:						
Recoveries	68	112	25	76	43	36
Transfers from valuation reserves	380				380	
All other	364	105	106	53	258	52
Total recoveries, transfers from valuation reserves and profits	2,882	415	1,037	234	1,845	181
Losses, charge-offs, and transfers to valuation reserves:						
On securities:						
Losses and charge-offs	889	476	341	204	548	272
Transfers to valuation reserves	363	22			363	22
On loans:						
Losses and charge-offs	172	272	53	127	119	145
Transfers to valuation reserves	1,223	1,035	820	928	403	107
All other	2,756	1,312	203	227	2,553	1,085
Total losses, charge-offs, and transfers to valuation reserves	5,403	3,117	1,417	1,486	3,986	1,631

[1] Number at end of period.

[2] Figures are averages of amounts reported for the June and December call dates in the year indicated and the December call date in the previous year.

TABLE NO. 36.—*Earnings, expenses, and dividends of banks in the District of Columbia, years ended Dec. 31, 1958 and 1957*—Continued

[In thousands of dollars]

	Years ended Dec. 31—					
	Total		National banks		Nonnational banks	
	1958	1957	1958	1957	1958	1957
Profits before income taxes	14, 989	14, 708	9, 619	9, 058	5, 370	5, 650
Taxes on net income: Federal	8, 527	7, 695	4, 787	4, 558	3, 740	3, 137
Net profits before dividends	6, 462	7, 013	4, 832	4, 500	1, 630	2, 513
Cash dividends	4, 839	4, 635	2, 899	2, 775	1, 940	1, 860
Memoranda items: Recoveries credited to valuation reserves (not included in recoveries above): On securities						
On loans	72	100	42	58	30	42
Losses charged to valuation reserves (not included in losses above): On securities		42				42
On loans	255	205	117	125	138	80
Stock dividends (increases in capital stock)	100	770		750	100	20
Ratios to gross earnings:	*Percent*	*Percent*	*Percent*	*Percent*	*Percent*	*Percent*
Salaries, wages and fees	31. 97	32. 11	31. 66	31. 28	32. 34	33. 16
Interest on time deposits	14. 55	14. 10	14. 17	13. 61	14. 98	14. 74
All other current expenses	22. 08	21. 05	20. 60	20. 50	23. 78	21. 74
Total current expenses	68. 60	67. 26	66. 43	65. 39	71. 10	69. 64
Net current earnings	31. 40	32. 74	33. 57	34. 61	28. 90	30. 36
Ratio of cash dividends to capital stock (par value)	15. 79	14. 80	15. 50	14. 28	16. 25	15. 66
Ratio of cash dividends to capital accounts	4. 33	4. 13	4. 53	4. 28	4. 13	3. 93

TABLE No. 37.—*Number of banks, capital stock, capital funds, net profits, interest and dividends, and ratios, all banks in the District of Columbia, years ended Dec. 31, 1930–58*

[In thousands of dollars. Figures for previous years published in report for 1940, p. 200]

Year	Number of banks	Capital[1] — Capital notes and debentures	Capital[1] — Preferred stock (par value)	Capital[1] — Common stock (par value)	Capital[1] — Total	Capital accounts[1]	Net profits before dividends	Interest and cash dividends — On capital notes and debentures	Interest and cash dividends — On preferred stock	Interest and cash dividends — On common stock	Ratios — Interest on capital notes and debentures to capital notes and debentures	Ratios — Cash dividends on preferred stock to preferred capital	Ratios — Cash dividends on common stock to common capital	Ratios — Total interest and cash dividends to capital accounts	Ratios — Net profits before dividends — To capital stock	Ratios — Net profits before dividends — To capital accounts
1930	39			24,008	24,008	52,638	2,983			2,755			11.48	5.23	12.43	5.67
1931	39			23,328	23,328	52,066	1,514			2,648			11.35	4.09	6.49	2.91
1932	34			23,072	23,072	50,062	1,218[2]			2,278			9.87	4.55	5.28[2]	2.43[2]
1933	21	300	1,575	19,216	19,516	41,119	2,186[2]		34	1,006		2.16	5.24	2.45	11.20[2]	5.32[2]
1934	22	1,340	1,650	18,345	21,260	39,849	416[2]	31	68	901	2.31	4.12	4.91	2.42	1.96[2]	1.04[2]
1935	22	1,790	1,650	18,235	21,675	40,843	2,501	77	68	996	4.30	4.12	5.46	2.79	11.54	6.12
1936	22	1,536	1,554	18,243	21,429	42,263	3,744	58	59	1,083	3.78	3.80	5.94	2.86	17.47	8.86
1937	22	1,419	1,355	18,250	21,223	44,365	2,966	47	50	1,194	3.31	3.69	6.54	2.83	13.98	6.69
1938	22	1,303	1,208	18,060	20,718	45,481	2,480	41	47	1,248	3.15	3.89	6.91	2.93	11.97	5.45
1939	22	1,295	1,288	17,300	19,625	46,966	3,455	40	56	1,379	3.09	4.35	7.97	2.94	17.45	7.36
1940	22	999	1,130	17,338	19,803	48,191	2,986	28	42	1,416	2.80	3.72	8.17	3.12	15.22	6.20
1941	22	604	969	17,490	19,224	49,499	3,283	24	38	1,442		3.92	8.24	3.11	17.08	6.63
1942	22	454	784	17,669	19,092	50,425	2,436	11	31	1,439	2.42	3.90	8.14	3.05	12.76	4.83
1943	22	400	317	17,768	18,962	51,447	2,468	17	16	1,432	4.25	3.05	8.06	2.95	13.02	4.80
1944	21	123	34	17,616	18,056	52,301	3,573	6	1	1,557	4.88	2.94	8.84	2.88	19.79	6.88
1945	20			17,833	17,867	55,255	5,485			1,610			9.03	2.92	30.70	9.93
1946	19			19,783	19,783	61,601	5,438			1,902			9.61	3.09	27.49	8.83
1947	19			20,750	20,750	65,468	4,991			2,198			10.59	3.36	24.05	7.62
1948	19			20,933	20,933	67,653	3,589			2,412			11.52	3.57	17.15	5.31
1949	19			21,017	21,017	69,635	5,083			2,653			12.62	3.81	24.19	7.30
1950	19			21,467	21,467	73,451	6,361			2,912			13.57	3.96	29.63	8.66
1951	19			22,333	22,333	78,295	5,800			3,014			13.50	3.85	25.97	7.41
1952	19			22,833	22,833	81,881	6,446			3,068			13.44	3.75	28.23	7.87
1953	19			23,000	23,000	85,707	7,143			3,166			13.77	3.69	31.06	8.33
1954	17			24,610	24,610	90,209	6,773			3,553			14.44	3.94	27.52	7.51
1955	17			27,440	27,440	96,050	7,388			3,941			14.36	4.10	26.92	7.69
1956	17			30,213	30,213	107,318	7,708			4,449			14.73	4.15	25.51	7.18
1957	16			31,307	31,307	112,236	7,013			4,635			14.80	4.13	22.40	6.25
1958	13			30,637	30,637	110,950	6,462			4,839			15.79	4.36	21.09	5.82

[1] Averages of amounts from reports of condition made in each year.
[2] Deficit.

TABLE No. 38.—*Total loans of banks in the District of Columbia, losses and recoveries on loans, and ratio of net losses or recoveries to loans, by calendar years 1939–58*

ALL BANKS

[In thousands of dollars]

Year	Total loans end of year	Losses and charge-offs	Recoveries	Net losses or recoveries (+)	Ratio of losses (or recoveries+) to loans
					Percent
1939	112, 470	257	137	120	.11
1940	128, 221	371	193	178	.14
1941	144, 649	332	277	55	.04
1942	118, 524	225	351	+126	+.11
1943	106, 789	237	297	+60	+.06
1944	110, 479	600	434	166	.15
1945	125, 302	195	300	+105	+.08
1946	175, 340	184	483	+299	+.17
1947	242, 755	303	529	+226	+.09
1948	270, 963	1 395	2 211	184	.07
1949	285, 399	1 574	2 304	270	.09
1950	347, 853	1 382	2 539	+157	+.05
1951	372, 607	1 475	2 315	160	.04
1952	420, 060	1 393	2 253	140	.03
1953	446, 861	1 579	2 406	173	.04
1954	501, 630	1 335	2 162	173	.03
1955	579, 680	1 360	2 243	117	.02
1956	631, 394	1 423	2 173	250	.04
1957	650, 210	1 477	2 212	265	.04
1958	670, 206	1 427	2 140	287	.04
Average for 1939–58	322, 070	376	298	78	.02

NATIONAL BANKS

Year	Total loans end of year	Losses and charge-offs	Recoveries	Net losses or recoveries (+)	Ratio of losses (or recoveries+) to loans
1939	51, 608	167	59	108	.21
1940	60, 059	178	119	59	.10
1941	68, 766	122	143	+21	+.03
1942	55, 876	112	147	+35	+.06
1943	51, 534	133	113	20	.04
1944	55, 181	110	141	+31	+.06
1945	67, 807	66	112	+46	+.07
1946	96, 720	62	211	+149	+.15
1947	131, 989	133	230	+97	+.07
1948	145, 299	1 264	2 100	164	.11
1949	145, 982	1 261	2 93	168	.11
1950	183, 547	1 166	2 180	+14	+.01
1951	199, 131	1 298	2 191	107	.05
1952	226, 337	1 279	2 102	177	.08
1953	245, 151	1 288	2 289	+1	
1954	300, 865	1 139	2 75	64	.02
1955	347, 098	1 206	2 123	83	.02
1956	378, 746	1 241	2 103	138	.04
1957	396, 165	1 252	2 134	118	.03
1958	376, 878	1 170	2 67	103	.03
Average for 1939–58	179, 237	182	137	45	.03

See footnotes at end of table.

TABLE No. 38.—*Total loans of banks in the District of Columbia, losses and recoveries on loans, and ratio of net losses or recoveries to loans, by calendar years 1939-58*—Continued

NONNATIONAL BANKS

[In thousands of dollars]

Year	Total loans end of year	Losses and charge-offs	Recoveries	Net losses or recoveries (+)	Ratio of losses (or recoveries+) to loans
					Percent
1939	60, 862	90	78	12	.02
1940	68, 162	193	74	119	.17
1941	75, 883	210	134	76	.10
1942	62, 648	113	204	+91	+.1
1943	55, 255	104	184	+80	+.14
1944	55, 298	490	293	197	.36
1945	57, 495	129	188	+59	+.10
1946	78, 620	122	272	+150	+.19
1947	110, 766	170	299	+129	+.12
1948	125, 664	[1] 131	[2] 111	20	.02
1949	139, 417	[1] 313	[2] 211	102	.07
1950	164, 306	[1] 216	[2] 359	+143	+.09
1951	173, 476	[1] 177	[2] 124	53	.03
1952	193, 723	[1] 114	[2] 151	+37	+.02
1953	201, 710	[1] 291	[2] 117	174	.09
1954	200, 765	[1] 196	[2] 87	109	.05
1955	232, 582	[1] 154	[2] 120	34	.01
1956	252, 648	[1] 182	[2] 70	112	.04
1957	254, 045	[1] 225	[2] 78	147	.06
1958	293, 328	[1] 257	[2] 73	184	.06
Average for 1939-58	142, 833	194	161	33	.02

[1] Excludes transfers to valuation reserves. [2] Excludes transfers from valuation reserves.

NOTE.—For prior figures beginning with year 1928 see Annual Report for 1947, p. 109.

TABLE No. 39.—*Total securities of banks in the District of Columbia, losses and recoveries on securities, and ratio of net losses or recoveries to securities, by calendar years 1939–58*

ALL BANKS

[In thousands of dollars]

Year	Total securities end of year	Losses and charge-offs	Recoveries	Net losses or recoveries (+)	Ratio of losses (or recoveries +) to securities
					Percent
1939	134, 137	1, 045	493	552	.41
1940	136, 389	732	351	381	.28
1941	158, 518	827	359	468	.30
1942	306, 889	466	262	204	.07
1943	433, 694	770	590	180	.04
1944	549, 977	639	459	180	.03
1945	719, 103	299	278	21	.002
1946	621, 710	205	125	80	.01
1947	547, 104	347	83	264	.05
1948	509, 545	[1] 201	[2] 88	113	.02
1949	534, 759	[1] 126	[2] 2	124	.02
1950	575, 500	[1] 169	[2] 2	167	.03
1951	601, 232	[1] 757		757	.13
1952	570, 881	[1] 711	[2] 8	703	.12
1953	548, 393	[1] 634	[2] 71	563	.10
1954	575, 323	[1] 164	[2] 34	130	.02
1955	543, 452	[1] 509	[2] 1	508	.09
1956	521, 085	[1] 1, 224		1, 224	.23
1957	514, 639	[1] 518	[2] 1	517	.10
1958	594, 931	[1] 889		889	.15
Average for 1939–58	484, 863	562	161	401	.08

NATIONAL BANKS

Year	Total securities end of year	Losses and charge-offs	Recoveries	Net losses or recoveries (+)	Ratio of losses (or recoveries +) to securities
1939	81, 270	883	394	489	.60
1940	81, 589	533	285	248	.30
1941	94, 880	617	242	375	.40
1942	203, 593	271	199	72	.04
1943	276, 495	641	469	172	.06
1944	341, 778	231	250	+19	+.01
1945	440, 209	182	173	9	.002
1946	372, 566	97	76	21	.01
1947	327, 705	166	16	150	.05
1948	308, 248	[1] 44	[2] 80	+36	+.01
1949	345, 537	[1] 24	[2] 1	23	.01
1950	379, 010	[1] 100		100	.03
1951	388, 279	[1] 540		540	.14
1952	361, 695	[1] 432	[2] 7	425	.12
1953	351, 994	[1] 265	[2] 67	198	.06
1954	378, 648	[1] 151	[2]	151	.04
1955	354, 373	[1] 167		167	.05
1956	348, 086	[1] 332		332	.10
1957	331, 406	[1] 204	[2] 1	203	.06
1958	350, 090	[1] 341		341	.10
Average for 1939–58	305, 873	311	113	198	.06

See footnotes at end of table.

TABLE No. 39.—*Total securities of banks in the District of Columbia, losses and recoveries on securities, and ratio of net losses or recoveries to securities, by calendar years 1939–58*—Continued

NONNATIONAL BANKS

[In thousands of dollars]

Year	Total securities end of year	Losses and charge-offs	Recoveries	Net losses or recoveries (+)	Ratio of losses (or recoveries +) to securities
					Percent
1939	52, 867	162	99	63	.12
1940	54, 800	199	66	133	.24
1941	63, 638	210	117	93	.15
1942	103, 296	195	63	132	.13
1943	157, 199	129	121	8	.01
1944	208, 199	408	209	199	.10
1945	278, 894	117	105	12	.004
1946	249, 144	108	49	59	.02
1947	219, 399	181	67	114	.05
1948	201, 297	157	[2] 8	149	.07
1949	189, 222	[1] 102	[2] 1	101	.05
1950	196, 490	[1] 69	[2] 2	67	.03
1951	212, 953	[1] 217		217	.10
1952	209, 186	[1] 279	[2] 1	278	.13
1953	196, 399	[1] 369	[2] 4	365	.19
1954	196, 675	[1] 13	[2] 34	+21	+.01
1955	189, 079	[1] 342	[2] 1	341	.18
1956	172, 999	[1] 892		892	.52
1957	183, 233	[1] 314		314	.17
1958	244, 841	[1] 548		548	.22
Average for 1939–58	178, 990	251	48	203	.11

[1] Excludes transfers to valuation reserves.   [2] Excludes transfers from valuation reserves.

NOTE.—For prior figures beginning with year 1928 see Annual Report for 1947, p. 110.

TABLE No. 40.—*Fiduciary activities of banks in the District of Columbia, Dec. 31, 1958*

	Total	National banks	Nonnational banks
Number of banks exercising fiduciary powers	6	3	3
Number with authority but not exercising fiduciary powers			
Total number authorized to exercise fiduciary powers	6	3	3
Total banking assets of banks authorized to exercise fiduciary powers	$1, 426, 311, 563	$876, 353, 405	$549, 958, 158
Personal account liabilities:			
Living trusts	277, 301, 147	118, 329, 589	158, 971, 558
Court accounts	41, 241, 704	13, 758, 131	27, 483, 573
Agency, escrow, custodian, etc	587, 599, 862	223, 775, 167	363, 824, 695
All other liabilities	5, 365, 224	2, 546, 038	2, 819, 186
Total liabilities	911, 507, 937	358, 408, 925	553, 099, 012
Number of personal accounts:			
Living trusts	3, 603	1, 348	2, 255
Court accounts	514	180	334
Agency, escrow, custodian, etc	2, 033	675	1, 358
Number of corporate trust bond issue accounts being administered	51	36	15
Number of all other accounts being administered [1]	284	105	179
Total number of accounts being administered	6, 485	2, 344	4, 141
Bond and debenture issues outstanding where bank acts as trustee	$259, 039, 700	$231, 114, 800	$27, 924, 900
Trust department gross earnings for year ended Dec. 31, 1958	$3, 017, 000	$995, 000	$2, 022, 000

[1] Corporate paying agency, depository, registrar, transfer agency, etc.

TABLE No. 41.—*Assets and liabilities of all active banks in the United States and possessions, by classes, Dec. 31, 1958*

[In thousands of dollars]

	Total all banks	National banks	All banks other than national	Banks other than national		
				State commercial[1]	Mutual savings	Private
Number of banks	14,034	4,585	9,449	8,866	520	63
ASSETS						
Loans and discounts:						
Real estate loans:						
Secured by farm land (including improvements)	1,523,272	561,970	961,302	906,635	52,753	1,914
Secured by residential properties (other than farm)	39,526,109	10,247,685	29,278,424	8,339,176	20,935,204	4,044
Secured by other properties	7,736,687	2,903,670	4,833,017	2,555,728	2,275,453	1,836
Loans to banks	723,230	266,478	456,752	456,434		318
Loans to brokers and dealers in securities	2,831,989	1,007,262	1,824,727	1,818,152		6,575
Other loans for the purpose of purchasing or carrying stocks, bonds, and other securities	1,865,753	794,360	1,071,393	1,049,366	11,574	10,453
Loans to farmers directly guaranteed by the Commodity Credit Corporation	814,039	345,137	468,902	467,846		1,056
Other loans to farmers (excluding loans on real estate)	4,179,107	2,039,164	2,139,943	2,132,042	1,466	6,435
Commercial and industrial loans (including open market paper)	40,771,061	22,402,978	18,368,083	18,216,205	83,060	68,818
Other loans to individuals for personal expenditures	21,034,372	11,443,539	9,590,833	9,377,508	204,458	8,867
All other loans (including overdrafts)	3,470,301	1,839,971	1,630,330	1,601,981	21,688	6,661
Total gross loans	124,475,920	53,852,214	70,623,706	46,921,073	23,585,656	116,977
Less valuation reserves	2,188,442	1,055,990	1,132,452	903,834	228,359	259
Net loans	122,287,478	52,796,224	69,491,254	46,017,239	23,357,297	116,718
Securities:						
U.S. Government obligations, direct and guaranteed	73,935,092	35,824,760	38,110,332	30,757,230	7,265,060	88,042
Obligations of States and political subdivisions	17,310,671	8,845,522	8,465,149	7,676,813	725,449	62,887
Other bonds, notes, and debentures	7,661,486	1,836,523	5,824,963	1,710,466	4,110,335	4,162
Corporate stocks, including stocks of Federal Reserve banks	1,417,734	281,419	1,136,315	265,784	862,386	8,145
Total securities	100,324,983	46,788,224	53,536,759	40,410,293	12,963,230	163,236
Currency and coin	3,451,865	1,675,827	1,776,038	1,629,437	143,782	2,819
Balances with other banks, including reserve balances and cash items in process of collection	46,695,132	25,188,993	21,506,189	20,647,459	777,203	81,477
Bank premises owned, furniture and fixtures	2,577,592	1,326,352	1,251,240	1,018,964	230,482	1,794
Real estate owned other than bank premises	66,443	33,575	32,868	23,494	9,229	145
Investments and other assets indirectly representing bank premises or other real estate	204,056	127,075	76,981	76,981		
Customers' liability on acceptances outstanding	867,765	321,852	545,913	532,799		13,114
Other assets	1,404,845	538,844	866,001	563,561	297,606	4,834
Total assets	277,880,159	128,796,966	149,083,193	110,920,227	37,778,829	384,137

See footnote at end of table

TABLE No. 41.—*Assets and liabilities of all active banks in the United States and possessions, by classes, Dec. 31, 1958*—Continued

[In thousands of dollars]

	Total all banks	National banks	All banks other than national	Banks other than national		
				State commercial [1]	Mutual savings	Private
LIABILITIES						
Demand deposits:						
Individuals, partnerships, and corporations	115,663,804	61,785,222	53,878,582	53,647,384	22,074	209,124
U.S. Government	4,308,234	2,313,912	1,994,322	1,990,678	3,330	314
States and political subdivisions	11,038,915	6,335,204	4,703,711	4,698,304	1,688	3,719
Banks in the United States	14,167,450	8,502,192	5,665,258	5,647,435	342	17,481
Banks in foreign countries	1,659,342	539,956	1,119,386	1,094,045		25,341
Certified and cashiers' checks, etc.	4,063,772	1,875,813	2,188,459	2,153,010	4,960	30,489
Total demand deposits	150,901,517	81,351,799	69,549,718	69,230,856	32,394	286,468
Time deposits:						
Individuals, partnerships, and corporations	94,012,283	32,614,707	61,397,576	27,377,756	33,992,773	27,047
U.S. Government	336,037	251,120	84,917	84,897	18	2
Postal savings	22,121	9,905	12,216	12,216		
States and political subdivisions	3,682,769	2,091,559	1,591,210	1,577,292	12,986	932
Banks in the United States	315,258	72,330	242,928	240,264	2,164	500
Banks in foreign countries	2,061,527	694,708	1,366,819	1,358,769		8,050
Total time deposits	100,429,995	35,734,329	64,695,666	30,651,194	34,007,941	36,531
Total deposits	251,331,512	117,086,128	134,245,384	99,882,050	34,040,335	322,999
Bills payable, rediscounts, and other liabilities for borrowed money	96,544	43,035	53,509	43,057	8,034	2,418
Acceptances executed by or for account of reporting banks and outstanding	907,608	330,616	576,992	560,705		16,287
Other liabilities	3,722,771	1,668,386	2,054,385	1,533,870	511,369	9,146
Total liabilities	256,058,435	119,128,165	136,930,270	102,019,662	34,559,738	350,850
CAPITAL ACCOUNTS						
Capital notes and debentures	57,689		57,689	57,689		
Preferred stock	19,216	3,492	15,724	15,724		
Common stock	5,491,152	2,947,787	2,543,365	2,537,812		5,553
Surplus	11,207,379	4,718,459	6,488,920	4,186,046	2,282,633	20,241
Undivided profits	4,257,667	1,711,435	2,546,232	1,825,773	718,829	1,630
Reserves and retirement account for preferred stock and capital notes and debentures	788,621	287,628	500,993	277,501	217,629	5,863
Total capital accounts	21,821,724	9,668,801	12,152,923	8,900,545	3,219,091	33,287
Total liabilities and capital accounts	277,880,159	128,796,966	149,083,193	110,920,227	37,778,829	384,137

[1] Includes stock savings banks.

TABLE No. 42.—*Assets and liabilities of all active banks in the United States and possessions, Dec. 31, 1958 (including national, State commercial, savings, and private banks)*

ASSETS

[In thousands of dollars]

Location	Population (approximate)	Number of banks	Loans and discounts, including overdrafts	U.S. Government obligations, direct and guaranteed	Obligations of States and political subdivisions	Other bonds, notes, and debentures	Corporate stocks, including stocks of Federal Reserve banks	Currency and coin	Balances with other banks including reserve balances and cash items in process of collection	Bank premises owned, furniture and fixtures	Real estate owned other than bank premises	Investments and other assets indirectly representing bank premises or other real estate	Customers' liability on acceptances outstanding	Other assets	Total assets
Maine	963,000	87	511,515	326,213	43,688	73,346	26,077	21,800	104,950	12,644	1,057	874		2,661	1,124,915
New Hampshire	592,000	109	523,529	247,656	28,945	32,762	38,325	11,326	78,478	12,291	1,141	96		1,761	976,310
Vermont	375,000	64	314,033	116,159	27,449	8,051	3,769	7,571	52,841	5,337	199	1,089		953	537,451
Massachusetts	4,904,000	356	5,975,837	3,237,352	385,495	432,595	267,772	115,583	1,263,772	98,404	2,968	1,423	31,003	45,152	11,857,356
Rhode Island	888,000	17	739,696	342,850	71,369	91,194	28,772	22,093	117,132	14,252	2,226	470	4,324	3,891	1,436,269
Connecticut	2,351,000	151	2,500,332	1,242,102	274,308	299,879	133,051	72,094	468,549	51,046	1,999	342	62	21,828	5,065,592
Total New England States	10,073,000	784	10,564,942	5,512,332	831,254	937,827	497,766	250,557	2,085,722	193,974	7,590	4,294	35,389	76,246	20,997,893
New York	16,350,000	561	36,572,157	14,223,401	3,386,773	2,659,894	491,798	422,165	11,222,630	512,219	5,910	10,032	608,972	559,192	70,675,143
New Jersey	5,844,000	283	3,669,837	2,380,494	876,427	372,213	39,629	146,332	1,014,510	99,627	1,374	784	221	36,841	8,638,289
Pennsylvania	11,201,000	750	7,524,734	4,335,871	1,284,147	937,213	81,603	267,983	2,651,472	186,359	7,450	10,665	7,008	60,541	17,355,136
Delaware	466,000	29	356,290	252,296	42,049	82,375	11,797	12,894	115,568	9,585	767	1,036		3,186	887,852
Maryland	3,001,000	149	1,228,729	1,009,732	172,229	147,122	6,518	56,461	449,127	29,863	785	477	335	50,254	3,151,632
District of Columbia	832,000	13	670,206	525,163	40,502	26,971	2,295	28,841	304,373	21,839	137	4,560		5,374	1,630,261
Total Eastern States	37,694,000	1,785	50,021,962	22,726,957	5,802,127	4,225,788	633,640	934,676	15,757,680	859,492	16,423	27,554	616,626	715,388	102,338,313
Virginia	4,008,000	312	1,434,081	954,410	221,722	72,342	5,286	70,992	604,551	43,549	1,165	4,521	238	6,902	3,419,759
West Virginia	1,982,000	183	470,107	501,543	76,621	12,652	2,885	34,902	251,123	13,027	557	1,270		3,771	1,368,458
North Carolina	4,610,000	203	1,182,213	739,356	261,202	107,120	4,131	77,320	592,281	36,886	608	568	200	19,601	3,021,486
South Carolina	2,434,000	144	384,103	289,683	82,231	30,515	1,305	31,011	208,793	11,954	386	68	1	3,259	1,043,309
Georgia	3,860,000	394	1,248,964	832,381	157,028	50,803	4,153	55,586	603,416	40,206	1,688	131	376	9,590	3,004,322

TABLE No. 42.—Assets and liabilities of all active banks in the United States and possessions, Dec. 31, 1958 (including national, State commercial, savings, and private banks)—Continued

ASSETS—Continued

[In thousands of dollars]

Location	Population (approximate)	Number of banks	Loans and discounts, including overdrafts	U.S. Government obligations, direct and guaranteed	Obligations of States and political subdivisions	Other bonds, notes, and debentures	Corporate stocks, including stocks of Federal Reserve banks	Currency and coin	Balances with other banks including reserve balances and cash items in process of collection	Bank premises owned, furniture and fixtures	Real estate owned other than bank premises	Investments and other assets indirectly representing bank premises or other real estate	Customers' liability on acceptances outstanding	Other assets	Total assets
Florida	4,581,000	280	1,708,496	1,565,817	341,086	49,701	5,773	97,024	1,014,300	70,729	2,155	14,091	619	17,969	4,887,760
Alabama	3,251,000	239	808,246	590,674	202,762	44,992	2,847	48,056	409,075	21,140	715	2,699	158	5,814	2,137,178
Mississippi	2,207,000	194	467,028	345,790	185,082	15,611	1,329	33,561	265,064	18,822	286	628	---------	2,980	1,336,181
Louisiana	3,147,000	186	1,083,515	879,546	260,953	22,425	4,485	59,312	690,007	30,781	585	4,235	3,491	10,379	3,049,724
Texas	9,525,000	968	5,015,157	2,954,056	707,536	220,273	23,259	176,798	3,217,990	205,605	8,823	9,722	52,178	29,435	12,620,832
Arkansas	1,768,000	237	447,340	338,464	136,598	20,364	1,445	25,651	287,791	13,144	472	40	---------	2,089	1,273,398
Kentucky	3,114,000	360	901,969	783,827	95,801	40,089	3,084	49,362	567,331	16,606	261	188	51	4,465	2,463,034
Tennessee	3,499,000	298	1,388,995	825,771	228,931	45,764	4,749	67,496	720,003	37,369	1,040	132	12,076	7,279	3,339,605
Total Southern States	47,986,000	3,998	16,540,214	11,601,318	2,957,553	732,651	64,731	827,071	9,431,725	559,818	18,751	38,293	69,388	123,533	42,965,046
Ohio	9,461,000	609	4,931,807	3,714,185	761,367	145,672	24,824	207,531	1,975,642	112,772	1,299	14,545	1,071	41,671	11,932,386
Indiana	4,641,000	463	1,742,904	1,839,359	252,569	61,215	6,068	103,255	905,219	43,473	636	1,135	43	12,611	4,968,487
Illinois	10,033,000	946	6,557,006	6,292,967	1,264,388	382,923	41,047	181,302	3,526,117	78,459	3,908	17,427	12,397	77,445	18,435,386
Michigan	7,986,000	393	3,847,920	2,979,141	826,173	41,054	13,009	144,345	1,280,619	91,212	1,661	6,692	175	30,793	8,962,794
Wisconsin	3,996,000	556	1,768,180	1,672,575	281,900	83,034	4,519	75,478	787,042	39,417	1,207	3,515	175	21,419	4,738,461
Minnesota	3,420,000	687	2,003,051	1,286,643	299,424	189,007	5,407	52,901	870,159	38,870	1,592	6,607	970	17,494	4,772,125
Iowa	2,835,000	669	1,400,095	1,041,660	283,296	43,097	2,680	53,351	583,489	17,924	1,132	2,938	75	4,376	3,434,113
Missouri	4,309,000	613	2,404,459	1,984,925	448,842	93,662	20,846	80,380	1,416,909	41,009	1,445	2,888	2,885	19,711	6,517,961
Total Middle Western States	46,701,000	4,936	24,355,422	20,811,455	4,417,959	1,039,664	118,400	898,543	11,345,196	463,136	12,880	55,747	17,791	225,520	63,761,713

North Dakota	656,000	155	251,197	333,217	74,218	54,976	554	8,494	100,327	6,346	297	250		2,294	832,160
South Dakota	705,000	172	286,244	303,190	43,929	21,933	771	9,318	112,687	5,889	382	273	55	3,025	787,641
Nebraska	1,474,000	423	700,402	554,059	113,904	21,713	2,207	19,881	398,903	10,821	117	1,002	3	4,250	1,827,314
Kansas	2,134,000	593	904,392	738,752	262,298	35,094	2,736	33,099	466,609	19,545	1,218	263	9	3,572	2,467,581
Montana	700,000	115	317,171	305,617	53,386	27,726	994	11,075	146,304	9,179	354	35		2,468	874,318
Wyoming	323,000	52	146,270	157,979	19,459	7,207	506	6,235	89,871	4,359	150			941	432,977
Colorado	1,744,000	175	871,461	581,606	81,912	9,727	4,177	26,004	444,212	14,523	605	1,704		8,933	2,044,864
New Mexico	861,000	53	273,427	237,976	32,052	3,342	644	13,658	141,675	10,005	128	142		1,283	714,332
Oklahoma	2,310,000	387	990,793	775,034	209,067	38,544	3,900	37,771	699,210	30,393	470	7,368	875	6,053	2,799,478
Total Western States	10,907,000	2,125	4,741,357	3,987,430	890,225	220,262	16,489	165,535	2,599,798	111,060	3,721	11,037	942	32,809	12,780,665
Washington	2,805,000	93	1,450,678	910,388	221,603	77,995	4,464	39,010	527,305	41,200	730	1,185	1,069	11,806	3,287,433
Oregon	1,797,000	56	895,623	633,394	217,579	19,965	2,878	19,678	363,627	30,439	1,027	65	33	9,834	2,194,142
California	14,637,000	124	11,514,627	6,596,335	1,673,088	339,781	72,291	207,711	3,893,932	252,371	3,504	50,106	123,461	136,345	24,863,552
Idaho	674,000	28	290,401	226,263	48,852	1,283	833	8,870	99,928	8,371	294	360		694	686,149
Utah	882,000	49	456,539	256,131	66,769	6,144	1,525	12,243	178,667	6,020	110	7,992		1,587	993,727
Nevada	271,000	6	162,004	128,407	41,650	8,658	443	7,176	44,181	6,628	11	220		2,541	401,919
Arizona	1,177,000	8	568,464	241,667	60,775	17,682	1,633	20,951	187,738	22,295	471	6,518	154	8,151	1,136,499
Total Pacific States	22,243,000	364	15,338,336	8,992,585	2,330,316	471,508	84,067	315,639	5,295,378	367,324	6,147	66,446	124,717	170,958	33,563,421
Total United States (exclusive of possessions)	175,604,000	13,992	121,562,233	73,632,077	17,229,434	7,627,700	1,415,093	3,392,021	46,515,499	2,554,804	65,512	203,371	864,853	1,344,454	276,407,051
Alaska	169,000	18	67,313	72,867	9,255	5,116	37	7,686	26,202	2,895	261	492		216	192,340
Canal Zone (Panama)	40,000	(1)	1,553					2,008	666	17				15,465	19,709
Guam	50,000	(2)	8,933					812	21	241	76			12,271	22,354
The Territory of Hawaii	590,000	10	288,862	148,995	37,179	5,554	1,584	24,328	104,846	12,716	341	25	459	2,942	627,831
Puerto Rico [3]	2,323,000	10	349,577	70,016	33,856	23,108	1,007	23,871	44,405	6,837	212	168	2,453	29,235	584,745
American Samoa	21,000	1	273	1,307				113	252	5				32	1,982
Virgin Islands of the United States	24,000	3	8,734	9,830	947	8	13	1,026	3,241	77	41			230	24,147
Total possessions	3,217,000	42	725,245	303,015	81,237	33,786	2,641	59,844	179,633	22,788	931	685	2,912	60,391	1,473,108
Total United States and possessions	178,821,000	14,034	122,287,478	73,935,092	17,310,671	7,661,486	1,417,734	3,451,865	46,695,132	2,577,592	66,443	204,056	867,765	1,404,845	277,880,159

[1] 2 branches of a national bank and 2 branches of a State member bank in New York.
[2] Branch of a national bank in California.
[3] Asset and liability items include data for branches of a national bank and a State member bank in New York.

TABLE No. 42.—Assets and liabilities of all active banks in the United States and possessions, Dec. 31, 1958 (including national, State commercial, savings, and private banks)—Continued

LIABILITIES

[In thousands of dollars]

Location	Demand deposits	Time deposits	Total deposits	Bills payable, rediscounts, and other liabilities for borrowed money	Acceptances executed by or for account of reporting banks and outstanding	Other liabilities	Capital stock [1]	Surplus	Undivided profits	Reserves and retirement account for preferred capital notes and debentures
Maine	352,729	650,985	1,003,714			10,682	21,080	49,814	35,939	3,595
New Hampshire	288,449	625,713	864,162	91		8,455	8,876	53,128	34,566	4,948
Vermont	140,206	346,619	486,825	2,175		4,994	12,733	17,049	13,170	2,622
Massachusetts	4,489,251	6,053,238	10,542,489	58	32,136	164,097	135,130	611,640	324,259	46,845
Rhode Island	483,709	805,581	1,289,290	760	4,324	20,997	22,060	84,444	14,700	454
Connecticut	1,724,636	2,841,295	4,565,931	1,914	62	58,437	67,181	232,023	118,127	21,917
Total New England States	7,428,980	11,323,431	18,752,411	4,998	36,522	267,662	267,060	1,048,098	540,761	80,381
New York	32,832,423	29,792,380	62,624,803	16,088	642,310	1,350,316	1,227,872	3,540,948	1,065,812	206,994
New Jersey	3,809,169	4,130,379	7,939,548	2,131	221	89,929	157,573	329,005	83,662	36,220
Pennsylvania	9,045,782	6,485,063	15,530,845	6,675	7,512	195,491	374,095	968,825	242,808	28,885
Delaware	496,230	293,287	789,517			10,334	14,771	57,732	15,054	444
Maryland	1,667,573	1,203,192	2,870,765	725	335	34,633	46,302	126,048	61,786	11,038
District of Columbia	1,120,105	383,628	1,503,733			16,495	29,770	59,100	16,369	4,794
Total Eastern States	48,971,282	42,287,929	91,259,211	25,619	650,378	1,697,198	1,850,383	5,081,658	1,485,491	288,375
Virginia	1,912,071	1,204,161	3,116,232	1,875	238	36,867	79,108	130,524	48,114	6,801
West Virginia	849,776	373,752	1,223,528	520		10,017	34,166	64,824	28,868	6,335
North Carolina	2,019,149	692,343	2,711,492	1,042	200	70,035	61,818	135,749	31,621	9,529
South Carolina	763,906	187,302	951,208		1	10,279	26,460	39,612	13,017	2,732
Georgia	2,048,569	669,169	2,717,738	1,278	376	41,464	70,098	107,121	39,930	26,317
Florida	3,293,136	1,205,290	4,498,426	4,600	639	53,787	127,300	140,232	44,621	18,155
Alabama	1,409,948	541,370	1,951,318	100	158	20,113	49,144	73,314	35,125	7,906
Mississippi	936,559	295,525	1,232,084	1,650		9,287	24,469	65,371	2,162	1,158
Louisiana	2,191,589	611,011	2,802,600	1,540	3,650	23,559	67,108	112,024	35,586	3,657
Texas	9,243,777	2,314,501	11,558,278	2,750	54,382	73,410	340,552	406,563	144,766	40,131
Arkansas	920,952	243,341	1,164,293			6,188	30,875	40,697	27,011	4,334
Kentucky	1,787,727	456,124	2,243,851	140	179	20,478	55,169	94,311	43,680	5,226
Tennessee	2,081,335	969,310	3,050,645	1,000	12,076	34,868	72,942	111,668	49,440	6,966
Total Southern States	29,458,494	9,763,199	39,221,693	16,495	71,899	410,352	1,039,209	1,522,010	543,941	139,447

Ohio	6,771,430	4,125,951	10,897,381	2,436	1,071	133,414	259,138	482,725	148,451	7,770
Indiana	3,091,140	1,464,434	4,555,574	250	43	50,231	95,337	168,730	85,664	12,658
Illinois	11,917,229	4,928,066	16,845,295	4,058	12,585	194,256	464,385	566,618	233,545	114,644
Michigan	4,464,867	3,725,187	8,190,054	185	175	137,605	189,167	296,267	127,878	21,463
Wisconsin	2,568,289	1,819,517	4,387,806	525	175	29,313	89,157	151,039	69,937	10,509
Minnesota	2,637,498	1,717,174	4,354,672	260	970	52,585	103,978	157,647	82,113	19,900
Iowa	2,242,865	903,674	3,146,539	865	75	11,192	68,879	106,526	88,735	11,302
Missouri	4,653,599	1,302,894	5,956,493	2,270	2,917	58,942	154,036	195,251	134,122	13,930
Total Middle Western States	38,346,917	19,986,897	58,333,814	10,849	18,011	667,538	1,424,077	2,124,803	970,445	212,176
North Dakota	486,877	277,141	784,018	200		6,617	15,903	23,186	16,130	6,106
South Dakota	502,744	224,634	727,378			5,850	13,928	21,388	16,564	2,533
Nebraska	1,479,677	181,201	1,660,878	8,541	55	10,613	42,046	56,976	41,078	7,127
Kansas	1,775,152	480,712	2,255,864	1,096	3	11,712	55,854	87,168	52,272	3,612
Montana	580,733	232,156	812,889	550	9	9,539	18,493	19,974	12,308	556
Wyoming	284,402	115,050	399,452	400		3,206	5,198	14,153	9,045	1,523
Colorado	1,340,367	534,341	1,874,708	1,786	3	21,551	50,684	60,255	31,665	4,212
New Mexico	511,207	156,709	667,916			5,545	14,920	15,862	5,324	4,765
Oklahoma	2,113,238	433,386	2,546,624	10,691	875	15,854	64,212	88,772	66,081	6,469
Total Western States	9,074,397	2,635,330	11,709,727	23,164	945	90,487	281,238	387,734	250,467	36,903
Washington	1,773,773	1,294,733	3,008,506	100	1,069	38,403	61,495	114,053	56,707	7,100
Oregon	1,166,592	832,727	1,999,319		33	33,215	49,545	60,202	51,397	431
California	12,058,152	10,729,424	22,787,576		125,684	432,351	466,050	730,231	310,457	11,203
Idaho	413,054	224,542	637,596			6,261	15,755	16,897	6,163	3,477
Utah	530,245	384,065	914,310			13,176	20,297	33,812	10,448	1,684
Nevada	227,395	147,679	375,074			4,039	8,086	8,664	5,999	57
Arizona	725,020	311,313	1,036,333		154	21,339	24,350	41,696	11,767	860
Total Pacific States	16,894,231	13,864,483	30,758,714	100	126,940	548,784	645,578	1,005,555	452,938	24,812
Total United States (exclusive of possessions)	150,174,301	99,831,269	250,035,570	81,225	904,695	3,682,021	5,505,545	11,169,858	4,244,043	782,064
Alaska	111,549	68,947	180,496			706	3,898	3,920	2,351	969
Canal Zone (Panama)	14,959	4,652	19,611			98				
Guam	12,173	9,613	21,786			568				
The Territory of Hawaii	317,404	252,258	509,662	244	459	7,217	16,862	21,190	8,601	3,596
Puerto Rico	258,939	221,209	480,148	15,075	2,454	31,759	39,090	12,036	2,340	1,843
American Samoa	728	1,054	1,782			31	100	25	5	
Virgin Islands of the United States	11,464	10,993	22,457			371	562	350	327	80
Total possessions	727,216	508,726	1,295,942	15,319	2,913	40,750	60,512	37,521	13,624	6,527
Total United States and possessions	150,901,517	100,429,995	251,331,512	96,544	907,608	3,722,771	5,558,057	11,207,379	4,257,667	788,621

1 Includes capital notes and debentures. (See classification on pp. 174 and 175.)

TABLE No. 42.—Assets and liabilities of all active banks in the United States and possessions, Dec. 31, 1958 (including national, State commercial, savings, and private banks)—Continued

[In thousands of dollars]

Location	Real estate loans			Loans to banks	Loans to brokers and dealers in securities	Other loans for the purpose of purchasing or carrying stocks, bonds, and other securities	Loans to farmers directly guaranteed by the Commodity Credit Corporation	Other loans to farmers (excluding loans on real estate)	Commercial and industrial loans (including open market paper)	Other loans to individuals for personal expenditures	All other loans (including overdrafts)	Total gross loans	Less valuation reserves	Net loans
	Secured by farm land (including improvements)	Secured by residential properties (other than farm)	Secured by other properties											
Maine	8,037	245,808	48,322	248	934	2,855	138	11,749	100,504	88,973	9,819	517,387	5,872	511,515
New Hampshire	3,337	326,270	66,637	250	1,681	1,459		3,676	62,180	58,785	3,510	527,785	4,256	523,529
Vermont	17,458	159,928	29,435		353	3,529		15,223	37,797	49,598	3,947	317,268	3,235	314,033
Massachusetts	10,452	3,201,902	519,329	5,160	27,050	23,827		9,559	1,478,827	687,476	92,421	6,056,003	80,166	5,975,837
Rhode Island	2,145	392,631	59,798		6,460	812		978	174,974	87,633	26,038	751,469	11,773	739,696
Connecticut	9,116	1,604,419	145,464		7,339	14,939		8,335	343,689	352,975	41,473	2,527,749	27,417	2,500,332
Total New England States	50,545	5,930,958	868,985	5,658	43,817	47,421	138	49,520	2,197,971	1,325,440	177,208	10,697,661	132,719	10,564,942
New York	59,085	15,329,016	2,125,246	510,271	1,797,930	495,216	398	88,440	12,739,810	3,027,042	1,094,909	37,267,363	695,206	36,572,157
New Jersey	14,147	1,774,119	302,119	575	89,035	25,784		16,294	656,201	794,036	74,321	3,746,631	76,794	3,669,837
Pennsylvania	78,411	2,275,861	516,424	4,337	67,216	127,302	89	83,317	2,723,057	1,581,487	221,737	7,679,238	154,504	7,524,734
Delaware	10,556	101,963	26,211		11,905	3,465	74	3,733	86,609	108,603	6,840	359,959	3,660	356,299
Maryland	26,145	489,535	107,264	1,605	17,725	38,948		17,824	241,261	264,444	39,989	1,244,740	16,011	1,228,729
District of Columbia	1,158	132,691	62,322	1,399	12,474	3,313		120	265,312	165,096	35,205	679,090	8,884	670,206
Total Eastern States	189,502	20,103,185	3,139,586	518,187	1,996,285	694,028	561	209,728	16,712,250	5,940,708	1,473,001	50,977,021	955,059	50,021,962
Virginia	43,009	321,548	97,532	2,342	11,270	12,136	1,039	50,002	390,017	475,981	47,154	1,452,030	17,949	1,434,081
West Virginia	12,072	140,490	41,008	250	584	8,584		7,778	94,436	163,946	10,147	479,295	9,188	470,107
North Carolina	38,659	113,680	67,471	3,127	21,381	30,337	3,463	35,572	476,224	385,365	25,891	1,208,104	25,891	1,182,213
South Carolina	11,407	46,437	28,978		3,334	8,399	5,507	12,452	137,058	119,321	17,346	390,239	6,136	384,103
Georgia	43,996	161,967	64,134	4,076	12,514	42,462	13,370	35,636	478,286	373,326	36,021	1,265,788	16,824	1,248,964
Florida	23,819	211,989	143,802	979	14,344	40,782	20	35,002	694,243	542,317	36,299	1,736,248	27,752	1,708,496
Alabama	25,759	103,768	44,550	1	3,649	6,120	18,816	25,002	288,647	267,094	34,322	827,727	19,481	808,246
Mississippi	30,502	44,562	29,412	601	7,101	11,462	12,436	34,109	183,420	113,930	11,112	478,647	11,619	467,028
Louisiana	24,598	135,068	87,729	2,163	8,258	8,205	7,099	34,225	494,846	225,399	81,483	1,099,073	15,558	1,083,515
Texas	42,291	247,140	198,382	2,939	43,136	234,277	207,715	289,152	2,496,411	1,172,470	167,671	5,101,584	86,427	5,015,157
Arkansas	25,843	47,613	38,882		3,641	4,816	34,358	47,598	134,291	114,823	6,316	452,181	4,841	447,340
Kentucky	68,782	148,670	59,498	140	5,213	11,017	1,882	69,128	262,329	258,527	32,213	917,153	15,184	901,969
Tennessee	51,224	134,179	66,054	2,449	24,340	15,355	20,472	53,228	583,834	432,906	29,983	1,414,024	25,029	1,388,995
Total Southern States	441,960	1,857,111	961,432	19,067	158,765	434,206	325,877	721,536	6,714,042	4,645,405	542,692	16,822,093	281,879	16,540,214

Ohio	4,931,807	95,192	5,026,999	173,375	1,196,433	1,383,307	106,611	6,154	185,696	125,466	1,185	352,352	1,389,185	107,235
Indiana	1,742,904	31,620	1,774,524	38,284	428,702	442,376	116,733	7,453	12,286	12,012	404	115,232	533,272	67,770
Illinois	6,557,006	180,203	6,737,209	260,161	1,139,709	3,292,961	302,339	32,660	205,464	283,766	11,240	256,753	890,292	61,864
Michigan	3,547,920	61,425	3,609,345	93,555	948,726	917,952	87,424	736	55,198	19,620		290,588	1,171,851	53,695
Wisconsin	1,768,180	42,041	1,810,221	99,421	318,502	482,400	100,326	114	22,788	17,830	519	148,762	539,686	79,873
Minnesota	2,003,051	26,109	2,029,160	50,834	374,239	544,215	211,026	34,656	15,077	17,171	1,222	103,990	619,574	63,156
Iowa	1,400,095	19,080	1,419,175	27,679	223,075	288,094	449,400	52,440	9,005	3,630	208	68,397	255,363	71,884
Missouri	2,404,459	32,763	2,437,222	61,622	557,600	841,722	160,983	29,389	48,329	25,328	3,112	142,165	507,077	59,895
Total Middle Western States	24,355,422	488,433	24,843,855	804,931	5,186,986	8,163,027	1,534,842	163,602	553,843	498,823	17,890	1,448,239	5,906,300	565,372
North Dakota	251,197	5,903	257,100	2,581	51,720	37,671	54,696	39,773	1,182			8,112	50,805	10,560
South Dakota	286,244	7,783	294,027	4,962	45,860	44,473	91,648	30,941	751	173		11,534	57,376	6,309
Nebraska	700,402	11,997	712,399	19,129	104,668	178,123	252,276	64,128	7,246	1,711	1,718	25,757	43,438	14,205
Kansas	904,392	8,824	913,216	15,099	169,091	235,193	241,744	97,695	6,168	3,889	307	30,050	86,417	27,563
Montana	317,171	7,387	324,558	3,029	89,083	64,491	58,373	19,084	1,668	1,000	8	14,266	44,558	4,558
Wyoming	146,270	2,043	148,313	337	28,201	38,343	33,193	1,859	819	3		11,575	31,745	2,238
Colorado	871,461	14,218	885,679	24,227	224,608	300,293	139,042	8,248	7,050	4,885	2,406	58,445	108,590	7,885
New Mexico	273,427	6,946	280,373	4,535	73,356	93,348	29,565	6,101	3,974	16,690		20,234	29,050	3,520
Oklahoma	990,793	13,475	1,004,268	33,271	246,238	415,446	105,785	43,578	7,258	13,463	762	51,616	65,842	21,009
Total Western States	4,741,357	78,576	4,819,933	107,170	1,032,825	1,407,381	1,006,322	311,407	36,116	41,814	5,201	231,589	542,231	97,877
Washington	1,450,678	23,071	1,473,749	40,200	283,188	483,541	66,864	5,115	7,541	6,485	113	109,582	449,640	21,480
Oregon	895,623	7,622	903,245	19,032	174,097	336,735	45,862	1,358	4,130	3,289		60,816	240,230	17,696
California	11,514,627	198,092	11,712,719	272,355	1,942,538	4,086,811	356,198	2,197	56,892	67,284	152,236	757,124	3,092,729	111,355
Idaho	290,401	4,770	295,171	3,566	63,740	62,145	50,776	2,825	873	68		14,709	93,196	3,273
Utah	456,539	6,127	462,666	10,769	100,699	136,141	32,672	590	3,388	3,344		34,316	133,271	7,476
Nevada	162,004	1,192	163,196	2,429	51,227	32,856	6,539		795	2,100	546	25,044	41,133	1,073
Arizona	568,464	4,831	573,295	4,673	153,758	173,770	79,801	369	950	9,869		9,571	135,738	4,250
Total Pacific States	15,338,336	245,705	15,584,041	353,024	2,769,247	5,311,099	638,712	12,454	74,569	92,439	152,895	1,011,162	5,000,937	166,603
Total United States (exclusive of possessions)	121,562,233	2,182,371	123,744,604	3,458,026	20,900,611	40,506,670	4,160,660	814,039	1,840,183	2,831,943	718,898	7,660,993	39,340,722	1,511,859
Alaska	67,313	2,462	69,775	749	16,424	18,214	240		72			11,444	22,301	331
Canal Zone (Panama)	1,553		1,553	182	191	1,180	1						2,049	
Guam	8,933		8,933		4,740	2,143								
The Territory of Hawaii	288,862	1,934	290,796	4,885	41,001	59,714	3,909		24,695	25	4,332	52,472	102,265	1,830
Puerto Rico	349,577	1,591	351,168	6,286	69,490	181,492	14,283		803	21		11,024	54,275	9,162
American Samoa	273		273	36	125	104	8							
Virgin Islands of the United States	8,734	84	8,818	137	1,790	1,544	6					754	4,497	90
Total possessions	725,245	6,071	731,316	12,275	133,761	264,391	18,447		25,570	46	4,332	75,694	185,387	11,413
Total United States and possessions	122,287,478	2,188,442	124,475,920	3,470,301	21,034,372	40,771,061	4,179,107	814,039	1,865,753	2,831,989	723,230	7,736,687	39,526,109	1,523,272

TABLE NO. 42.—Assets and liabilities of all active banks in the United States and possessions, Dec. 31, 1958 (including national, State commercial, savings, and private banks)—Continued

[In thousands of dollars]

Location	Capital			Demand deposits						Time deposits					
	Capital notes and debentures	Preferred stock	Common stock	Individuals, partnerships, and corporations	U.S. Government	States and political subdivisions	Banks in United States	Banks in foreign countries	Certified and cashiers' checks, etc.[1]	Individuals, partnerships, and corporations	U.S. Government	Postal savings	States and political subdivisions	Banks in United States	Banks in foreign countries
Maine		100	20,980	287,182	10,226	33,517	11,835	9	9,960	645,443	1,520	7	3,985	30	
New Hampshire		1,102	8,876	183,176	8,287	25,523	12,126		9,337	624,354	745	10	604		
Vermont		200	11,631	113,571	4,286	16,255	1,790		4,304	343,045	148	3	3,383	40	
Massachusetts			134,930	3,433,892	130,164	347,180	427,336	29,825	120,854	5,997,440	7,561	1,060	15,066	861	31,250
Rhode Island			22,040	407,369	14,844	32,337	9,447	1,730	17,982	802,127	1,349	159	1,921		25
Connecticut			67,181	1,449,691	58,340	103,804	54,713	68	58,020	2,835,988	1,763	40	2,441	1,063	
Total New England States		1,402	265,658	5,874,881	226,147	558,616	517,247	31,632	220,457	11,248,397	13,086	1,279	27,400	1,994	31,275
New York	48,054	1,853	1,177,965	23,763,264	1,146,861	1,109,313	3,728,500	1,317,085	1,767,400	27,506,795	45,702		328,468	233,327	1,678,088
New Jersey	8,301	3,848	145,424	3,109,796	112,054	371,282	91,412	623	124,002	4,058,074	8,386		63,632	282	25
Pennsylvania		261	373,834	7,452,713	270,821	403,016	742,643	26,408	150,181	6,333,882	5,054	1,020	132,053	6,654	6,400
Delaware			14,771	429,468	22,188	27,120	6,836		10,618	267,521	920		24,846		
Maryland		55	46,247	1,330,450	45,977	159,442	112,951	1,258	17,495	1,178,986	8,729	19	15,225	233	1,450
District of Columbia			29,770	995,385	22,630	133	70,153	6,400	25,404	363,306	18,216	656			
Total Eastern States	56,355	6,017	1,788,011	37,081,076	1,620,531	2,070,306	4,752,495	1,351,774	2,095,100	39,708,564	86,987	1,695	564,224	240,496	1,685,963
Virginia	1,080		78,028	1,460,520	54,907	142,185	207,012	306	47,141	1,092,272	20,335	1,667	88,578	1,309	
West Virginia			34,166	660,760	22,332	102,255	48,302		16,127	369,913	693	307	2,757	82	
North Carolina	30		61,788	1,484,349	50,145	151,915	297,053	63	35,624	599,826	8,190	3,988	77,949	2,390	
South Carolina	50		26,410	619,219	21,401	83,372	24,647		15,287	160,257	5,767	7	18,866	2,405	
Georgia			70,098	1,467,480	50,016	220,372	274,945	158	35,398	645,213	6,382	1,246	14,988	1,340	
Florida	650		128,630	2,443,735	57,115	390,838	354,727	5,137	41,564	1,097,899	8,724	1,758	94,421	2,488	
Alabama			49,144	1,071,957	33,450	194,064	94,939	531	15,007	526,722	4,474	46	8,697	1,431	
Mississippi	220		24,249	651,057	16,386	181,233	81,875	3	6,005	276,106	2,107		897	16,415	
Louisiana	47		67,061	1,497,279	33,410	334,870	291,116	7,951	26,963	587,538	3,699	401	17,250	623	1,500
Texas			340,552	6,815,564	160,236	644,348	1,423,440	18,949	181,240	1,912,115	15,900	1,159	375,263	5,064	5,000
Arkansas			30,875	732,969	14,871	81,478	80,902		10,732	240,211	858	445	1,612	215	
Kentucky	50		55,119	1,406,734	45,698	108,754	210,042	44	16,455	427,112	4,095	20	24,728	169	
Tennessee			72,942	1,441,143	44,626	184,850	390,967	1,685	18,064	916,798	1,341	226	49,200	1,745	
Total Southern States	2,127		1,037,082	21,752,766	604,593	2,820,754	3,779,967	34,827	465,587	8,851,982	82,565	11,270	775,206	35,676	6,500
Ohio	100	365	258,673	5,453,879	241,528	559,076	380,650	7,417	128,880	3,935,524	3,125	871	185,931	500	
Indiana	244	25	95,068	2,394,516	81,095	411,258	141,761	503	62,007	1,398,405	3,465	1,638	59,009	1,917	
Illinois		2,000	462,385	9,224,644	366,118	656,253	1,456,045	43,690	170,479	4,655,358	11,252	1,044	226,112	3,000	31,300

Michigan	415	3,015	186,152	3,590,668	179,369	385,802	224,975	8,902	75,151	3,511,187	2,692	59	210,429	820	
Wisconsin		1,900	86,842	2,063,227	81,899	169,393	189,376	2,707	61,687	1,791,188	3,462	1,136	22,807	424	500
Minnesota	300	150	103,528	1,891,989	79,871	240,576	381,642	4,077	39,343	1,682,903	2,095	256	31,849	71	
Iowa		435	68,444	1,752,752	50,765	245,423	163,584		30,341	900,267	1,576	195	1,571	65	
Missouri	275	370	153,391	3,360,051	105,905	326,578	820,434	3,632	36,999	1,203,759	4,208	574	94,083	270	
Total Middle Western States	1,334	8,260	1,414,483	29,731,726	1,186,550	2,994,359	3,758,467	70,928	604,887	19,078,591	31,875	5,773	831,791	7,067	31,800
North Dakota			15,903	387,831	10,375	70,170	13,411	20	5,070	213,992	375	6	62,743	25	
South Dakota			13,928	415,637	10,308	60,523	11,737		4,539	206,628	1,049	7	16,919	31	
Nebraska		10	42,046	1,153,042	36,654	111,981	164,278	51	13,671	179,476	201	34	1,478	12	
Kansas			55,844	1,265,437	39,309	343,463	108,908	10	18,025	420,627	3,598	60	56,420	7	
Montana			18,493	458,449	12,707	71,313	30,447		7,817	219,053	296	4	12,538		
Wyoming		100	5,098	210,835	5,777	49,334	15,697		2,759	106,261	1,257	23	7,509	265	
Colorado			50,684	1,075,151	36,801	80,291	129,340		18,723	494,934	2,201	10	37,004	192	
New Mexico			14,920	373,832	20,796	93,166	16,826	61	6,587	131,663	3,157	313	21,481	95	
Oklahoma			64,212	1,597,440	50,274	211,548	226,981	238	26,757	422,617	4,817	112	4,806	1,034	
Total Western States		110	281,128	6,937,654	223,001	1,091,789	717,625	380	103,948	2,395,251	16,951	569	220,898	1,661	
Washington			61,495	1,461,915	42,107	171,661	70,945	6,251	20,894	1,222,743	6,486	10	1,123	471	
Oregon		1,200	49,545	916,825	22,526	161,315	28,021	1,738	36,167	774,229	229	14	57,458	797	3,900
California			464,850	9,930,364	292,140	762,440	455,324	152,995	464,889	9,314,634	58,641	220	1,034,287	25,065	296,577
Idaho		100	15,755	318,464	10,206	78,747	3,416		5,674	223,126	1,391	11	14		
Utah			20,197	389,307	6,674	78,483	43,910	1	8,338	340,223	2,391	680	40,621	150	
Nevada			8,086	161,421	6,753	53,263	1,217		4,820	136,450	1,937		9,292		
Arizona			24,350	591,468	11,341	84,929	14,000	6,010	17,272	280,553	2,295	27	23,438		5,000
Total Pacific States		1,300	644,278	13,769,764	391,747	1,390,838	616,833	166,995	558,054	12,291,958	73,370	962	1,166,233	26,483	305,477
Total United States (exclusive of possessions)	57,689	19,216	5,430,640	115,147,867	4,252,569	10,926,662	14,142,634	1,656,536	4,048,033	93,574,743	304,834	21,548	3,585,752	313,377	2,061,015
Alaska			3,898	80,996	14,329	12,106	2,773		1,345	44,042	9,745	27	15,133		
Canal Zone (Panama)				7,056	7,390		103	311	99	1,517	3,135				
Guam				5,515	4,386	2,058			214	7,348	391		1,874		500
The Territory of Hawaii			16,862	231,314	23,971	43,633	12,543	2,066	3,877	196,578	8,596	496	46,034	54	
Puerto Rico			39,090	185,548	5,258	48,318	9,397	368	10,050	178,834	9,336	50	31,182	1,807	
American Samoa			100	401	137	126		61	3	886			168		
Virgin Islands of the United States			562	5,107	194	6,012			151	8,335			2,626	20	12
Total possessions			60,512	515,937	55,665	112,253	24,816	2,806	15,739	437,540	31,203	573	97,017	1,881	512
Total United States and possessions	57,689	19,216	5,491,152	115,663,804	4,308,234	11,038,915	14,167,450	1,659,342	4,063,772	94,012,283	336,037	22,121	3,682,769	315,258	2,061,527

¹ Includes dividend checks, letters of credit and travelers' checks sold for cash, and amounts due to reserve agents (transit account).

TABLE No. 43.—Assets and liabilities of active national banks, Dec. 31, 1958

ASSETS

[In thousands of dollars]

Location	Number of banks	Loans and discounts, including overdrafts	U.S. Government obligations, direct and guaranteed	Obligations of States and political subdivisions	Other bonds, notes and debentures	Corporate stocks, including stocks of Federal Reserve banks	Currency and coin	Balances with other banks including reserve balances and cash items in process of collection	Bank premises owned, furniture and fixtures	Real estate owned other than bank premises	Investments and other assets indirectly representing bank premises or other real estate	Customers' liability on acceptances outstanding	Other assets	Total assets
Maine	29	154,124	95,894	13,776	8,092	711	8,125	53,258	5,457	289	258		1,213	341,197
New Hampshire	51	132,459	74,512	15,766	3,253	636	7,810	58,993	3,925	205	56		525	298,140
Vermont	32	107,652	58,566	11,945	3,775	417	3,719	30,647	2,364	81	598		489	220,253
Massachusetts	107	1,808,323	932,468	192,294	29,298	9,683	53,932	827,948	36,739	307	658	28,462	16,581	3,936,693
Rhode Island	4	271,327	137,122	43,560	2,588	1,272	10,252	64,421	7,821	107		4,279	2,096	544,845
Connecticut	30	537,957	317,419	119,255	9,533	3,638	31,346	224,024	17,392	928	342	59	5,840	1,267,733
Total New England States	253	3,011,842	1,615,981	396,596	56,539	16,357	115,184	1,259,291	73,698	1,917	1,912	32,800	26,744	6,608,861
New York	258	5,639,091	2,791,584	961,533	149,958	35,115	106,613	2,170,817	107,061	1,675	3,778	86,387	99,687	12,153,299
New Jersey	167	1,618,820	1,214,566	497,840	90,323	7,476	80,115	563,887	50,880	807	603	134	14,686	4,140,137
Pennsylvania	485	3,735,515	2,378,182	768,291	152,132	22,150	145,828	1,465,381	105,278	2,378	3,349	5,824	28,503	8,812,811
Delaware	7	14,189	12,117	2,696	643	94	725	4,903	558				22	35,947
Maryland	53	359,941	349,751	77,463	20,516	1,858	20,386	222,210	11,829	360	363	199	3,390	1,068,266
District of Columbia	5	376,878	304,462	28,141	15,951	1,536	16,011	162,745	15,476	137			2,088	923,425
Total Eastern States	975	11,744,434	7,050,662	2,335,964	429,523	68,229	369,678	4,589,943	291,082	5,357	8,093	92,544	148,376	27,133,885
Virginia	131	817,199	544,651	125,022	43,982	3,642	37,863	371,870	24,796	847	1,620	238	3,976	1,975,706
West Virginia	77	240,504	272,902	36,134	8,464	1,707	17,707	142,520	7,442	119	367		2,347	730,006
North Carolina	43	305,057	197,978	49,050	15,875	1,481	20,889	162,100	9,448	76	432	150	2,069	764,481
South Carolina	25	254,381	181,184	37,603	9,852	1,086	16,687	145,326	8,624	174			2,674	657,416
Georgia	52	696,092	417,141	84,094	20,071	2,743	20,359	349,046	22,409	870		1	3,925	1,616,750
Florida	103	1,103,148	970,401	208,915	34,242	5,038	53,655	760,520	42,883	1,273	13,566	138	11,852	3,205,631
Alabama	69	598,936	400,045	142,664	27,351	2,582	31,654	311,296	15,587	403	2,437	155	4,999	1,538,109
Mississippi	27	133,769	98,534	41,253	3,259	732	8,082	86,500	4,673	10	500		977	378,289
Louisiana	41	723,383	576,141	127,256	17,297	3,910	28,064	470,378	19,416	297	2,825	3,416	8,254	1,980,637
Texas	458	3,934,359	2,285,940	511,789	140,498	17,905	112,099	2,634,362	158,630	6,876	8,525	51,066	25,088	9,887,737
Arkansas	55	224,438	171,099	72,849	7,787	1,155	11,469	149,298	8,183	269	40		1,693	648,280
Kentucky	88	334,116	308,862	51,668	16,966	1,504	19,379	214,678	8,141	49		39	2,235	958,119
Tennessee	75	959,678	573,346	136,809	25,529	4,062	41,317	540,733	23,976	209	182	11,852	5,475	2,322,986
Total Southern States	1,244	10,325,060	6,998,224	1,625,106	371,173	47,640	419,524	6,338,597	354,208	11,502	30,494	67,055	75,564	26,664,147

Ohio	228	2,224,974	1,913,642	366,035	56,175	10,812	96,375	1,071,659	63,321	805	3,301	374	17,898	5,825,371
Indiana	123	1,022,380	1,002,652	151,042	36,866	4,833	56,557	596,863	28,692	374	325	9	8,938	2,909,531
Illinois	395	4,778,748	4,264,808	787,219	236,667	23,719	118,399	2,655,123	49,236	2,055	3,584	10,195	55,260	12,985,013
Michigan	75	1,716,712	1,419,620	379,078	23,051	7,202	63,817	703,200	37,664	987	6,434	70	18,481	4,378,316
Wisconsin	97	769,994	718,649	105,153	42,164	3,232	27,347	438,095	18,003	689		58	8,250	2,131,634
Minnesota	179	1,219,272	757,555	185,051	65,687	5,143	28,027	688,597	25,297	1,315	6,506	946	13,322	2,996,718
Iowa	97	405,921	329,175	86,907	15,826	1,537	15,831	242,181	6,567	946	1,357	60	2,965	1,109,273
Missouri	75	911,841	708,458	128,411	24,039	4,068	23,124	629,007	13,220	1,023	1,148	518	8,038	2,452,895
Total Middle Western States	1,269	13,049,842	11,114,559	2,188,896	500,475	60,546	429,477	7,026,725	242,000	8,194	22,655	12,230	133,152	34,788,751
North Dakota	38	134,902	135,627	24,041	15,168	532	4,000	57,030	4,159	280	250		1,871	377,860
South Dakota	34	159,161	138,756	22,713	10,177	631	4,140	60,655	4,444	348	238		2,731	403,994
Nebraska	123	487,435	346,536	90,100	14,813	1,975	12,290	309,368	8,604	81	1,000	55	3,453	1,275,733
Kansas	169	467,350	400,202	123,123	30,511	2,310	16,418	283,963	13,761	659	181		2,717	1,341,195
Montana	41	156,849	156,773	23,901	12,981	563	5,125	74,898	5,584	232	23	9	1,531	438,469
Wyoming	25	108,811	108,968	14,219	5,640	423	4,480	66,012	3,457	96			908	313,014
Colorado	77	611,535	413,575	56,124	7,153	2,359	17,276	336,885	10,949	227	1,142		5,339	1,462,564
New Mexico	27	191,348	167,774	19,303	2,469	594	7,723	107,015	6,316	62	100		716	503,420
Oklahoma	197	787,896	614,297	163,901	33,702	3,788	26,943	605,417	27,432	384	6,999	875	5,214	2,276,848
Total Western States	731	3,105,287	2,482,531	537,425	132,614	13,175	98,395	1,901,243	84,706	2,369	9,933	939	24,480	8,393,097
Washington	25	1,090,842	685,593	185,653	34,947	3,961	30,985	467,432	35,812	720	480	1,062	10,108	2,547,595
Oregon	11	740,727	534,110	196,094	16,660	2,796	14,255	326,516	26,382	278	58	8	8,967	1,896,851
California	46	8,512,791	4,677,145	1,205,110	264,886	65,325	149,912	2,875,698	181,392	2,908	41,697	115,052	101,640	18,193,556
Idaho	9	213,865	180,694	34,877	75	684	5,974	73,512	6,902	59	34		294	516,970
Utah	7	229,704	111,984	36,478	3,659	843	5,148	82,106	1,255	22	6,000		405	477,604
Nevada	3	110,804	87,539	37,813	8,390	330	4,468	29,954	4,307	10	220		2,085	285,920
Arizona	3	452,965	166,066	43,114	11,523	1,483	15,562	147,809	16,958	12	5,160	154	5,564	866,350
Total Pacific States	104	11,381,698	6,443,131	1,739,139	340,140	75,422	226,304	4,003,027	272,988	4,009	53,649	116,276	129,063	24,784,846
Total United States (exclusive of possessions)	4,576	52,618,163	35,705,088	8,823,126	1,830,464	281,369	1,658,562	25,118,826	1,318,682	33,348	126,736	321,844	537,379	128,373,587
Alaska	7	52,402	55,944	6,869	3,784	37	6,082	20,860	2,413	186	339	8	168	149,084
The Territory of Hawaii	1	120,745	57,717	14,580	2,273		10,649	47,034	5,232				1,136	259,374
Virgin Islands of the United States	1	4,914	6,011	947	2	13	534	2,273	25	41			161	14,921
Total possessions	9	178,061	119,672	22,396	6,059	50	17,265	70,167	7,670	227	339	8	1,465	423,379
Total United States and possessions	4,585	52,796,224	35,824,760	8,845,522	1,836,523	281,419	1,675,827	25,188,993	1,326,352	33,575	127,075	321,852	538,844	128,796,966

TABLE No. 43.—*Assets and liabilities of active national banks, Dec. 31, 1958*—Continued

LIABILITIES

[In thousands of dollars]

Location	Demand deposits	Time deposits	Total deposits	Bills payable, rediscounts, and other liabilities for borrowed money	Acceptances executed by or for account of reporting banks and outstanding	Other liabilities	Capital stock [1]	Surplus	Undivided profits	Reserves and retirement account for preferred stock
Maine	185,339	120,736	306,075			3,898	11,250	12,476	6,369	1,129
New Hampshire	211,561	53,993	265,554			1,985	6,469	15,080	7,440	1,412
Vermont	77,766	120,254	198,020	200		2,900	6,745	7,237	3,973	1,378
Massachusetts	2,990,938	503,098	3,494,036		29,564	57,913	83,688	191,614	62,326	17,552
Rhode Island	255,163	233,827	488,990		4,279	8,229	12,645	25,292	5,365	45
Connecticut	880,293	271,384	1,151,677	1,500	59	17,265	33,323	46,532	15,598	1,779
Total New England States	4,601,060	1,303,292	5,904,352	1,700	33,902	92,190	154,120	298,231	101,071	23,295
New York	7,492,190	3,196,043	10,688,233	6,882	89,435	296,274	354,044	547,286	159,262	11,883
New Jersey	2,187,403	1,634,898	3,822,301	1,942	134	38,397	86,559	134,965	46,667	9,172
Pennsylvania	4,995,872	2,826,509	7,822,381	4,850	6,210	101,175	227,081	509,073	128,803	13,238
Delaware	17,582	14,238	31,820			85	775	2,400	793	74
Maryland	733,114	244,403	977,517	500	199	8,199	17,815	44,485	13,580	5,971
District of Columbia	651,460	200,828	852,288			7,534	18,100	33,100	9,981	2,422
Total Eastern States	16,077,621	8,116,919	24,194,540	14,174	95,978	451,664	704,374	1,271,309	359,086	42,760
Virginia	1,143,161	659,975	1,803,136	875	238	16,867	43,571	78,967	27,538	4,514
West Virginia	463,399	195,627	639,026	250		4,293	17,346	32,965	12,755	3,371
North Carolina	528,675	163,955	692,630	200	150	10,332	15,515	34,615	9,388	1,651
South Carolina	500,478	103,160	603,638		1	8,505	12,059	24,584	6,911	1,718
Georgia	1,191,699	277,414	1,469,113	850		24,286	33,957	57,352	6,596	14,596
Florida	2,237,000	715,107	2,952,107	3,475	145	36,811	76,710	93,559	27,754	15,070
Alabama	1,043,830	361,709	1,405,539	100	155	16,491	34,020	53,180	21,750	6,874
Mississippi	261,754	88,320	350,074			2,577	7,093	18,029	287	229
Louisiana	1,461,248	356,940	1,818,188	1,040	3,575	15,984	37,938	80,623	22,603	686
Texas	7,307,786	1,741,794	9,049,580		53,270	57,272	267,826	329,906	101,062	28,821
Arkansas	468,148	124,158	592,306			4,602	16,655	22,203	10,800	1,714
Kentucky	685,716	186,482	872,198		39	7,381	23,175	37,295	15,890	2,141
Tennessee	1,533,298	591,052	2,124,350		11,852	22,483	47,530	84,246	28,396	4,129
Total Southern States	18,826,192	5,565,693	24,391,885	6,790	69,425	227,884	633,395	947,524	301,730	85,514

Ohio	3,705,415	1,606,911	5,312,326	1,711	374	67,440	138,121	223,643	78,192	3,564
Indiana	1,894,044	772,134	2,666,178		9	30,014	56,403	105,608	42,072	9,247
Illinois	8,746,108	3,098,578	11,844,686	375	10,383	142,780	351,273	430,872	145,584	59,060
Michigan	2,530,339	1,468,334	3,998,673		70	76,215	77,236	158,682	62,232	5,208
Wisconsin	1,309,170	666,014	1,975,184		58	18,412	36,755	72,070	24,033	5,122
Minnesota	1,954,127	768,163	2,722,290		946	42,973	72,281	99,862	48,582	9,784
Iowa	790,518	233,704	1,024,222		60	5,553	19,298	34,649	22,287	3,004
Missouri	1,895,924	366,207	2,262,131	200	532	18,529	52,603	81,016	34,300	3,784
Total Middle Western States	22,825,645	8,980,045	31,805,690	2,286	12,432	401,916	803,970	1,206,402	457,282	98,773
North Dakota	231,149	117,890	349,039			5,110	6,960	10,815	5,267	669
South Dakota	253,029	121,311	374,340			4,981	6,998	11,795	5,285	595
Nebraska	1,044,804	120,412	1,165,216	7,010	55	7,787	26,815	38,427	25,395	5,028
Kansas	1,008,323	220,745	1,229,068	225		8,266	29,625	48,205	23,709	2,097
Montana	289,727	116,487	406,214	450	9	6,614	9,408	9,442	6,059	273
Wyoming	205,518	83,270	288,788	400		2,831	3,528	10,402	5,909	1,156
Colorado	988,779	359,189	1,347,968			11,680	32,930	45,302	22,441	2,243
New Mexico	367,329	104,922	472,251			3,961	9,850	10,780	3,584	3,429
Oklahoma	1,755,214	314,997	2,070,211	10,000	875	12,579	50,777	74,850	51,898	5,658
Total Western States	6,143,872	1,559,223	7,703,095	18,085	939	63,809	176,891	260,018	149,112	21,148
Washington	1,592,586	743,376	2,335,962		1,062	30,755	53,500	78,525	46,092	1,699
Oregon	1,030,407	694,986	1,725,393		8	30,298	40,840	52,435	47,756	121
California	8,751,100	7,901,386	16,652,486		116,708	337,407	330,784	525,830	223,601	6,740
Idaho	309,279	172,686	481,965			4,227	11,525	12,045	4,029	3,179
Utah	252,102	184,725	436,827			6,633	9,950	17,500	5,058	1,636
Nevada	160,464	106,806	267,270			2,612	5,450	5,550	4,981	57
Arizona	554,723	238,351	793,074		154	16,109	17,480	31,170	8,353	10
Total Pacific States	12,650,661	10,042,316	22,692,977		117,932	428,841	469,529	723,055	339,870	13,442
Total United States (exclusive of possessions)	81,125,051	35,567,488	116,692,539	43,035	330,608	1,665,504	2,942,279	4,706,539	1,708,151	284,932
Alaska	86,906	54,123	141,029		8	648	2,750	2,670	1,547	440
The Territory of Hawaii	133,149	105,396	238,545			2,037	6,000	9,000	1,608	2,176
Virgin Islands of the United States	6,693	7,322	14,015			197	250	250	129	80
Total possessions	226,748	166,841	393,589		8	2,882	9,000	11,920	3,284	2,696
Total United States and possessions	81,351,799	35,734,329	117,086,128	43,035	330,616	1,668,386	2,951,279	4,718,459	1,711,435	287,628

[1] See classification on pp. 182 and 183.

TABLE No. 43.—Assets and liabilities of active national banks, Dec. 31, 1958—Continued

[In thousands of dollars]

Location	Real estate loans — Secured by farm land (including improvements)	Real estate loans — Secured by residential properties (other than farm)	Real estate loans — Secured by other properties	Loans and discounts — Loans to banks	Loans to brokers and dealers in securities	Other loans for the purpose of purchasing or carrying stocks, bonds, and other securities	Loans to farmers directly guaranteed by the Commodity Credit Corporation	Other loans to farmers (excluding loans on real estate)	Commercial and industrial loans (including open market paper)	Other loans to individuals for personal expenditures	All other loans (including overdrafts)	Total gross loans	Less valuation reserves	Net loans
Maine	2,494	31,876	11,351		364	1,609	137	6,735	57,602	38,641	5,775	156,584	2,460	154,124
New Hampshire	1,169	22,795	6,652	250	1,681	1,145		3,046	51,323	43,843	2,804	134,708	2,249	132,459
Vermont	7,511	37,564	8,346			1,294		7,780	17,839	26,467	2,263	109,064	1,412	107,652
Massachusetts	2,516	142,440	103,251	3,769	12,500	12,481		6,781	1,106,954	400,442	63,697	1,854,831	46,508	1,808,323
Rhode Island	1,574	106,863	23,264		4,307	187		853	86,012	36,892	14,338	274,290	2,963	271,327
Connecticut	1,329	125,425	33,842		5,491	2,784		4,256	184,378	164,118	28,963	550,576	12,619	537,957
Total New England States	16,593	466,963	186,706	4,019	24,343	19,500	137	29,451	1,504,108	710,403	117,830	3,080,053	68,211	3,011,842
New York	24,259	694,162	194,631	80,263	365,193	47,012	93	49,644	3,003,937	1,140,357	193,740	5,793,291	154,200	5,639,091
New Jersey	10,898	572,400	145,958		32,626	13,831		12,931	377,286	445,980	44,537	1,656,447	37,627	1,618,820
Pennsylvania	58,386	896,105	286,082	656	19,033	32,808	75	68,046	1,602,668	720,367	125,087	3,809,313	73,798	3,735,515
Delaware	1,779	5,895	572			44		862	3,144	1,734	159	14,189		14,189
Maryland	10,521	66,605	34,243	75	3,068	28,932		7,522	108,622	89,752	14,055	363,395	3,454	359,941
District of Columbia	185	78,260	38,334	1,399	3,534	2,914		38	170,572	70,835	18,185	384,256	7,378	376,878
Total Eastern States	106,028	2,313,427	699,820	82,393	423,454	125,541	168	139,043	5,266,229	2,469,025	395,763	12,020,891	276,457	11,744,434
Virginia	19,784	180,024	56,372	2,172	7,191	7,969	489	27,826	241,518	251,316	32,632	827,293	10,094	817,199
West Virginia	4,026	70,596	19,007	50	287	3,173		3,153	56,460	84,718	4,145	245,615	5,111	240,504
North Carolina	5,161	18,447	12,392	49	7,381	14,383	421	8,015	119,340	116,922	8,615	311,126	6,069	305,057
South Carolina	2,666	16,646	19,832		2,774	4,187	1,182	4,546	113,495	77,622	15,231	258,181	3,800	254,381
Georgia	8,154	44,535	30,905	3,643	9,820	29,187	1,993	10,776	324,208	214,809	26,385	704,415	8,323	696,092
Florida	6,941	113,921	77,398	960	11,984	34,457		12,535	489,549	347,031	25,295	1,120,071	16,923	1,103,148
Alabama	7,571	62,752	30,093	1	3,589	4,693	11,217	17,478	247,314	198,388	31,299	614,395	15,459	598,936
Mississippi	3,416	10,820	10,756	50	582	1,451	996	6,097	56,520	40,778	5,483	136,949	3,180	133,769
Louisiana	4,858	57,485	45,827	2,163	8,132	6,503	1,836	10,501	398,240	129,210	66,534	731,289	7,906	723,383
Texas	28,028	174,949	145,266	2,789	42,853	213,138	139,103	186,342	2,117,211	805,960	152,046	4,007,685	73,326	3,934,359
Arkansas	8,058	18,136	16,647		2,574	917	7,263	19,771	87,559	62,896	3,159	226,980	2,542	224,438
Kentucky	15,470	47,765	22,949		2,075	2,508		28,201	109,618	103,404	7,869	340,168	6,052	334,116
Tennessee	12,295	56,096	41,337	2,449	21,151	12,384	12,357	22,553	505,510	269,894	21,792	977,818	18,140	959,678
Total Southern States	126,428	872,172	528,781	14,326	120,393	334,950	177,166	357,794	4,866,542	2,702,948	400,485	10,501,985	176,925	10,325,060

	1	2	3	4	5	6	7	8	9	10	11	12	13	14
Ohio	2,224,974	45,993	2,270,967	91,474	626,790	735,017	44,659	3,913	29,828	37,399	1,123	141,780	514,486	44,498
Indiana	1,022,380	18,273	1,040,653	31,608	250,755	328,676	29,771	2,047	8,611	11,817	395	65,330	291,674	19,969
Illinois	4,778,748	138,865	4,917,613	222,028	789,290	2,624,613	151,875	12,792	116,525	230,961	10,585	174,264	554,302	30,372
Michigan	1,716,712	34,448	1,751,160	48,971	446,535	575,679	15,927	127	22,430	11,981	------	118,745	501,021	9,444
Wisconsin	769,994	21,069	791,063	71,036	153,404	254,070	16,673	31	15,551	16,043	506	43,986	208,875	10,888
Minnesota	1,219,272	16,800	1,236,072	44,759	266,162	477,595	67,544	6,947	12,062	11,050	1,110	54,642	282,795	11,406
Iowa	405,921	7,221	413,142	17,390	71,014	102,870	97,135	9,253	3,361	2,353	------	22,085	77,356	10,325
Missouri	911,841	11,411	923,252	26,211	211,862	400,104	50,530	4,894	22,615	14,985	872	38,219	145,184	7,776
Total Middle Western States	13,049,842	294,080	13,343,922	553,477	2,816,112	5,498,630	474,114	40,004	230,983	336,589	14,591	659,051	2,575,693	144,678
North Dakota	134,902	3,417	138,319	1,407	34,713	28,916	19,700	11,838	908	158	------	5,928	32,493	2,416
South Dakota	159,161	5,634	164,795	4,186	32,532	33,795	36,245	9,591	390	------	------	7,305	38,060	2,533
Nebraska	487,435	8,507	495,942	15,886	79,539	154,512	151,158	27,743	6,789	1,711	1,718	20,607	29,228	7,101
Kansas	467,350	5,073	472,423	10,104	95,409	165,843	101,697	31,039	3,342	3,854	291	14,271	35,535	11,038
Montana	156,849	3,497	160,346	1,930	55,125	32,345	21,667	5,192	456	1,000	------	6,872	33,917	1,842
Wyoming	108,811	1,581	110,392	257	22,310	31,337	20,955	1,351	584	------	------	8,604	23,708	1,286
Colorado	611,535	9,232	620,767	18,450	130,156	233,148	102,797	5,113	4,305	3,280	------	44,858	73,055	5,605
New Mexico	191,348	5,122	196,470	3,683	49,481	64,926	17,787	5,486	3,516	16,690	------	12,699	20,382	1,820
Oklahoma	787,896	11,121	799,017	31,914	175,522	373,464	64,676	23,619	6,356	13,275	750	43,073	51,348	15,020
Total Western States	3,105,287	53,184	3,158,471	87,767	674,787	1,118,286	536,682	120,972	26,646	39,968	2,759	164,217	337,726	48,661
Washington	1,090,842	21,273	1,112,115	38,719	253,248	442,995	57,647	1,777	6,920	6,157	100	59,920	227,656	16,976
Oregon	770,727	6,438	777,165	16,215	151,389	310,293	39,949	1,061	3,347	3,117	------	47,699	189,137	14,958
California	8,512,791	146,397	8,659,188	215,905	1,403,264	3,077,706	282,971	2,193	31,422	38,752	147,744	482,156	2,899,931	77,144
Idaho	213,865	3,475	217,340	2,701	44,590	42,386	30,392	1,387	175	52	------	10,341	83,644	1,672
Utah	229,704	2,531	232,235	4,534	42,691	75,005	12,877	248	1,886	2,462	------	17,283	72,435	2,814
Nevada	110,804	526	111,330	1,683	36,848	18,096	2,368	------	297	2,100	------	15,807	33,693	438
Arizona	452,965	3,410	456,375	1,735	108,913	141,563	71,988	24	949	9,869	546	6,502	110,504	3,782
Total Pacific States	11,381,698	184,050	11,565,748	281,492	2,040,943	4,108,044	498,192	6,690	44,996	62,509	148,390	639,708	3,617,000	117,784
Total United States (exclusive of possessions)	52,618,163	1,052,907	53,671,070	1,836,814	11,414,218	22,361,889	2,035,276	345,137	782,616	1,007,256	266,478	2,878,283	10,182,981	560,172
Alaska	52,402	2,214	54,616	539	13,537	15,130	20	------	55	------	------	8,581	16,648	106
The Territory of Hawaii	120,745	869	121,614	2,554	15,356	25,315	3,862	------	11,689	6	------	16,317	44,913	1,602
Virgin Islands of the United States	4,914	------	4,914	64	428	694	6	------	------	------	------	489	3,143	90
Total possessions	178,061	3,083	181,144	3,157	29,321	41,139	3,888	------	11,744	6	------	25,357	64,704	1,798
Total United States and possessions	52,796,224	1,055,990	53,852,214	1,839,971	11,443,539	22,402,978	2,039,164	345,137	794,360	1,007,262	266,478	2,903,670	10,247,685	561,970

TABLE No. 43.—*Assets and liabilities of active national banks, Dec. 31, 1958*—Continued

[In thousands of dollars]

Location	Capital		Demand deposits						Time deposits					
	Preferred stock	Common stock	Individuals, partnerships, and corporations	U.S. Government	States and political subdivisions	Banks in United States	Banks in foreign countries	Certified and cashiers' checks, etc.[1]	Individuals, partnerships, and corporations	U.S. Government	Postal savings	States and political subdivisions	Banks in United States	Banks in foreign countries
Maine		11,250	154,795	4,939	13,854	7,666	9	4,076	118,525	1,404	7	800		
New Hampshire		6,469	161,569	7,363	22,067	11,621		8,941	52,851	745	10	387		
Vermont		5,945	64,327	2,277	7,303	1,262		2,597	119,416	94	3	741	581	31,250
Massachusetts	800	83,688	2,229,277	90,272	222,243	354,606	28,040	66,500	452,076	7,293	1,041	10,857		
Rhode Island		12,645	211,150	7,637	22,073	2,939	1,143	10,221	232,695	460	24	648	10	
Connecticut		33,323	741,014	33,042	43,296	28,439	60	34,442	268,832	1,748		794		
Total New England States	800	153,320	3,562,132	145,530	330,836	406,533	29,252	126,777	1,244,395	11,744	1,085	14,227	591	31,250
New York	229	353,815	5,712,460	252,224	344,648	585,109	246,467	351,282	2,716,364	22,808		107,448	25,624	323,799
New Jersey	638	85,921	1,771,205	64,810	240,543	42,479	142	68,224	1,597,474	8,180		29,241	53	3
Pennsylvania	50	227,031	4,068,341	165,387	244,867	404,966	20,984	91,327	2,750,093	3,354	684	60,922	5,056	6,400
Delaware		775	16,632	355	200			395	14,096			142		
Maryland		17,815	550,592	26,304	83,268	68,448	246	4,256	237,096	4,916		2,371	20	
District of Columbia		18,100	571,858	15,371	104	49,029	4,310	10,788	190,851	9,321	656			
Total Eastern States	917	703,457	12,691,088	524,451	913,630	1,150,031	272,149	526,272	7,505,974	48,579	1,340	200,124	30,703	330,199
Virginia		43,571	854,611	37,207	77,927	139,510	227	33,679	597,001	15,882	111	46,102	879	
West Virginia		17,346	347,766	11,997	59,145	35,382		9,109	193,611	653	171	1,139	53	
North Carolina		15,515	433,858	15,536	40,807	24,151	25	14,298	137,141	3,681		22,203	930	
South Carolina		12,059	396,697	14,008	61,673	14,748		13,292	89,561	4,943	2	8,269	385	
Georgia		33,957	802,452	30,035	116,894	216,993	52	24,373	266,973	3,769	756	5,913	3	
Florida	200	76,510	1,569,990	38,719	282,225	314,359	4,305	27,402	646,849	8,243	61	58,355	1,599	
Alabama		34,020	786,510	24,958	127,638	91,384	531	12,809	349,768	4,035	10	690	1,206	
Mississippi		7,093	175,485	5,294	45,674	33,784		1,517	78,248	2,072		110	7,890	
Louisiana		37,938	1,008,982	24,884	171,545	229,132	7,951	18,754	347,605	1,232	51	6,552		1,500
Texas		267,826	5,187,184	134,173	469,749	1,350,060	18,317	148,303	1,412,093	15,786	1,143	302,708	5,064	5,000
Arkansas		16,655	352,259	8,021	34,890	66,599		6,379	122,190	826	24	963	155	
Kentucky		23,175	573,643	18,179	32,152	55,132	1,658	6,610	175,566	635	15	10,166	100	
Tennessee		47,530	990,651	34,314	113,793	379,220		13,662	559,037	1,305	165	30,190	355	
Total Southern States	200	633,195	13,480,088	398,285	1,634,112	2,950,454	33,066	330,187	4,975,643	63,062	2,509	499,360	18,619	6,500

Ohio	25	138,121	2,863,024	130,169	364,813	262,944	4,154	80,311	1,513,061	1,774	190	91,521	365	
Indiana		56,378	1,429,199	50,907	234,050	132,730	503	46,655	730,522	3,280	1,478	36,709	145	
Illinois	1,500	349,773	6,562,286	275,271	487,241	1,288,662	39,790	122,858	2,915,636	11,165	1,004	139,473	500	30,800
Michigan		77,236	2,014,593	129,871	166,015	179,271	7,408	33,181	1,370,837	1,595	29	95,558	315	
Wisconsin	50	36,705	1,002,206	47,461	71,964	147,949	2,647	36,943	653,073	3,405	957	7,725	354	500
Minnesota		72,281	1,337,133	62,780	145,340	377,879	4,077	26,918	753,620	2,083	68	12,371	21	
Iowa		19,298	547,825	19,120	69,940	141,868		11,765	231,465	1,551	53	635		
Missouri		52,603	1,264,135	47,134	113,640	453,820	1,592	15,603	338,870	2,944	28	24,265	100	
Total Middle Western States	1,575	802,395	17,020,401	762,713	1,653,003	2,955,123	60,171	374,234	8,507,084	27,797	3,807	408,257	1,800	31,300
North Dakota		6,960	198,216	6,323	12,973	10,675	20	2,942	114,305	353	6	3,201	25	
South Dakota		6,998	206,399	5,108	29,055	9,786		2,681	111,922	1,032		8,357		
Nebraska		26,815	773,741	26,766	72,948	160,528	51	10,770	118,928	201	29	1,254		
Kansas		29,625	694,482	23,865	181,787	96,928		11,261	193,942	3,569	39	23,192	3	
Montana		9,408	228,601	6,719	34,590	15,283		4,534	111,101	131		5,255		
Wyoming		3,528	147,831	4,601	36,076	14,863		2,147	76,235	1,243	18	5,774		
Colorado		32,930	800,201	29,038	47,757	98,089	61	13,633	334,765	1,250	10	23,164		
New Mexico		9,850	258,884	16,860	70,352	16,482		4,751	89,704	1,009	11	14,153	45	
Oklahoma		50,777	1,305,497	44,660	162,669	221,453	238	20,697	305,783	3,901	97	4,282	934	
Total Western States	176,891	4,613,852	163,940	648,207	644,087	370	73,416	1,456,685	12,689	210	88,632	1,007	3,900	
Washington		53,500	1,312,007	37,604	152,089	67,338	6,061	17,487	731,500	6,466	10	1,110	390	
Oregon		40,840	810,691	19,213	140,073	25,331	1,656	33,443	649,512	229	14	45,181	50	
California		330,784	7,132,566	214,218	642,775	267,222	130,086	364,233	6,777,253	55,607	202	763,127	19,150	286,047
Idaho		11,525	236,374	5,708	61,003	2,244		3,950	171,294	1,381	11			
Utah		9,950	194,176	5,819	31,243	15,717		5,147	166,203	2,305	670	15,547		
Nevada		5,450	114,308	5,380	37,680	289		2,807	96,024	1,880		8,902		
Arizona		17,480	451,154	8,706	62,590	12,236	5,884	14,153	215,569	2,295	27	15,460		5,000
Total Pacific States		469,529	10,251,276	296,648	1,127,453	390,377	143,687	441,220	8,807,355	70,163	934	849,327	19,590	294,947
Total United States (exclusive of possessions)	3,492	2,938,787	61,618,837	2,291,567	6,307,241	8,496,605	538,695	1,872,106	32,497,136	234,034	9,885	2,059,927	72,310	694,196
Alaska		2,750	64,192	12,013	7,186	2,288		1,227	34,341	9,679	10	10,093		
The Territory of Hawaii		6,000	98,692	10,177	17,807	3,299	1,261	1,913	77,796	7,407	10	19,683	20	500
Virgin Islands of the United States		250	3,501	155	2,970			67	5,434			1,856		12
Total possessions		9,000	166,385	22,345	27,963	5,587	1,261	3,207	117,571	17,086	20	31,632	20	512
Total United States and possessions	3,492	2,947,787	61,785,222	2,313,912	6,335,204	8,502,192	539,956	1,875,313	32,614,707	251,120	9,905	2,091,559	72,330	694,708

1 Includes dividend checks, letters of credit and travelers' checks sold for cash, and amounts due to Federal Reserve banks (transit account).

TABLE No. 44.—Assets and liabilities of all active banks other than national, Dec. 31, 1958 (includes State commercial, mutual savings, and private banks)

ASSETS

[In thousands of dollars]

Location	Number of banks	Loans and discounts, including overdrafts	U.S. Government obligations, direct and guaranteed	Obligations of States and political subdivisions	Other bonds, notes and debentures	Corporate stocks, including stocks of Federal Reserve banks	Currency and coin	Balances with other banks including reserve balances and cash items in process of collection	Bank premises owned, furniture and fixtures	Real estate owned other than bank premises	Investments and other assets indirectly representing bank premises or other real estate	Customers' liability on acceptances outstanding	Other assets	Total assets
Maine	58	357,391	230,319	29,912	65,254	25,366	13,765	51,692	7,187	768	616		1,448	783,718
New Hampshire	58	391,070	173,144	13,179	29,509	37,689	3,516	19,485	8,366	936	40		1,236	678,170
Vermont	32	206,381	57,593	15,504	4,276	3,352	3,852	22,194	2,973	118	491		464	317,198
Massachusetts	249	4,167,514	2,304,884	193,201	403,297	258,089	61,651	435,824	61,665	2,661	765	2,541	28,571	7,920,663
Rhode Island	13	468,369	205,728	27,809	88,606	27,500	11,841	52,711	6,431	119	470	45	1,795	891,424
Connecticut	121	1,962,375	924,683	155,053	290,346	129,413	40,748	244,525	33,654	1,071		3	15,988	3,797,859
Total New England States	531	7,553,100	3,896,351	434,658	881,288	481,409	135,373	826,431	120,276	5,673	2,382	2,589	49,502	14,389,032
New York	303	30,933,066	11,431,817	2,425,240	2,509,936	456,683	315,552	9,051,813	405,158	4,235	6,254	522,585	459,505	58,521,844
New Jersey	116	2,051,017	1,165,928	378,587	281,890	32,153	66,217	450,623	48,747	567	181	87	22,155	4,498,152
Pennsylvania	265	3,789,219	1,957,689	515,856	785,081	59,453	122,155	1,186,091	81,081	5,072	7,316	1,274	32,038	8,542,325
Delaware	22	342,110	240,179	39,353	81,732	11,703	12,169	110,665	9,027	767	1,036		3,164	851,905
Maryland	96	868,788	659,981	94,766	126,606	4,660	36,075	226,917	18,034	425	114	136	46,864	2,083,366
District of Columbia	8	293,328	220,701	12,361	11,020	759	12,830	141,628	6,363		4,560		3,286	706,836
Total Eastern States	810	38,277,528	15,676,295	3,466,163	3,796,265	565,411	564,998	11,167,737	568,410	11,066	19,461	524,082	567,012	75,204,428
Virginia	181	616,882	409,759	96,700	28,360	1,644	33,129	232,681	18,753	318	2,901		2,926	1,444,053
West Virginia	106	229,603	228,641	40,487	4,188	1,385	17,195	108,603	5,585	438	903		1,424	638,452
North Carolina	160	877,156	541,378	212,152	91,245	2,650	56,731	430,181	27,262	532	136	50	17,532	2,257,005
South Carolina	119	129,722	108,499	44,628	20,663	219	14,324	63,467	3,506	212	68		585	385,893
Georgia	342	552,872	415,240	72,934	30,732	1,410	35,227	254,370	17,797	818	131	376	5,665	1,387,572
Florida	177	605,348	595,416	132,171	15,459	735	43,369	253,780	27,846	882	525	481	6,117	1,682,129
Alabama	170	209,310	190,629	60,098	16,456	265	16,402	97,809	5,553	282	262		2,003	599,069
Mississippi	167	333,259	247,256	143,829	13,537	597	25,479	178,564	14,149	276	128	3	815	957,892
Louisiana	145	360,132	303,405	133,897	4,928	575	31,248	219,629	11,365	298	1,410	75	2,125	1,069,087
Texas	510	1,080,798	668,116	195,747	79,775	5,354	64,099	583,628	46,975	1,947	1,197	1,112	4,347	2,733,095
Arkansas	182	222,902	167,365	43,933	32,387	290	14,182	138,493	4,961	203	6		396	625,118
Kentucky	272	567,853	474,965	63,749	3,381	1,280	29,983	352,653	8,465	212	132	12	2,230	1,504,915
Tennessee	223	429,317	252,425	92,122	20,367	687	26,179	179,270	13,393	831		224	1,804	1,016,619
Total Southern States	2,754	6,215,154	4,603,094	1,332,447	361,478	17,091	407,547	3,093,128	205,610	7,249	7,799	2,333	47,969	16,300,899

Ohio	381	2,706,833	1,800,543	395,332	89,497	14,012	111,156	903,983	49,451	494	11,244	697	23,773	6,107,015
Indiana	340	720,524	836,707	101,527	24,349	1,235	46,698	308,356	14,781	262	810	34	3,673	2,058,956
Illinois	551	1,778,258	2,028,189	477,169	146,256	17,328	62,903	870,994	29,223	1,853	13,843	2,202	22,185	5,450,373
Michigan	318	1,831,208	1,559,521	447,095	146,870	5,807	80,528	575,419	53,548	674	258	105	12,312	4,584,478
Wisconsin	459	908,186	953,926	176,747	40,870	1,287	48,131	348,947	21,414	518	3,515	117	13,169	2,606,827
Minnesota	508	783,779	529,088	114,373	123,320	264	24,874	181,562	13,573	277	101	24	4,172	1,775,407
Iowa	572	994,174	712,485	196,389	27,271	1,143	37,520	341,308	11,587	186	1,581	15	1,411	2,324,840
Missouri	538	1,492,618	1,276,467	320,431	69,623	16,778	57,256	787,902	27,789	422	1,740	2,367	11,673	4,065,066
Total Middle Western States	3,667	11,305,580	9,696,896	2,229,063	539,189	57,854	469,066	4,318,471	221,136	4,686	33,092	5,561	92,368	28,972,962
North Dakota	117	116,295	197,590	50,177	39,808	22	4,494	43,297	2,187	17			413	454,300
South Dakota	138	127,083	164,434	27,216	11,756	140	5,178	52,032	1,445	34	35		294	388,647
Nebraska	300	212,967	207,500	23,804	6,900	232	7,591	89,535	2,217	36	2		797	551,581
Kansas	424	437,042	338,550	139,175	4,583	426	16,681	182,646	5,784	559	82	3	855	1,126,386
Montana	74	160,322	148,844	29,485	14,745	431	5,950	71,406	3,595	122	12		937	435,849
Wyoming	27	37,459	49,011	5,240	1,567	83	1,755	23,859	902	54			33	119,963
Colorado	98	259,926	108,031	25,788	2,574	1,818	8,728	107,327	3,574	378	562		3,594	582,300
New Mexico	26	82,079	70,202	12,749	873	50	5,935	34,660	3,689	66	42		567	210,912
Oklahoma	190	202,897	160,737	45,166	4,842	112	10,828	93,793	2,961	86	369		839	522,630
Total Western States	1,394	1,636,070	1,504,899	352,800	87,648	3,314	67,140	698,555	26,354	1,352	1,104	3	8,329	4,387,568
Washington	68	359,836	224,795	35,950	43,048	503	8,025	59,873	5,388	10	705	7	1,698	739,838
Oregon	45	124,896	99,284	21,485	3,305	82	5,423	37,111	4,057	749	7	25	867	297,291
California	78	3,001,836	1,919,190	467,978	74,895	6,966	57,799	1,018,234	70,979	596	8,409	8,409	34,705	6,669,996
Idaho	19	76,536	45,190	13,975	1,208	149	2,896	26,416	1,469	235	326		400	169,179
Utah	42	226,835	144,147	30,291	2,485	682	7,095	96,561	4,765	88	1,992		1,182	516,123
Nevada	3	51,200	40,868	3,837	268	113	2,708	14,227	2,321	1			456	115,999
Arizona	5	115,499	75,601	17,661	6,159	150	5,389	39,929	5,357	459	1,358		2,587	270,149
Total Pacific States	260	3,956,638	2,549,454	591,177	131,368	8,645	89,335	1,292,351	94,336	2,138	12,797	8,441	41,895	8,778,575
Total United States (exclusive of possessions)	9,416	68,944,070	37,926,989	8,406,308	5,797,236	1,133,724	1,733,459	21,396,673	1,236,122	32,164	76,635	543,009	807,075	148,033,464
Alaska	11	14,911	16,923	2,386	1,332		1,604	5,342	482	75	153		48	43,256
Canal Zone (Panama)	(1)	1,553					2,008	666	17				15,465	19,709
Guam	(2)	8,933					812	21	241				12,271	22,354
The Territory of Hawaii	9	168,117	91,278	22,599	3,281	1,584	13,679	57,812	7,484	76	25	451	1,806	368,457
Puerto Rico [3]	10	349,577	70,016	33,856	23,108	1,007	23,871	44,405	6,837	341	168	2,453	29,235	584,745
American Samoa	1	273	1,307				113	252	5	212			32	1,982
Virgin Islands of the United States	2	3,820	3,819	6			492	968	52				69	9,226
Total possessions	33	547,184	183,343	58,841	27,727	2,591	42,579	109,466	15,118	704	346	2,904	58,926	1,049,729
Total United States and possessions	9,449	69,491,254	38,110,332	8,465,149	5,824,963	1,136,315	1,776,038	21,506,139	1,251,240	32,868	76,981	545,913	866,001	149,083,193

1 2 branches of a national bank and 2 branches of a national bank in California.

2 Branch of a national bank in California.

3 Asset and liability items include data for branches of a national bank and a State member bank in New York.

NOTE.—Figures obtained from the Federal Deposit Insurance Corporation.

TABLE No. 44.—Assets and liabilities of all active banks other than national, Dec. 31, 1958 (includes State commercial, mutual savings, and private banks)—Continued

LIABILITIES

[In thousands of dollars]

Location	Demand deposits	Time deposits	Total deposits	Bills payable, rediscounts, and other liabilities for borrowed money	Acceptances executed by or for account of reporting banks and outstanding	Other liabilities	Capital stock [1]	Surplus	Undivided profits	Reserves and retirement account for preferred stock and capital notes and debentures
Maine	167,390	530,249	697,639	91	----	6,784	9,830	37,338	29,570	2,466
New Hampshire	26,888	571,720	598,608	1,975	----	6,470	2,407	38,048	27,126	3,536
Vermont	62,440	226,365	288,805	58	----	2,094	5,988	9,812	9,197	1,244
Massachusetts	1,498,313	5,550,140	7,048,453	760	2,572	106,184	51,442	420,026	261,933	29,293
Rhode Island	228,546	571,754	800,300	----	45	12,768	9,415	59,152	9,335	409
Connecticut	844,343	2,569,911	3,414,254	414	3	41,172	33,858	185,491	102,529	20,138
Total New England States	2,827,920	10,020,139	12,848,059	3,298	2,620	175,472	112,940	749,867	439,690	57,086
New York	25,340,233	26,596,337	51,936,570	9,206	552,875	1,054,042	873,528	2,993,662	906,550	195,111
New Jersey	1,621,766	2,495,481	4,117,247	189	87	51,532	71,014	194,040	36,995	27,048
Pennsylvania	4,049,910	3,658,554	7,708,464	1,825	1,302	94,316	147,014	459,752	114,005	15,647
Delaware	478,648	279,049	757,697	----	----	10,249	13,996	55,332	14,261	370
Maryland	934,459	958,789	1,893,248	225	136	26,434	28,487	81,563	48,206	5,067
District of Columbia	468,645	182,800	651,445	----	----	8,961	11,670	26,000	6,388	2,372
Total Eastern States	32,893,661	34,171,010	67,064,671	11,445	554,400	1,245,534	1,146,009	3,810,349	1,126,405	245,615
Virginia	768,910	544,186	1,313,096	1,000	----	20,000	35,537	51,557	20,576	2,287
West Virginia	386,377	178,125	564,502	270	----	5,724	16,820	31,859	16,113	3,164
North Carolina	1,490,474	528,388	2,018,862	842	50	59,703	46,303	101,134	22,233	7,878
South Carolina	263,428	84,142	347,570	----	----	1,774	14,401	15,028	6,106	1,014
Georgia	856,870	391,755	1,248,625	428	376	17,178	36,141	49,769	23,334	11,721
Florida	1,056,136	490,183	1,546,319	1,125	494	16,976	50,590	46,673	16,867	3,085
Alabama	366,118	179,661	545,779	----	3	3,622	15,124	20,134	13,375	1,032
Mississippi	674,805	207,205	882,010	1,650	----	6,710	17,376	47,342	1,875	929
Louisiana	730,341	254,071	984,412	500	75	7,575	29,170	31,401	12,983	2,971
Texas	1,935,991	572,707	2,508,698	2,750	1,112	16,138	72,726	76,657	43,704	11,310
Arkansas	452,804	119,183	571,987	----	----	1,586	14,220	18,494	16,211	2,620
Kentucky	1,102,011	269,642	1,371,653	140	140	13,097	31,994	57,016	27,790	3,085
Tennessee	548,087	378,258	926,295	1,000	224	12,385	25,412	27,422	21,044	2,837
Total Southern States	10,632,302	4,197,506	14,829,808	9,705	2,474	182,468	405,814	574,486	242,211	53,933

Ohio	3,066,015	2,519,040	5,585,055	725	697	65,974	121,017	259,082	70,259	4,206
Indiana	1,197,096	692,300	1,889,396	250	34	20,217	38,934	63,122	43,592	3,411
Illinois	3,171,121	1,829,488	5,000,609	3,683	2,202	51,476	113,112	135,746	87,961	55,584
Michigan	1,934,528	2,256,853	4,191,381	185	105	61,390	111,931	137,585	65,646	16,255
Wisconsin	1,259,119	1,153,503	2,412,622	525	117	10,901	52,402	78,785	45,904	5,387
Minnesota	683,371	949,011	1,632,382	260	24	9,612	31,697	57,785	33,531	10,116
Iowa	1,452,347	669,970	2,122,317	665	15	5,639	49,581	71,877	66,448	8,298
Missouri	2,757,675	936,687	3,694,362	2,270	2,385	40,413	101,433	114,235	99,822	10,146
Total Middle Western States	15,521,272	11,006,852	26,528,124	8,563	5,579	265,622	620,107	918,401	513,163	113,403
North Dakota	255,728	159,251	414,979	200		1,507	8,943	12,371	10,863	5,437
South Dakota	249,715	103,323	353,038			869	6,930	9,593	11,279	1,938
Nebraska	434,873	60,789	495,662	1,531		2,826	15,231	18,549	15,683	2,099
Kansas	766,829	259,967	1,026,796	871	3	3,446	26,229	38,963	28,563	1,515
Montana	291,006	115,669	406,675	100		2,925	9,085	10,532	6,249	1,283
Wyoming	78,884	31,780	110,664			375	1,670	3,751	3,136	367
Colorado	351,588	175,152	526,740	1,786	3	9,871	17,754	14,953	9,224	1,969
New Mexico	143,878	51,787	195,665			1,584	5,070	5,082	2,175	1,336
Oklahoma	358,024	118,389	476,413	591		3,275	13,435	13,922	14,183	811
Total Western States	2,930,525	1,076,107	4,006,632	5,079	6	26,678	104,347	127,716	101,355	15,755
Washington	181,187	491,357	672,544	100	7	7,648	7,995	35,528	10,615	5,401
Oregon	136,185	137,741	273,926		25	2,917	8,705	7,767	3,641	310
California	3,307,052	2,828,038	6,135,090		8,976	94,944	135,266	204,401	86,856	4,463
Idaho	103,775	51,856	155,631			2,034	4,230	4,852	2,134	298
Utah	278,143	199,340	477,483			6,543	16,312	16,312	5,390	48
Nevada	66,931	40,873	107,804			1,427	2,636	3,114	1,018	
Arizona	170,297	72,962	243,259			5,230	6,870	10,526	3,414	850
Total Pacific States	4,243,570	3,822,167	8,065,737	100	9,008	120,743	176,049	282,500	113,068	11,370
Total United States (exclusive of possessions)	69,049,250	64,293,781	133,343,031	38,190	574,087	2,016,517	2,565,266	6,463,319	2,535,892	497,162
Alaska	24,643	14,824	39,467			58	1,148	1,250	804	529
Canal Zone (Panama)	14,959	4,652	19,611			98				
Guam	12,173	9,613	21,786			568				
The Territory of Hawaii	184,255	146,862	331,117	244	451	5,180	10,862	12,190	6,993	1,420
Puerto Rico	288,939	221,209	480,148	15,075	2,454	31,759	39,090	12,036	2,340	1,843
American Samoa	728	1,054	1,782			31	100	25	5	39
Virgin Islands of the United States	4,771	3,671	8,442			174	312	100	198	
Total possessions	500,468	401,885	902,353	15,319	2,905	37,868	51,512	25,601	10,340	3,831
Total United States and possessions	69,549,718	64,695,666	134,245,384	53,509	576,992	2,054,385	2,616,778	6,488,920	2,546,232	500,993

¹ Includes capital notes and debentures.   (See classification on pp. 190 and 191.)

TABLE No. 44.—Assets and liabilities of all active banks other than national, Dec. 31, 1958 (includes State commercial, mutual savings, and private banks)—Continued

[In thousands of dollars]

Location	Real estate loans			Loans to banks	Loans to brokers and dealers in securities	Other loans for the purpose of purchasing or carrying stocks, bonds, and other securities	Loans to farmers directly guaranteed by the Commodity Credit Corporation	Other loans to farmers (excluding loans on real estate)	Commercial and industrial loans (including open-market paper)	Other loans to individuals for personal expenditures	All other loans (including overdrafts)	Total gross loans	Less valuation reserves	Net loans
	Secured by farm land (including improvements)	Secured by residential properties (other than farm)	Secured by other properties											
Maine	5,543	213,932	36,971	248	570	1,246	1	5,014	42,902	50,332	4,044	360,803	3,412	357,391
New Hampshire	2,168	303,475	59,985			314		630	10,857	14,942	706	393,077	2,007	391,070
Vermont	9,947	122,364	21,089		353	2,235		7,443	19,958	23,131	1,684	208,204	1,823	206,381
Massachusetts	7,036	3,059,462	416,078	1,391	14,550	11,346		2,778	371,873	287,034	28,724	4,201,172	33,658	4,167,514
Rhode Island	571	285,768	36,534		2,153	625		2,125	88,962	50,741	11,700	477,179	8,810	468,369
Connecticut	7,787	1,478,994	111,622		1,948	12,155		4,079	159,311	188,857	12,520	1,977,173	14,798	1,962,375
Total New England States	33,952	5,463,995	682,279	1,639	19,474	27,921	1	20,069	693,863	615,037	59,378	7,617,608	64,508	7,553,100
New York	34,826	14,634,854	1,930,615	430,008	1,432,737	448,204	305	38,796	9,735,873	1,886,685	901,169	31,474,072	541,006	30,933,066
New Jersey	3,249	1,201,719	156,161	575	56,409	11,953		3,363	278,915	348,056	29,784	2,090,184	39,167	2,051,017
Pennsylvania	20,025	1,379,756	230,342	3,681	48,183	94,494	14	15,271	1,120,389	861,120	96,650	3,869,925	80,706	3,789,219
Delaware	8,777	96,068	25,639		11,905	3,421			83,465	106,869	6,681	345,770	3,660	342,110
Maryland	15,624	422,980	73,021	1,530	14,657	10,016	74	10,302	132,639	174,692	25,934	881,345	12,557	868,788
District of Columbia	973	54,431	23,988		8,940	399		82	94,740	94,261	17,020	294,834	1,506	293,328
Total Eastern States	83,474	17,789,758	2,439,766	435,794	1,572,831	568,487	393	70,685	11,446,021	3,471,683	1,077,238	38,956,130	678,602	38,277,528
Virginia	23,225	141,524	41,160	170	4,079	4,167	550	22,176	148,499	224,665	14,522	624,737	7,855	616,882
West Virginia	8,046	69,594	22,001	200	297	5,411		4,625	37,976	79,228	6,002	233,680	4,077	229,603
North Carolina	33,498	95,233	55,079	3,078	14,000	16,154	3,042	27,557	356,884	268,443	24,010	896,978	19,822	877,156
South Carolina	8,741	29,791	9,146		560	4,212	4,325	7,906	23,563	41,699	2,115	132,058	2,336	129,722
Georgia	35,842	117,432	33,229	433	2,694	13,275	11,377	24,860	154,078	158,517	9,636	561,373	8,501	552,872
Florida	16,878	98,068	66,404	19	2,360	6,325	20	15,119	204,694	195,286	11,004	616,177	10,829	605,348
Alabama	18,187	41,016	14,457		60	1,427	7,549	17,524	41,383	68,706	3,023	213,332	4,022	209,310
Mississippi	27,086	33,742	18,656	551	6,519	10,011	11,440	28,012	126,900	73,152	5,629	341,698	8,439	333,259
Louisiana	19,740	77,883	41,902	150	126	1,702	5,263	13,724	96,156	96,189	14,949	367,784	7,652	360,132
Texas	14,263	72,191	53,116		283	21,139	68,612	102,810	379,200	366,510	15,625	1,093,899	13,101	1,080,798
Arkansas	17,785	29,477	16,235		1,067	3,899	27,095	27,827	46,732	51,927	3,157	225,201	2,299	222,902
Kentucky	53,312	100,905	36,549	140	3,138	8,563	1,323	40,927	152,711	155,123	24,344	576,985	9,132	567,853
Tennessee	38,929	78,083	24,717		3,189	2,971	8,115	30,675	78,324	163,012	8,191	436,206	6,889	429,317
Total Southern States	315,532	984,939	432,651	4,741	38,372	99,256	148,711	363,742	1,847,500	1,942,457	142,207	6,320,108	104,954	6,215,154

Location	1	2	3	4	5	6	7	8	9	10	11	12	13	14
Ohio	62,737	874,699	210,572	62	88,067	155,868	2,241	61,952	648,290	569,643	81,901	2,756,032	49,199	2,706,833
Indiana	47,801	241,598	49,902	9	195	3,675	5,406	86,962	113,700	177,947	6,676	733,871	13,347	720,524
Illinois	31,492	335,990	82,489	655	52,805	88,039	19,868	150,464	668,342	350,419	38,133	1,819,596	41,338	1,778,258
Michigan	44,251	670,830	141,843		7,639	32,768	609	71,497	342,273	501,891	44,584	1,858,185	26,977	1,831,208
Wisconsin	68,985	330,811	104,776	13	1,787	7,237	83	83,653	228,330	165,098	28,385	1,019,158	20,972	998,186
Minnesota	51,750	336,779	49,348	112	121	3,015	27,709	143,482	66,620	108,077	6,075	793,088	9,309	783,779
Iowa	61,159	178,007	46,312	208	1,277	5,644	43,187	352,265	155,224	152,061	10,289	1,006,083	11,859	994,174
Missouri	52,119	361,893	103,946	2,240	10,343	25,714	24,495	110,453	441,618	345,738	35,411	1,513,970	21,352	1,492,618
Total Middle Western States	420,694	3,330,607	789,188	3,299	162,234	322,860	123,598	1,060,728	2,664,397	2,370,874	251,454	11,499,933	194,353	11,305,580
North Dakota	8,144	18,312	2,184			274	27,935	34,996	8,755	17,007	1,174	118,781	2,486	116,295
South Dakota	3,776	19,316	4,229			361	21,330	55,403	10,678	13,328	776	129,232	2,149	212,083
Nebraska	7,104	14,210	5,150	16	15	457	36,385	101,118	23,611	25,129	3,293	216,457	3,490	212,967
Kansas	16,525	50,882	15,779	8		2,826	66,656	140,047	69,350	73,682	4,995	440,793	3,751	437,042
Montana	2,746	35,051	7,394		35	1,212	13,892	36,706	32,146	33,958	1,099	164,212	3,890	160,322
Wyoming	952	8,037	2,971			235	508	12,238	7,006	5,891	80	37,921	462	37,459
Colorado	2,280	35,535	13,587	2,406	1,605	2,745	3,135	36,245	67,145	94,452	5,777	264,912	4,986	259,926
New Mexico	1,700	8,668	7,535			458	615	11,778	28,422	23,875	852	83,903	1,824	82,079
Oklahoma	5,989	14,494	8,543	12	188	902	19,959	41,109	41,982	70,716	1,357	205,251	2,354	202,897
Total Western States	49,216	204,505	67,372	2,442	1,846	9,470	190,435	469,640	289,095	358,038	19,403	1,661,462	25,392	1,636,070
Washington	4,504	221,984	49,662	13	328	621	3,338	9,217	40,546	29,940	1,481	361,634	1,798	359,836
Oregon	2,738	51,093	13,117		172	783	297	5,913	26,442	22,708	2,817	126,080	1,184	124,896
California	34,211	1,007,798	274,968	4,492	28,532	25,470	4	73,227	1,009,105	539,274	56,450	3,053,531	51,695	3,001,836
Idaho	1,601	9,552	4,368		16	698		20,384	19,759	19,150	865	77,831	1,295	76,536
Utah	4,662	60,836	17,033		882	1,502	1,438	19,795	61,136	58,008	6,235	230,431	3,596	226,835
Nevada	635	7,440	9,237			498	342	4,171	14,760	14,379	746	51,866	666	51,200
Arizona	468	25,234	3,069			1	345	7,813	32,207	44,845	2,938	116,920	1,421	115,499
Total Pacific States	48,819	1,383,937	371,454	4,505	29,930	29,573	5,764	140,520	1,203,955	728,304	71,532	4,018,293	61,655	3,956,638
Total United States (exclusive of possessions)	951,687	29,157,741	4,782,710	452,420	1,824,687	1,057,567	468,902	2,125,384	18,144,831	9,486,393	1,621,212	70,073,534	1,129,464	68,944,070
Alaska	225	5,653	2,863			17		220	3,084	2,887	210	15,159	248	14,911
Canal Zone (Panama)									1,180	191	182	1,553		1,553
Guam								1	2,143	4,740		8,933		8,933
The Territory of Hawaii	228	2,049	36,155	4,332	19	13,006		47	34,399	25,645	2,331	169,182	1,065	168,117
Puerto Rico	9,162	57,352	11,024		21	803		14,283	181,492	69,490	6,286	351,168	1,591	349,577
American Samoa		54,275						8	104	125	36	273		273
Virgin Islands of the United States		1,354	265						850	1,362	73	3,904	84	3,820
Total possessions	9,615	120,683	50,307	4,332	40	13,826		14,559	223,252	104,440	9,118	550,172	2,988	547,184
Total United States and possessions	961,302	29,278,424	4,833,017	456,752	1,824,727	1,071,393	468,902	2,139,943	18,368,083	9,590,833	1,630,330	70,623,706	1,132,452	69,491,254

TABLE No. 44.—Assets and liabilities of all active banks other than national, Dec. 31, 1958 (includes State commercial, mutual savings, and private banks)—Continued

[In thousands of dollars]

Location	Capital				Demand deposits						Time deposits					
	Capital notes and debentures	Preferred stock	Common stock	Individuals, partnerships, and corporations	U.S. Government	States and political subdivisions	Banks in United States	Banks in foreign countries	Certified and cashiers' checks, etc.[1]		Individuals, partnerships, and corporations	U.S. Government	Postal savings	States and political subdivisions	Banks in United States	Banks in foreign countries
Maine		100	9,730	132,387	5,287	19,663	4,169		5,884		526,918	116		3,185	30	
New Hampshire			2,407	21,607	924	3,456	505		396		571,503			217		
Vermont		302	5,686	49,244	2,009	8,952	528		1,707		223,629	54	19	2,642	40	
Massachusetts		200	51,242	1,204,615	39,892	124,987	72,730	1,785	54,354		5,545,364	268	135	4,209	280	
Rhode Island			9,415	196,219	7,207	10,264	6,508	587	7,761		569,432	889	40	1,273		25
Connecticut			33,858	708,677	25,298	60,508	26,274	8	23,578		2,567,156	15		1,647	1,053	
Total New England States	48,054	602	112,338	2,312,749	80,617	227,780	110,714	2,380	93,680		10,004,002	1,342	194	13,173	1,403	25
New York	8,301	1,624	824,150	18,050,804	894,637	784,665	3,143,391	1,070,618	1,416,118		24,790,431	22,894		221,020	207,703	1,354,289
New Jersey		3,210	39,503	1,338,591	47,244	130,739	48,933	481	55,778		2,460,600	186		34,391	279	25
Pennsylvania		211	146,803	3,384,372	105,434	158,149	337,677	5,424	58,854		3,583,789	1,700	336	71,131	1,598	
Delaware			13,996	412,836	21,833	26,920	6,836		10,223		253,425	920		24,704		
Maryland		55	28,432	779,858	19,673	76,174	44,503	1,012	13,239		941,890	3,813	19	12,854	213	
District of Columbia			11,670	423,527	7,259	29	21,124	2,090	14,616		172,455	8,895				1,450
Total Eastern States	56,355	5,100	1,084,554	24,389,988	1,096,080	1,156,676	3,602,464	1,079,625	1,568,828		32,202,590	38,408	355	364,100	209,793	1,355,764
Virginia		1,080	34,457	605,909	17,700	64,258	67,502	79	13,462		495,271	4,453	1,556	42,476	430	
West Virginia		30	16,820	312,994	10,335	43,110	12,920		7,018		176,302	40	136	1,618	29	
North Carolina		50	46,273	1,050,491	34,609	111,108	272,902	38	21,326		462,685	4,509	3,988	55,746	1,460	
South Carolina			14,351	222,522	7,333	21,699	9,899		1,975		70,696	824	5	10,597	2,020	
Georgia			36,141	665,028	19,081	103,678	57,952	106	11,025		378,240	2,613	490	9,075	1,337	
Florida		450	50,140	873,745	18,396	108,633	40,368	832	14,162		451,040	481	1,697	36,066	889	
Alabama			15,124	285,447	8,492	66,426	3,555		2,198		176,954	439	36	2,007		
Mississippi		220	17,156	475,572	11,092	135,559	48,091	3	4,488		197,858	35		787	8,525	
Louisiana		47	29,123	488,297	8,526	135,325	61,984	632	8,209		239,933	2,467	350	10,698	623	
Texas			72,726	1,628,380	26,063	174,599	73,380		32,937		500,022	114	16	72,555		
Arkansas			14,220	380,710	6,850	46,588	14,303	44	4,353		118,021	32	421	649	60	
Kentucky		50	31,944	833,091	27,519	76,602	154,910	27	9,846		251,546	3,460	5	14,562	69	
Tennessee			25,412	450,492	10,312	71,057	11,747		4,402		357,761	36	61	19,010	1,390	
Total Southern States		1,927	403,887	8,272,678	206,308	1,186,642	829,513	1,761	135,400		3,876,339	19,503	8,761	275,846	17,057	

Ohio	100	365	120,552	2,590,855	111,359	194,263	117,706	3,263	48,569	2,422,463	1,351	681	94,410	135	
Indiana	244		38,690	965,317	30,188	177,208	9,031	3,900	15,352	667,883	185	160	22,300	1,772	
Illinois		500	112,612	2,662,358	90,847	169,012	197,383	1,494	47,621	1,739,722	87	40	86,639	2,500	500
Michigan	415	3,015	108,916	1,576,075	49,498	219,787	45,704	60	41,970	2,140,350	1,097	30	114,871	505	
Wisconsin	300	1,850	50,137	1,061,021	34,438	97,429	41,427		24,744	1,138,115	57	179	15,082	70	
Minnesota		150	31,247	554,856	17,091	95,236	3,763		12,425	929,283	12	188	19,478	50	
Iowa		435	49,146	1,204,927	31,645	175,483	21,716		18,576	668,802	25	142	19,936	65	
Missouri	275	370	100,788	2,095,916	58,771	212,938	366,614	2,040	21,396	864,889	1,264	546	69,818	170	
Total Middle Western States	1,334	6,685	612,088	12,711,325	423,837	1,341,356	803,344	10,757	230,653	10,571,507	4,078	1,966	423,534	5,267	500
North Dakota			8,943	189,615	4,052	57,197	2,736		2,128	99,687	22	7	59,542	81	
South Dakota			6,930	209,238	5,200	31,468	1,951		1,858	94,706	17	7	8,562	747	
Nebraska		500	15,231	379,301	9,888	39,033	3,750		2,901	60,548		5	224	31	
Kansas			26,219	570,955	15,444	161,676	11,980	10	6,764	226,685	29	21	33,228	12	
Montana		10	9,085	229,848	5,988	36,723	15,164		3,283	107,952	165	4	7,288	4	
Wyoming			1,570	63,004	1,176	13,258	834		612	30,026	14	5	1,735	265	
Colorado		100	17,754	274,950	7,763	32,534	31,251		5,090	160,169	951		13,840	192	
New Mexico			5,070	114,948	3,936	22,814	344		1,836	41,959	2,148	302	7,328	50	
Oklahoma			13,435	291,943	5,614	48,879	5,528		6,060	116,834	916	15	524	100	
Total Western States	110		104,237	2,323,802	59,061	443,582	73,538	10	30,532	938,566	4,262	359	132,266	654	
Washington			7,995	149,908	4,503	19,572	3,607	190	3,407	491,243	20		13	81	
Oregon			8,705	106,134	3,313	21,242	2,690	82	2,724	124,717			12,277	747	
California		1,200	134,066	2,797,798	77,922	119,665	188,102	22,909	100,656	2,537,381		18	271,160	5,915	10,530
Idaho			4,230	82,090	1,045	17,744	1,172		1,724	51,832	3,034		14		
Utah		100	10,247	195,131	4,387	47,240	28,193	1	3,191	174,020	10	10	25,074	150	
Nevada			2,636	47,113	1,294	15,583	928		2,013	40,426	86		390		
Arizona			6,870	140,314	2,635	22,339	1,764	126	3,119	64,984	57		7,978		
Total Pacific States	1,300		174,749	3,518,488	95,099	263,385	226,456	23,308	116,834	3,484,603	3,207	28	316,906	6,893	10,530
Total United States (exclusive of possessions)	57,689	15,724	2,491,853	53,529,030	1,961,002	4,619,421	5,646,029	1,117,841	2,175,927	61,077,607	70,800	11,663	1,525,825	241,067	1,366,819
Alaska			1,148	16,804	2,316	4,920	485	311	118	9,701	66	17	5,040		
Canal Zone (Panama)				7,056	7,390		103		99	1,517					
Guam				5,515	4,386	2,058			214	7,348	391		168		
The Territory of Hawaii			10,862	132,622	13,794	25,826	9,244	805	1,964	118,782	3,135		1,874	54	
Puerto Rico			39,090	185,548	5,258	48,318	9,397	368	10,050	178,834	1,189	486	26,351	1,807	
American Samoa			100	401	137	126			3	886	9,336	50	31,182		
Virgin Islands of the United States			312	1,606	39	3,042		61	84	2,901			770		
Total possessions			51,512	349,552	33,320	84,290	19,229	1,545	12,532	319,969	14,117	553	65,385	1,861	
Total United States and possessions	57,689	15,724	2,543,365	53,878,582	1,994,322	4,703,711	5,665,258	1,119,386	2,188,459	61,397,576	84,917	12,216	1,591,210	242,928	1,366,819

[1] Includes dividend checks, letters of credit and travelers' checks sold for cash, and amounts due to reserve agents (transit account).

Table No. 45.—Assets and liabilities of active State commercial banks, Dec. 31, 1958 [1]

ASSETS

[In thousands of dollars]

Location	Number of banks	Loans and discounts, including overdrafts	U.S. Government obligations, direct and guaranteed	Obligations of States and political subdivisions	Other bonds, notes, and debentures	Corporate stocks, including stocks of Federal Reserve banks	Currency and coin	Balances with other banks, including reserve balances and cash items in process of collection	Bank premises owned, furniture and fixtures	Real estate owned other than bank premises	Investments and other assets indirectly representing bank premises or other real estate	Customers' liability on acceptances outstanding	Other assets	Total assets
Maine	26	163,923	111,929	16,478	5,446	1,527	11,217	39,870	4,933	337	616	--------	1,079	357,355
New Hampshire	24	72,207	34,053	5,889	4,164	4,146	1,899	7,624	1,809	99	40	--------	210	132,140
Vermont	26	112,496	43,894	15,063	2,309	1,297	3,293	19,629	1,927	76	491	--------	398	200,873
Massachusetts	63	801,738	586,862	135,498	26,685	4,568	39,478	342,584	25,984	230	765	2,541	8,932	1,975,865
Rhode Island	5	203,000	107,037	22,206	8,593	2,725	8,882	44,321	3,581	91	470	45	1,143	402,094
Connecticut	48	548,930	344,225	119,115	14,402	8,047	28,815	194,873	18,434	244	--------	3	2,705	1,279,793
Total New England States	192	1,902,294	1,228,000	314,249	61,599	22,310	93,584	648,901	56,668	1,077	2,382	2,589	14,467	4,348,120
New York	173	15,866,170	7,832,047	1,930,458	399,258	105,849	237,009	8,516,121	269,933	496	6,254	509,476	250,175	35,923,246
New Jersey	95	1,279,439	875,469	340,903	64,229	10,463	58,764	415,923	37,146	512	181	87	14,322	3,097,438
Pennsylvania	253	2,877,158	1,627,098	442,124	134,012	34,090	113,895	1,156,438	70,897	4,923	7,316	1,274	23,351	6,492,576
Delaware	20	307,307	217,771	25,000	6,354	4,033	11,950	104,951	7,656	583	1,036	--------	3,159	689,800
Maryland	89	564,477	488,065	87,619	39,118	4,660	33,510	211,445	14,713	317	114	136	9,855	1,454,029
District of Columbia	8	293,328	220,701	12,361	11,020	759	12,830	141,628	6,363	--------	4,560	--------	3,286	706,836
Total Eastern States	638	21,187,879	11,261,151	2,838,465	653,991	159,854	467,958	10,546,506	406,708	6,831	19,461	510,973	304,148	48,363,925
Virginia	181	616,882	409,759	96,700	28,360	1,644	33,129	232,681	18,753	318	2,901	--------	2,926	1,444,053
West Virginia	106	229,603	228,641	40,487	4,188	1,385	17,195	108,603	5,585	438	903	--------	1,424	638,452
North Carolina	160	877,156	541,378	212,152	91,245	2,650	56,731	430,181	27,262	532	136	--------	17,532	2,257,005
South Carolina	119	129,722	108,499	44,628	20,663	219	14,324	63,467	3,506	212	68	50	585	385,893
Georgia	311	548,530	414,772	72,855	30,675	1,410	34,596	250,758	17,630	766	131	--------	5,562	1,378,061
Florida	177	605,348	595,416	132,171	15,459	735	43,369	233,780	27,846	882	525	376	6,117	1,682,129
Alabama	170	209,310	190,629	60,098	17,641	265	16,402	97,809	5,553	282	262	481	815	599,069
Mississippi	167	333,259	247,256	143,829	12,352	597	25,479	178,564	14,149	276	128	3	2,003	957,892
Louisiana	145	360,132	303,405	133,697	5,128	575	31,248	219,629	11,365	298	1,410	75	2,125	1,069,087
Texas	501	1,064,677	652,036	188,688	77,407	5,227	63,028	592,786	46,313	1,919	1,197	1,107	4,325	2,678,710
Arkansas	182	222,902	167,365	63,749	12,577	290	14,182	138,493	4,961	203	--------	--------	396	625,118
Kentucky	272	567,853	474,965	44,133	23,123	1,280	29,983	352,653	8,465	212	6	12	2,230	1,504,915
Tennessee	223	429,317	252,425	92,122	20,235	687	26,179	179,270	13,393	831	132	224	1,804	1,016,619
Total Southern States	2,714	6,194,691	4,586,546	1,325,309	359,053	16,964	405,845	3,078,674	204,781	7,169	7,799	2,328	47,844	16,237,003

Ohio	378	2,507,502	1,728,081	363,405	47,589	8,546	107,945	884,037	46,437	480	11,244	697	22,203	5,758,166
Indiana	331	688,634	810,695	98,037	22,011	1,208	46,094	303,875	14,375	223	810	34	3,462	1,989,458
Illinois	551	1,778,258	2,028,159	477,169	146,256	17,328	62,903	870,994	29,223	1,853	13,843	2,202	22,185	5,450,373
Michigan	318	1,831,208	1,559,521	447,095	18,003	5,807	80,528	575,419	53,548	674	258	105	12,312	4,584,478
Wisconsin	455	987,316	944,978	174,890	30,964	1,234	47,835	347,066	51,169	508	3,515	117	13,139	2,581,751
Minnesota	507	579,081	502,278	91,705	61,850	264	24,381	174,820	12,787	238	101	24	2,933	1,450,462
Iowa	564	988,386	708,282	196,075	27,264	1,143	37,361	339,377	11,312	186	1,581	15	1,411	2,312,373
Missouri	538	1,492,618	1,276,467	320,431	69,623	16,778	57,256	787,902	27,789	422	1,740	2,367	11,673	4,065,066
Total Middle Western States	3,642	10,852,983	9,558,461	2,198,807	432,560	52,308	464,323	4,283,490	216,640	4,584	33,092	5,561	89,318	28,192,127
North Dakota	117	116,295	197,590	50,177	39,808	22	4,494	43,297	2,187	17			413	454,300
South Dakota	138	127,083	164,434	21,216	11,756	140	5,178	52,032	1,445	34	35		294	383,647
Nebraska	300	212,967	207,500	23,804	6,900	232	7,591	89,535	2,217	36	2		797	551,581
Kansas	424	437,042	338,550	139,175	4,583	426	16,681	182,646	5,784	559	82	3	855	1,126,386
Montana	74	160,322	148,844	29,485	14,745	431	5,950	71,406	3,595	122	12		937	435,849
Wyoming	27	37,459	49,011	5,240	1,567	83	1,755	23,859	902	54			33	119,963
Colorado	98	259,926	168,031	25,788	2,574	1,818	8,728	107,327	3,574	378	562		3,594	582,300
New Mexico	26	82,079	70,202	12,749	873	50	5,935	34,660	3,689	66	42		567	210,912
Oklahoma	190	202,897	160,737	45,166	4,842	112	10,828	93,793	2,961	86	369		839	522,630
Total Western States	1,394	1,636,070	1,504,899	352,800	87,648	3,314	67,140	698,555	26,354	1,352	1,104	3	8,329	4,387,568
Washington	64	129,001	119,242	33,499	2,460	301	7,021	51,038	3,818	10	705	7	625	347,727
Oregon	44	95,734	90,488	21,101	517	82	5,153	35,775	3,935	439	7	25	600	253,916
California	78	3,001,836	1,919,190	467,978	74,895	6,966	57,799	1,018,234	70,979	596	8,409	8,409	34,705	6,669,996
Idaho	19	76,536	45,569	13,975	1,208	149	2,896	26,416	1,469	235	326		400	169,179
Utah	42	226,835	144,147	30,291	2,485	682	7,095	96,561	4,765	88	1,992		1,182	516,123
Nevada	3	51,200	40,868	3,837	268	113	2,708	14,227	2,321	1			456	115,999
Arizona	5	115,499	75,601	17,661	6,159	150	5,389	39,929	5,357	459	1,358		2,587	270,149
Total Pacific States	255	3,696,641	2,435,105	588,342	87,992	8,443	88,061	1,282,180	92,704	1,828	12,797	8,441	40,555	8,343,089
Total United States (exclusive of possessions)	8,835	45,470,558	30,574,230	7,617,972	1,682,843	263,193	1,586,911	20,538,306	1,003,855	22,841	76,635	529,895	504,661	109,871,832
Alaska	10	14,591	16,648	2,386	1,234		1,562	5,060	473	24	153		48	42,179
Canal Zone (Panama)	(2)	1,553					2,008	666	17				15,465	19,709
Guam	(3)	8,933					812	21	241	76			12,271	22,354
The Territory of Hawaii	9	168,117	91,278	22,599	3,281	1,584	13,679	57,812	7,484	341	25	451	1,806	368,457
Puerto Rico [4]	10	349,577	70,016	33,856	23,108	1,007	23,871	44,405	6,837	212	168	2,453	29,235	584,745
American Samoa	1	273	1,307				113	252	5				32	1,982
Virgin Islands of the United States	1	3,637	3,819				481	937	52				43	8,969
Total possessions	31	546,681	183,068	58,841	27,623	2,591	42,526	109,153	15,109	653	346	2,904	58,900	1,048,395
Total United States and possessions	8,866	46,017,239	30,757,230	7,676,813	1,710,466	265,784	1,629,437	20,647,459	1,018,964	23,494	76,981	532,799	563,561	110,920,227

1 Includes stock savings banks.
2 2 branches of a national bank and 2 branches of a State member bank in New York.
3 Branch of a national bank in California.

4 Asset and liability items include data for branches of a national bank and a State member bank in New York.

TABLE No. 45.—Assets and liabilities of active State commercial banks, Dec. 31, 1958—Continued

LIABILITIES

[In thousands of dollars]

Location	Demand deposits	Time deposits	Total deposits	Bills payable, rediscounts, and other liabilities for borrowed money	Acceptances executed by or for account of reporting banks and outstanding	Other liabilities	Capital stock 1	Surplus	Undivided profits	Reserves and retirement account for preferred stock and capital notes and debentures
Maine	167,379	154,918	322,297	50		4,244	9,830	10,780	9,346	808
New Hampshire	26,876	91,114	117,990			977	2,407	5,943	4,280	543
Vermont	62,435	120,189	182,624	50		1,344	5,988	6,022	4,235	610
Massachusetts	1,497,931	263,758	1,761,689	300	2,572	36,008	51,442	82,053	34,597	7,204
Rhode Island	228,286	128,958	357,244		45	7,454	9,415	22,359	5,306	271
Connecticut	842,068	313,348	1,155,416	214	3	19,186	33,823	50,999	18,405	1,747
Total New England States	2,824,975	1,072,285	3,897,260	614	2,620	69,213	112,905	178,156	76,169	11,183
New York	25,122,833	6,464,575	31,587,408	1,454	536,593	690,724	870,828	1,587,726	595,374	53,139
New Jersey	1,603,698	1,235,603	2,839,301	189	87	37,343	71,014	107,060	36,764	5,680
Pennsylvania	4,044,806	1,760,362	5,805,168	1,825	1,302	79,698	147,014	337,561	108,870	11,138
Delaware	478,641	136,344	614,985			10,230	13,996	36,441	14,035	113
Maryland	930,653	395,656	1,326,309	225	136	16,027	28,487	60,108	17,770	4,967
District of Columbia	468,645	182,800	651,445			8,961	11,670	26,000	6,388	2,372
Total Eastern States	32,649,276	10,175,340	42,824,616	3,693	538,118	842,983	1,143,009	2,154,896	779,201	77,409
Virginia	768,910	544,186	1,313,096	1,000		20,000	35,537	51,557	20,576	2,287
West Virginia	386,377	178,125	564,502	270		5,724	16,820	31,859	16,113	3,164
North Carolina	1,490,474	528,388	2,018,862	842	50	59,703	46,303	101,134	22,233	7,878
South Carolina	263,428	84,142	347,570			1,774	14,401	15,028	6,106	1,014
Georgia	849,264	391,178	1,240,442	412	376	17,170	35,452	49,369	23,153	11,687
Florida	1,056,136	490,183	1,546,319	1,125	494	16,976	50,590	46,673	16,867	3,085
Alabama	366,118	179,661	545,779		3	3,622	15,124	20,134	13,375	1,032
Mississippi	674,805	207,205	882,010	1,650		6,710	17,376	47,342	1,875	929
Louisiana	730,341	254,071	984,412	500	75	7,575	29,170	31,401	12,983	2,971
Texas	1,895,058	565,304	2,460,362	2,750	1,107	16,112	71,237	73,373	42,966	10,803
Arkansas	452,804	119,183	571,987			1,586	14,220	18,494	16,211	2,620
Kentucky	1,102,011	269,642	1,371,653	140	140	13,097	31,994	57,016	27,790	3,085
Tennessee	548,037	378,258	926,295	1,000	224	12,385	25,412	27,422	21,044	2,837
Total Southern States	10,583,763	4,189,526	14,773,289	9,689	2,469	182,434	403,636	570,802	241,292	53,392

Ohio	3,064,991	2,202,077	5,267,068	725	697	60,770	121,017	234,807	69,905	3,177
Indiana	1,186,461	640,173	1,826,634	250	34	20,178	38,859	57,934	42,928	2,641
Illinois	3,171,121	1,829,488	5,000,609	3,683	2,202	51,476	113,112	135,746	87,961	55,584
Michigan	1,934,528	2,256,853	4,191,381	185	105	61,390	111,931	137,585	65,646	16,255
Wisconsin	1,259,119	1,130,604	2,389,723	525	117	10,714	52,402	77,167	45,724	5,379
Minnesota	682,966	647,691	1,330,657	260	24	8,654	31,697	40,785	30,572	7,813
Iowa	1,442,192	668,373	2,110,565	665	15	5,639	49,366	71,670	66,233	8,220
Missouri	2,757,675	936,687	3,694,362	2,270	2,385	40,413	101,433	114,235	99,822	10,146
Total Middle Western States	15,499,053	10,311,946	25,810,999	8,563	5,579	259,234	619,817	869,929	508,791	109,215
North Dakota	255,728	159,251	414,979	200		1,507	8,943	12,371	10,863	5,437
South Dakota	249,715	103,323	353,038			869	6,930	9,593	11,279	1,938
Nebraska	434,873	60,789	495,662	1,531	3	2,826	15,231	18,549	15,683	2,099
Kansas	766,829	259,967	1,026,796	871		3,446	26,229	38,963	28,563	1,515
Montana	291,006	115,669	406,675	100		2,925	9,085	10,532	6,249	283
Wyoming	78,884	31,780	110,664			375	1,670	3,751	3,136	367
Colorado	351,588	175,152	526,740	1,786	3	9,871	17,754	14,953	9,224	1,969
New Mexico	143,878	51,787	195,665			1,584	5,070	5,082	2,175	1,336
Oklahoma	358,024	118,389	476,413	591		3,275	13,435	13,922	14,183	811
Total Western States	2,930,525	1,076,107	4,006,632	5,079	6	26,678	104,347	127,716	101,355	15,755
Washington	181,163	134,263	315,426	100	7	3,370	7,995	13,036	6,996	797
Oregon	136,184	97,161	233,345		25	1,918	8,705	6,730	2,923	270
California	3,307,052	2,828,038	6,135,090		8,976	94,944	135,266	204,401	86,856	4,463
Idaho	103,775	51,856	155,631			2,034	4,230	4,852	2,134	298
Utah	278,143	199,340	477,483			6,543	10,347	16,312	5,390	48
Nevada	66,931	40,873	107,804			1,427	2,636	3,114	1,018	
Arizona	170,297	72,962	243,259			5,230	6,870	10,526	3,414	850
Total Pacific States	4,243,545	3,424,493	7,668,038	100	9,008	115,466	176,049	258,971	108,731	6,726
Total United States (exclusive of possessions)	68,731,137	30,249,697	98,980,834	27,738	557,800	1,496,008	2,559,763	4,160,470	1,815,539	273,680
Alaska	23,894	14,613	38,507			57	1,098	1,225	773	519
Canal Zone (Panama)	14,959	4,652	19,611			98				
Guam	12,173	9,613	21,786			568				
The Territory of Hawaii	184,255	146,862	331,117	244	461	5,180	10,862	12,190	6,993	1,420
Puerto Rico	258,939	221,209	480,148	15,075	2,454	31,759	39,090	12,036	2,340	1,843
American Samoa	728	1,054	1,782			31	100	25	5	39
Virgin Islands of the United States	4,771	3,494	8,265			169	312	100	123	
Total possessions	499,719	401,497	901,216	15,319	2,905	37,862	51,462	25,576	10,234	3,821
Total United States and possessions	69,230,856	30,651,194	99,882,050	43,057	560,705	1,533,870	2,611,225	4,186,046	1,825,773	277,501

1 Includes capital notes and debentures. (See classification on pp. 198 and 199.)

TABLE No. 45.—Assets and liabilities of active State commercial banks, Dec. 31, 1958—Continued

[In thousands of dollars]

Location	Real estate loans — Secured by farm land (including improvements)	Real estate loans — Secured by residential properties (other than farm)	Real estate loans — Secured by other properties	Loans to banks	Loans to brokers and dealers in securities	Other loans for the purpose of purchasing or carrying stocks, bonds, and other securities	Loans to farmers directly guaranteed by the Commodity Credit Corporation	Other loans to farmers (excluding loans on real estate)	Commercial and industrial loans (including open market paper)	All other loans to individuals for personal expenditures	All other loans (including overdrafts)	Total gross loans	Less valuation reserves	Net loans
Maine	4,327	48,239	18,293	248	570	989	1	5,007	42,813	43,985	2,525	166,997	3,074	163,923
New Hampshire	800	45,282	10,460			248		550	6,570	8,834	230	72,474	267	72,207
Vermont	6,450	48,508	12,425		353	384		6,148	19,217	19,345	1,874	114,204	1,708	112,496
Massachusetts	1,448	109,968	58,511	1,391	14,550	9,074		2,778	371,621	225,751	23,534	818,626	16,888	801,738
Rhode Island	300	33,680	26,300		2,153	303		2,125	87,171	45,284	11,700	207,016	4,016	203,000
Connecticut	2,324	166,744	36,686		1,848	10,507		4,041	157,364	166,839	12,337	558,690	9,760	548,930
Total New England States	15,649	452,421	162,675	1,639	19,474	21,505	1	18,649	684,756	509,538	51,700	1,938,007	35,713	1,902,294
New York	27,091	1,167,891	357,621	429,690	1,426,187	432,887		38,795	9,629,555	1,831,943	888,334	16,230,299	364,129	15,866,170
New Jersey	3,099	484,334	102,679	575	56,409	11,908	305	3,363	278,915	344,631	29,767	1,315,680	36,241	1,279,439
Pennsylvania	19,255	510,838	185,728	3,681	48,183	94,440	14	15,120	1,119,218	858,841	95,266	2,950,584	73,426	2,877,158
Delaware	8,107	61,985	25,569		11,905	3,421	74	2,871	83,323	106,802	6,681	310,738	3,431	307,307
Maryland	14,437	161,796	49,827	1,530	14,657	10,016		10,302	132,561	154,258	25,526	574,910	10,433	564,477
District of Columbia	973	54,431	23,988		8,940	399		82	94,740	94,261	17,020	294,834	1,506	293,328
Total Eastern States	72,962	2,441,275	745,412	435,476	1,566,281	553,071	393	70,533	11,338,312	3,390,736	1,062,594	21,677,045	489,166	21,187,879
Virginia	23,225	141,524	41,160	170	4,079	4,167	550	22,176	148,499	224,665	14,522	624,737	7,855	616,882
West Virginia	8,046	69,894	22,001	200	297	5,411		4,625	37,976	79,228	6,002	233,680	4,077	229,603
North Carolina	33,498	95,233	55,079	3,078	14,000	16,154	3,042	27,557	356,884	268,443	24,010	896,978	19,822	877,156
South Carolina	8,741	29,791	9,146		560	4,212	4,325	27,906	23,563	41,699	2,115	132,058	2,336	129,722
Georgia	34,851	116,611	32,877	433	2,669	13,275	11,377	24,571	153,563	157,281	9,522	557,030	8,500	548,530
Florida	16,878	98,068	66,404	19	2,360	6,325	20	15,119	204,694	195,286	11,004	616,177	10,829	605,348
Alabama	18,187	41,016	14,457		60	1,427	7,599	17,524	41,333	68,706	3,023	213,332	4,022	209,310
Mississippi	27,086	33,742	18,656	551	6,519	10,011	11,440	28,012	126,900	73,152	5,629	341,698	8,439	333,259
Louisiana	19,740	77,583	41,902		126	1,702	5,263	13,724	96,606	96,189	14,949	367,784	7,652	360,132
Texas	13,977	71,179	52,466	150	283	21,061	67,841	101,032	373,290	361,406	15,093	1,077,778	13,101	1,064,677
Arkansas	17,785	29,477	16,235		1,067	3,899	27,095	27,827	46,732	51,927	3,157	225,201	2,299	222,902
Kentucky	53,312	100,905	36,549	140	3,138	8,563	1,273	40,927	152,711	155,123	24,344	576,985	9,132	567,853
Tennessee	38,929	78,083	24,717		3,189	2,971	8,115	30,675	78,324	163,012	8,191	436,206	6,889	429,317
Total Southern States	314,255	983,106	431,649	4,741	38,347	99,178	147,940	361,675	1,841,075	1,936,117	141,561	6,299,644	104,953	6,194,691

(Note: the column headings for the following table appear on the preceding page; columns are numbered 1–14 here for reference.)

	1	2	3	4	5	6	7	8	9	10	11	12	13	14
Ohio	59,275	724,477	208,514	62	88,067	155,868	2,241	61,952	620,730	551,903	77,050	2,550,139	42,637	2,507,502
Indiana	45,322	216,802	47,348	9	195	3,558	5,344	86,378	113,132	176,912	6,674	701,674	13,040	688,634
Illinois	31,492	335,990	82,489	655	52,805	88,939	19,868	150,464	668,342	350,419	38,133	1,819,596	41,338	1,778,258
Michigan	44,251	670,530	141,843		7,639	32,768	609	71,497	342,273	501,891	44,584	1,858,185	26,977	1,831,208
Wisconsin	68,932	320,872	103,992	13	1,787	7,237	83	83,653	228,330	165,028	28,360	1,008,287	20,971	987,316
Minnesota	34,026	162,444	33,428	112	121	3,015	27,709	143,482	66,620	107,945	6,075	584,977	5,896	579,081
Iowa	61,170	177,576	46,160	208	1,277	5,644	42,964	348,587	154,751	151,655	10,233	1,000,225	11,859	988,366
Missouri	52,119	361,893	103,946	2,240	10,343	25,714	24,495	110,453	441,618	345,738	35,411	1,513,970	21,352	1,492,618
Total Middle Western States	396,587	2,970,884	767,720	3,299	162,234	322,743	123,313	1,056,466	2,635,796	2,351,491	246,520	11,037,053	184,070	10,852,983
North Dakota	8,144	18,312	2,184			274	27,935	34,996	8,755	17,007	1,174	118,781	2,486	116,295
South Dakota	3,776	19,316	4,229		15	361	21,350	55,403	10,678	13,328	776	129,232	2,149	127,083
Nebraska	7,104	14,210	5,150			457	36,385	101,118	23,611	25,129	3,293	216,457	3,490	212,967
Kansas	16,525	50,882	15,779	16	35	2,826	66,656	140,047	69,350	73,682	4,995	440,793	3,751	437,042
Montana	2,746	35,051	7,394	8		1,212	13,892	36,706	32,146	33,958	1,099	164,212	3,890	160,322
Wyoming	952	8,037	2,971		3	235	508	12,238	7,006	5,891	80	37,921	462	37,459
Colorado	2,280	35,535	13,587	2,406	1,605	2,745	3,135	36,245	67,145	89,452	5,777	264,912	4,986	259,926
New Mexico	1,700	8,668	7,535			458	615	11,778	28,422	28,875	852	83,903	1,824	82,079
Oklahoma	5,989	14,494	8,543	12	188	902	19,959	41,109	41,982	70,716	1,357	205,251	2,354	202,897
Total Western States	49,216	204,505	67,372	2,442	1,846	9,470	190,435	469,640	289,095	358,038	19,403	1,661,462	25,392	1,636,070
Washington	4,036	31,065	11,468	13	328	621	3,338	9,217	40,546	28,937	1,130	130,699	1,698	129,001
Oregon	2,738	24,647	10,499		172	783	297	5,913	26,442	22,607	2,817	96,915	1,181	95,734
California	34,211	1,007,798	274,968	4,492	28,532	25,470	4	73,227	1,009,105	539,274	56,450	3,053,531	51,695	3,001,836
Idaho	1,601	9,552	4,368		16	698	1,438	20,384	19,759	19,150	865	77,831	1,295	76,536
Utah	4,662	60,836	17,033		882	1,502	342	19,795	61,136	58,008	6,235	230,431	3,596	226,835
Nevada	635	7,440	9,237			498		4,171	14,760	14,379	746	51,866	666	51,200
Arizona	468	25,234	3,069			1	345	7,813	32,207	44,845	2,938	116,920	1,421	115,499
Total Pacific States	48,351	1,166,572	330,642	4,505	29,930	29,573	5,764	140,520	1,203,955	727,200	71,181	3,758,193	61,552	3,696,641
Total United States (exclusive of possessions)	897,020	8,218,763	2,505,470	452,102	1,818,112	1,035,540	467,846	2,117,483	17,992,989	9,273,120	1,592,959	46,371,404	900,846	45,470,558
Alaska	225	5,496	2,814			17		220	3,048	2,835	184	14,839	248	14,591
Canal Zone (Panama)									1,180	191	182	1,553		1,553
Guam								1	2,143	4,740		8,933		8,933
The Territory of Hawaii	228	2,049	36,155	4,332	19	13,006		47	34,399	25,645	2,331	169,182	1,065	168,117
Puerto Rico	9,162	57,352	11,024		21	803		14,283	181,492	69,490	6,286	351,168	1,591	349,577
American Samoa		54,275						8		125	36	273		273
Virgin Islands of the United States		1,241	265						954	1,362	3	3,721	84	3,637
Total possessions	9,615	120,413	50,258	4,332	40	13,826		14,559	223,216	104,388	9,022	549,669	2,988	546,681
Total United States and possessions	906,635	8,339,176	2,555,728	456,434	1,818,152	1,049,366	467,846	2,132,042	18,216,205	9,377,508	1,601,981	46,921,073	903,834	46,017,239

TABLE No. 45.—Assets and liabilities of active State commercial banks, Dec. 31, 1958—Continued

[In thousands of dollars]

Location	Capital			Demand deposits						Time deposits					
	Capital notes and debentures	Preferred stock	Common stock	Individuals, partnerships, and corporations	U.S. Government	States and political subdivisions	Banks in United States	Banks in foreign countries	Certified and cashiers' checks, etc.¹	Individuals, partnerships, and corporations	U.S. Government	Postal savings	States and political subdivisions	Banks in United States	Banks in foreign countries
Maine		100	9,730	132,387	5,280	19,663	4,169		5,880	153,817	103		998		
New Hampshire			2,407	21,607	914	3,456	505		394	90,955			159		
Vermont		302	5,686	49,244	2,008	8,952	528		1,703	118,188	54	19	1,920	27	
Massachusetts		200	51,242	1,204,615	39,512	124,937	72,730	1,785	54,352	259,127	268	135	4,064	280	
Rhode Island			9,415	196,219	7,187	10,263	6,508	587	7,522	126,636	889	40	1,273		25
Connecticut			33,823	707,082	25,092	60,508	26,274	8	23,104	312,770	15		523		
Total New England States		602	112,303	2,311,154	79,993	227,779	110,714	2,380	92,955	1,061,493	1,329	194	8,937	307	25
New York	48,054	1,624	821,150	17,907,971	892,550	764,565	3,126,436	1,045,277	1,386,034	4,667,219	22,894		221,020	207,203	1,346,239
New Jersey	8,301	3,210	59,503	1,322,923	47,137	130,504	48,908	481	53,745	1,207,666	186	336	27,717	9	25
Pennsylvania		211	146,803	3,379,626	105,138	158,112	337,677	5,424	58,829	1,685,651	1,700		71,077	1,598	
Delaware			13,996	412,836	21,833	26,920	6,836		10,216	110,792	920				
Maryland		55	28,432	777,802	19,599	76,167	44,186	1,012	11,887	378,765	3,813	19	24,632	205	
District of Columbia			11,670	423,527	7,259	29	21,124	2,090	14,616	172,455	8,895		12,854		1,450
Total Eastern States	56,355	5,100	1,081,554	24,224,685	1,093,516	1,156,297	3,585,167	1,054,284	1,535,327	8,222,548	38,408	355	357,300	209,015	1,347,714
Virginia		1,080	34,457	605,909	17,700	64,258	67,502	79	13,462	495,271	4,453	1,556	42,476	430	
West Virginia			16,820	312,994	10,335	43,110	12,920		7,018	176,302	40	136	1,618	29	
North Carolina		30	46,273	1,050,491	34,609	111,108	272,902	38	21,326	462,685	4,509	3,988	55,746	1,460	
South Carolina		50	14,351	222,522	7,333	21,699	9,899		1,975	70,696	824	5	10,397	2,020	
Georgia			35,452	657,444	19,081	103,678	57,952	106	11,003	377,663	2,613	490	9,075	1,337	
Florida		450	50,140	873,745	18,396	108,633	40,368	832	14,162	451,050	481	1,697	36,066	889	
Alabama			15,124	285,447	8,492	66,426	3,555		2,198	176,954	439	36	2,007	225	
Mississippi		220	17,156	475,572	11,092	135,559	48,091	3	4,488	197,858	35		787	8,525	
Louisiana		47	29,123	488,297	8,526	163,325	61,984		8,209	239,933	2,467	350	10,698	623	
Texas			71,237	1,591,177	25,812	172,244	72,854	632	32,339	493,348	112	16	71,828		
Arkansas			14,220	380,710	6,850	46,588	14,303		4,353	118,021	32	421	649	60	
Kentucky		50	31,944	833,091	27,519	76,602	154,910	44	9,845	251,546	3,460	5	14,562	69	
Tennessee			25,412	450,492	10,312	71,057	11,747	27	4,402	357,761	36	61	19,010	1,390	
Total Southern States		1,927	401,709	8,227,891	206,057	1,184,287	828,987	1,761	134,780	3,869,088	19,501	8,761	275,119	17,057	
Ohio	100	365	120,552	2,589,923	111,359	194,263	117,706	3,263	48,477	2,107,169	1,351	681	92,741	135	
Indiana	244		38,615	957,015	30,058	175,108	9,031		15,249	616,112	185	160	21,936	1,760	
Illinois		500	112,612	2,662,358	90,847	169,012	197,353	3,900	47,621	1,739,722	87	40	86,639	2,500	500

Michigan	415	3,015	108,916	1,576,075	49,498	219,787	45,704	1,494	41,970	2,140,350	1,097	30	114,871	505
Wisconsin	300	1,850	50,137	1,061,021	34,438	97,429	41,427	60	24,744	1,115,239	52	179	15,064	70
Minnesota		150	31,247	554,856	17,091	95,236	3,763		12,020	627,963	12	188	19,478	50
Iowa		435	48,931	1,195,169	31,645	175,086	21,716		18,576	667,205	25	142	936	65
Missouri	275	370	100,788	2,095,916	58,771	212,938	366,614	2,040	21,396	864,889	1,264	546	69,818	170
Total Middle Western States	1,334	6,685	611,798	12,692,333	423,707	1,338,859	803,344	10,757	230,053	9,878,649	4,073	1,966	421,503	5,255
North Dakota		8,943	189,615	57,197	4,052	19,572	2,736		2,128	99,687	22	7	59,542	31
South Dakota		6,930	209,238	31,468	5,200	21,242	1,951		2,690	94,706	17	5	8,562	12
Nebraska		15,231	379,301	39,033	9,888	119,665	3,750		100,656	60,548	29	21	224	4
Kansas	10	26,219	570,955	161,676	15,444	36,723	11,980		15,164	226,685	29	21	33,228	265
Montana		9,085	229,848	5,988	7,763	13,258	834		612	107,952	14	5	7,283	
Wyoming		1,570	63,004	1,176		32,534			5,090	30,026	951		1,735	
Colorado		17,754	274,950	3,936		22,814	31,251		1,836	160,169	2,148	302	13,840	192
New Mexico	100	5,070	114,948	5,614		48,879	344		6,060	41,959	916		7,328	50
Oklahoma		13,435	291,943				5,528			116,834		15	524	100
Total Western States	110	104,237	2,323,802	443,582	73,538		10		30,532	938,566	4,262	359	132,266	654
Washington		7,995	149,908	4,479	19,572	17,744	1,045		3,407	134,180	20		13	50
Oregon		8,705	106,134	3,312	21,242				2,724	84,918		18	12,243	
California	1,200	134,066	2,797,798	77,822	119,656	188,102	22,909		100,656	2,537,381	3,034		271,160	5,915
Idaho	100	4,230	82,090	1,045	17,744				1,724	51,832	10	10	14	
Utah		10,247	195,131	4,387	47,240				3,191	174,020	86		25,074	150
Nevada		2,636	47,113	1,294	15,583				2,013	40,426	57		390	
Arizona		6,870	140,314	2,635	22,339				3,119	64,984			7,978	
Total Pacific States	1,300	174,749	3,518,488	95,074	263,385	226,456	23,308		116,834	3,087,741	3,207	28	316,872	6,115
Total United States (exclusive of possessions)	57,689	15,724	2,486,350	53,298,353	1,957,408	4,614,189	5,628,206	1,092,500	2,140,481	27,058,085	70,780	11,663	1,511,997	238,403
Alaska		1,098	16,283		4,745	485			115	9,580	66	17	4,950	
Canal Zone (Panama)			7,056		2,390	103		311	99	1,517				
Guam			5,515		2,058				214	7,348	391		1,874	
The Territory of Hawaii		10,862	132,622		13,794	25,826	9,244	805	1,964	118,782	3,135	486	26,351	54
Puerto Rico		39,090	185,548		5,258	48,318	9,397	368	10,050	178,834	1,189	50	31,182	1,807
American Samoa			401		137	126		61	3	886			168	
Virgin Islands of the United States		312	1,606		39	3,042							770	
Total possessions		51,462	349,031	33,270	84,115	19,229	1,545		12,529	319,671	14,117	553	65,295	1,861
Total United States and possessions	57,689	2,537,812	53,647,384	1,990,678	4,698,304	5,647,435	1,094,045	2,153,010	27,377,756	84,897	12,216	1,577,292	240,264	1,358,769

Grand-total column (rightmost): Total Middle Western States 500; Total Western States 10,530; Total Pacific States 10,530; Total United States (exclusive of possessions) 1,358,769; Total United States and possessions 1,358,769.

¹ Includes dividend checks, letters of credit and travelers' checks sold for cash, and amounts due to reserve agents (transit account).

TABLE No. 46.—Assets and liabilities of active mutual savings banks, Dec. 31, 1958

[In thousands of dollars]

ASSETS

Location	Number of banks	Loans and discounts, including overdrafts	U.S. Government obligations, direct and guaranteed	Obligations of States and political subdivisions	Other bonds, notes, and debentures	Corporate stocks, including stocks of Federal Reserve banks	Currency and coin	Balances with other banks, including reserve balances and cash items in process of collection	Bank premises owned, furniture and fixtures	Real estate owned other than bank premises	Investments and other assets indirectly representing bank premises or other real estate	Customers' liability on acceptances outstanding	Other assets	Total assets
Maine	32	193,468	118,390	13,434	59,808	23,839	2,548	11,822	2,254	431			369	426,363
New Hampshire	34	318,863	139,091	7,290	25,345	33,543	1,617	11,861	6,557	837			1,026	546,030
Vermont	6	93,885	13,699	441	1,967	2,055	559	2,565	1,046	42			66	116,325
Massachusetts	186	3,365,776	1,718,022	57,703	376,612	253,521	22,173	93,240	35,081	2,431			19,639	5,944,798
Rhode Island	8	265,369	98,691	5,603	80,013	24,775	2,959	8,390	2,850	28			652	489,330
Connecticut	71	1,412,315	579,862	35,938	275,891	121,351	11,876	49,301	15,156	827			13,278	2,515,795
Total New England States	337	5,649,676	2,667,755	120,409	819,636	459,084	41,732	177,179	63,544	4,596			35,030	10,038,641
New York	128	14,984,004	3,543,381	440,339	2,109,336	342,882	78,175	473,362	134,465	3,739			204,630	22,314,313
New Jersey	21	771,578	290,459	37,684	217,661	21,600	7,453	34,700	11,601	55			7,833	1,400,714
Pennsylvania	7	907,844	324,632	73,088	650,836	25,312	7,914	28,429	10,119	135			8,686	2,036,995
Delaware	2	34,803	22,408	14,353	75,378		219	5,714	1,371	184			5	162,105
Maryland	7	304,311	171,916	7,147	87,488	7,670	2,565	15,472	3,321	108			37,009	629,337
Total Eastern States	165	17,002,540	4,352,796	572,611	3,140,699	397,554	96,326	557,677	160,877	4,221			258,163	26,543,464
Ohio	3	199,331	72,462	1,927	41,908	5,466	3,211	19,946	3,014	14			1,570	348,849
Indiana	4	30,002	21,940	3,142	2,334	27	459	3,576	384	39			208	62,111
Wisconsin	4	10,870	8,948	1,857	906	53	276	1,881	245	10			30	25,076
Minnesota	1	204,698	26,810	22,668	61,470		493	6,742	786	39			1,239	324,945
Total Middle Western States	12	444,901	130,160	29,594	106,618	5,546	4,439	32,145	4,429	102			3,047	760,981
Washington	4	230,835	105,553	2,451	40,588	202	1,004	8,835	1,570				1,073	392,111
Oregon	1	29,162	8,796	384	2,788		270	1,336	62	310			267	43,375
Total Pacific States	5	259,997	114,349	2,835	43,376	202	1,274	10,171	1,632	310			1,340	435,486
Total United States (exclusive of possessions)	519	23,357,114	7,265,060	725,449	4,110,329	862,386	143,771	777,172	230,482	9,229			297,580	37,778,572
Virgin Islands of the United States	1	183			6		11	31					26	257
Total United States and possessions	520	23,357,297	7,265,060	725,449	4,110,335	862,386	143,782	777,203	230,482	9,229			297,606	37,778,829

TABLE No. 46.—*Assets and liabilities of active mutual savings banks, Dec. 31, 1958*—Continued

LIABILITIES

[In thousands of dollars]

Location	Demand deposits	Time deposits	Total deposits	Bills payable, rediscounts, and other liabilities for borrowed money	Acceptances executed by or for account of reporting banks and outstanding	Other liabilities	Surplus [1]	Undivided profits	Reserves
Maine	11	375,331	375,342	41		2,540	26,558	20,224	1,658
New Hampshire	12	480,606	480,618	1,975		5,493	32,105	22,846	2,993
Vermont	5	106,176	106,181	8		750	3,790	4,962	634
Massachusetts	382	5,286,382	5,286,764	460		70,176	337,973	227,336	22,089
Rhode Island	260	442,796	443,056			5,314	36,793	4,029	138
Connecticut	720	2,256,213	2,256,933	200		21,984	134,163	84,124	18,391
Total New England States	1,390	8,947,504	8,948,894	2,684		106,257	571,382	363,521	45,903
New York	2,481	20,112,674	20,115,155	5,350		354,233	1,391,862	310,873	136,840
New Jersey	18,068	1,259,878	1,277,946			14,189	86,980	231	21,368
Pennsylvania	288	1,891,842	1,892,130			14,611	120,669	5,135	4,450
Delaware	7	142,705	142,712			19	18,891	226	257
Maryland	3,806	563,133	566,939			10,407	21,455	30,436	100
Total Eastern States	24,650	23,970,232	23,994,882	5,350		393,459	1,639,857	346,901	163,015
Ohio	1,024	316,963	317,987			5,204	24,275	354	1,029
Indiana	4,900	51,172	56,072			22	4,788	502	727
Wisconsin		22,899	22,899			187	1,802	180	8
Minnesota	405	301,320	301,725			988	17,000	2,959	2,303
Total Middle Western States	6,329	692,354	698,683			6,371	47,865	3,995	4,067
Washington	24	357,094	357,118			4,278	22,492	3,619	4,604
Oregon	1	40,580	40,581			999	1,037	718	40
Total Pacific States	25	397,674	397,699			5,277	23,529	4,337	4,644
Total United States (exclusive of possessions)	32,394	34,007,764	34,040,158	8,034		511,364	2,282,633	718,754	217,629
Virgin Islands of the United States		177	177			5		75	
Total United States and possessions	32,394	34,007,941	34,040,335	8,034		511,369	2,282,633	718,829	217,629

[1] Includes guaranty fund.

TABLE No. 46.—Assets and liabilities of active mutual savings banks, Dec. 31, 1958—Continued

[In thousands of dollars]

Location	Real estate loans — Secured by farm land (including improvements)	Real estate loans — Secured by residential properties (other than farm)	Real estate loans — Secured by other properties	Loans to banks	Loans to brokers and dealers in securities	Other loans for the purpose of purchasing or carrying stocks, bonds, and other securities	Loans to farmers directly guaranteed by the Commodity Credit Corporation	Other loans to farmers (excluding loans on real estate)	Commercial and industrial loans (including open market paper)	Other loans to individuals for personal expenditures	All other loans (including overdrafts)	Total gross loans	Less valuation reserves	Net loans
Maine	1,216	165,693	18,678			257		7	89	6,347	1,519	193,806	338	193,468
New Hampshire	1,308	258,193	49,525			66		80	4,287	6,608	476	320,603	1,740	318,863
Vermont	3,497	73,856	8,664			1,851		1,295	741	3,786	310	94,000	115	93,885
Massachusetts	6,488	2,949,494	357,567			2,272			252	61,283	5,190	3,382,546	16,770	3,365,776
Rhode Island	271	252,088	10,234			322			1,791	5,457		270,163	4,794	265,369
Connecticut	5,459	1,311,918	74,874			1,648		27	1,606	21,665	156	1,417,353	5,038	1,412,315
Total New England States	18,299	5,011,242	519,542			6,416		1,409	8,766	105,146	7,651	5,678,471	28,795	5,649,676
New York	7,735	13,466,963	1,572,994			4,996		1	45,403	54,237	8,315	15,160,644	176,640	14,984,004
New Jersey	150	717,385	53,482			45				3,425	17	774,504	2,926	771,578
Pennsylvania	570	808,193	44,154						850	1,357		915,124	7,280	907,844
Delaware	670	34,083	70						142	67		35,032	229	34,803
Maryland	1,187	261,134	23,194						78	20,434	408	306,435	2,124	304,311
Total Eastern States	10,312	15,347,758	1,693,894			5,041		1	46,473	79,520	8,740	17,191,739	189,199	17,002,540
Ohio	3,462	150,222	2,058						27,560	17,740	4,851	205,893	6,562	199,331
Indiana	2,435	24,230	2,443						261	746		30,288	286	30,002
Wisconsin	53	9,939	784					56		70	25	10,871	1	10,870
Minnesota	17,724	174,335	15,920			117				132		208,111	3,413	204,698
Total Middle Western States	23,674	358,726	21,205			117		56	27,821	18,688	4,876	455,163	10,262	444,901
Washington	468	190,919	38,194					56		1,003	351	230,935	100	230,835

Oregon		26,446	2,618						101		29,165	3	29,162
Total Pacific States	468	217,365	40,812						1,104	351	260,100	103	259,997
Total United States (exclusive of possessions)	52,753	20,935,091	2,275,453		11,574		1,466	83,060	204,458	21,618	23,585,473	228,359	23,357,114
Virgin Islands of the United States		113								70	183		183
Total United States and possessions	52,753	20,935,204	2,275,453		11,574		1,466	83,060	204,458	21,688	23,585,656	228,359	23,357,297

TABLE No. 46.—*Assets and liabilities of active mutual savings banks, Dec. 31, 1958*—Continued

[In thousands of dollars]

Location	Demand deposits					Certified and cashiers' checks, etc.[1]	Time deposits					
	Individuals, partnerships, and corporations	U.S. Government	States and political subdivisions	Banks in United States	Banks in foreign countries		Individuals, partnerships, and corporations	U.S. Government	Postal savings	States and political subdivisions	Banks in United States	Banks in foreign countries
Maine		7				4	373,101	13		2,187	30	
New Hampshire		10				2	480,548			58		
Vermont		1				4	105,441			722	13	
Massachusetts		380				2	5,286,237			145		
Rhode Island		20	1			239	442,796					
Connecticut	40	206				474	2,254,036			1,124	1,053	
Total New England States	40	624	1			725	8,942,159	13		4,236	1,096	
New York	141	2,084				256	20,112,674			6,674	270	
New Jersey	15,668	107	235	25		2,033	1,252,934			54		
Pennsylvania		288					1,891,788			72		
Delaware						7	142,633				8	
Maryland	2,056	74	7	317		1,352	563,125					
Total Eastern States	17,865	2,553	242	342		3,648	23,963,154			6,800	278	
Ohio	932					92	315,294			1,669		
Indiana	3,237	128	1,445			90	50,931			229	12	
Wisconsin							22,876			18		
Minnesota						405	301,320	5				
Total Middle Western States	4,169	128	1,445			587	690,421	5		1,916	12	
Washington		24					357,063			34	31	
Oregon		1					39,799				747	
Total Pacific States		25					396,862			34	778	
Total United States (exclusive of possessions)	22,074	3,330	1,688	342		4,960	33,992,596	18		12,986	2,164	
Virgin Islands of the United States							177					
Total United States and possessions	22,074	3,330	1,688	342		4,960	33,992,773	18		12,986	2,164	

[1] Includes dividend checks, letters of credit and travelers' checks sold for cash, and amounts due to reserve agents (transit account).

TABLE No. 47.—*Assets and liabilities of active private banks, Dec. 31, 1958*

ASSETS

[In thousands of dollars]

Location	Number of banks	Loans and discounts, including overdrafts	U.S. Government obligations, direct and guaranteed	Obligations of States and political subdivisions	Other bonds, notes, and debentures	Corporate stocks	Currency and coin	Balances with other banks, including reserve balances and cash items in process of collection	Bank premises owned, furniture and fixtures	Real estate owned other than bank premises	Investments and other assets indirectly representing bank premises or other real estate	Customers' liability on acceptances outstanding	Other assets	Total assets
Connecticut	2	1,130	596		53	15	57	351	64				5	2,271
New York	2	82,892	56,889	54,443	1,342	7,952	368	62,330	760			13,109	4,700	284,285
Pennsylvania	5	4,217	5,959	644	233	51	346	1,224	65	14			1	12,754
Total Eastern States	7	87,109	62,348	55,087	1,575	8,003	714	63,554	825	14		13,109	4,701	297,039
Georgia	31	4,342	468	79	57		631	3,612	167	52			103	9,511
Texas	9	16,121	16,080	7,059	2,368	127	1,071	10,842	662	28		5	22	54,385
Total Southern States	40	20,463	16,548	7,138	2,425	127	1,702	14,454	829	80		5	125	63,896
Indiana	5	1,888	4,072	348	4		145	905	22				3	7,387
Michigan														
Iowa	8	5,808	4,203	314	7		159	1,931	45					12,467
Total Middle Western States	13	7,696	8,275	662	11		304	2,886	67				3	19,854
Total United States (exclusive of possessions)	62	116,398	87,767	62,887	4,064	8,145	2,777	81,195	1,785	94		13,114	4,834	383,060
Alaska	1	320	275		98		42	282	9	51				1,077
Total United States and possessions	63	116,718	88,042	62,887	4,162	8,145	2,819	81,477	1,794	145		13,114	4,834	384,137

TABLE No. 47.—*Assets and liabilities of active private banks, Dec. 31, 1958*—Continued

LIABILITIES

[In thousands of dollars]

Location	Demand deposits	Time deposits	Total deposits	Bills payable, rediscounts, and other liabilities for borrowed money	Acceptances executed by or for account of reporting bank and outstanding	Other liabilities	Capital stock	Surplus	Undivided profits	Reserves
Connecticut	1,555	350	1,905			2	35	329		
New York	214,919	19,088	234,007	2,402	16,282	9,085	3,000	14,074	303	5,132
Pennsylvania	4,816	6,350	11,166			7		1,522		59
Total Eastern States	219,735	25,438	245,173	2,402	16,282	9,092	3,000	15,596	303	5,191
Georgia	7,606	577	8,183	16		8	689	400	181	34
Texas	40,933	7,403	48,336		5	26	1,489	3,284	738	507
Total Southern States	48,539	7,980	56,519	16	5	34	2,178	3,684	919	541
Indiana	5,735	955	6,690			17	75	400	162	43
Michigan										
Iowa	10,155	1,597	11,752				215	207	215	78
Total Middle Western States	15,890	2,552	18,442			17	290	607	377	121
Total United States (exclusive of possessions)	285,719	36,320	322,039	2,418	16,287	9,145	5,503	20,216	1,599	5,853
Alaska	749	211	960			1	50	25	31	10
Total United States and possessions	286,468	36,531	322,999	2,418	16,287	9,146	5,553	20,241	1,630	5,863

TABLE No. 47.—Assets and liabilities of active private banks, Dec. 31, 1958—Continued

[In thousands of dollars]

Location	Real estate loans — Secured by farm land (including improvements)	Real estate loans — Secured by residential properties (other than farm)	Real estate loans — Secured by other properties	Loans to banks	Loans to brokers and dealers in securities	Other loans for the purpose of purchasing or carrying stocks, bonds, and other securities	Loans to farmers directly guaranteed by the Commodity Credit Corporation	Other loans to farmers (excluding loans on real estate)	Commercial and industrial loans (including open market paper)	Other loans to individuals for personal expenditures	All other loans (including overdrafts)	Total gross loans	Less valuation reserves	Net loans
Connecticut	4	332	62					11	341	353	27	1,130		1,130
New York	200	725	460	318	6,550	10,321			60,915	505	4,520	83,129	237	82,892
Pennsylvania						54		151	321	922	1,384	4,217		4,217
Total Eastern States	200	725	460	318	6,550	10,375		151	61,236	1,427	5,904	87,346	237	87,109
Georgia	991	821	352		25		771	289	515	1,236	114	4,343	1	4,342
Texas	286	1,012	650			78		1,778	5,910	5,104	532	16,121		16,121
Total Southern States	1,277	1,883	1,002		25	78	771	2,067	6,425	6,340	646	20,464	1	20,463
Indiana	44	566	111				62	528	307	289	2	1,909	21	1,888
Michigan	389	431	152				223	3,678	473	406	56	5,808		5,808
Iowa														
Total Middle Western States	433	997	263				285	4,206	780	695	58	7,717	21	7,696
Total United States (exclusive of possessions)	1,914	3,887	1,787	318	6,575	10,453	1,056	6,435	68,782	8,815	6,635	116,657	259	116,398
Alaska		157	49						36	52	26	320		320
Total United States and possessions	1,914	4,044	1,836	318	6,575	10,453	1,056	6,435	68,818	8,867	6,661	116,977	259	116,718

TABLE No. 47.—*Assets and liabilities of active private banks, Dec. 31, 1958*—Continued

[In thousands of dollars]

Location	Demand deposits						Time deposits					
	Individuals, partnerships, and corporations	U.S. Government	States and political subdivisions	Banks in United States	Banks in foreign countries	Certified and cashiers' checks, etc.¹	Individuals, partnerships, and corporations	U.S. Government	Postal savings	States and political subdivisions	Banks in United States	Banks in foreign countries
Connecticut	1,555						350					
New York	142,692	3	100	16,955	25,341	29,828	10,538				500	8,050
Pennsylvania	4,746	8	37			25	6,350					
Total Eastern States	147,438	11	137	16,955	25,341	29,853	16,888				500	8,050
Georgia	7,584					22	577					
Texas	37,203	251	2,355	526		598	6,674	2		727		
Total Southern States	44,787	251	2,355	526		620	7,251	2		727		
Indiana	5,065	2	655			13	840			115		
Michigan												
Iowa	9,758		397				1,597					
Total Middle Western States	14,823	2	1,052			13	2,437			115		
Total United States (exclusive of possessions)	208,603	264	3,544	17,481	25,341	30,486	26,926	2		842	500	8,050
Alaska	521	50	175			3	121			90		
Total United States and possessions	209,124	314	3,719	17,481	25,341	30,489	27,047	2		932	500	8,050

¹ Includes dividend checks, letters of credit and travelers' checks sold for cash, and amounts due to reserve agents (transit account).

TABLE No. 48.—*Per capita demand and time deposits of individuals, partnerships, and corporations in all active banks, Dec. 31, 1958*

Location	Population (approximate)	Deposits of individuals, partnerships, and corporations (in thousands)			Per capita		
		Total	Demand	Time	Total	Demand	Time
Maine	963,000	932,625	287,182	645,443	$968.46	$298.22	$670.24
New Hampshire	592,000	807,530	183,176	624,354	1,364.07	309.42	1,054.65
Vermont	375,000	456,616	113,571	343,045	1,217.64	302.86	914.78
Massachusetts	4,904,000	9,431,332	3,433,892	5,997,440	1,923.19	700.22	1,222.97
Rhode Island	888,000	1,209,496	407,369	802,127	1,362.05	458.75	903.30
Connecticut	2,351,000	4,285,679	1,449,691	2,835,988	1,822.92	616.63	1,206.29
Total New England States	10,073,000	17,123,278	5,874,881	11,248,397	1,699.92	583.23	1,116.69
New York	16,350,000	51,270,059	23,763,264	27,506,795	3,135.78	1,453.41	1,682.37
New Jersey	5,804,000	7,167,870	3,109,796	4,058,074	1,226.53	532.13	694.40
Pennsylvania	11,201,000	13,786,595	7,452,713	6,333,882	1,230.84	665.36	565.48
Delaware	466,000	696,989	429,468	267,521	1,495.69	921.61	574.08
Maryland	3,001,000	2,509,436	1,330,450	1,178,986	836.20	443.34	392.86
District of Columbia	832,000	1,358,691	995,385	363,306	1,633.04	1,196.38	436.66
Total Eastern States	37,694,000	76,789,640	37,081,076	39,708,564	2,037.18	983.74	1,053.44
Virginia	4,008,000	2,552,792	1,460,520	1,092,272	636.92	364.40	272.52
West Virginia	1,982,000	1,030,673	660,760	369,913	520.02	333.38	186.64
North Carolina	4,610,000	2,084,175	1,484,349	599,826	452.10	321.98	130.12
South Carolina	2,434,000	779,476	619,219	160,257	320.24	254.40	65.84
Georgia	3,860,000	2,112,693	1,467,480	645,213	547.33	380.18	167.15
Florida	4,581,000	3,541,634	2,443,735	1,097,899	773.11	533.45	239.66
Alabama	3,251,000	1,598,679	1,071,957	526,722	491.75	329.73	162.02
Mississippi	2,207,000	927,163	651,057	276,106	420.10	295.00	125.10
Louisiana	3,147,000	2,084,817	1,497,279	587,538	662.48	475.78	186.70
Texas	9,525,000	8,727,679	6,815,564	1,912,115	916.29	715.54	200.75
Arkansas	1,768,000	973,180	732,969	240,211	550.44	414.58	135.86
Kentucky	3,114,000	1,833,846	1,406,734	427,112	588.90	451.75	137.15
Tennessee	3,499,000	2,357,941	1,441,143	916,798	673.89	411.87	262.02
Total Southern States	47,986,000	30,604,748	21,752,766	8,851,982	637.78	453.31	184.47
Ohio	9,461,000	9,389,403	5,453,879	3,935,524	992.43	576.46	415.97
Indiana	4,641,000	3,792,921	2,394,516	1,398,405	817.26	515.95	301.31
Illinois	10,033,000	13,880,002	9,224,644	4,655,358	1,383.43	919.43	464.00
Michigan	7,986,000	7,101,855	3,590,668	3,511,187	889.29	449.62	439.67
Wisconsin	3,996,000	3,854,415	2,063,227	1,791,188	964.57	516.32	448.25
Minnesota	3,420,000	3,574,892	1,891,989	1,682,903	1,045.29	553.21	492.08
Iowa	2,855,000	2,653,019	1,752,752	900,267	929.25	613.92	315.33
Missouri	4,309,000	4,563,810	3,360,051	1,203,759	1,059.13	779.77	279.36
Total Middle Western States	46,701,000	48,810,317	29,731,726	19,078,591	1,045.17	636.64	408.53

TABLE NO. 48.—*Per capita demand and time deposits of individuals, partnerships, and corporations in all active banks, Dec. 31, 1958*—Continued

Location	Population (approximate)	Deposits of individuals, partnerships, and corporations (in thousands)			Per capita		
		Total	Demand	Time	Total	Demand	Time
North Dakota	656,000	601,823	387,831	213,992	917.41	591.20	326.21
South Dakota	705,000	622,265	415,637	206,628	882.65	589.56	293.09
Nebraska	1,474,000	1,332,518	1,153,042	179,476	904.01	782.25	121.76
Kansas	2,134,000	1,686,064	1,265,437	420,627	790.10	592.99	197.11
Montana	700,000	677,502	458,449	219,053	967.86	654.93	312.93
Wyoming	323,000	317,096	210,835	106,261	981.72	652.74	328.98
Colorado	1,744,000	1,570,085	1,075,151	494,934	900.28	616.49	283.79
New Mexico	861,000	505,495	373,832	131,663	587.10	434.18	152.92
Oklahoma	2,310,000	2,020,057	1,597,440	422,617	874.48	691.53	182.95
Total Western States	10,907,000	9,332,905	6,937,654	2,395,251	855.68	636.07	219.61
Washington	2,805,000	2,684,658	1,461,915	1,222,743	957.10	521.18	435.92
Oregon	1,797,000	1,691,054	916,825	774,229	941.04	510.20	430.84
California	14,637,000	19,244,998	9,930,364	9,314,634	1,314.82	678.44	636.38
Idaho	674,000	541,590	318,464	223,126	803.55	472.50	331.05
Utah	882,000	729,530	389,307	340,223	827.13	441.39	385.74
Nevada	271,000	297,871	161,421	136,450	1,099.15	595.65	503.50
Arizona	1,177,000	872,021	591,468	280,553	740.88	502.52	238.36
Total Pacific States	22,243,000	26,061,722	13,769,764	12,291,958	1,171.68	619.06	552.62
Total United States (exclusive of possessions)	175,604,000	208,722,610	115,147,867	93,574,743	1,188.59	655.72	532.87
Alaska	169,000	125,038	80,996	44,042	739.87	479.27	260.60
Canal Zone (Panama)	40,000	8,573	7,056	1,517	214.33	176.40	37.93
Guam	50,000	12,863	5,515	7,348	257.26	110.30	146.96
The Territory of Hawaii	590,000	427,892	231,314	196,578	725.24	392.06	333.18
Puerto Rico	2,323,000	364,382	185,548	178,834	156.86	79.87	76.99
American Samoa	21,000	1,287	401	886	61.29	19.10	42.19
Virgin Islands of the United States	24,000	13,442	5,107	8,335	560.08	212.79	347.29
Total possessions	3,217,000	953,477	515,937	437,540	296.39	160.38	136.01
Total United States and possessions	178,821,000	209,676,087	115,663,804	94,012,283	1,172.54	646.81	525.73

TABLE No. 49.—*Officials of State banking departments and number of each class of active banks in December 1958*

| Location | Names of officials | Titles | Total number of banks | State commercial [1] | | | Mutual savings | | | Private |
| | | | | Insured | | Non-insured | Insured | | Non-insured | Non-insured |
				Members Federal Reserve System	Non-members Federal Reserve System		Members Federal Reserve System	Non-members Federal Reserve System		
Maine	Carleton L. Bradbury	State Bank Commissioner	58	6	14	6		22	10	
New Hampshire	Winfield J. Phillips	Bank Commissioner	58	1	14	9		12	22	
Vermont	Alexander H. Miller	Commissioner of Banking and Insurance	32	1	24	1		6		
Massachusetts	Edward A. Counihan III	Commissioner of Banks	249	23	35	5		8	178	
Rhode Island	Alexander Chmielewski	Bank Commissioner	13	1	2	2		7	1	
Connecticut	Henry H. Pierce, Jr.	do	121	11	29	8		6	65	2
Total New England States			531	43	118	31		61	276	2
New York	George A. Mooney	Superintendent of Banks	303	118	46	9		128		2
New Jersey	Charles R. Howell	Commissioner of Banking and Insurance	116	55	37	3		21		
Pennsylvania	Robert L. Myers	Secretary of Banking	265	78	167	8		7		5
Delaware	Randolph Hughes	State Bank Commissioner	22	2	17	1		2		
Maryland	William H. Kirkwood, Jr.	Bank Commissioner	96	12	76	1		6	1	
District of Columbia			8	4	4					
Total Eastern States			810	269	347	22		164	1	7
Virginia	Logan R. Ritchie	Commissioner of Banking	181	71	110					
West Virginia	Donald L. Taylor	do	106	35	68	3				
North Carolina	Ben R. Roberts	Commissioner of Banks	160	4	155	1				
South Carolina	C. V. Pierce	Chief Bank Examiner	119	6	106	7				
Georgia	A. P. Persons	Superintendent of Banks	342	13	291	7				31
Florida	Ray E. Green	State Commissioner of Banking	177	12	160	5				
Alabama	Lonnie W. Gentry	Superintendent of Banks	170	24	146					
Mississippi	W. P. McMullan, Jr.	State Comptroller	167	8	156	3				
Louisiana	J. W. Jeansonne	State Bank Commissioner	145	11	133	1				
Texas	J. M. Falkner	Commissioner, Department of Banking	510	117	371	13				9
Arkansas	Dick Simpson	State Bank Commissioner	182	20	157	5				
Kentucky	Earle Combs	Commissioner, Department of Banking	272	20	241	11				

See footnotes at end of table.

TABLE No. 49.—*Officials of State banking departments and number of each class of active banks in December 1958*—Continued

Location	Names of officials	Titles	Total number of banks	State commercial [1] — Insured — Members Federal Reserve System	State commercial [1] — Insured — Nonmembers Federal Reserve System	State commercial [1] — Noninsured	Mutual savings — Insured — Members Federal Reserve System	Mutual savings — Insured — Nonmembers Federal Reserve System	Mutual savings — Noninsured	Private — Noninsured
Tennessee	M. A. Bryan	Superintendent of Banks	223	8	208	7				
Total Southern States			2,754	349	2,302	63			1	40
Ohio	R. E. McDaniel	Superintendent of Banks	381	157	220	1	1	3		
Indiana	Joseph McCord	Director, Department of Financial Institutions	340	109	[2]220	3		3		4
Illinois	Elbert S. Smith	Auditor of Public Accounts	551	129	416	6				
Michigan	Alonzo L. Wilson	Commissioner, State Banking Department	318	150	166	2				
Wisconsin	G. M. Matthews	Commissioner of Banks	459	63	387	5				
Minnesota	I. C. Rasmussen	do	508	30	467	10	2	1	1	
Iowa	Joe H. Gronstal	Superintendent of Banks	572	71	460	33				
Missouri	G. H. Bates	Commissioner of Finance	538	97	423	[3]18				8
Total Middle Western States			3,667	806	2,759	78	3	8	1	12
North Dakota	G. H. Russ, Jr.	State Examiner	117	2	112	3				
South Dakota	Gordon H. Maxam	Superintendent of Banks	138	26	112					
Nebraska	J. Floyd McLain	Director of Banking	300	17	244	39				
Kansas	J. A. O'Leary	State Bank Commissioner	424	43	345	36				
Montana	R. E. Towle	Superintendent of Banks	74	44	29	1				
Wyoming	Norris E. Hartwell	State Examiner	27	14	13					
Colorado	Frank E. Goldy	State Bank Commissioner	98	17	63	18				
New Mexico	F. F. Weddington	State Bank Examiner	26	8	18					
Oklahoma	Carl B. Sebring	Bank Commissioner	190	27	156	7				
Total Western States			1,394	198	1,092	104				
Washington	Joseph C. McMurray	Supervisor of Banking	68	10	52	2				2
Oregon	J. F. M. Slade	Superintendent of Banks	45	6	36	2				
California	William A. Burkett	do	78	25	48	5		4		
Idaho	R. U. Spaulding	Commissioner of Finance	19	8	11			1		
Utah	Seth H. Young	Bank Commissioner	42	13	24	5				

Nevada	Grant L. Robison	Superintendent of Banks	3	2	1	1				
Arizona	D. O. Saunders	do	5	1	3	1				
Total Pacific States			260	65	175	15	3	5		61
Total United States (exclusive of possessions)			9,416	1,730	6,793	313		238	278	
Alaska	Secretary, Territorial Banking Board		11		6	4				
The Territory of Hawaii	Supervising Bank Examiner		9		3	6				
Puerto Rico	Secretary of the Treasury		10		7	3				
American Samoa			1			1				
Virgin Islands of the United States			2		1				1	
Total possessions			33		17	14			1	
Total United States and possessions			9,449	1,730	6,810	327	3	238	279	62

[1] Includes stock savings banks.
[2] Includes 1 private bank.
[3] Includes 1 trust company which is a member of the Federal Reserve System.

TABLE No. 50.—Assets and liabilities of all active banks, Dec. 31, 1936 to 1958

[Amounts in thousands of dollars]

	Number of banks	Loans and discounts, including overdrafts	U.S. Government obligations, direct and guaranteed	Other bonds, stocks, and securities	Cash	Balances with other banks [1]	Other assets	Total assets	Capital [2]	Surplus and undivided profits [3]	Total deposits	Bills payable and rediscounts, etc.	Other liabilities
1936	15,704	21,613,328	17,497,059	10,700,905	1,025,586	15,871,668	3,402,165	70,110,711	3,293,014	4,849,310	61,155,014	57,247	756,126
1937	15,463	22,342,879	16,660,068	9,828,984	907,871	15,065,962	3,271,994	68,077,758	3,223,110	4,949,834	59,109,903	50,816	744,095
1938	15,265	21,535,406	18,002,042	9,664,255	(4)	18,373,644	3,258,252	70,833,599	3,192,493	5,016,435	61,907,761	36,612	680,298
1939	15,096	22,374,700	19,447,464	9,348,161	1,196,539	22,197,935	3,010,458	77,575,257	3,125,524	5,169,647	68,566,043	25,551	688,492
1940	14,956	23,967,476	21,028,798	9,499,776	1,407,364	26,846,418	2,822,070	85,571,902	3,070,519	5,339,039	76,407,885	25,060	729,399
1941	14,885	26,838,365	25,553,809	9,035,537	1,545,018	25,942,377	2,538,588	91,463,694	3,034,361	5,460,776	82,233,260	22,593	702,704
1942	14,722	24,001,146	46,059,111	8,312,249	1,463,836	27,371,581	2,334,654	109,542,577	2,985,391	5,619,637	100,265,638	18,638	653,273
1943	14,621	23,674,539	66,259,384	7,466,862	1,612,252	26,999,933	2,109,008	128,121,978	3,011,600	6,034,091	118,336,126	51,650	688,511
1944	14,579	26,101,639	86,414,755	7,596,205	1,801,370	29,175,791	1,857,424	152,947,184	3,052,950	6,640,166	142,310,824	125,624	817,620
1945	14,598	30,466,867	101,904,073	8,611,660	2,025,088	33,589,693	1,753,694	178,351,075	3,187,368	7,424,243	166,530,093	227,150	982,221
1946	14,633	35,822,868	87,093,517	9,543,221	2,221,793	32,995,748	1,729,215	169,406,362	3,299,469	8,138,479	156,801,396	48,403	1,118,615
1947	14,755	43,231,136	81,636,988	10,760,398	2,392,970	36,167,173	1,835,487	176,024,102	3,342,600	8,654,798	162,728,682	74,614	1,223,408
1948	14,735	48,452,162	74,462,553	11,470,848	2,145,156	37,490,869	2,053,761	176,075,430	3,423,195	9,130,608	162,041,389	64,320	1,415,918
1949	14,705	49,828,162	78,753,673	12,682,551	2,185,256	34,490,538	2,102,933	180,043,113	3,548,731	9,616,859	165,244,044	27,195	1,606,284
1950	14,666	60,711,146	73,188,217	14,816,545	2,343,064	38,892,739	2,288,962	192,240,673	3,670,249	10,245,616	176,120,158	94,407	2,110,043
1951	14,636	60,000,966	71,595,087	15,991,176	2,880,421	42,826,197	2,558,776	203,862,623	3,840,006	10,866,262	186,603,665	44,008	2,508,682
1952	14,596	75,928,803	72,872,466	17,449,091	2,938,679	42,825,197	2,677,998	214,830,603	4,016,796	11,437,192	196,431,336	196,234	2,749,025
1953	14,538	80,920,155	78,004,064	18,452,644	2,690,476	43,301,133	2,895,929	221,132,803	4,173,707	12,035,657	201,978,297	66,803	2,878,339
1954	14,388	86,058,272	70,309,691	20,519,756	2,657,128	42,097,116	3,348,420	232,684,756	4,428,194	12,936,050	212,030,341	32,915	3,257,256
1955	14,265	100,575,185	70,575,281	20,754,037	2,873,239	45,105,892	3,486,967	243,105,011	4,706,970	13,503,336	221,391,573	174,195	3,328,937
1956	14,188	110,632,011	66,795,281	20,556,588	3,484,476	46,352,257	4,144,714	251,965,327	5,007,583	14,342,869	228,578,958	88,202	3,947,715
1957	14,103	115,759,782	66,066,124	23,051,813	3,532,901	46,006,103	4,770,796	259,187,519	5,308,140	15,228,280	234,178,092	97,990	3,375,017
1958	14,034	122,287,478	73,935,092	26,389,891	3,451,865	46,695,132	5,120,701	277,880,159	5,568,057	16,253,667	251,331,512	96,544	4,630,379

[1] Includes reserve balances and cash items in process of collection.
[2] Includes capital notes and debentures in banks other than national.
[3] Includes reserve accounts.
[4] Not called for separately. Included with "Balances with other banks."

Back figures.—See reference in heading of table 46, p. 190, in 1963 annual report, to reports containing figures since 1834. (Comparable figures for years prior to 1936 covered June 30 only.)

NOTE.—Reciprocal interbank demand balances with banks in the United States are reported net beginning with the year 1942.

TABLE No. 51.—*Assets and liabilities of all active national banks, Dec. 31, 1936 to 1958*

[Amounts in thousands of dollars]

	Number of banks	Loans and discounts, including overdrafts	U.S. Government obligations, direct and guaranteed	Other bonds, stocks, and securities	Cash	Balances with other banks[1]	Other assets	Total assets	Capital	Surplus and undivided profits[2]	Total deposits	Bills payable and rediscounts, etc.	Other liabilities
1936	5,331	8,271,210	8,085,554	4,094,490	518,503	8,462,578	1,032,327	31,064,662	1,598,815	1,572,195	27,608,397	3,495	281,760
1937	5,266	8,813,547	8,072,882	3,690,122	422,490	8,128,003	977,186	30,104,230	1,577,831	1,666,367	26,540,694	10,839	308,499
1938	5,230	8,489,120	8,705,959	3,753,234	555,304	9,151,105	1,011,455	31,666,177	1,570,622	1,757,522	28,050,676	5,608	281,749
1939	5,193	9,043,632	9,073,935	3,737,641	615,698	11,887,915	960,436	35,319,257	1,532,903	1,872,215	31,612,992	2,882	298,265
1940	5,150	10,027,773	9,752,605	3,915,435	718,799	14,401,268	918,082	39,733,962	1,527,237	2,009,161	35,852,424	3,127	342,013
1941	5,123	11,751,792	12,073,052	3,814,456	786,501	14,215,429	897,004	43,538,234	1,515,794	2,133,305	39,554,772	3,778	330,585
1942	5,087	10,200,798	23,825,351	3,657,437	733,499	15,516,771	847,122	54,780,978	1,503,682	2,234,673	50,648,816	3,516	390,291
1943	5,046	10,133,532	34,178,555	3,325,698	807,969	15,272,695	813,468	64,531,917	1,531,515	2,427,927	60,156,181	8,155	408,139
1944	5,031	11,497,802	43,478,789	3,543,540	904,500	16,732,749	792,479	76,949,859	1,566,905	2,707,960	72,128,937	54,180	491,877
1945	5,023	13,948,042	51,467,706	4,143,903	1,008,644	19,170,145	797,316	90,535,756	1,658,839	2,996,898	85,242,947	77,969	559,103
1946	5,013	17,309,767	41,843,532	4,799,284	1,094,721	18,972,446	830,513	84,850,263	1,756,621	3,393,178	79,049,839	20,047	630,578
1947	5,011	21,480,457	38,825,435	5,184,531	1,168,042	20,907,548	880,987	88,447,000	1,779,766	3,641,558	82,275,356	45,135	705,185
1948	4,997	23,818,513	34,980,263	5,248,090	1,040,763	21,983,506	1,063,917	88,135,052	1,828,759	3,842,129	81,648,016	41,330	774,818
1949	4,981	23,928,293	38,270,523	5,937,227	1,059,663	19,985,295	1,058,178	90,239,179	1,916,340	4,018,001	83,344,318	7,562	952,958
1950	4,965	29,277,480	35,691,560	7,331,063	1,147,069	22,666,366	1,126,555	97,240,093	2,001,650	4,327,339	89,529,632	76,644	1,304,828
1951	4,946	32,423,777	35,156,343	7,887,274	1,418,564	24,593,594	1,259,008	102,738,560	2,105,345	4,564,773	94,431,561	15,484	1,621,397
1952	4,916	36,119,673	35,936,442	8,355,843	1,446,134	24,953,269	1,321,382	108,132,743	2,224,852	4,834,369	99,257,776	75,525	1,739,825
1953	4,864	37,944,146	35,588,763	8,621,470	1,292,254	25,253,264	1,416,802	110,116,699	2,301,757	5,107,759	100,947,233	14,851	1,745,099
1954	4,796	39,827,678	39,506,599	9,425,259	1,279,171	24,442,726	1,668,736	116,150,569	2,485,844	5,618,398	106,145,813	11,098	1,889,416
1955	4,700	43,559,726	33,690,806	9,166,524	1,388,250	24,375,190	1,569,791	113,750,287	2,472,624	5,463,305	104,217,989	107,796	1,488,573
1956	4,659	48,248,332	31,680,085	8,823,307	1,706,507	25,375,990	1,867,761	117,701,982	2,638,108	5,834,024	107,494,823	18,654	1,716,373
1957	4,627	50,502,277	31,333,076	9,643,633	1,734,533	25,130,601	2,173,520	120,522,640	2,806,213	6,287,004	109,436,311	38,324	1,954,788
1958	4,585	52,796,224	35,824,760	10,963,464	1,675,827	25,188,993	2,347,698	128,796,966	2,951,279	6,717,522	117,086,128	43,035	1,999,002

1 Includes reserve balances and cash items in process of collection.
2 Includes reserve accounts.

Back figures.—See reference in heading of table 47, p. 191, in 1953 annual report, to reports containing figures since 1863.

NOTE.—Reciprocal interbank demand balances with banks in the United States are reported net beginning with the year 1942.

TABLE No. 52.—Assets and liabilities of all active banks other than national, Dec. 31, 1936 to 1958

[Amounts in thousands of dollars]

	Number of banks	Loans and discounts, including overdrafts	U.S. Government obligations, direct and guaranteed	Other bonds, stocks, and securities	Cash	Balances with other banks [1]	Other assets	Total assets	Capital stock	Capital notes and debentures	Surplus and undivided profits [2]	Total deposits	Bills payable and rediscounts, etc.	Other liabilities
1936	10,373	13,342,118	8,811,505	6,606,415	507,083	7,409,090	2,369,838	39,046,049	1,489,354	204,845	3,277,115	33,546,617	53,752	474,366
1937	10,197	13,529,332	8,587,186	6,138,862	485,381	6,987,959	2,294,808	37,973,528	1,471,533	173,746	3,283,467	32,569,209	39,977	435,596
1938	10,035	13,046,286	9,296,083	5,911,021	(3)	8,667,235	2,246,797	39,167,422	1,459,015	162,856	3,258,913	33,857,085	31,004	398,549
1939	9,903	13,331,068	10,373,529	5,610,520	580,841	8,310,020	2,050,022	42,256,000	1,450,873	141,748	3,297,432	36,953,051	22,669	390,227
1940	9,806	13,939,703	11,276,198	5,584,341	688,565	10,445,150	1,903,988	45,837,940	1,420,148	123,134	3,329,878	40,555,461	21,933	387,386
1941	9,762	15,086,573	13,480,757	5,221,081	758,517	11,726,948	1,641,584	47,915,460	1,410,373	108,194	3,327,471	42,678,488	18,815	372,119
1942	9,635	13,800,348	22,233,760	4,654,812	730,337	11,854,810	1,487,532	54,761,599	1,382,507	99,202	3,384,964	49,616,822	15,122	262,982
1943	9,575	13,541,007	32,080,829	4,141,164	804,283	11,727,238	1,295,540	63,590,061	1,389,943	90,142	3,606,164	58,179,945	43,495	280,372
1944	9,548	14,603,837	42,935,966	4,052,665	896,870	12,443,042	1,064,945	75,997,325	1,403,725	82,320	3,932,206	70,181,887	71,444	325,743
1945	9,575	16,518,825	50,436,367	4,467,757	1,016,444	14,419,648	956,378	87,815,319	1,456,449	72,080	4,427,345	81,287,146	149,181	423,118
1946	9,620	18,513,101	45,249,985	4,743,937	1,127,072	14,023,302	898,702	84,556,099	1,475,054	67,794	4,745,301	77,751,557	28,356	488,037
1947	9,744	21,750,679	42,811,503	5,575,867	1,224,928	15,259,625	954,500	87,577,102	1,500,807	62,027	5,013,240	80,453,326	29,479	518,223
1948	9,738	24,634,230	39,482,290	6,222,758	1,104,393	15,506,863	989,844	87,940,378	1,546,005	48,431	5,288,479	80,393,373	22,990	641,100
1949	9,724	25,899,869	40,483,150	6,745,324	1,125,593	14,505,243	1,044,755	89,803,934	1,583,954	48,437	5,598,858	81,899,726	19,633	653,326
1950	9,701	31,433,666	37,496,657	7,485,482	1,195,995	16,226,373	1,162,407	95,000,580	1,621,492	47,107	5,918,277	86,590,526	17,963	805,215
1951	9,690	35,577,189	36,438,744	8,103,902	1,471,857	18,232,603	1,299,768	101,124,063	1,695,205	39,456	6,301,489	92,172,104	28,524	887,285
1952	9,680	39,809,130	37,074,393	9,093,248	1,492,545	17,871,928	1,356,616	106,697,860	1,745,470	46,474	6,602,823	97,173,580	120,313	1,009,200
1953	9,674	42,976,009	37,283,703	9,831,174	1,398,222	18,047,869	1,479,127	111,016,104	1,828,615	43,335	6,927,898	101,031,064	51,952	1,133,240
1954	9,592	46,230,594	38,497,065	11,094,497	1,377,957	17,654,390	1,679,684	116,534,187	1,896,592	45,758	7,317,652	101,884,528	21,817	1,367,840
1955	9,565	57,015,459	36,618,885	11,587,513	1,484,989	20,730,702	1,917,176	129,354,724	2,183,182	51,164	8,040,031	117,173,584	66,399	1,840,364
1956	9,529	62,383,679	35,115,196	11,733,281	1,747,969	21,006,267	2,276,953	134,263,345	2,319,177	50,298	8,508,845	121,084,135	69,548	2,231,342
1957	9,476	65,257,505	34,728,048	13,408,180	1,798,368	20,875,502	2,597,276	138,664,879	2,452,897	49,030	8,941,276	124,741,781	59,666	2,420,229
1958	9,449	69,491,254	38,110,332	15,426,427	1,776,038	21,506,139	2,773,003	149,083,193	2,559,089	57,689	9,536,145	134,245,384	53,509	2,631,377

1 Includes reserve balances and cash items in process of collection.
2 Includes reserve accounts.
3 Not called for separately. Included with "Balances with other banks."

Back figures.—See reference in heading of table 48, p. 192, in 1953 annual report, to reports containing figures since 1834. (Comparable figures for years prior to 1936 covered June 30 only.)

NOTE.—Reciprocal interbank demand balances with banks in the United States are reported net beginning with the year 1942.

TABLE NO. 53.—*National bank placed in charge of receiver during year ended Dec. 31, 1958*[1]

Name of bank: First National Bank, Halfway, Oregon

(Receivership No. 2970)

Charter number_____	11466
Date of organization_____	Sept. 22, 1919
Date receiver appointed_____	Mar. 17, 1958
Capital stock at date of failure_____	$25, 000
Deposits at date of failure_____	$1, 368, 000

[1] Data as to liquidation unavailable inasmuch as direction or supervision by the Secretary of the Treasury or the Comptroller of the Currency of liquidation by the Federal Deposit Insurance Corporation as receiver of national banks terminated as of the close of business Sept. 20, 1950, by the Federal Deposit Insurance Act of 1950 (Public Law 797) approved Sept. 21, 1950.

TABLE No. 54.—*Bank suspensions since inauguration of Federal deposit insurance, years ended Dec. 31, 1934 to 1958*

Year ended Dec. 31—	Number					Capital stock (in thousands of dollars) [1]					Deposits (in thousands of dollars)				
	All banks	Member banks		Nonmember banks		All banks	Member banks		Nonmember banks		All banks	Member banks		Nonmember banks	
		National	State	Insured	Noninsured		National	State	Insured	Noninsured		National	State	Insured	Noninsured
1934	57	1	----	8	48	3,822	25	----	416	3,381	36,939	42	----	1,912	34,985
1935	34	4	----	22	8	1,518	405	----	633	480	10,101	5,399	----	3,763	939
1936	44	1	----	40	3	1,961	88	----	1,678	195	11,323	524	----	10,207	592
1937	58	3	2	47	6	3,435	685	671	2,004	75	16,169	3,825	1,708	10,156	480
1938	56	1	1	47	7	2,467	25	25	2,052	365	13,837	36	211	11,721	1,869
1939	42	4	3	25	10	5,309	220	3,600	1,204	285	34,980	1,323	24,629	6,589	2,439
1940	22	1	----	18	3	1,587	82	----	1,452	53	5,944	257	----	5,341	346
1941	8	1	----	6	1	496	360	----	118	18	3,723	3,141	----	503	79
1942	9	----	----	6	3	327	----	----	272	55	1,702	----	----	1,375	327
1943	4	2	----	2	----	708	650	----	58	----	6,300	5,059	----	1,241	----
1944	1	----	----	1	----	32	----	----	32	----	405	----	----	405	----
1945	----	----	----	----	----	----	----	----	----	----	----	----	----	----	----
1946	----	----	----	----	----	----	----	----	----	----	----	----	----	----	----
1947	1	----	----	----	1	125	----	----	----	125	167	----	----	----	167
1948	----	----	----	----	----	----	----	----	----	----	----	----	----	----	----
1949	4	----	----	----	4[2]	120	----	----	----	120	2,443	----	----	----	2,443
1950	1	----	----	----	1	52	----	----	37	15	42	----	----	----	42
1951	3	----	----	----	3	750	----	200	550	----	3,113	----	----	----	3,113
1952	3	----	----	1	2	45	----	----	25	20	1,414	----	----	1,279	135
1953	4	----	1	1	2[3]	140	75	----	65	----	44,802	----	19,478	24,934	390
1954	3	----	----	1	2	550	280	----	250	20	2,880	----	----	930	1,950
1955	4	2	----	2	----	303	250	35	----	18	6,498	4,606	----	1,892	----
1956	3	1	----	1	1	----	----	----	----	----	11,823	6,520	----	4,703	600
1957	3	1	1	----	1	----	----	----	----	----	12,869	10,451	1,163	----	1,255
1958	8	4	----	1	3[4]	210	25	----	75	110	6,287	1,368	----	2,787	2,132
Total	372	26	8	229	109	23,957	3,170	4,531	10,921	5,335	233,761	42,551	47,189	89,738	54,283

[1] Includes capital notes and debentures, if any, outstanding at date of suspension.
[2] Includes 2 private banks without capital.
[3] Includes 1 private bank for which capital and deposit figures are not available.
[4] Includes 3 private banks for which capital figures are not available.

NOTE.—Figures for banks other than national furnished by Board of Governors of the Federal Reserve System, and represent associations closed to the public, either temporarily or permanently, by supervisory authorities or directors of the banks on account of financial difficulties. In the case of national bank suspensions these represent actual failures for which receivers were appointed.

INDEX

United States Government securities:

U. S. GOVERNMENT PRINTING OFFICE: 1959